The book "Innovative Creativit
definitive record on the subject.
business practices, humanitie
theories, and even religions, to
aspect of this exploration of
approach, delving into the

consciousness. With the brilliance of an incredibly gifted mind, the authors unravel the intricate puzzle of creativity. They guide us through the seemingly impossible task of grasping the intangible essence of innovative creativity, revealing that creativity flourishes when consciousness is temporarily dissolved. Perhaps, in this mystical revelation, lies the profound reason why we must experience the death of old ideas and habits to truly embrace creativity.

Understanding creativity is no small feat—it is akin to comprehending the creation of our universe from nothingness, to a realm where even quantum mechanics falters. In this unfathomable ocean of knowledge, the "practical" chapters on the self, human operation, and the art of quieting our minds, stories and conversations become invaluable. These chapters offer a tangible lifeline amidst the boundless sea of possibilities, providing practical insights that illuminate our understanding of creativity.

Prepare to be enthralled as you embark on this extraordinary odyssey through the pages of "Innovative Creativity." It promises to reshape your perception, challenge your beliefs, and unlock the limitless potential of your own creative genius.

- Rongbin W.B. Lee, Emeritus Professor, Founding Director of the Knowledge Management and Innovation Research Centre of The Hong Kong Polytechnic University

Innovative Creativity *offers an exploration into the multifaceted world of creativity, intertwining concepts of knowledge, innovation, and consciousness, with each chapter guiding the reader through the intricate relationship between information, creativity, and the transformative power of knowledge. The book's unique structure, starting from foundational concepts and gradually exploring the deeper aspects of creativity and consciousness, is both educational and inspirational. The inclusion of practical exercises such as 'Humility' and 'Quieting the Mind'* ***invites readers to engage actively with the material,*** *making the journey personal and introspective. This book uses a holistic approach, looking at creativity through various perspectives—from neuroscience to spirituality, and emphasizes the importance of balance, mindfulness, and self-awareness. In summary, this book is not just a read;* ***it's an experience****. It's a must-have for anyone looking to deepen their understanding of creativity, whether a novice seeking inspiration or a seasoned professional aiming to enrich their creative process and understanding.*

- Vincent Ribiére, Ph.D., D.Sc., Managing Director and Co-Founder of the Institute for Knowledge and Innovation Southeast Asia (IKI-SEA). Director of the KIM Ph.D. Program, Bangkok University, Thailand

A few exceptional geniuses can think innovatively to generate new ideas, find unorthodox solutions of existing problem(s), and think out of the box to develop radically different ideas which no one else has ever thought of before. They, however, are in the minority. While opportunities are there for everyone to capture ideas, only a few can make this happen. In the knowledge economy, organizations and businesses survive by constantly innovating processes and products for competitive advantage, which requires cultivating and practicing a culture of creativity and innovation. Human minds are fundamentally creative but that creativity needs to be channelized for significant value creation within the organization. This generates a need for innovative creativity, which can be an extremely difficult task for the organization. This book on Innovative Creativity—by two well-known and renowned experts on Tacit Knowledge Management (TKM), Alex Bennet and Aurthur Shelly, and including a case example researched by Charles Dhewa—explores how human minds can become more creative and innovative by providing tools, and discussing disciplines and processes for individuals and groups to develop the ability to achieve and demonstrate extraordinary creativity. "Innovative Creativity" is an essential book for seekers of knowledge and the pursuit of creativity and innovation.

- Dr. Rajat Baisya, Professor & Head (Retd) Department of Management Studies, Indian Institute of Technology, Delhi; President, Project & Technology Management Foundation; Chairman, Strategic Consulting Group Pvt. Ltd., India

The mind is an incredible gift, capable of surprising leaps of thought. The authors—Dr. Alex Bennet, Dr. Arthur Shelley, and soon-to-be Dr. Charles Dhewa—use their cutting-edge skills to explore our minds through the magical synthesis of creativity, showing value to individuals, groups, and organizations. This book guides the reader through an enlightened journey combining knowledge and creativity to reach innovation. They teach many possible ways to enlarge creative thinking such as using pattern thinking, engaging levels of consciousness and the unconscious, and accessing creativity through sleep and mindfulness, all the while enlarging creative possibilities. Add in neuroscience findings about our brains and bodies to further explain their teachings. Imagine using the period between sleep and wakefulness for problem solving. Imagine strengthening your intuition and using it to connect to new ideas. Imagine sharing your ideas with others and multiplying them, enlarging them exponentially. The authors connect the dots between all of these processes and give you the tools to gain extraordinary creativity. Dr. Alex Bennet and Dr. Arthur Shelley have both been recognized as in the Top 50 Most Influential People in the World in Tacit Knowledge Management (TKM). We are in good hands as together we explore Innovative Creativity.

- Susan Dreiband, former CKO of the U.S. Forest Service, Reiki Master and Truth Seeker, USA

This Book—"Innovative Creativity: Creating with Innovation in Mind"—is a fourth volume from a series which was initiated with the book "Unleashing the Human Mind: A Consilience Approach to Managing Self" published in 2022, and continued with "Reblooming the Knowledge Movement: The Democratization of Organizations" and "INside Innovation: Looking from the Inside Out" published in 2023, where the protagonist author is Alex Bennet. This volume attains an apogee in the development of various series of concepts, strategies and forms to approach the complexity and multifaceted kind of minds, consciousness and their manifestations. There are reflexive results both at the individual level, incentivized to follow various useful ways, strategies or techniques for a dynamic, inter-correlative and adaptive connection with reality, and also at the collective level as the sum of physical individual organisms which form a new organism with its own characteristics and behaviors. In the first volume, the authors explain why it is necessary to unleash the mind from its stagnant state and engage it in an active attitude in the same cadency with the changes underway in personal life and society. In the second, the authors refer to the role of knowledge and its effect in the reblooming of society. And in the third, the authors explore the effect of one's own internal motivation and vision, conducting a personal evolution. In this fourth volume, the authors approach innovative creativity, the highest form of co-participation in the driving of our own destiny. Therefore, these challenging proposals by themselves invite the readers to open their minds and interests for opening the pages of this volume.

- **Professor Dr. Florin Gaiseanu, Science of Information and Technology, Bucharest (Romania) and Barcelona (Spain), Honor and Honorable Member of the Editorial Board of International Journals in Europe and USA.ng edge**

Innovation requires creativity. We are creative by nature, even as we struggle with leveraging it in organisational structures that limit our curiosity and learning. Alex Arthur and Charles bring organisational creativity to life by illuminating the interrelatedness of knowledge and learning, so essential to organisational transformation and change. Ultimately, it is people who lead change, and creativity is in abundance, even as it is largely untapped, in organisations. A deeply rewarding read for any change consultant."

- **Dr. Karuna Ramanathan, Organisational Transformation Consultant-Coach, Singapore**

*I would strongly recommend to anyone who wants to step into the tacit knowledge management (TKM) field, you should read this book **"Innovative Creativity"**. It explores the root causes of tacit knowledge and creativity, providing useful tools and patterns with practical exercises which you can easily use in your daily work for TKM.*

- **Fisher YU, Secretary-General of *GO-TKM*, the world's largest not-for-profit organization for tacit knowledge management, Brussels, Belgium.**

This book is a living model of Innovative Creativity. The authors provide a wholistic and comprehensive approach to understanding innovative creativity from multiple perspectives while forging their own unique perspective. They describe in rich detail the facets of creativity and the dynamics of transforming information into knowledge, and knowledge and creativity into innovation. Each chapter describes one or more key concepts, presents a framework for understanding the interplay of those concepts, and reinforces the learning with powerful exercises to build the reader's capacity for creativity. The learning is further reinforced by multiple examples, tools and a concluding case study. In this way, the book inspires and empowers the reader to be creative by renewing the mind, expanding the heart, and increasing interaction and collaboration with others.

A key theme runs through the book: Creativity is a choice. One choice is to stop learning and activating the creativity inherently within us. The other choice is to intentionally utilize our remarkable ability to continuously create reality inwardly and co-create reality as we interact with others and the environment. The authors caution that if innovative creativity is to serve the greater good, it requires a healthy, open mind and a compassionate, humble heart. Innovative Creativity powerfully and persuasively calls us to tap into a new way of thinking and creating. As we share and collaborate with others who are likeminded, we transform our world into a haven of oneness, beauty, compassion, and service within our organizations, community, and nations.

- Dr. Joyce Avedisian, Avedisian Management Consultants, Author, USA

You can never ask for more from the book, even though you would not have expected less. With the volatile, uncertain, complex, and ambiguous world of today, this book is the springboard for whosoever desires to find solutions to world challenges innovatively and creatively. This book is also a stopgap for those who seek to understand the relationship between information, creativity, knowledge and innovation.

- Muktar Ahmad, KIM PhD Student, IKI-SEA, Bangkok Unviersity; Chartered Banker, Human Resource Expert, Training facilitator, and Program Development Manager, Central Bank of Nigeria, Africa

Dr. Alex's and her co-authors' "Innovative Creativity" is like a flashlight in a dark room for anyone who's ever felt stuck creatively. It's filled with relatable examples, easy-to-digest concepts, and hands-on tips that feel more like a chat with a wise friend than a lecture. As a PhD student under her guidance, I've seen these principles come to life in her seminars. This book is a must-have if you want to light up your creative journey. Trust me, it's a game changer in understanding creativity in a fun, approachable way!

- Zhenggang Zhao, Founder of Asia Connet PTE LTD, Singapore

This book provides profound food for thought. "Innovative Creativity" is not just another book on creativity and innovation. Instead, it is a deep ocean of complex thoughts about the interrelationship of creativity, innovation, knowledge, wisdom and intelligence among various other facets of human life. A key takeaway from the book is that "creativity can't exist without knowledge and knowledge can't exist without creativity" and that "knowledge is an action lever for innovation". The distinction between knowledge (described by the authors as the capacity -- potential or actual -- to take effective action) and knowing ("seeing beyond images, hearing beyond words, sensing beyond appearances and feeling beyond emotions") and how both knowledge and knowing are prerequisites for innovation and creativity have been very well brought out. The authors have gone into various dimensions of tacit knowledge and their connection with intuition (which may be an earned, revealed or controlled intuition) and how this has a bearing on creativity. While presenting various perspectives on creativity as described in different streams of literature, the authors make the point that imagination is a direct player in the creativity process and that innovative creativity is the sum total of creative imagination, empathy and energy. The book weaves a thread around various interrelated concepts impinging on creativity. These include the concepts of the creative leap, story thinking, pattern thinking, emotional intelligence, synthesis, synchronicity, hemispheric balance, and the value role of attention and intention, among others.

A beauty of the book is its compilation of exercises, which the reader can experiment with to understand the nuances of various concepts that have been covered. I particularly liked the exercises on "humility", "sleep on it", "quieting the mind", "listening to feelings" and "imagining". Further, in order to explain the interrelationships between various concepts, the authors have created figures which vividly illustrate the complexity of these interrelationships.

It is often said that the more we know, the more we discover our ignorance. While that may be true, the authors rightfully proclaim that knowledge begets knowledge. As a reader, I feel overwhelmed with the new knowledge about innovative creativity that this book has created for me.

- Prof. (Dr.) Surinder Batra, former Dean (Academics) & Professor, Institute of Management Technology, Ghaziabad, India

When I look back at more than 25 years of seeing organizations tackling various phases of knowledge management and innovation efforts in the Department of Defense, Federal Government, and in Private Industry environments there have been many successes, but I have yet to see any truly achieve the real potential of what could be possible. I see this book, Innovative Creativity, as setting a course to pull together the forces of deep creative thinking, understanding the integration of innovation, and setting the foundation of a knowledge management effort to set a course for success. If I were designing a curriculum, this book would be one of the core reading requirements to spark deeper thought on the kind of creative thought needed to meet future challenges in a complex world.

- Michael C. Dorohovich, Lieutenant Colonel, U.S. Army, Retired; former GDIT KM Program Manager supporting the Defense Acquisition University, USA

This book masterfully teaches the theory while offering practical insights on implementation. It deconstructs the discipline of innovative creativity into its constituent concepts, enriching our understanding and deepening our knowledge of each aspect. It aids in connecting the dots, yet thoughtfully entrusts us, the readers, with the responsibility of innovativel creativity, encouraging us to weave these elements into a cohesive paradigm for our individual and collective benefit.

- Dr. Moria Levy, CEO ROM Global, ISO30401 project leader, KMGN chair 2022, Israel

It definitely takes a genius, brilliant, and very rich mind to bring in and weave together such a broad scope of wisdom, and present an all-embracing view of the interdependences with respect to ***Innovative Creativity****. Not only did I experience great joy and the feeling of love when reading this deep, tightly woven and enriching book, but also deep mental satisfaction through the continuous intellectual stimulation and knowledge enhancement. It was just like listening to a beautiful musical masterpiece,* ***scritto in vivacissimo, fortissimo e assai con brio****, orchestrated by Dr. Alex Bennet, Dr. Arthur Shelley, and Charles Dhewa.*

To add to the many facets of the book, I would like to contribute the following quote from Thaye Dorje, His Holiness the 17th Gyalwa Karmapa: "Inner Wealth is our mind, our consciousness. I believe that this mind is like a wish-fulfilling jewel. If you know how to utilize this mind, it can produce the most beneficial effects. The best way to utilize and develop this mind is to absorb knowledge, and the most important kind of knowledge is the one that makes us a kind person, a decent person, a person worthy of respect." It is difficult to find a book that honors all the profound but extraordinary facets of life and brings in and connects higher knowledge and wisdom to beautifully present the way things are, the true being of our existence. I thank the authors for enriching our minds and lives with this outstanding contribution.

- Jacqueline Guth, KIM PhD student at IKI-SEA, Bangkok University; Head of Quality and KM at two Healthcare Centers, Switzerland

Perfectly timed release. Go grab it! Now! Have the "First-Reader's" advantage! Within a single day, at a slow reading pace, one can finish-off reading the superbbbly effective, hands-on exercises in this new book INNOVATIVE CREATIVITY by the gifted and prolific authors and specialists, Dr. Alex Bennet and Dr. Arthur Shelley. Then, instantaneously, start applying them to your own life, work, and network, and let yourself and your community feel the magic first-hand! The topic of this book is the inevitably necessary subject we've been waiting for, emerging from within the huge bouquet of wonderfully useful books which Dr. Alex Bennet has gifted to the world of learning professionals and students—all those who are mindfully keeping in tandem with the latest in KM and Innovation. At the onslaught of the thrustful wave of advancements and releases in Artificial Intelligence, having the skill of Innovative Creativity may be the only differentiating capability between a top excelling Talent and the rest of the world!

- ABI Sarkar, Entrepreneur, JOBexo, Author in English/Hindi/ Thai of *Talent-Evaluator*. India

Never before in human history, has an existential threat of a global scale as the climate crisis compromised the future of civilization as we know it. The paradigms that brought us here are not the ones that can take us out of it. We must now imagine the worst that might happen and then imagine how best to cope with it. That is probably the largest leap of imagination ever imposed upon the possibility of a human future. This book is as timely as it is relevant for nourishing our creative imagination potential. It helps connect the spheres of unbound creativity with those of actionable knowledge and social innovation. This rare accomplishment is welcome for being at once imaginative and feasible.

- **Dr. Francisco Javier Carrillo, President of the World Capital Institute and Emeritus Professor of Knowledge Based Development at Technólogico de Monterrey, Mexico**

We are the masters of our work because I am that I am. Whether we believe in The Divine infinitely creating-Creator or the constant expanding universe, we have the innate necessity to create or co-create in order to survive and thrive. Dr. Alex Bennet is a true inspiration and a remarkable author of various topics that caresses the study of the mind and brain's plasticity and development. In Innovative Creativity she and her co-author Dr. Arthur Shelley support what multiple conducted studies have found, much like physical fitness, that keeping the brain flexible and challenged to innovative ideas leads to mental fitness. An active mind leads to a stronger immune system, emotional stability and wellbeing. Undoubtedly, stimulating creativity plays a roll on shifting the mind from a latent stage to potentializing productivity, bringing personal fulfillment, self-recognition and self-actualization. Innovative Creativity should be a book Inculcated from early education and required throughout the educational systems and included as a corporate fundamental. Pushing the mind on innovative creativity will help engender a healthier planetary social-political relationships where making peace dominates making war.

- **Dr. Alexandra Paulhiac, Oriental Medicine; Diplomat of Neuro Acupuncture; Functional Medicine Physician; Director, Mountain Quest Wellness Center, USA**

Einstein professed in his book Cosmic Religion, "At times I feel certain I am right without knowing the reason." Given as of 2023 we know Einstein's theory of relativity has proven correct to 14 decimal places; it seems he really did know something. This tacit nature of knowledge, both personally and across groups and societies, has led some experts to claim we can never accurately define knowledge, but in this insightful book, Bennet, Shelley and Dhewa draw from neuroscience, indigenous knowledge, successful case studies and even spiritual practices to make the point that we don't have to define knowledge alone to take advantage of it. By defining it in relation to innovation and creativity, we can enhance our thinking to new levels of impact and flow, both in our personal and professional lives.

- **Stuart French, Knowledge Manager, Victorian County Fire Authority, Australia**

Innovative Creativity

Creating with Innovation in Mind

Dr. Alex Bennet, Mountain Quest Institute
Dr. Arthur Shelley, Intelligent Answers
with Charles Dhewa, Knowledge Transfer Africa

FIRST EDITION (Softback)

MQIPress
Frost, West Virginia
303 Mountain Quest Lane, Marlinton, WV 24954
United States of America
Telephone: 304-799-7267
eMail: alex@mountainquestinstitute.com
www.mountainquestinn.com
www.MQIPress.com

ISBN 978-1-949829-71-6

The mind is a wonderful thing.
Entangled with living,
Engendering thought,
Who knows what the next thought will bring?

Prologue

Creativity is our life partner, encapsulated within magic and mystery. We humans have been creating since our dawn. Creativity has many life partners, and comes in a legion of ways. While many adhere to the maxim: "If it isn't broke, leave it alone;" I say: If it isn't broke, break it! How else can we move on to something new? Creativity comes from necessity, dreams, fantasies, greed, curiosity, and many other human impulses. Then there is luck, serendipity, collaboration, policies, muses, discoveries of old and new books, ruins, cultures, and grand gestures – to name but a few. Creativity is part of our human DNA, and will exist as long as we exist.

Michael Stankosky
Doctor of Science & Master of Arts
Professor Emeritus
George Washington University

Contents

Preface

There are so many wonderful books on creativity! Would that we could touch them and immediately "know" what is in them, and then use our incredible human synthesizing skills to connect all the learning that is best for us and plan our actions accordingly. Maybe one day this will happen! But not today.

So why another book? Ah, but that's the beauty of creativity. There is ALWAYS something new. Just like people. No two people are—or ever have been—alike; there's always something unique about each of us! And so it is with creativity. Even when we THINK we are doing something exactly the same, whenever a human is involved in the doing or thinking, there's always something that's different! Different situations. Different contexts. And lots of different ways of thinking to explore! We're these amazing complex adaptive systems, and "change" is our middle name. Come to think of it, creativity is like complexity. It's a multiplier. The more things we create, the more there is to create.

Do you know that for hundreds, thousands, maybe even millions of years ideas were not really valued. I mean, some really good ideas like fire certainly caught on, but it took civilization a long time before realizing that it *must value ideas*. In an interview with General Eisenhower right before he was elected US president, David Lawrence reported him saying: "I want new ideas. I don't know what the future has in store for me, but if I am called to a high position of responsibility, I will want new ideas." It didn't take long before creative thinking was becoming a prized and profit-producing possession for individuals, organizations, and countries. And then it was. For example, in the Spring of 2010, IBM—the international technology and consulting firm—released a study crossing 33 industries engaging 1500 chief executive officers from 60 countries which cited creativity as the **single most important leadership competency**.[1]

Everyone needs new ideas. Just think how boring life would be without them! Fortunately, this is one need pretty much everyone can resolve, although in some people that creative power lies dormant, waiting. Ideas are all around us and within us in every moment of life, just waiting for us to feel, hear, or catch sight of, and for some to smell and taste. Looking at the top ten countries in terms of the number of patents filed in 2021 alone, there were 695,400 filed in China, 595,700 in the U.S., 502,600 in Japan, 206,780 in South Korea, 173,220 in Germany, 58,410 in the United Kingdom, 53,860 in Switzerland, 44,520 in Sweden, and 41,270 in the Netherlands. In 2022, Indian and Chinese innovators soared to record highs, increasing by 31.6% and 3.1%, respectively.

Out of a total of 3,457,400 filed patents internationally in 2022, 1.58 million were filed in China, and around 505,000 in the U.S., 405,000 in Japan, 272,000 in the Republic of Korea, and nearly 156,000 in Germany. And those are just the ideas that people thought powerful enough to warrant patents!

The large majority of those patentable ideas—which means that they've resulted in innovation—follow the interest, passion, focus, and joy of the creator. This is not surprising. Focus brings limits, which enable us to dig down deeper into the knowledge domain of interest, passion keeps us digging, and joy is both an incentive to keep going *and* a reward. Crawford goes even further, suggesting that you begin to think "in terms of your great ambitions, your desires, and your plans for the future. If these things have been implanted in your mind, it is probable that your activity will gravitate in such directions."[2] This is the power of intent. And once you start, you keep going! Ideas beget ideas, one idea jumping out from another, with all of that stuff that is the product of our deep dive into a domain of knowledge emerging to bisociate with stuff in the context of where we situate ourselves. And so, the jumps (or leaps) continue, with really good ideas often representing many successive jumps. We once asked a scientist friend how on earth he had 80 patents, and he simply said, "They just keep emerging, connecting to each other, and then disconnecting and standing in their own light."

Even when these ideas jump out from other ideas, *they are all different*. They are products of mental activity *and* intuition and we already know that we all think, feel, and act differently, so our ideas are different. They are concepts or notions, or maybe a mental image or picture, a vision, or maybe they relate to a plan or a standard, or … and the list goes on. They are the ideas that pop in and out of our minds, sometimes entangled with everyday monkey chatter and other times pure and clear and beautiful.

How do we get these ideas? We're going to talk a lot about that in this book. But looking through the vast number of books on this topic, they seem to follow two paths: *inspiration* and *technique*, although these can certainly overlap. We describe creativity as the bisociation of two or more things, and that certainly can be caused by either inspiration or technique. Yet creativity is generally *more* than the combining of two or more things. On the technique side, way back in the 1950's, Crawford outlined a process involving three steps: (1) look at one thing (can be either a process or an idea), (2) then select one unusual or strong attribute of that thing, and (3) then apply that attribute to something else.[3] Note the caveat that these "things" have to have a relationship of some nature with each other.

Crawford goes on further to say that there are five controlling factors to our choice of attributes: money-making and commercial possibilities, labor-saving possibilities, preservation and well-being of ourselves and others, beauty and appeal to the senses, and the current of the world's thinking.[4] We would add the excitement of innovating, of contributing something new, of making a difference in the world! This shifting of attributes from one thing to another has had a lot of success in the past. Try it.

As he concludes, you now have a creation, and even in 1954 when his book *The Techniques of Creative Thinking* was published, Crawford vigorously stated, "Creative thinking is today's most prized, profit-producing possession for any individual, corporation, or country. It has the capacity to change you, your business, and the world."[5] Little did he know how true those words would still reverberate in the 21st century!

Knowledge Capacities, discussed in depth in Chapter 1, have an underlying theme similar to Crawford's technique, perhaps with a little different twist. Instead of shifting a specific attribute from one thing to another, knowledge capacities are a shift in your perception, the *way* you look at something. One example is shifting frames of reference. There is limited mental capacity in a single viewpoint or frame of reference. Confusion, paradoxes and riddles are not made by external reality or the situation; they are created by our own limitations in thinking, language, and perspective or viewpoint. When addressing an issue or opportunity in an organizational setting, approaches to shifting your frame of reference might include looking at the issue from the viewpoint of different stakeholders; exploring the issue from the inside out as well as the outside in; or looking at the issue through the lens of simplicity, complicity, and then complexity. Another example is the use of McCabe's Dihedral Group Theory, which echoes the mathematical thought processes used by Steve Jobs.[6] The point is that when you look from different directions you perceive differences, *which combine thoughts in different ways,* leading to new ideas.

To enrich your creativity techniques, in this text we introduce John Lewis' *Story Thinking* with the visualization of the *structure of story* underlying both creativity and innovation. Story Thinking breaks Aristotle's description of the natural story-telling pattern into a six-phase cycle: Automation, Disruption, Investigation, Ideation, Expectation, and Affirmation (ADIIEA). (See Chapter 8.)

And then, there is the other path, that of inspiration. Indeed, for many people who create successful innovation, their bright ideas come suddenly, perhaps waking in the middle of the night with solutions in mind, and having the ability to translate those ideas into something useful. With few exceptions, these ideas are in the knowledge domain of their interest and passion, a domain on which they have focused and engaged for a number of years. In other words, they PREPARED themselves in their knowledge domain of passion … *they were ready to receive big ideas and knew what to do with those ideas when they got them.* In this regard, there is clearly value in well-invested age. Older men and women get a break here since "the further we progress along the great path of time and the older we are, the greater perspective we have looking backwards",[7] although, of course, this is highly dependent on the health and openness to learning of the individual. You will note the element of wisdom that snuck into the end of this paragraph. And, yes, wisdom joins intuition and imagination as powerful human forces accelerating innovative creativity.

There are those who choose to become the fullness of who they are, that is, to embrace *both* ways of knowing and creating—the mental technique and the intuitive inspiration. Einstein saw this as he wrote in his book *Cosmic Religion* that: *Imagination embraces the entire world, stimulating progress, giving birth to evolution. It is, strictly speaking, a real factor in scientific research.*[8] It is at this nexus, this point of creative tension, that something can emerge that is greater than either approach could bring forth by itself. And it is at this intersection that we begin with the big idea of Innovative Creativity.

A Bit About Structure

Somewhere along the way, life began to be all about unfolding, with little bits of information emerging here and there and a large part of our learning was the discovery of how all these sometimes disparate pieces fit together. You will find this to be the case with this book. Deep dives into a topic and then moving right into various other topics, leaving you, the reader to "connect the dots" as you move through the text. Now, there are hints along the way as a number of subjects emerge again and again throughout the book. For example, when indexing there were some concepts—intent/intention, intuition, patterns, self, tacit knowledge, thinking and thought, truth and wisdom—woven throughout.

Then, finally, at the end, following a case study, a chapter actually entitled "Connecting the Dots", which provides a model and a brief recapping of core ideas as well as a few additional thoughts. Creativity itself is about connecting the dots, brining two or more ideas together to achieve something new. And that is what we are asking you to do. Make the ideas that resonate with you your own, and use them to explore your own unique Innovative Creativity journey.

That said, just prior to publication, a colleague and friend, Dr. Moria Levy, CEO of ROM Global, noted that the enriching ideas might be easier to consume if there was a better understanding of the big picture from the beginning. She provided an illustration to share how she saw the larger pieces fitting together, and so I share that now with you.

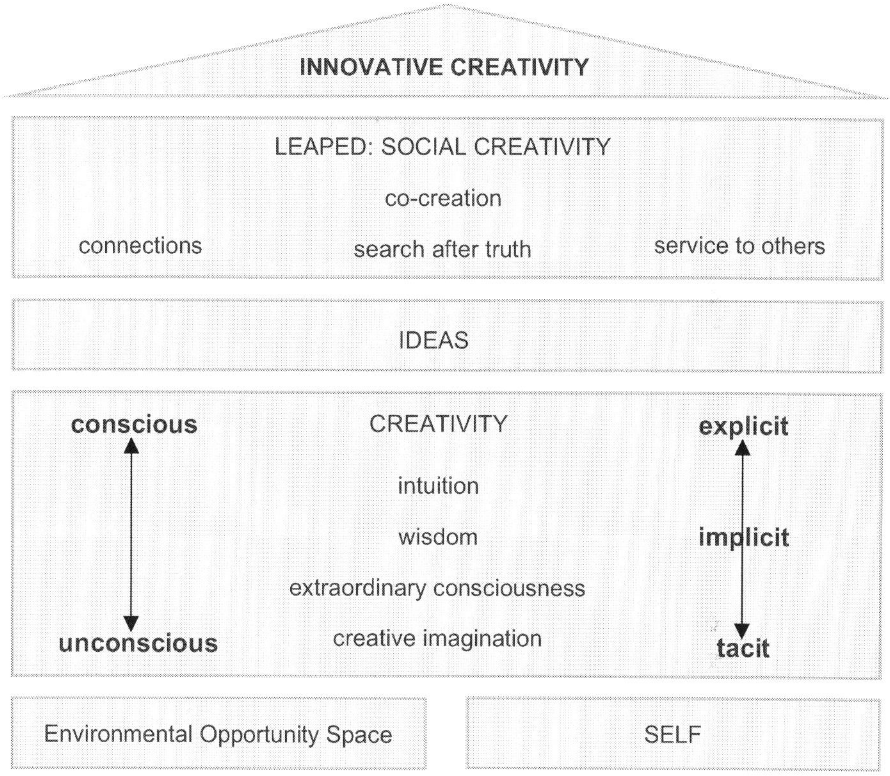

Basics: Exploring Creativity

While the sequential organization of the chapters is not directly tied to this model, it provides a good way to look at the relationships of core topics. Working through SELF and the Environmental Opportunity Space, it acknowledges the human power of creative imagination, wisdom, and extraordinary consciousness as we access our tacit knowledge and tap into the larger sphere of intuition, emerging ideas and opening to the creative leap, which is very much augmented by our social connections, driven by our search for truth, and accelerated through service to others. And with that thought, we begin.

There is a space between man's imagination
and man's attainment that may only
be traversed by his longing.

Kahlil Gibran
Sand and Foam

Foreword

To be sure, in this timely and inspired volume Alex Bennet, Arthur Shelley, and Charles Dhewa provide an expansive view of human ingenuity. Joining in, from the onset in the Prologue, Michael Stankosky includes in granite stone clarity, insight into this human quality. In stride with his preeminent work over decades on the nature of knowledge, he places creativity front and center as an inherent human function. Cautiously, he advises that it is also *encapsulated within magic and mystery*. In this book, the authors may in fact know where a good portion of the *magic* and *mystery* comes from and belongs.

Historically and well into our times, these views present a paradigm shift of epic proportion. Human intelligence is on the rise! Not that we're getting smarter; rather, we are rising to better understand what we are, how we think, how we learn, how we choose, and what and how we can create. In that regard, I would share a few historical perspectives for reflection and then a slight glimpse of creativity vis-a-vis the new era of human intelligence as we peruse the insightful approach of these three harbingers of creativity and innovation.

In researching the etymology of creativity, one finds that the emergence of root words are sparse and lacking. In fact, we may surmise that humans have been hesitant to recognize our faculty for being creative. There is *creare* and *creo* from Latin for "to create", and *facere* for "to make" and *creatives* for "creative", *Krelnein* or *Krainein* from Greek for "to fulfill", and *merake* for "doing things with love or soul—putting yourself into something". Indeed, while there are many words and meanings of words that could be considered in tracing the language spectrum, they do not begin to resonate with the magnitude of the modern usage of *creativity*. In great measure, earlier related language was reserved across religions and cultures for the activities and realms of divine beings. Accordingly, not attributing creating and creativity to humans was, and may still be, a way to elevate the divine and diminish mortals.

Across annals of history, we recorded and gathered religious and philosophical insights depicting human nature and its creations. Vast vestiges, memorials and records represent human legacies of civilizations, governing and economic systems, sciences, structures and infrastructures, and literature, music, and bodies of beliefs. We carved and we painted, and generations stand in awe of those creations. Imagine $450 million for a single portrait by an artist from five centuries ago and $30 million for one of the artist's notebooks; and only now is the cosmic merit of the artist brilliantly revealed.[9] Across time, Leonardo da Vinci adds a grand key, "Though human ingenuity may make various inventions … it will never devise any invention more beautiful, nor more simple, nor more to the purpose than Nature does; because in her inventions nothing is wanting, and nothing is superfluous."[10] History has considered human brilliance as anomalies for so long. Now, with modern capabilities to explore within us, what then do we make of the human brain-mind/heart-soul with which we are endowed? When we appreciate nature as an example, not just a metaphor, our questions become more like nature—innumerable and infinitely varied. Variety is the crowning evidence of existence and most likely of creation and creativity.

When my wife and I married in 1968, all we had was a Blue Chevy Nova and our wedding rings. The first impactful experience we shared was my service in a distant battlefield. Somehow, to help lift us from that harsh reality, we purchased a 54-volume set of the Great Books of the Western World.[11] This collection was compiled under the advice of some of the most learned scholars of the time. Two volumes entitled *A Syntopicon* carefully reviewed 102 selected topics. See the list at en.wikipedia.org, topic under Contents: *A Syntopicon*. Fast forward to 1984 when I was serving as a consultant to the Commanding General, Fort Belvoir, Virginia. There, I had the opportunity to design and develop, with special colleagues, a unique think tank for providing unprecedented ability to solve complex issues rapidly and effectively. To that end, my attention was drawn to the world-changing use of personal computers and to the escalating dynamic of creativity processes in complex decision-making.

To increase my understanding of creativity, I turned to the 102 topics in *A Syntopicon*. Alas, there was no listing for Creativity, even though there were topics like Habit and Reasoning. Then, as I read in the introductory volume, "The Great Conversation", I was struck by three affirmative statements about the nature of meaningful thinking at work: Speaking of the worker in the workplace—"He will develop all the meaning there is in his work and go on to see to it that it has more and better meaning."[12]; "An axiomatic educational proposition is that what is honored in a country will be cultivated there."[13]; and "We cannot admit that ordinary people cannot have a good education, because we cannot agree that democracy must involve a degradation of the human ideal.... We cannot concede that the conquest of nature, the conquest of drudgery, and the conquest of political power must lead in combination to triviality in education and hence in all the other occupations of life. The aim of education is wisdom, and each must have the chance to become as wise as he can."[14] There we had it—affirmations about deeper thinking, even at work, but no reference to creativity. One thing was certain, there was a lot to think about. How to think about it all was still a formidable challenge.

I continued my interest in creativity with a limited 1950's perspective. It expanded by orders of magnitude during the subsequent decades. Fortunately, there were impressions from my background that nudged me in curious directions. At the age of 16, I read how Einstein envisioned following a beam of light across the universe and how that momentary experience served as an epiphany for his conception of the theory of relatively. I wondered how the mind could process that to any useful conclusion. In my twenties, my religious upbringing solidified around a positive regard for the capacities of our brains and minds. Then, in the 1970's as an immense range of creativity resources unfolded, a growing number of 20th Century thought leaders emerged under the caveat of the creativity discipline. And in the shifting of leading global economies from industrial-based to information-based and knowledge-based, a wave of creativity perspectives and resources unfolded for engaging employees in deeper thinking and productivity at work. A major change of view of the role of employees, especially in America, was characterized by Peter Drucker's observation about employees evolving from being expenses to employees as assets, and then to employees as investors.[15] Along with this evolution emerged the contemporary role of *knowledge worker*. At the same time, people in general were gradually accepting that they had abilities to think in a variety of imaginative, constructive, new, innovative, and creative ways. Given the convergence in various countries and economies, especially again in America and in the western and democratic nations, numerous brilliant creativity thought leaders, prolific theorists and authors, scientists across disciplines, centers of university research and studies, consulting, and business development activities produced a firestorm of the new appreciation of human brain power. The impact blossomed in education systems, in Wall Street, and in the entrepreneurial climate and economies of the industrial age of the middle half of the 20th Century. As WWII ended with the victories of freedom-loving nations, veterans and workers from hyper-focused wartime engines of invention and productivity infused a heightened sense of rebuilding everything better and better in the last half of the 20th Century and innovation and creativity blossomed.

Some would venture to say that the genesis of creativity was cultivated during the Renaissance with grand manifestations of human achievement. Clearly, the amazing achievements of that era begin to add humans to the realm of creators, albeit at an earthly level. In any case, at the beginning of the 20th Century we still had the majority of our populations engaged with producing food for our life sustenance. Then, almost miraculously, by the end of the century only a few percent of us were required to do that. The rest of us were engaged in creating thousands of new things and our brain-mind/heart-soul capacities were enveloped with the notion of creativity. Still, we were not clear about this *magical and mysterious* power. Is it organized within our brains and minds to function concurrently as we process learning and knowledge? Is it easily engaged, or do you have to methodically engage it? Is it localized or systemic? Is it a core process throughout the subfunctions of the brain-mind development, or is it selectively distributed, genetic or acquired? At this point, two decades into the 21st Century, the questions about creativity are multiplying exponentially and they will likely abound for decades to come.

More than ever, *How do we release the Genie from the lamp?* How do we tap the next level of creativity and innovation that are needed here on Planet Earth? There are so many human needs. Ironically, the more we discover, the more apparent the challenges become; even our achievements illuminate unforeseen expectations. As we shift here to the vantage point of Mountain Quest Institute (MQI), we concede that the *Wishful Genie Paradigm* is not an answer. Moreover, the MQI groundbreaking work in *Innovative Creativity: Creating with Innovation in Mind* beckons us to deepen and broaden our innate creativity capacities in a fresh and expansive way to summon the genius within each of us.

These authors draw from a deep aquifer of research with advanced concepts and models founded in a consilience approach that coalesces many disciplines and sciences. Their systemic approach orchestrates creativity capacities with the flow of information and knowledge deep within. In Chapter 7 they even look to drawing from the quantum level. At that depth we may tap crescendos of our brain/mind performance for innovation. The added value of IC is that it has significantly rich implied and projected capabilities. It is well enough conceived and developed to keep pace with rapidly progressing human augmentation technologies needed for making strides vis-à-vis innovative efforts and ambitions. Second, and more importantly, it has in its DNA the genetic coding, so to speak, to influence the rapidly evolving quantum revolution.

The marathon is on. Artificial Intelligence shifts to Augmented Intelligence; Digital Computing shifts to Quantum Computing; Human Intelligence shifts from a subset of the neuroscience family of research to an emerging and expansive range of comprehensive human consciousness. In the research, the prominence of creativity is increasing to the point where there is a wide range of schools of thought even about the primary relationship of creativity and intelligence.

As you engage the set of chapters before you, what will you experience? What will capture your imagination? What will you return back to from time to time? What will you choose to learn more about to empower your life interests?

What will encourage you to wonder deeply about and engage your brain-mind/heart-soul potential?

My Hope—The U.S. National Library of Medicine reports there are more than 600 neurologic diseases. You would recognize many of them—people all around us deal with them. For example, by 2050 the number of Americans alone with Alzheimer's or other dementias could double to 13 million. The cost of that care now exceeds $300 billion per year. IC can help reduce this.

What do you hope for? What does your SELF think about? Try Exercise 5 in Chapter 4: *Who is My SELF?* Remember, Innovative Creativity encourages and helps us to see how we are co-creators. These MQI authors know about this—in this book they share *deep knowledge* of it!

Robert Turner
Co-Author, *Reblooming the Knowledge Movement: The Democratization of Organizations* and *Unleashing the Human Brain: A Consilience Approach to Managing Self*

Freeing
Preparing
IC
Accessing
Focusing

Chapter 1
Introduction

Innovative Creativity is purposefully engaging your creativity with innovation in mind. Grammatically and conceptually, it can be thought of in two ways, and both will be explored in this book. From one perspective, "Innovative Creativity" means that we are going to take an *innovative approach to exploring creativity*. And indeed, we are! There is so much that has been written through the years about creativity, and that writing emerges from so many fields of study, so many different viewpoints. This, of course, is a good thing, providing a rich array of offerings to a diversity of people who, along with their unique self-created models of the world and ways of understanding and learning, demand different approaches and viewpoints. As we write in the beginning of *Unleashing the Human Mind* by Bennet, Bennet and Turner:

> *Increasingly, we recognize that we are infinitely complex beings with immense physical, mental, emotional and spiritual capacities. Presiding over our human systems,* ***our human brains are fully integrated, biological, and extraordinary organs that are preeminent in the known Universe.***[16]

There are several points in this quote important to this introduction. First, the recognition that we are infinitely complex beings. There is so much "more" to us than we have discovered, and still there is so much that we HAVE discovered, enough to "know" that we HAVE immense physical, mental, emotional and spiritual capacities. So, in this book, while focusing on creativity, we are going to integrate our physical, mental, emotional and spiritual capabilities, pushing the edges of everyday thought to more fully engage our human potential.

This requires a consilience approach. Consilience means a "jumping together" of knowledge through the dynamic linking of ideas, facts and theories *across disciplines* to create a common groundwork of explanation.[17] While certainly a large amount of research on creativity has been done in the area of psychology and related disciplines, creativity is a phenomenon that requires exploration across disciplines. As Nobel Prize-winning immunologist Peter Medawar said,

> *The analysis of creativity in all its forms is beyond the competence of any one accepted discipline. It requires a consortium of talents: psychologists, biologists, philosophers, computer scientists, artists, and poets would all expect to have their say. That "creativity is beyond analysis" is a romantic illusion we must now outgrow.*[18]

We agree that understanding creativity requires exploring it across disciplines. In this book we pull thoughts from various fields including education, learning, cognitive psychology, sociology, biology, decision science, management, neuroscience, systems and complexity, spirituality, and many more sub-fields, and do NOT embrace a specific argument or approach to creativity, although there are certainly many to choose from! Only—and here is the rub—in all the materials we are going to explore, what makes sense and what proves useful will be determined by YOU with your unique beliefs, feeling of self, capabilities, and capacity for learning, all complimented by a true sense of humility.[19] So, in a sense, this book is yours.

The potential offered through humility is a human gift in a changing, complex and uncertain world. *You cannot learn if you already have all the answers*. Humility is so important to our learning potential that we've included a short exercise below. From an individual perspective, humility means having an accurate view of yourself, neither too high nor too low; recognizing your strengths and abilities as well as your weaknesses and limitations, and being honest about those to yourself and others. From a collective viewpoint, this means being other-oriented, focused beyond self. This would include development of empathy, knowing the needs and wants of others, and taking those into consideration in your decisions and actions. When taking creativity to the level of innovation, creating something useful to yourself and others, it is easy to recognize how very important it is to *understand the needs and wants of others*!

* * * * *

EXERCISE 1: *Humility*

STEP (1) To increase humility, first *open your mind* to accept that, by nature, at this point of development human beings have egos and desires, both of which can have strong emotional tags connected to them. Yet it can be rather difficult for an individual to recognize egotism and arrogance in themselves. Remember, the personality, not the self, is often in control, so an individual may or may not be aware of their projection or position. This is potentially true of the individual with whom you are interacting, as well as yourself.

STEP (2) Second, *assume the other is right*. Set aside personal opinions and beliefs for the moment, accept what is being said, the idea or concept, and reflect on this new perspective in the search for truth. While this may prove quite difficult for an individual who is highly dependent on ego and arrogance to survive in what can be a challenging world, almost every individual has someone or something they love more than themselves. Try imagining that this new idea is coming from that someone whom you love, respect, and trust, or that it is associated with something that you love. This simple trick will help increase your ability to engage humility.

STEP (3) Adopting this new idea or concept, *try to prove it is right*, pulling up as many examples as you can and testing the logic of it. If all the examples you can pull up fit this new perspective, then you have discovered a new level of truth. If the examples contradict the concept, then bring in your previous ideas and test the logic of those. Again, if the examples do not all fit, continue your search for a bigger concept that conveys a higher level of truth. The critical element in this learning approach is giving up your way of thinking so that you can understand thoughts different than your own, discovering new truths. Then you can compare the various concepts, asking which is more complete or how they potentially work together.

One issue that may emerge is the inclination for people to think how they feel first, then think about the logical part to determine truth. This "feeling" has already biased their higher conceptual thinking, which may result in it being untrue. As we expand in consciousness, it is necessary for us to develop a new sense of self that does not require us to be right in order to feel good about our self.

STEP (4) Once we come to a conclusion, we need to take action. It is time to affirm our incorrectness, as appropriate, to those with whom we have potentially lacked humility, and to *show gratitude for them sharing their thoughts with us*. Note that the expression of appreciation and gratitude reduces forces. It is not enough to say that you were wrong, *nor is that an important issue*. What *is* important is to acknowledge that someone else is right, and that you are appreciative of learning from them.

STEP (5) Finally, *ensure that your motive for adopting humility is your search for truth*. Motive eventually comes out, and the wrong motive will defeat the purpose at hand. In this search for truth, you are using mental discipline to develop greater wisdom. While it is difficult to overcome the urge to "look good" and to be "righter" than others, remember, when we are "full" there is no room for new thought. When choosing humility as part of our learning journey, we discover that it is not about being right, rather it is about the continuous search for higher truth.

* * * * *

And that brings us to the second way of thinking about "Innovative Creativity", which is the ability to APPLY your creativity to life situations whether personal or professional, the creation of something useful, whether described as a design or theory, a process, or a product. Some experts already define that as part of creativity, believing that creativity should also have utility and lead to a new product or process, that is, innovation. We're going to explore the diversity of thought around creativity and innovation in Chapter 2. For now, let's agree that innovation means the creation of new ideas and the transformation of those ideas into useful applications; thus, the combination of creativity and contribution as operational values promote innovation.[20]

Throughout all our life experiences, humans are always looking for relationships among things—thoughts, events, happenings, and people. We are on a grand search for patterns, for *creative association.*[21] In our attempt to understand the wholeness of a topic, we are usually led to the idea of systems thinking.[22] This extension of cause-and-effect thinking shows us that effects provide a feedback loop into the next cause, helping us to understand that what we call an "effect" is actually *part* of the next "cause". We move to symbiotic thinking when we realize that the very concept of "cause" cannot exist without the concept of "effect". This deeper relationship is not from causality, *but from existence.*

Would the concept of "day" exist if not also for the concept of "night"? Would we have a need for the term "summer" if not also for the term "winter"? The very existence of a thing or idea *requires* the existence of something else. Space cannot exist without objects, and objects must be enclosed by space. As we develop our symbiotic thinking, we see that "supply and demand" is not just a single business concept, but two concepts where each exists because the other exists. And we begin to understand the nature of quantum physics, where two states must exist at the same time. This leads us to the larger understanding that *the need to create cannot exist without the need to receive that which is created*, that which is innovation. Innovative Creativity fully includes the desire to use one's creativity for individual and collective benefit.

Linking Information, Knowledge, Creativity, and Innovation

A brief understanding of terms will help establish this link. Information exists, it has a physical aspect, physically encoded as *patterns of organization.*

Organization itself can be defined as "the physical expression of a system containing information."[23] Organization means the existence of a non-random pattern of particles and energy fields or the sub-units comprising any system such that "the intricate organization of matter and energy which makes possible that phenomenon which we call life, is itself a product of the vast store of information contained within the system itself."[24] In short, information is a basic property of the Universe, as fundamental as matter and energy, and interconvertible with energy.

As we are continuously reminded in today's environment, it is critical to be able to recognize the truth of information, that is, the accuracy of information we are using from any source. And it is important to reach this conclusion not based on belief but rather on personal testing, which can occur through past experiences or through creating new circumstances which logically challenge the information in order to prove its validity. Note that when information is *effectively applied* it is knowledge. Knowledge is the capacity (potential or actual) to take effective action[25] or, as Plato forwarded, justified true belief. A belief is justified as "true" when it is acted upon and the expected result occurs. All knowledge is comprised of information that is synthesized to help improve the activity of energy, and while it produces a "result" of some nature, the result itself is not knowledge, but a product of knowledge, which is effectively applied information.

Similarly, creativity is a capacity. Creativity—which is considered from a number of viewpoints in Chapter 2—comes, at least at the present time, exclusively from people, a CAPACITY to see new ideas from associating internal and external information. In turn, innovation is *applied creativity* in concert with knowledge. As an idea generator, knowledge is the currency of creativity and innovation, and knowledge cannot exist without information.

As can be seen, information, knowledge, creativity and innovation have an entangled relationship. Knowledge is effectively applying information (in terms of producing the expected result). Innovation is effectively applying creativity (in terms of a useful design, process or product).

Knowledge = Information + Effective Action (Potential or Actual)

Innovation = Knowledge + Creativity + Useful Application

While knowledge comes from the past and creativity requires knowledge, both knowledge and creativity are capacities which can be applied in the present (actual) or engaged in the future (potential). They have a symbiotic relationship, that is, knowledge cannot exist without creativity (see the section on

Knowledge as a Creative Process below), and creativity cannot exist without knowledge. Further, they both emerge from the associative patterning process of the brain, that is, the unique complexing of external and internal information (organized patterns). This important concept will come up throughout this text.

In Figure 1, there is a dotted line between knowledge and creativity, which when combined lead to innovation. It has long been recognized that there is a tension between knowledge and innovation, that creative thinking goes beyond knowledge. As Weisberg suggests, "Knowledge may provide the basic elements, the building blocks out of which are constructed new ideas, but in order for these building blocks to be available, the mortar holding the old ideas together must not be too strong."[26] The intent is that while universally acknowledging that it is necessary to have knowledge of a field if you wish to discover something novel within that field, simultaneously, if you have locked into specific ideas and are not open to learning, you will never be able to move beyond stereotyped responses.[27] This stresses the importance of humility, mind open to learning, as necessary to creativity.

Note that innovation is not necessarily an immediate result. As Fritz Machlup said in the early 1960's in his seminal work on the knowledge economy, "We shall have to bring out clearly that this is not a simple unidirectional flow from one stage to the next, from inception to development, to eventual adoption, but there are usually cross-currents, eddies, and whirlpools."[28]

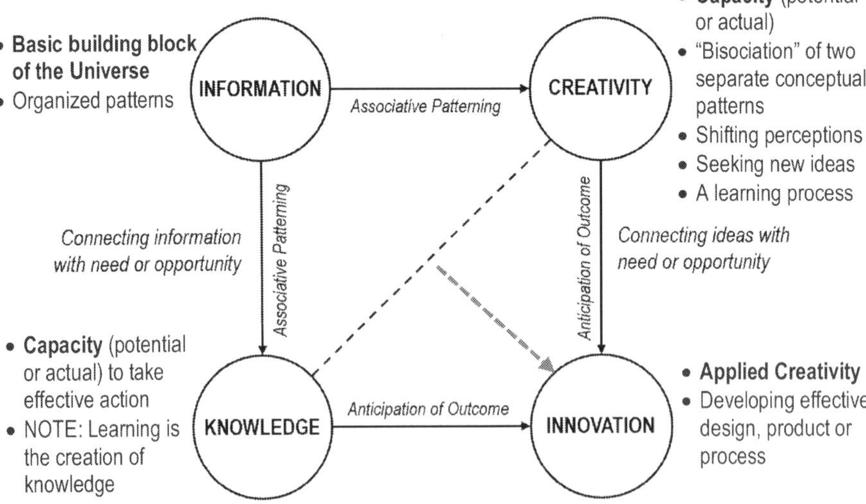

Figure 1. *Exploring the relationships among information, knowledge, creativity and innovation.*

Past experiences, feelings, knowledge, goals, and the situation at hand all influence how creative an individual will, or can, be. It is the context of the activity or situation at hand (need, challenge, etc.) that triggers the putting things together (bisociation) in an unusual way to create (and recognize) something that may be new and potentially useful (innovation). Thus, knowledge—context sensitive and situation dependent (temporal) and a trigger for creativity—serves as an action lever for innovation.

Knowledge as a Creative Process

As can be seen, information and knowledge are foundational to Innovative Creativity. The flow of knowledge, as the capacity to take effective action, is in reality the flow of information with enough context and understanding built around that information—entangled with the sensemaking capability of the user—such that the user can effectively create or re-create the necessary or desired knowledge and act on that information.

The idea of "re-creating" requires a deeper understanding of knowledge from the viewpoint of the mind/brain. Knowledge can be considered as having two parts, knowledge (informing) and knowledge (proceeding), which builds on the distinction made by Ryle[29] between "knowing that" and "knowing how. Remember, knowledge is both the *potential* and *actual* capacity to take effective action. Knowledge (informing) is the information (or content) part of knowledge. While this information part of knowledge is still generically information (represented by organized patterns), it is special because of its structure and relationship with other information. Knowledge (informing) consists of information that may represent understanding, meaning, insights, expectations, intuition, theories, and principles that support or lead to effective action. It is considered knowledge when used *as part of the knowledge process*.

Knowledge (proceeding) represents the *process* and *action* part of knowledge. It is the process of selecting and associating the relevant information—literally, knowledge (informing)—from which *specific actions can be identified and implemented*, that is, actions that result in some level of anticipated outcome. There is considerable precedent for considering knowledge as a process versus an outcome of some action. For example, Kolb[30] forwards in his theory of experiential learning that knowledge retrieval, creation, and application requires engaging knowledge as a process, not a product. Bohm reminds us that "the actuality of knowledge is a living process that is taking place right now" and that we are taking part in this process.[31] Note that the process our minds use to find, create, and semantically mix the information needed to take effective action, whether used in decision-making or in creating innovation, is often unconscious and difficult to communicate to someone else; therefore, by definition, tacit. See Chapter 9.

Recognizing that knowledge is context sensitive and situation dependent in terms of relevancy, we can now also recognize that knowledge relates not only to its information content, knowledge (informing), but also to the efficacy and usefulness of that information content in terms of the situation at hand, knowledge (proceeding). This means that while the content may be constant, when you change the context the effectiveness of the content in that new context may be entirely different. The greater the complexity of a situation, the greater the potential number of patterns and relationships of patterns that make knowledge relevant to that situation, and the less likely that knowledge would apply to different situations.

From the viewpoint of the mind/brain, any knowledge that is being "re-used" is actually being "re-created" and, in an area of continuing interest, most likely complexed over and over again as new and different incoming information is associated with internal information. Further, if knowledge (informing) is different, there is a good chance that knowledge (proceeding) will be different, that is, the *process* of pulling up and sequencing associated knowledge (informing) and semantically complexing it with incoming information to make it comprehensive is going to vary. In essence, every time we apply knowledge, whether informing or proceeding, it is to some extent new knowledge because the human mind—unlike an information management system—*unconsciously tailors what is emerging as knowledge to the situation at hand*! This is the individuated art of knowledge (proceeding).[32]

Another important element of this process is the way information is stored in the brain, which takes invariant form. The mind doesn't store memories like a computer, that is, exactly storing everything that comes in. For example, when you see a picture, only about 20 percent (the core) of what you are seeing is represented in the image in your brain; the other 80 percent of that image comes from information, ideas, and feelings already in your brain.[33] This particular phenomenon of relating external and internal forms of experience is called appresentation.[34] As Moon explains: "Appresentation is the manner in which a part of something that is perceived as an external experience can stimulate a much more complete or richer internal experience of the 'whole' of that thing to be conjured up."[35] This tells us that while indeed our unconscious is trying to simplify life by using solutions that have worked before, those solutions are being complexed with incoming information and shifted to fit the situation and context at hand. This also leads us to understand that there is an *existential* element engaged with experiential learning.

The above discussion brings home the fact that the mind/brain develops robustness and deep understanding derived from its capacity to use past learning and memories to complete incoming information instead of storing all the details. This provides the ability to create and store higher level patterns while simultaneously semantically complexing incoming information with internal memories, adapting those memories to the situation at hand, *which may be an identified need or opportunity*. So, from a high-level perspective, we now understand that knowledge is itself *a creative process*, and that the bisociation of two (or more) separate conceptual patterns—which *is* by definition the creative process—is an everyday occurrence. In Chapter 2 we take a deeper dive into different ways to think about creativity.

<<<<<<<>>>>>>>

INSIGHT: **Knowledge, which itself is a creative process, is a trigger for creativity and an action-lever for innovation.**

<<<<<<<>>>>>>>

Knowledge Capacities

If your thought appears locked when addressing an issue or opportunity, shifting the direction from which you look can trigger new thought, not necessarily looking for new facts, but for a *new way of looking at that which is already known*. Knowledge Capacities, mental techniques for shifting focused thinking, can do just that.

Knowledge Capacities are sets of ideas and ways of acting that are more general in nature than competencies, more core to a way of thinking and being, that change our reference points. *They provide different ways for us to think and create, to perceive and operate, in the world around us.* Developed by combining senses, Knowledge Capacities complement six different ways that humans creatively operate in the world. These are: looking and seeing, feeling and touching, perceiving and representing, knowing and sensing, hearing and listening, and acting and being.[36] Each of these sets has two concepts introduced because, while they are related, there is clarity added by coupling the concepts. Each area is briefly addressed below. See Figure 2.

With our compliments (and apologies) to *Encarta World English Dictionary*, we attach specific meanings to these six ways humans operate in the world, meanings that suggest ways of observing and processing the events that occur in our lives. Knowledge Capacities are all about expanding the way we see those events in order to raise our awareness and, in relation to Innovative Creativity, *offering new ideas and an expanded set of potential solutions.*

Looking and Seeing: To direct attention toward something in order to consider it; to have a clear understanding of something. (*Examples*: Shifting Frames of Reference, Reversal)

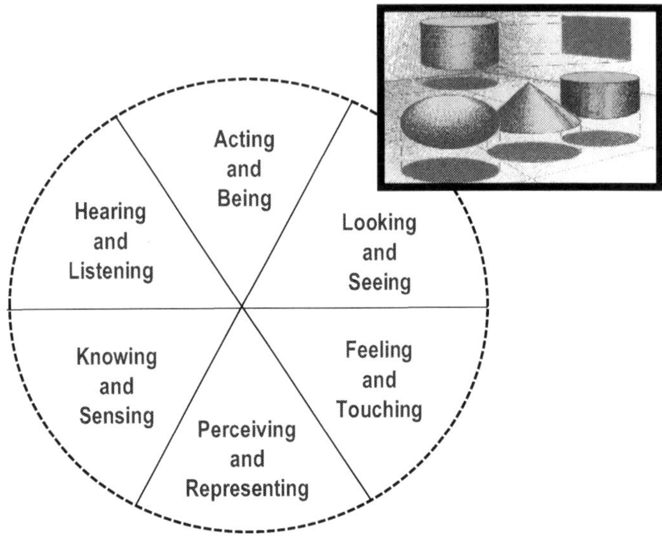

Figure 2. *Ways humans operate in the world.*

Feeling and Touching: The sensation felt when touching something; to have an effect or influence on somebody or something; to consider the response of others being touched. (*Example*: Emotional Intelligence)

Perceiving and Representing: To acquire information about the surrounding environment or situation; mentally interpreting information; an impression or attitude; ability to notice or discern. (*Examples*: Learning How to Learn, Comprehending Diversity, Symbolic Representation)

Knowing and Sensing: Showing intelligence; understanding something intuitively; detecting and identifying a change in something. (*Example*: Engaging Tacit Knowledge)

Hearing and Listening: To be informed of something, especially being told about it; making a conscious effort to hear, to concentrate on somebody or something; to pay attention and take it into account. (*Example*: Active Listening, Humility)

Acting and Being: To do something to change a situation; to serve a particular purpose; to provide information (identity, nature, attributes, position or value); to have presence, to live; to happen or take place; to have a particular quality or attribute. (*Examples*: Orchestrating Drive, Instinctual Harnessing, Organizational Zoo)

To build a further understanding, some short examples of Knowledge Capacities are provided as Appendix A. Specifically, these examples include: Learning How to Learn (perceiving and representing); Shifting Frames of Reference (seeing and looking); Reversal (seeing and looking); Comprehending Diversity (perceiving and representing); Orchestrating Drive (acting and being); and Symbolic Representation (perceiving and representing). Humility (hearing and listening) was introduced at the beginning of this chapter.

As we mature and age—and as our senses lose some of their effectiveness—the ways we perceive and operate in the world change, and with them a preference for *higher engagement of the intuitive* emerges. Thus, for example, the Knowledge Capacity of "Knowing and Sensing" would dominate decision-making. This is consistent with the neuroscience finding that despite certain cognitive losses, the engaged, mature brain can make effective decisions at more intuitive levels.[37] Consider how this "knowing" affects the creative mind as we age. Appendix B offers a larger treatment of Knowing.

Differentiating Knowledge and Knowing

Knowledge begets knowledge, and in a global interactive environment, the more that is understood, the more that can be created and understood. This is how our personal learning system works. And as we tap into our internal resources, *knowledge enables knowing, and knowing inspires the creation of knowledge*. Since there is only so much room in our conscious mind at any given time, as we expand our knowledge that which is well "known" becomes embedded in the unconscious.

The concept of "knowing", which largely follows the path of intuition, is not easy to define, since the word and concept are used in so many different ways by different people. Note that this diversity is an indicator of the importance of the concept. We consider knowing as a sense that is supported by our tacit knowledge, that is, those connections among thoughts that drive actions but cannot be expressed by the individual with that knowledge, often engaging feelings as intuitive "nudges". (A deeper discussion of tacit knowledge is in Chapter 9.) In a poetic sense, knowing could be described as *seeing beyond images, hearing beyond words, sensing beyond appearances, and feeling beyond emotions.*

A framework for knowing[38] developed by Bennet focuses on methods to increase individual sensory capabilities, specifically referring to our five external senses and to the ability to consciously integrate these sensory inputs with our tacit knowledge, both that knowledge created by past learning experiences (earned intuitive knowledge) and its entanglement with the flow of spiritual tacit knowledge (revealed intuitive knowledge) continuously available to each of us. Cognitive capabilities engaged include listening, noticing, scanning, sensing, patterning, and integrating. Cognitive processes engaged include visualizing, intuiting, valuing, choosing, and setting intent. (See Appendix B.)

Figure 3 is a nominal graphic showing the continuous feedback loops between knowledge and knowing. Thinking about (potential) and experiencing (actual) effective action (knowledge) supports development of embodied, intuitive and affective tacit knowledges.

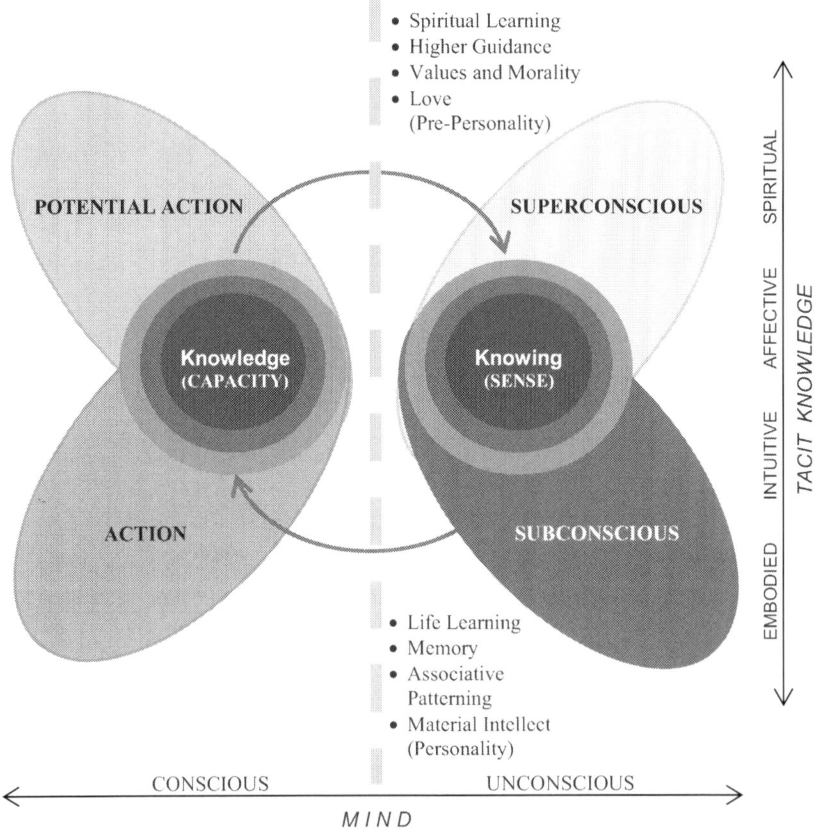

Figure 3. *The Knowledge and Knowing Loop.*

When we recognize and use our sense of knowing—regardless of its origin—we are tapping into our tacit knowledge (intuition) to inform our creativity, decisions, and actions. In turn, the feedback from taking action expands our knowledge base, much of which over time will become future tacit resources. Since our internal sense of knowing draws collectively from all areas of our tacit knowledge, the more we open to this inner sense, respond accordingly, and observe and reflect on feedback, the more our inner resources move beyond limited perceptions which may be connected to embedded beliefs and mental models, which are often remnants of childhood experiences.

The *subconscious* and *superconscious* are both part of our unconscious resources, with the subconscious directly supporting the embodied mind/brain and the superconscious (related to the larger field, whether you prefer to call that an energy field, information field, consciousness field, quantum field, or God field) is focused on tacit resources involving larger moral aspects, the emotional part of human nature, and higher development of our mental faculties.[39] When engaged by an intelligent mind which has moved beyond logic into whole thought (combining concepts and events and moving toward wisdom) based on recognition of a connected and interdependent humanity, these resources are immeasurable. Innovation results from whole thought. (Chapter 4 provides a deeper treatment of whole thought.) Thus, knowing—driven by the unconscious as an integrated unit—is the sense gained from experience that resides in the subconscious part of the mind AND the energetic connection our mind enjoys with the superconscious, although most of the time the *why* we know is tacit. As Einstein professed in his book *Cosmic Religion*, "At times I feel certain I am right without knowing the reason."[40]

In Figure 3, the superconscious is described with the terms spiritual learning, higher guidance, values and morality, and love. It is also characterized as "pre-personality" to emphasize that there are no personal translators such as beliefs and mental models attached to this form of knowing. The flow of information from the superconscious is very much focused on the moment at hand and does not bring with it any awareness patterns that could cloud the creative decision-maker's full field of perception.

In contrast, the memories stored in the subconscious are very much a part of the individual personality, and may be heavily influenced by individual perceptions and feelings at the time they were formed as well as when they are later triggered. Descriptive terms for the subconscious include life learning, memory, associative patterning, and material intellect.

Note that the subconscious is an autonomic system serving a life-support function, and thus the human subconscious is in service to the conscious mind.

It is not intended to dominate choices and decision-making, but rather to support those functions, including creativity. The subconscious expands as it integrates and connects (complexes) all that we put into it through our five perceived externally-connected senses (this is the process of associative patterning). *Note that it is at the conscious mind level that we develop our intellect and make the creative choices that serve as the framework for our subconscious processing.* Full use of your creative mind is your choice.

The Magical Synthesis

In 1976 Silvano Arieti published a book titled *Creativity: The Magical Synthesis*, which was the natural outcome of his many years of clinical research on the intrapsychic and interpersonal perspectives of cognition. He saw creativity as a prerogative, the ability to take that which is already existing and available and change it in unpredictable ways, an enlargement of human experience.[41] In that process an additional bond is established between the world and human existence, with each creative experience a variation of that bond. When confronted with something witty or comical, we laugh. With a great work of art, we experience aesthetic pleasure. With expressions of philosophy or religion, we may have a feeling of transcendence. And with a new scientific innovation may come the qualities of usefulness, understanding and predictability. Responses to our Innovative Creativity range from the physiological to the spiritual, from the practical to the theoretical. In Arieti's words,

> *Creative work thus may be seen to have a dual role: at the same time as it enlarges the universe by adding or uncovering new dimensions, it also enriches and expands man, who will be able to experience these new dimensions inwardly. It is committed not just to the visible but, in many cases, to the invisible as well.*[42]

This work, then, contends that creativity, and the innovation emerging from that creativity, must be considered from both the viewpoint of unity, in itself, and culture, as part of a larger whole. The creative process moves beyond free images and ideas floating in the head and beyond the qualities of uniqueness, originality, and divergence. It is—as Crawford and Arieti and so many other exploring minds have forwarded—necessary to engage the mental *and* the intuitive, both techniques *and* imagination.

So how does synthesis fit into this magical intersection? Synthesis—the human ability to knit together information from disparate sources into a coherent whole—is an important creative capability. Both simplification and explanation, synthesis enables the ability to decide what information to heed, what can be ignored, and how to organize (connect and integrate) and communicate what is important. It could arguably be said that synthesis is a necessary skill for living.

There are literally thousands—and probably more—approaches to synthesis. While certainly some level of synthesis skills are innate, this skillset can be honed. For example, early development and expansion of this skillset comes with doing book reviews, identifying plots, describing characters, linking character traits and actions to the purpose you think the author is trying to convey, and so on, including looking for relationships, solving word problems, identifying themes, considering cause and effect, and exploring structure and message. During research studies, to interpret meaning in qualitative approaches, researchers search for themes and descriptions, often winnowing through large amounts of data for what is most important to their research. Experts "chunk" ideas and concepts, creating understanding through the development of significant patterns useful for solving problems and anticipating future behavior within their area of focus.

For example, a study of chess players showed that master players—or experts—examined the chessboard patterns over and over again, studying them, looking at nuances, trying small changes to perturb the outcome (sense and response), generally "playing with" and studying these patterns.[43] In other words, using long-term working memory, pattern recognition, and chunking rather than logic as a means of understanding. An important insight from this study is the recognition that *when facing complex problems which do not allow reasoning or cause-and-effect analysis because of their complexity, the solution may lie in synthesis*, studying patterns and chunking those patterns, organizing at several levels to enable a tacit capacity to create solutions. This was demonstrated in the movie *A Beautiful Mind* staring Russell Crowe as a brilliant mathematician on the brink of international acclaim who becomes entangled in a mysterious conspiracy. In Chapter 2 we will talk more about the human search for patterns.

Chapter 2
Exploring Creativity

Creativity is the emergence of new or original patterns, which may be ideas, concepts, or actions. Mihaly Csikszentmihalyi, Professor of Psychology at the University of Chicago, notes that the term creativity originally meant to bring into existence something genuinely new valued enough to be added to the culture. His systems model of creativity reflects this approach.[44] Focusing on the importance of relativity, quantum physicist Amit Goswami offers his definition as the creation of something new in an entirely new context.[45]

Newness of the context is key. Since knowledge is context-sensitive and situation-dependent, every time we pull up what we perceive as "knowledge" (the capacity to take effective action) it is "new". As introduced in Chapter 1, knowledge (informing) and knowledge (proceeding) are specifically tailored to the instant at hand. This means that we as living humans acting and interacting are in a continuous state of creativity and change. This is consistent with theoretical biologist Rupert Sheldrake forwarding that creativity is a profound mystery precisely *because* it involves the appearance of patterns that never existed before.[46]

The idea of creativity as both mysterious and divine goes back to Plato, whose beautiful words example the creativity at the heart of the poet: "For the poet is an airy thing, a winged and a holy thing; and he cannot make poetry until he becomes inspired and goes out of his senses and no mind is left in him ... not by art, then, they make their poetry ... but by divine dispensation."[47] The romantic could substitute the word "exceptional" for "divine", glorifying creative people as gifted with talent (insight or intuition) that others lack, or perceive they lack.

Csikszentmihalyi points out that if we acknowledge that creativity involves "newness", the only way to tell that an idea is new is in reference to some standards, a social evaluation. As he says, "Therefore, creativity does not happen inside people's heads, but in the interaction between a person's thoughts and a sociocultural context", which is what makes creativity not an individual phenomenon, but systemic. Thus, as introduced above, Csikszentmihalyi uses the term "creative" to infer bringing into existence something he terms as "genuinely" new, that is, something of paramount significance valued enough to be added to the culture. This emphasizes H-creativity (historical) versus P-creativity (personal), which we talk about later in this chapter. From this viewpoint, Csikszentmihalyi's perspective is:

> *Creativity is any act, idea, or product that changes an existing domain, or that transforms an existing domain into a new one. And the definition of a creative person is: someone whose thoughts or actions change a domain, or establish a new domain ... In other words, a personal trait of "creativity" is not what determines whether a person will be creative. What counts is whether the novelty he or she produces is accepted for inclusion in the domain.* [48]

Similarly, Gardner[49] believes that understanding creativity entails analysis at the subpersonal, personal, impersonal and multipersonal levels. Subpersonal includes biologically oriented questions such as those related to genetics and neurobiology. Personal addresses the cognitive, including "personality, motivational, social and affect aspects of creators".[50] Impersonal would include the specific domain or discipline engaged. Multipersonal would include the social relationships, which from Gardner's viewpoint refers to "individuals and institutions sanctioned to evaluate the appropriateness and quality of the contribution at hand".[51] As a part of Innovative Creativity, the "multipersonal" focus is rather on the social aspects in terms of contribution to and discovery of ideas, which will be discussed further in Chapter 7.

Reaching even further in terms of exploring creativity, Feldman says we should conceptualize creativity as involving multiple dimensions, and he suggests "at least" addressing the following: (1) cognitive processes, (2) social/emotional processes, (3) family aspects (growing up and current), (4) education and preparation (formal and informal), (5) characteristics of the domain and field, (6) social/cultural contextual aspects, and (7) historical forces, events, trends.[52]

While we admire these author's systemic approach, acknowledging the importance of this viewpoint, and thus have shared several examples with you, Innovative Creativity embraces the P-creativity (psychological or personal) viewpoint that *everyone is creative* while simultaneously recognizing that an individual's creativity (1) generally occurs in the domain of that individual's focus (passion, interest, over time) and (2) does NOT occur in isolation, but is very much affected by an individual's relationship network (see Chapter 7). Indeed, as previously noted, knowledge itself is a creative process, it is *ever created new and specific to the situation and context at hand*. And only the individual can judge the significance of that knowledge (the ability to take effective action, or "justified true belief") to their life path. Further, for purposes of this discussion, both knowledge and creativity are considered human capacities, very much associated with a sociocultural context in terms of relativity.[53]

However, there certainly is a recognized difference in terms of wider application and long-term potential value between P-Creativity and H-Creativity (historic). Figure 4 is an attempt to capture that relationship honoring Csikszentmihalyi and Gardner's systemic approach (which informs H-Creativity) while simultaneously staying focused on the innate ability of every individual to create. Recall that, like knowledge, we consider creativity a capacity, with knowledge resulting in effective action and, when used in support of innovation, creativity resulting in production of something useful. That "something useful" may be at the individual, group, or world level. And when it affects the larger "field", that is, moves beyond the local application with recognized newness and quality by members of the larger field, then that "something useful" moves into the domain of H-Creativity.

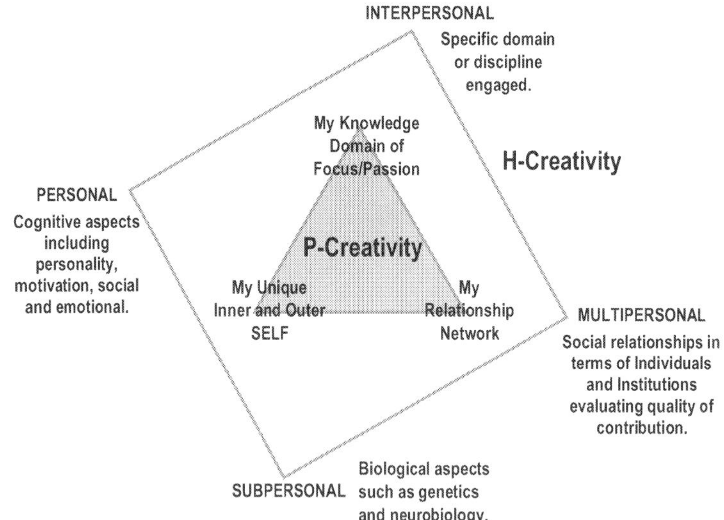

Figure 4. *Relationship between P-Creativity (inside the square) and H-Creativity (outside the square).*[54]

For purposes of this book, we use the definition of creativity defined by psychiatrist Nancy Andreason.[55] Thus, we see creativity as *emerging new or original ideas or seeing new patterns in some domain of knowledge*. In other words, creativity can be considered as *the ability to perceive new relationships and new possibilities*, seeing things from a different frame of reference, realizing new ways of understanding, or having insight. Regardless of the domain of knowledge which you engage, creativity is all about perceiving new patterns in the mind, and innovation is about the useful application of those patterns.

The Search for Patterns

Underlying the physical Universe there is energy and patterns of energy. Humans are ALWAYS looking for relationships among things—events, happenings, people, thoughts, life experiences. We are part of the grand search for patterns, for creative association.[56] The human mind has actually evolved to discover patterns. And, *the human mind yearns for the beauty of order and pattern*. With each person's pattern detection and formulation system fueled by all that it is to be human, an entangled matrix of thoughts, feelings and experiences emerge within and without throughout life. Around us weave the energies of probability, randomness and chaos married to characteristics of change, uncertainty and unpredictability. Just as we take the events of our lives and create a story of us, whether real or imaginary, *we discover and invent the patterns which we seek,* driven by the need for structure, connections and meaning.

The term "pattern" comes from the French word *patron*, which refers to a specific theme that reoccurs in events, objects or movement. Patterns can be based on repetition (the same thing appearing again and again), periodicity (recurrence at regular intervals), similarity (likeness, qualities or features in common), or symmetry (balanced proportions, exact correspondence in position) and translation (a change in form or state, transference to a different place).

If a specific pattern or set of patterns is not random, then it contains information. However, whether a specific non-random pattern is *recognized as information* and can be used to create knowledge depends on the individual sensing the pattern. For example, if the pattern is a Chinese symbol and the observer does not understand Chinese and is not capable of interpreting the pattern of the symbol, then the observer acquires no information from that symbol. However, to a Chinese observer the same symbol may contain huge significance and meaning.

Building on this idea, any given pattern may contain different information for different observers, with various people having different interpretations, that is, perceiving different information from the same pattern. These differences happen for a number of reasons. First, we tend to see what we are looking for, what we are interested in, or what strikes an emotional chord in us.

Since no two people are alike (different DNA, beliefs, passions, etc.), the things we are looking for, interested in, or emotionally charged about can be quite different. Second, the interpretation and meaning of incoming patterns are very much a function of preexisting patterns in the brain. This understanding makes it clear why preparation in a domain of knowledge is critical to Innovative Creativity. In short,

> *Each new development or bit of creation starts from something else. It does not come out of a blue sky. You make use of that which has already entered the mind, or that which you cause to enter the mind. That is the real reason, the great reason for accumulating knowledge.*[57]

Pattern Thinking

An approach to studying the changing times and the content and context of a situation for which you seek a solution—what is called "knowledging"[58]—is to identify patterns of change and the underlying principles or environmental drivers that are generating the change, unpredictability and apparent complexity. Much of this kind of knowledge resides in the unconscious, particularly if you have previously and deliberately looked for these characteristics. Thus, you may not be consciously aware of them (this knowledge is tacit) but your unconscious can, and often will, be aware of them as you observe and study a situation, creating knowledge in the form of understanding.

As we are exposed to more diverse and varying conditions, the brain creates new patterns and strengths of connections and thereby *changes its physiological structure*.[59] It is also true that the structure of the brain—containing a huge number of networks of neurons—significantly influences how incoming signals representing new thoughts (patterns composed of networks of neurons) are formed. Through the process of associative patterning, these new patterns entering the brain associate or connect with patterns already in the brain. Thus, thought affects the structure of the brain, and the structure of the brain affects thought.

Pattern thinking is not primarily thinking *through* patterns, although over time this will occur. Rather, *it is using your inside world to look for patterns in the outside world*, and bringing them into your conscious awareness. The outer world (what we perceive as reality) is based on our inner models, with everything that we perceive fabricated in the brain.[60] The intent of pattern thinking is to let the pattern emerge as a mode of understanding a situation, purposefully thinking about external patterns in order to better anticipate and respond to change, that is, to expand understanding, solve problems, create new ideas, and improve our capacity to forecast the outcomes of decisions.

Thinking *about* patterns is different than thinking *with* patterns. If you start with a specific pattern in mind, no doubt you will find it. This is the same phenomenon that occurs when you purchase a new car and you begin seeing similar cars every time you are on the freeway, although you'd never noticed them before! However, pattern emergence can be stimulated by other patterns. For example, the systems thinking approach developed by Peter Senge is based on matching a recurring set of relationships (archetypes) to a situation at hand.[61] While this force-fitting can certainly help facilitate an understanding of causal relationships in simple and complicated situations, it does not work well in complex relationships because of the need to over-simplify in order to fit the archetype.

Complexity infers difficulty in understanding something due to the large number of unpredictable and nonlinear relationships. Yet, once you have used the models of complexity over and over again, you begin to think systems and *discover system patterns beyond the archetypes*. Both systems thinking and complexity thinking are forms of pattern thinking, enabling a person to build the ability to recognize, comprehend and learn how to influence complex systems, and find creative solutions to complex issues. An excellent treatment of "Systems and Complexity Thinking" by Dr. David Bennet, a nuclear physicist and neuroscientist, is included as Chapter 19 in *Reblooming the Knowledge Movement: The Democratization of Organizations*.[62]

From the neuroscience perspective, pattern thinking involves mental exercise that stimulates the brain. The best mental exercise is new learning in multiple areas of the brain, acquiring new knowledge and doing things you've never done before.[63] Making new connections, seeing new relationships, and bringing patterns into our conscious stream of thoughts does just that.

* * * * *

Exercise 2: *Thinking Patterns*

This tool is focused on tapping into the innate human ability to recognize patterns.

STEP (1) Find a place where you will not be disturbed and briefly close your eyes and take several deep breaths. Open your eyes. Then sit comfortably, ready to take notes.

STEP (2) Consider the group of things or series of incidents in which you are searching for connections. If this is a group of things, briefly write down each item's characteristics such as how it looks and what it is made of, how it is created/developed, its purpose, how it is used, etc. If this is a series of incidents, briefly write down for each incident the subject (who or what) and the event (action occurring) and any descriptive adjectives that come to mind describing the incident, the people involved, the place and timing, the outcome, and the why (if known).

STEP (3) Look across the group and consider the *differences* among the things or incidents. Note these as characteristics.

STEP (4) Look across the group and consider the *similarities* among the things or incidents. Note these as characteristics.

STEP (5) Considering both differences and similarities, identify categories into which these differences and/or similarities could fall. Keep searching until you can bring two or more characteristics of *different things or incidents* together into a category. Repeat until you have discovered all the categories that connect the things or incidents.

STEP (6) Now, look at how the categories fit together OR don't fit together. *ASK*: How do these things relate? Are these different things the same *types* of things? Are there patterns emerging? Is something missing?

STEP (7) Repeat Steps 3-6, ever grouping in higher-level categories (concepts), until you are satisfied you have discovered all there is to discover. Then, go do something entirely different, perhaps play a game of golf or enjoy a pleasant meal with a friend or take a nap. In other words, let your unconscious take the lead, and be prepared to take notes when perhaps the next day some new idea regarding the group or series of incidents pops up in your head.

HINT: This process works well in a facilitated collaborative group looking from multiple frames of reference!

* * * * *

There is a reminder in this exercise that bears repeating. STEP (7) asked that you be prepared to take notes when new ideas pop into your head. It is important to build your personal Idea Book and, just as you deposit money in a savings account for the future, to deposit ideas in your Idea Book. As we will repeat several times in this text: *ideas beget ideas*. And often a big idea arrives in small bites, little ideas that build up over time to a big idea. Looking to the future, capture those pleasant and worthwhile ideas that may come with real results down the road. Because these often arrive while you are in an expanded state of consciousness, they may—like dreams—be difficult to remember when everyday responsibilities engage your attention. So, if you are serious about fully engaged your creativity capabilities, it's time for you to start your personal Idea Book, and have it handy as you go about everyday living. One of the authors used to keep an idea book beside the bed, often waking up at night to write things down, except having to learn to do this in the dark so as not to wake his wife. One night, emerging from a dream with ideas exploding, he wrote frantically in the dark a whole page of "stuff". Content, he went back to bed. Next morning, he discovered that the pen he had used had no ink!!

Everyone is Creative

Margaret Boden, a Research Professor of Cognitive Science in the Department of Informatics at the University of Sussex, says yes, and we agree. **Everyone is creative**. As introduced earlier in this text, Boden breaks creative thought (or creative people) into two types: P-creative (psychological or personal) and H-creative (historical).[64] *P-creative ideas* are fundamentally novel with respect to the individual mind, the person who has them, and *H-creative ideas* are historically grounded, fundamentally novel with respect to the whole of recorded human history. The point here is that the H-creative ideas, which by definition are also P-creative, are the ones that are socially recognized as creative, but P-creative ideas are *possible and occur throughout life in every human being*. They are part of learning and growing.

It would be difficult to cover the many approaches that have been taken to explore the subject of human creativity. Just to provide an idea of the massive amount of research, these include mystical approaches such as Rudyard Kipling's Daemon;[65] pragmatic approaches such as the lateral thinking of Edward DeBono;[66] and the psychodynamic approach introduced by Freud, the relation of the poet to day-dreaming. In *Collected papers*,[67] psychometric approaches involved laboratory testing are exampled by Guilford[68] and Torrance;[69] cognitive approaches included those forwarded by Finke, Ward and Smith,[70] which describe a generative phase and exploratory phase to creativity; social-personality approaches focused on personality and motivational variables in combination with the sociocultural environment as exampled by Amabile[71] and Eysenck;[72] evolutionary approaches instigated by Campbell[73] and picked up by Perkins[74] and Simonton,[75] referencing two steps to creativity, blind variation and selective retention; and confluence approaches such as the work forwarded by Csikszentmihalyi,[76] Amabile,[77] and Gruber.[78] THAT is a whole lot of creativity! Maybe BECAUSE everyone is creative, we keep coming up with different ways to DESCRIBE creativity. That makes sense. How do *you* describe it?

Ultimately, Sternberg, who takes a confluence approach integrating all the other approaches, says that *creativity is a choice*. In his words, it is a decision which has three parts: "The decision to be creative, the decision of how to be creative, and implementation of these decisions."[79] Thus, he agrees that *creativity can be developed.* Sternberg forwards an investment theory of creativity, requiring a confluence of six interrelated resources: intellectual abilities, knowledge, styles of thinking, personality, motivation and environment. His bottom line is that creative intelligence is just a *part* of human creativity. More is needed. As he describes that more, "Creativity also involves aspects of knowledge, styles of thinking, personality, and motivation, as well as these psychological components *in interaction and the environment.* An individual with the intellectual skills for creativity but without the other personal attributes is unlikely to do creative work."[80]

Neuroscience findings in the Mountain Quest Institute research on the Intelligent Complex Adaptive Learning System (ICALS)[81] support that everyone is creative and creativity is a choice. We will explore these ideas further in the following chapter. What we do know now is that creativity is an inherent capability of every mind/brain.[82]

<<<<<<<>>>>>>>

INSIGHT: **Creativity is a choice; creativity can be developed. It is an inherent capability of every mind/brain.**

<<<<<<<>>>>>>>

In introducing creativity, it was important to immediately connect creativity to patterns. Learning consists of building new patterns within the mind that represent ideas, concepts, and capabilities, and processes that are internally imagined (creative imagination), or represent some interpretation of external reality. Associative patterning, the human ability to complex incoming information previously stored in the brain, was introduced above. This is consistent with Stonier—who was a biologist, philosopher, information theorist, educator and pacifist—that thinking involves *the association of different patterns within the mind/brain.*[83] Since memory is distributed throughout the brain, these associative processes may contain *random associations* that can result in new ideas, concepts, or approaches. This is considered ordinary creativity and can be very valuable as a form of self-learning.

These new patterns may represent insights, increased understanding of a situation, clarification of the meaning of a situation, or even that new solution you've been hunting for! They may come from the unconscious mind "playing with" ideas during the night. This is most likely the source of the adage, "We need to sleep on it." Since much thinking is done by the unconscious during sleep, this process is useful for coming up with creative ideas.

* * * * *

EXERCISE 3: *Sleep on It*

Sleeping on a question or problem can yield an answer the next morning. This is a particularly powerful way to access tacit knowledge.

STEP (1) Prime your conscious mind. Early in the evening, prior to going to bed, take a focused period of time to "brainstorm" with yourself. *Ask* yourself a lot of questions *related* to the task at hand. Reflect carefully on the questions and be patient. This is the process of active reflection.

STEP (2) Before going to bed, ensure that you have a pen and paper available beside the bed, accessible without you getting up. Write the specific problem or question you want to address on this pad of paper.

STEP (3) Tell yourself, as you fall asleep at night, to work on that specific problem or question, then clear your mind and sleep.

STEP (4) When you wake up the next morning, but before you get up, lie in bed and ask the same question, listening patiently to your own quiet, passive thoughts. Frequently, but not always, the answer will emerge.

STEP (5) Write the answer down quickly before it is lost from the conscious mind (as with dreams).

Another aspect of this approach is useful when a group or team is tackling a difficult problem. Often, the answers from the team can be improved if, rather than acting on the immediate responses, *let the team sleep on the problem* and review the answers they come up with in the morning. What happens is that while you sleep the unconscious mind is processing the information taken in that day, keeping the valuable (in terms of individuated preferences) information and discarding that which doesn't make sense or is not important to you. The unconscious is also working on solutions to issues or problems that have come up. When the team gets back together the next day, there will be new ideas and thoughts, and a clearer vision of the best way ahead.

* * * * *

Extraordinary Creativity

We are now prepared to explore the idea of *extraordinary creativity*, which describes the creativity of individuals who have the capacity to *repeatedly create novel ideas or processes that push the limits of understanding or application.* These are the "truly creative" people who keep an open mind, maintain a high curiosity, and investigate multiple paths toward new possibilities. They have a particular mental capability and capacity for challenging the status quo and seeing things from unique perspectives.[84] (See the discussion of Knowledge Capacities in Chapter 1 and Appendix A.) These are largely (but not always) the people who would fall into Csikszentmihalyi's definition of creativity, creative with historical significance, AND "some persons brimming with brilliance whom everyone thinks of as being exceptionally creative" but never leave behind an accomplishment or even any trace of their existence, "except, perhaps, in the memories of those who have known them."[85] Since innovation can be design, process or product focused, producing something that is useful, the latter group might well be considered as engaging Innovative Creativity if the memory of their creativity—perhaps their creative way of thinking, feeling, and acting—proved "useful" to those who remembered.

<<<<<<>>>>>>

INSIGHT: **Truly creative people keep an open mind, maintain a high curiosity, and investigate many paths toward new possibilities.**

<<<<<<>>>>>>

In her research, Andreasen specifically calls out ordinary and extra-ordinary creativity.[86] Behavioral aspects of highly creative people include personality and cognitive traits such as openness to experience, curiosity, and a tolerance of ambiguity. She also describes highly creative people as often receiving their ideas as flashes of insights "through moments of inspiration, or by going into a state at the edge of chaos, where ideas float, soar, collide, and connect".[87] (See the discussions of "flow" in Chapter 10 and "revealed intuition" in Chapter 11.) Further,

> *We have learned that this creative state arises from a mind and brain that are rich in associative links that encourage new combinations to occur freely. And we have learned that the brain is plastic—that we can change, and hopefully improve, our brains by exercising them. We have also learned that all of us possess, at a minimum, something I have called ordinary creativity. To call it ordinary is not to diminish it. The fact that we can generate novel speech "on the fly" is a testament to the "extraordinary ordinary creativity of our glorious human brains".*[88]

Note the reference to the human associative patterning process.

On the other hand, extraordinary creativity, as Andreasen concludes, is at least sometimes based on a "qualitatively different neural process than ordinary creativity" and at least sometimes arises from that "over the precipice component of human thought that we call the unconscious".[89] Thus, the unconscious mental life appears to be highly relevant to extraordinary creativity.

There is no doubt the highly creative person is endowed with a very active, intense imagination. (See Chapter 5 on Creative Imagination.) Whereas most people check their imagination in deference to a perceived reality, the highly creative person follows a different course. As Arieti describes, "He feels himself to be in a state of turmoil, restlessness, deprivation, emptiness, and unbearable frustration unless he expresses his inner life in one or another creative way."[90] This is a powerful motivation to create!

And here we can learn from Csikszentmihalyi's research into what he describes as the creative personality. He calls out ten traits, which are synthesized below.[91] Creative people …

- Have high physical energy while also often quiet and at rest, working long hours with great concentration yet having an aura of freshness and enthusiasm.
- Are both smart and naïve.
- Combine playfulness and discipline, responsibility and irresponsibility.
- Alternate between imagination and fantasy (at one end) and a rooted sense of reality (at the other end).
- Harbor opposite tendencies between extroversion and introversion.
- Are simultaneously remarkably humble and proud.
- Escape rigid gender role stereotyping.
- Are both traditional and conservative, rebellious and iconoclastic.
- Are passionate about their work while also extremely objective.
- Are open and sensitive, which exposes them to suffering and pain AND a great deal of enjoyment.

Noting the polarities, this is an intriguing list of characteristics. Csikszentmihalyi feels these contrasting personality traits are telling characteristics of creative people, and that the "novelty that survives to change a domain is usually the work of someone who can operate at both ends of these polarities."[92]

As forwarded by Andreasen and others, and introduced earlier, ideas are often received through flashes of insights and moments of inspiration.

Inspiration has historically been described as a transfusion of soul or breath of divinity from the gods received by some fortunate individual. Today, inspiration is described as an experience of insight that cuts across categories or *leaps over* normal steps of reasoning, what we call the creative leap. In this experience there is a psychological element that we are abandoning our thought to another force, a powerful *flow* of ideas. This concept of flow will come up repeatedly in the discussion of creativity, as indeed it should!

This type of experience does not appear to be designed or purposed; in fact, to labor or work toward it can move us in the opposite direction. However, English Professor Robert Grudin thinks that we can practice *deserving it* through embedding habits in our daily lives. Describing these habits as a demanding and integral code, Grudin collectively calls these habits the *ethics of inspiration*. This utopian code includes: love of one's work, fidelity, concentration, love of problems, a sense of the openness of thought, boldness, innocence, an uncensored mind, civility, gentleness, and liberty. This is a good set. As Grudin describes, "It is a garden of mind, recalling Eden, Rousseau's vision of philosophy as a recapturing of nature, and Milton's idea that the purpose of education was to rebuild the ruins of the Fall."[93]

Extraordinarily creative people "go into a state *at the edge of chaos*, where ideas float, soar, collide and collect."[94] While this state may result in something of value becoming a reality, all too often the flash is there and then gone, disappearing into a field of ideas to which we may or may not again connect. This is what can be referred to as uncontrolled intuition. What we are searching for is how the individual can, at will, take the creative leap and *purposefully* tap into the field of ideas. This is the capacity for controlled intuition (see Chapter 12).

The really interesting news is that ordinary people can become extraordinarily creative! Further, they can become an inspiration to others, who in turn can become extraordinarily creative. As R.D. Green writes,

> *When we think about inspiration, what inspires us most are ordinary people who have done extraordinary things. We appreciate when someone has the ability and willingness to be selfless, creative, innovative, or just dares to be different .... The beautiful thing about inspiration of this kind is that 'ordinary' part .... [E]ach of them came from backgrounds of great poverty and difficulty. Each of them faced giant mountains to climb. They managed to reach the summit of those mountains not simply because they were great leaders, but because they were not afraid to be who they were. They were authentic.*[95]

<<<<<<<>>>>>>>

INSIGHT: **Ordinary people can become extraordinarily creative.**

<<<<<<<>>>>>>>

There are many techniques, both individual and group processes, that serve to open the mind to new possibilities and stimulate creative thinking. Such processes use all forms of learning with some being from concrete experience, dialogue, or social interaction; others from internal reflection and comprehension. In all of these approaches, if learners understand the dangers of assuming they already "know" the answer, choosing to deliberately keep an open mind improves the efficiency and effectiveness of learning and creativity. This is why the human gift of humility brought up throughout this text is so important. *Becoming aware that every healthy mind is capable of creativity, and that the guidelines and practices of creative thinking are available to anyone*, opens the door to enhanced individual and organizational creativity and learning capacity. When open to learning, intelligence follows creativity.

Chapter 3
Creativity as an Aspect of Consciousness

Let's further explore the role of consciousness in creativity and take a look at what we have learned about creativity from recent neuroscience research.

While the exact definition of consciousness is still in dispute among experts in a myriad of fields, we each have personal experience with consciousness. We give up consciousness every time we go to sleep. Yet in the morning, we pick it up as if nothing happened in between. And in our lives, we see consciousness as a march of sequential events, interplaying on multiple levels, that arise either from the environment getting our attention, or from our own internal ruminations. Consciousness involves "wakefulness, receiving and responding to sensory inputs, imagination, inner experience, and volition."[96]

As a few more points of reference, Searle focuses on consciousness as a "real biological phenomenon" which "consists of inner, qualitative, subjective, unified states of sentience, awareness, thoughts and feelings."[97] He includes dreams as a *form* of consciousness, which are tied to the creative imagination (see Chapter 5). And Rollo May sees consciousness as the awareness of the dialectical tensions between possibilities and limitations.[98]

Creativity operates in both the middle of and around the fringes of consciousness. Hobson says that creativity is inherent in the basic operation of the nervous system.[99] Andreasen sees the brain as a "self-organizing system that can create novel linkages on a millisecond time scale".[100] Christos says that it stands to reason from a scientific perspective that individual creativity is a function of the brain (and what is stored in it), but the question is *how* this occurs.

> *I believe the answer is related to the fact that memory is stored distributively in wide areas of the brain in such a way that different memories overlap each other or use common neurons and synapses for their storage and representation. The overlapping store of memory in common areas naturally gives rise ... to new states or memories that were not intentionally stored in the network.*[101]

New research led by Hawkins and published as *A Thousand Brains: A New Theory of Intelligence* confirms Christos' belief.[102] Knowledge in the brain is indeed distributed across somewhere around 150,000 cortical columns (which are in the neocortex, the organ of intelligence) in different random locations, with thousands upon thousands of neural connections, associating and creating patterns through neuronal firings among axons and dendrites.

Christos also says that the human brain has a natural capacity to be creative, the ability to generate something entirely new—its own information or memory-like states—not formally acquired from the overlapping storage of memory. This overlapping storage of memory gives rise to what Christos calls "spurious memories", new states or memories not intentionally stored in the network. While spurious memories may possess some subtle combinations of stored memories, they

> *... have the capacity to generate new ideas that combine different bits of information... [and[may be extremely useful (and possibly essential), not just for creativity but also so that a neural network can learn something new, adapt, generalize, classify, think, and make new associations.*[103]

These spurious states made up of an endless variety of combinations of features of stored memories may very well be what we call creativity. They "clearly give the brain added flexibility to adapt and to develop nonbiological abilities".[104]

Tallis says that creativity works more efficiently when consciousness has been—at least temporarily—dissolved.[105] This is not a new idea. In Poincaré's discussion about his own experiences with creativity,[106] he advocates a volleying back and forth between the conscious mind and the unconscious mind, the value of which is affirmed through neuroscience findings from the ICALS study highlighted at the end of this chapter and in Chapter 8. As Christos describes this process:

> [Poincaré] *asserts that new ideas are often generated through a process whereby a problem reverts from the conscious mind (required to initiate the "search") to the unconscious mind (required to generate new ideas) and back to the conscious mind (required to ascertain the usefulness of the ideas generated by the unconscious mind).*[107]

Expanding on this relationship, Andreasen[108] offers that "there is a resonance between an inspired nonrational state and a more rational state in which the details were elaborated." While Amen does not address this "volleying", he does say that creative people slip into a state of intense concentration and focus that is similar to an unconscious state, where a person is no longer in touch with reality. But he adds, "In a subjective sense … the creative individual is moving into another reality that is actually more real … a place where words, thoughts, and ideas float freely, collide, and ultimately coalesce." [109] Amen.

The Role of the Unconscious

Arthur Koestler, who immersed himself in the ideological and social conflicts of the 20th century, went beyond describing creativity as inspirational and romantic, and tried to understand *how creativity happens*. He felt that IT WAS AN ACT OF INTUITION.

> *The moment of truth, the sudden emergence of a new insight, is an act of intuition. Such intuition gives the appearance of miraculous flashes, or short circuits of reasoning. In fact, they may be likened to an immersed chain, of which only the beginning and the end are visible above the surface of consciousness. The diver vanishes at one end of the chain and comes up at the other end, guided by invisible links.*[110]

While Koestler's words reiterate earlier observations and insinuate more, they do not *explain* the more.

These flashes of insight, which represent the "creative leap" discussed in Chapter 13, may very well be connected to the strength of the associative patterning process, which can change the physiology of the brain. Begley says that it "has become a truism that the better connected a brain is the better it is, period, enabling the mind it runs to connect new facts with old, to retrieve memories, and even to see links among seemingly disparate facts, the foundation for creativity".[111]

Andreasen forwards Davidson's work with Buddhist monks to suggest that meditation, in this study non-referential meditation, created high levels of gamma synchrony. This "gamma power" was the greatest "in the association cortices that are the reservoir of creativity—frontal, temporal, and parietal association regions". She concluded that people can change their brains by "training them in the practice of meditation, so that they improve the quality of their moment-to-moment awareness not only during meditation but also during the routine of everyday life."[112]

There are other ways to open the brain that are quite different from meditation. These methodologies focus on achieving an intentional focus on an object (referential) or on a state (nonreferential) through "just thinking". As an example, one way of increasing the creative state of mind is "random episodic silent thought" (REST). Sound can also play a role in opening the brain, specifically, in opening the connection between the conscious and unconscious mind. Pinker notes that neuroscience has slowly begun to recognize the capability of internal thoughts and external information such as sound to affect the physical structure of the brain—its synaptic connection strengths, its neuronal connections, and the growth of additional neurons.[113] Hemispheric synchronization—the use of sound coupled with a binaural beat to bring both hemispheres of the brain into unison—is an example.[114] (See the discussion of hemispheric synchronization in Chapter 4).

French mathematician Henri Poincaré suggests that creativity *tugs* on the unconscious. He builds on the four stages of creativity identified by Gram Wallas in his book, *The Art of Thought,* published in 1926.[115] These are: preparation, incubation, illumination, and verification. The initial phase, *preparation*, is the conscious probing of a problem or an idea. This usually emerges from the field on which you are focusing, that is, your chosen work focus, hopefully an area in which you have passion.

The second phase, *incubation*, occurs while the conscious mind is focused elsewhere, and may last for minutes, months, or years. During this time, the unconscious mind may well be contemplating the challenge and trying to make sense of the situation. Poincaré credited this phase with the novelties denied through waking, rational thought. These first two phases (preparation and incubation) work together, that is, as an individual embeds themselves in a domain of knowledge, over time both continuous learning and incubation are occurring in preparation for the third phase.

The flash of insight, or tug, comes in the third phase, *illumination*, when creative thoughts burst through the unconscious stirring of incubation into the conscious. As Poincaré expressed, "ideas rose in crowds; I felt them collide until pairs interlocked, so to speak, making a stable combination."[11] For the chemist Kekule von Stradonitz, he was able to discover the structure of the benzene molecule during a dream. For Mozart, his music came to him in a semi-conscious state. Peter Ilich Tchaikovsky says that this "germ", which represents a future composition, comes suddenly and unexpectedly. It "takes root with extraordinary force and rapidity, shoots up through the Earth, puts forth branches and leaves, and finally blossoms. I cannot define the creative process in any way but this simile."[11]

The fourth phase, *verification* or *validation*, is where the idea can be explored and tested. If it doesn't meet up to expectations, then the cycle begins again. Underlying all this, of course, is an openness to new ways of doing things. These four phases lay the foundation for the creative process, with illumination linked to the moment of intuition, with preparation and incubation setting the stage, and verification refining the product.

Five years later Rossman, a chemical engineer and psychologist,[118] studied the creative process of 710 inventors and expanded Wallas' four phases to seven more pragmatic steps:

1. Observation of a need or difficulty
2. Analysis of the need
3. A survey of all available information
4. A formulation of all objective solutions
5. A critical analysis of advantages and disadvantages of these solutions
6. The birth of the new idea—the invention
7. Experimentation[119]

With Wallas' four-phase model considered foundational (as it still is today), 22 years later Osborn, an advertising executive, also divided the creative process into seven stages,[120] although his terminology was quite different than that of Rossman. As he described these seven stages:

1. Orientation: pointing to the problem
2. Preparation: gathering pertinent data
3. Analysis: breaking down the relevant material
4. Ideation: coming up with alternative ideas
5. Incubation: "letting up" to invite illumination
6. Synthesis: putting the pieces together
7. Evaluation: judging the resulting ideas[121]

This process was further refined by Osbourn's colleagues, Isakson and Parnes, who developed the Creative Problem Solving (CPS) model, which was used for instructional seminars.[122] This model had six steps:

1. Objective-Finding: List broad objectives, goals or purposes, then select best statement;
2. Data-Finding: List data dealing with each chosen objective, then select most pertinent;
3. Problem-Finding: List problems or challenges for attainment of each objective, then select most promising definition for creative attack;
4. Idea-Finding: List ideas, alternatives, approaches, strategies, means or options for handling chosen challenge, then cull out those that are most interesting or promising;

5. Solution-Finding: List criteria for evaluating culled-out ideas, then choose criteria use them to and evaluate the chosen ideas;
6. Acceptance-Finding: List ways of implementing the ideas, then develop plans, carry them out, obtain feedback and monitor results.[123]

Over the following years other voices such as Taylor[124] and Stein[125] forwarded theory largely built on or related to Wallas' four phases. This is not surprising, since this same four-phase process can be effectively moved through to solve pretty much any problem or issue. It wasn't until 1964 that Koestler published *The Act of Creation* with the fundamental concept of bisociation, which underlies the creative process. For Koestler, bisociation is any mental occurrence that is simultaneously associated with two (or more) habitually incompatible contexts.[126]

Poincaré visualized the creative thought mechanism of the unconscious as similar to the workings of the atom.

> *Figure the future elements of our combinations as something like the hooked atoms of Epicurus. During the complete repose of the mind, these atoms are motionless, they are, so to speak, hooked to the wall ...; On the other hand, during a period of apparent rest and unconscious work, certain of them are detached from the wall and put in motion. They flash in every direction ... [like] a swarm of gnats, or, if you prefer a more learned comparison, like the molecules of gas in the kinematic theory of gases. Then their mutual impacts may produce new combinations.*[127]

While we can now see that the creative process is certainly more than a simple combination, just putting two things together, it indeed requires two or more information inputs for bisociation, offering the potential for emergence, for something "magical" to happen.

<<<<<<<>>>>>>>

INSIGHT: **Henri Poincaré visualized the creative thought mechanism of the unconscious as similar to the workings of the atom.**

<<<<<<<>>>>>>>

Staying with Poincaré's analogy, he notes that the role of preliminary conscious work is that of mobilizing certain of these atoms,

> *... to unhook them from the wall and put them in swing ... After this shaking up imposed upon them by our will, these atoms do not return to their primitive rest. They freely continue their dance. Now, our will did not choose them at random; it pursued a perfectly determined aim. The*

mobilized atoms are therefore not any atoms whatsoever; they are those from which we might reasonably expect the desired solution. [128]

Agreeing that creativity is an aspect of consciousness, Scott Jeffrey, a student of David Hawkins, says that creativity is governed by impersonal attractor fields of varying strengths within the Universal Consciousness.[129] Thus, creativity is the result of the assimilation and progressive *organization of information*, what could be described as evolutionary learning, which in turn produces the linear from the ever-present field of the nonlinear. We're going to explore that further.

Levels of Consciousness

There are five circumstances that create *cradles of creativity*. These are (1) an atmosphere of intellectual freedom and excitement; (2) a critical mass of creative minds; (3) free and fair competition; (4) mentors and patrons; and (5) at least some economic prosperity.[130] The first item—focused on the individual—is related to the level of consciousness, which determines an individual's ability to respond. Intellectual freedom and excitement require conscious awareness of a need or opportunity as a starting point. Equally important is the amount and accuracy of information that the individual is able to sense and synthesize into knowledge.

Murray Gell-Mann demonstrates a cradle of creativity by describing a shared experience in conceiving creative ideas. He was one of a small group of physicists, biologists, painters and poets that came together in 1970 to talk about their experiences in getting creative ideas. As Murray describes, "The accounts all agreed to a remarkable extent. We had each found a contradiction between the established way of doing things and something we needed to accomplish: in art, the expression of a feeling, a thought, an insight; in theoretical science, the explanation of some experimental facts in the face of an accepted 'paradigm' that did not permit such an explanation."[131]

Each person had started with a focus on a problem and the difficulties they were trying to overcome in their field of focus, a field in which each was an "expert". When further conscious thought was deemed useless, that stopped, although each continued to carry the problem around with them. Then, suddenly, while doing something quite different—shaving, cooking, or engaged in simple conversation—an idea just popped into thought. **Thus, the unconscious appears to play an essential role in creativity**.

There are levels of consciousness. In the *Great Chain of Being*, levels of consciousness range from matter to body to mind to soul[132] and span the spectrum from subconscious to self-conscious to superconscious.[133] Wilber has developed over 100 models of these levels, with different human constructs, pointing out that each individual has different capacities, intelligences, and functions, causing each to move thorough the developmental levels at different rates.[134]

Hawkin's levels of consciousness are represented by calibrated levels correlated with a specific process of consciousness, an increase in intelligence related to emotions, perceptions, attitudes, worldviews, and spiritual beliefs, which can be thought of as indicators of consciousness development.[135] As the culmination of research over a 20-year period involving thousands of people of all ages and personality types, Hawkins mapped the energy field of human consciousness, with levels ranging from 0 to 1,000. While there are many other models, we will use this one to further explore human consciousness.

Let's first look at the indicators that occur at various levels of consciousness development. The progression is as follows: 20 (Shame); 30 (Guilt); 50 (Apathy); 75 (Grief); 100 (Fear); 125 (Desire); 150 (Anger); 175 (Pride); 200 (Courage); 250 (Neutrality); 310 (Willingness); 350 (Acceptance); 400 (Reason); 500 (Love); 540 (Joy); 600 (Peace); 700-1,000 (Enlightenment). Note that the 200 level—that associated with integrity and courage—serves as a critical response point, a balance point between negative and positive indicators.

What is specific to our focus on creativity is that the higher the consciousness level the greater the energy focused on creativity. This should not be surprising. The heavy negative emotions and feelings at the lower levels of consciousness do not leave much room for creative thought. In Hawkins' scale, as people move from the lower negative emotions into courage (200), the well-being of others becomes increasingly more important. By the 500 level—that of love—"the happiness of others emerges as the essential motivating force."[136] This, in turn, offers insight into the relationship of expanded consciousness and creativity, a higher awareness of the needs and desires of others, which is one element of the bisociation process leading to innovation.

Herein we have discovered a prerequisite for self which is necessary for Innovative Creativity: CONSCIOUSNESS EXPANSION. And before we leave this all too brief treatment of the conscious and unconscious in relation to creativity, let's explore some neuroscience findings in this regard, and maybe add a few practical tools as well.

Nurturing Our Creativity

Neuroscience research since the turn of the century has emerged findings that help us to understand how to nurture our creativity. In the Mountain Quest Institute ICALS research study exploring experiential learning through the expanding lens of neuroscience, creativity emerged as one of 13 primary areas of focus. While some of these findings are embedded in support of topic areas throughout this book, they are briefly summarized below: (1) an enriched environment can produce a personal internal reflective world of imagination and creativity; (2) conscious and unconscious patterns are involved with creativity; (3) the unconscious produces flashes of insight; (4) volleying between conscious and unconscious thinking increases creativity; (5) meditation quiets the mind; (6) extraordinary creativity can be developed; (7) the free flow and randomness of mixing patterns can create new patterns; and (8) accidental associations occur.[137] (See Figure 5.) Each of these findings will be expanded on below.

CONSCIOUS

- An enriched environment can produce a personal internal reflective world of imagination and creativity.
- Meditation quiets the mind.

UNCONSCIOUS

- The unconscious mind is always processing.
- Free flow and randomly mixing patterns to create new patterns
- Accidental associations
- Flashes of insight

- Conscious and unconscious patterns are involved with creativity.
- Volleying between the conscious and unconscious increases creativity.
- Mirror neurons

Figure 5. *Neuroscience findings.*

(1) An enriched environment can produce a personal internal reflective world of imagination and creativity. This item is part of the environment, and as such may affect concrete experience and active experimentation associated with experiential learning. A rich environment entering the mind/brain/body through experiences increases the formation and survival of new neurons, stimulating the mind to associate patterns and create new possibilities. The literature suggests that an enriched environment contains many interesting and thought-provoking ideas, pictures, books, statues, etc. James Byrnes, a professor of human development, says that in an enriched environment there are physiological changes in the brain, specifically, thicker cortices are created, cell bodies are larger, and dendritic branching in the brain is more extensive.[138] These changes have been directly connected to higher levels of intelligence.[139] Note that in today's world, the context of an enriched environment includes augmentation of the mind/brain with technologies.[140] The context of an enriched environment is discussed further in Chapter 4.

(2) Conscious and unconscious patterns are involved with creativity. Creative insight is the result of searching for new relationships between concepts in one domain with those in another domain.[141] It creates recognition and understanding of a problem within the situation, including the how and why of the past and current behavior of the situation. It is often the result of intuition, competence, and the identification of patterns, themes and cue sets.[142] Insight may also provide patterns and relationships that will anticipate the future behavior of a situation. In other words, while we are consciously searching for answers to an issue or opportunity, *our unconscious is also supplying information to assist in this search*.

(3) The unconscious produces flashes of insight. As previously introduced—and described by many researchers in the areas of creativity—spurious memories can generate new ideas that combine in different ways to create new associations.[143] This relates to uncontrolled intuition. We can find these flashes fascinating and exciting, even when we don't fully understand them!

(4) Volleying between the conscious and the unconscious increases creativity. "New ideas are generated through the process of shifting from conscious to unconscious as the mind contemplates and searches for solutions."[144] This switching process makes use of the memories and knowledge in the unconscious and the goals and thinking of the conscious mind, increasing the chances of associating conscious ideas to create new ones. While this occurs regularly in the transition from the waking state to the sleeping state (and vice versa), to do this while awake requires some level of control and discipline in implementation. For example, those who have learned how to meditate can do this at will, which brings us to the next finding.

(5) Meditation quiets the mind. Again, meditation requires some level of control and discipline, and it can significantly enhance the ability to focus attention. In this context, quieting the mind means to reduce the noise that "bedevils the untrained mind, in which an individual's focus darts from one sight or sound or thought to another like a hyperactive dragonfly, and replace it with attentional stability and clarity."[145] Quieting the mind allows the mind to focus attention on potential relationships that may create new ideas. Here is an exercise that can help.

* * * * *

EXERCISE 4: *Quieting the Mind*

STEP (1) *Location*. Find a quiet and comfortable place to sit or lie for a half hour (or more), keeping a pen and pad of paper nearby for emerging thoughts. This may be inside or outside, depending on your comfort level.

STEP (2) *Clearing your mind*. Close your eyes and use your imagination to create a mental exercise that will allow you to empty your mind of past and present worries and concerns. As an example, here is an exercise adapted from The Monroe Institute.[146] Imagine a large box with a heavy lead top, which is open.

(a) In your hands is a checklist. On that checklist are all the incidents in your life that have troubled or bothered you in any way, the names of any people with whom you have had an altercation, all the worries that are currently on your mind, and any future commitments that are prominent in your mind. You do not have to bring these things into conscious thought. Just acknowledge that the list is complete, fold it up and put it in the box.

(b) Now, do a quick scan of your body for any aches and pains. Focus on the place where the ache or pain is manifesting, imagine it as clay, and reach in (mentally) and pull out all the clay, rolling it into a ball and bouncing it into your box. Do this for each area where an ache or pain is manifesting.

(c) Next, do a quick scan for fear, all fears, large or small, wherever fear resides in your body. Focus on each place and, imagining the fear as a stream of yellow, orange or red light, stream it into the box.

(d) Next, focus inside your brain and imagine all the monkey chatter underway as old-fashioned tickertape, the stuff you've seen in the movie *Miracle on 24th Street* being thrown out of windows during the Macy's holiday parade. Grab two or three big handfuls of this tickertape to clear out the monkey chatter, putting it in the box.

(e) Finally, reach inside your chest, pull out your ego, and put it inside the box. Don't worry, you can always retrieve it later (or the part of it you choose to retrieve).

(f) Now, close that heavy lead top and push the box around behind you. Imagine a vacuum cleaner hose coming from that box to your left shoulder.

Should any negative image, ache, fear or monkey chatter come up during your quiet time, just send it up that vacuum cleaner hose into your box.

STEP (3) *Float.* For those who regularly meditate, clearing your mind may have already taken you into a place of floating, a quiet mind state. One way to achieve this is to focus on the *Fontanelle*, the soft spot at the top (center) of your head that served you as an infant. This focus is not accomplished by thought, but rather a feeling of the inner eyes looking upward. This becomes easier with practice.

STEP (4) Once you have discovered this quiet place, relax and enjoy it, letting free-flowing thoughts and visuals play in this space, opening your eyes and briefly jotting down notes when something of meaning to you emerges, then continuing your float. A common visual during this event is the opening and dissolving of colorful energy bubbles. Enjoy the energy while allowing your body to relax.

STEP (5) When you feel complete, bring your awareness back to your outer enriched environment, knowing that you can return to this quiet place whenever you choose.

* * * * *

(6) Extraordinary creativity can be developed. A basic operation of the brain is that of associating patterns within the mind to create new patterns (thoughts, ideas, and concepts), what is referred to as ordinary creativity. As we have forwarded, everyone possesses ordinary creativity,[147] the creation of new ways of doing things in their daily lives through discussing new ideas and developing insights and deeper understanding. In this sense, *all learning is creating*. Recall that *extraordinary creativity*, introduced in Chapter 2, refers to highly creative people who often receive ideas through flashes of insights and moments of inspiration. The really good news is that this can be developed.

(7) Free-flow and randomly mixing patterns create new patterns. This relates directly to creativity and is one way to describe the interaction among neuronal networks and patterns to create new ideas. As described, this is a random emergent process stimulated by the continuous activity of the mind. While this activity is outside of conscious internal focusing or environmental external triggering, *it is based on past exposure, experience and learning*; thus, future activity can be nurtured. The "fun" events of today can lead to the "creative" events of tomorrow.

<<<<<<<>>>>>>>

INSIGHT: **The fun events of today can lead to the creative events of tomorrow.**

<<<<<<<>>>>>>>

(8) Accidental associations can create new patterns. As an extension to (7) above, this makes the point that creativity can happen by accident within an active mind that plays with ideas, connections, and their relationships.

As a summary ...

We can now clearly see from a neuroscience perspective that **everyone has the capacity for creativity and that creativity is a choice**. And through exploring findings from neuroscience, we begin to understand potential ways of tapping into our creativity. The two summary paragraphs introduced above bear repeating here:

Since both conscious and unconscious patterns are involved in creativity, it just makes sense that *volleying between the conscious and unconscious increases creativity*. It also makes sense that the environment in which you are conscious is enriched, while simultaneously using meditation to quiet the mind, *moving from an outer enriched state to an inner enriched state*.

Recognizing that humans are multidimensional and that the unconscious brain is always processing, randomly mixing patterns to create new patterns, it can be seen that **the experiences to which we expose ourselves and the people with whom we interact directly impact our creativity**. Even when we are consciously unaware of our surroundings and the activities underway, information is being received and processed. This understanding led to the development of Relationship Network Management, an important personal and professional skillset at all levels of the organization, which is described in detail in Chapter 7, explored in Exercise 11, and supported by Appendix C. Remember, even when we are consciously unaware of our surroundings and with other activities underway, information is being received and processed. *Our movements and the conversations of our everyday lives really count!*

Chapter 4

The Prerequisites of SELF

Be the change that you wish to see in the world.
Mahatma Gandhi

It's difficult to perceive how to introduce in a few paragraphs the concept of self, much less in terms of the prerequisites for creativity. In fact, it is impossible, so we're going to assume each of you is a student of self, and perhaps we can plant a few ideas that are pertinent to the topic at hand and point out additional resources should you wish to dive deeper into a very deep topic, that is, YOU!

We recently published somewhat of a tome called *Unleashing the Human Mind: A Consilience Approach to Managing Self*. Then, hoping to make this information more accessible to a broader audience, Arthur Shelley's beloved OrgZoo critters (emerging in management literature some 20 plus years ago) joined the Mountain Quest team on a learning quest up the mountain. Thus, a companion book, a Field Guide, *Unleashing the Human Mind: An OrgZoo Quest* came into being, necessitating pulling core ideas from the larger book ... and so we did. Here is an exercise planted at the beginning of the Field Guide which begins to answer the question at hand: "Who is my SELF?"

* * * * *

EXERCISE 5: *Who is My SELF?*

Who we are, our SELF, ultimately comes down to the choices of what we *think, feel and do*. As we expand our understanding of self, let's start with a simple exercise that explores the instant at hand, that is, where we are, what our environment is, and how we feel about our SELF in this moment of life, the

NOW. When repeated, this exercise will help you realize the many beautiful moments in your life.

STEP (1) As you move forward, you will want to experience this exercise several times during a single day, or perhaps once a week over a given time frame, such that you capture the variety of your life experience. If you have an alarm/alert on your watch or cell phone, you can set it to go off as a reminder. Then, when the alarm goes off, or when it is close to the set time, turn it off, stop whatever you are doing, and go to Step (2).

STEP (2) You are not in a hurry and you are in a quiet place. Stand up. With your eyes open, slowly turn completely around, scanning things that are close to you, say within five or six feet. Spend a moment thinking about each thing that comes into view. About each, ***reflect:*** How is this useful? Who created this? Does it serve a purpose? Do the pieces all fit together well? Are the colors pleasing? Allow yourself to be fully in the NOW; FEEL into the item upon which you are focusing, and allow each item their moment of importance.

STEP (3) Slowly, take a second complete turn. This time focus further out—into the distance—reflecting on all that comes into view. If you are outside, you may wish to take a third turn to reflect on the far distance. FEEL the energy around you and, again, give every item that comes into focus its special moment in time.

STEP (4) Close your eyes, and consider all of the things you have brought into your focus and *how they all fit together*. Now, imagine yourself as the model in a famous artist's painting, a *Carletti*, with all of the things around you of significance to the painting. What story do they tell? What is your relationship to these items? What do these things that surround you tell you about the figure in the middle of the painting that is YOU.

STEP (5) Taking a deep breath, leap into the future, say 100 years forward. Using your creative imagination, picture yourself in the middle of an art auction, and *there in front of you is the picture of YOU and all those things surrounding you*. Many people in the room are bidding, and the price gets higher and higher. As the people continue bidding, you look closely at the painting, and you begin to see *why* they are bidding. There is a relationship between the person in the painting that is YOU and all those things that surround you. They look REAL and yet there is an invisible energy that says more than the picture. You look closely at your painted face, captured with the eyes closed, and see a *wonder* expressed there. You note that the artist has captured the *knowing* that is occurring in the moment at hand. Even with the eyes closed, this figure has *full awareness of who they are and where they are*. The bids continue to go higher and higher.

STEP (6) Still in that place, you hear the auctioneer pause and say: "Is there another bid? This is a *Carletti*, a moment of beauty. The summation of the parts work together in such a way that nothing needs to be added, taken away or altered. The artist has captured a perfect life moment."

STEP (7) Still in that future place, you push your hand into your pocket and pull out a credit card with no limits, recognizing that in this place, at this future moment, you are wealthy and have the means to purchase this painting if you choose … *Do you choose to do so?*

REFLECT: What have you learned about your SELF from this exercise?

* * * * *

This concept of "self" is complex, and, indeed, the human is a complex adaptive system. A complex system has a large number of interrelated parts which may or may not have nonlinear relationships, feedback loops and dynamic uncertainties difficult to understand and predict. Complex adaptive systems also have emergent properties which make the whole of the system (you) much more than the sum of its parts! For example, consciousness is emergent. An adaptive system—which can be responsive or proactive—improves its ability to survive and grow through internal adjustments. Complex adaptive systems operate at some level of perpetual disequilibrium, necessary for adapting but which contributes to unpredictable behavior. *Life is all about adapting*—which requires creativity—and we can all agree that it certainly is complex!

One of the ways the human adapts is through the plasticity of the brain, which means you have a brain that is malleable or pliable. Plasticity is a result of the connections between neural patterns in the mind and the physical world, which means that what we think and believe actually impacts our physical bodies! It's sort of a tit-for-tat kind of thing. The structure of our brain affects our thoughts, and our thoughts affect the structure of our brain. While we introduced this concept earlier, you will see it repeated several times throughout this text because it's so important to understand. This is interesting to think about in terms of our capacity for creativity, which is the bisociation of two or more ideas. It just makes sense that the more you learn the more ideas you have to bisociate, and continuous learning in your area of focus provides greater opportunity to solve issues and engage challenges in that domain as the future unfolds.

Self—an emergent quality of humans—is the totality of the conscious and unconscious mind, the brain, and the body, inclusive of everything it is to be human. From a quantum field perspective, the mind can be considered a field of potential—of possibilities—where at least half of the field has chosen to head the same direction. The mind is the seat of consciousness, enabling awareness of our self as a knower, an observer, and a learner, and as one who takes action, with our neurons forming a continuous memory of thoughts and actions, creating a coherent story of who we are.[148] Moving through various life experiences, the individual singles out and accentuates what is significant and connects these events to historic events to create a narrative unity, what can be described as a *fictionalized history*. This autobiographical self—the idea of who we are, the image we build up of ourselves and where we fit socially—is created over years of experiences and constantly being remodeled, a product of continuous learning in an experiential life.[149] Thus, *the story of self lives in the mind*—the what, why and how of your life.

Within each of us, embedded across cortical columns in the neocortex, is a personal ever-changing representation and models of the world[150] which are self-created. As noted previously, the neocortex is the organ of intelligence, which receives input from movement, generates behaviors, and predicts the next input. Reference frames within the cortical columns enable the ability to perceive shapes, changes, and locations relative to each other, providing the flexibility to bisociate ideas and process and navigate change.

While this self-created, ever-updating world model within our head does enable some "control" of the "external world", the creativity of the inner world does not follow causal laws (laws of antecedent causation, or cause and effect) and is *largely subject to our passion and direction*. At its best, inner creativity contributes to ennoblement of our character, the releasing of negative thought and emotions to allow creative freedom through the free-flow of ideas. "Since this inner life of man is truly creative, there rests upon each person the responsibility of choosing as to whether this creativity shall be spontaneous and wholly haphazard or controlled, directed, and constructive. How can a creative imagination produce worthy children when the stage whereon it functions is already preoccupied by prejudice, hate, fears, resentments, revenge, and bigotries?"[151]

Creativity requires freedom of thought, which can be greatly retarded by our preconceived opinions, settled ideas, and long-term prejudices. These handicaps can push unfinished creative thought into our consciousness, causing conceptual confusion. Indeed, while ideas may be stimulated by the outer world, ideals and values emerge from the creative realms of the inner world.

Thus, it is necessary to balance the inner and outer worlds. Balancing our inner and outer worlds is the middle way of the Buddha, and the golden mean of Aristotle. Carl Jung saw synchronicity as an example of how the inner and outer worlds can participate with each other. (See Chapter 11.)

An Enriched Environment

Arieta—who is rapidly becoming one of my favorite authors writing about creativity—says there are two kinds of prerequisites from which the creative process unfolds, contingencies and imagination.[152] Contingencies include all that is external to the creative person. His point is that new things cannot emerge out of nothing. Thus, the importance of preparation, not only in the domain of interest and passion—which is critical—but also in terms of exposure to an environment that stimulates creativity.

We often think of nature as an enriched environment, and indeed for the creative mind this is often the case. In an indoors setting, space design and plants, art and furnishings help create an enriched environment, and "toys" of various types can stimulate the mind. In today's environment, augmentation plays a key role, including virtual reality technologies as well as social media platforms that may stimulate and support learning and the creation of new ideas. As can be seen through inclusion of social media, an enriched environment is also focused on the social aspects, that is, engagement with other people. People do not learn in isolation—it is important to understand that humans are social beings—but are very much engaged in a continuous process of social learning.

The environment can also be considered in terms of external and internal. The biology, physiology, function, and form of the mind/brain/body affect an individual's creativity. For example, affective attunement contributes to the evolution and sculpting of the brain. "Affective" refers to feelings and attitudes and "attunement" infers being in harmony with or resonating with another. Affective attunement is a shared state, a vibrational entrainment inclusive of understanding another's needs and feelings that opens the door to learning and the sharing of ideas. As Johnson forwards, "According to social cognitive neuroscience, the brain actually needs to seek out an affectively attuned other if it is to learn."[153] Cozolino says that for complex levels of thought—those that involve higher brain functions and potential changes in neural networks such as creativity—learning cannot be accomplished when an individual feels anxious and defensive. A safe and empathic relationship can establish an emotional and neurobiological context that is conducive to neural reorganization. "It serves as a buffer and scaffolding within which an adult can better tolerate the stress required for neural reorganization."[154] As Taylor bluntly explains,

> *Adults who would create (or recreate) neural networks associated with development of a more complex epistemology need emotional support for the discomfort that will also certainly be part of that process.*[155]

Environmental influences such as nutrition, stress and emotions affect creativity. For example, there is an optimum level of stress for each individual. As has been discovered through neuroscience research, moderate levels of arousal (a state of high attention without debilitating anxiety) initiate neural plasticity by producing neurotransmitters and growth hormones, which literally build connections. Learning and creativity are enhanced through the production of dopamine, serotonin, norepinephrine and endogenous endorphins. For example, excitement can serve as a strong motivation to drive people to learn and create, but cannot be so strong that it becomes high stress moving toward anxiety. As Cozolino and Sprokay offer, "We appear to experience optimal development and integration in a context of nurturance and optimal stress".[156]

While we have emphasized the importance of a trusted other and an enriched environment when exploring new ideas, Caine and Caine remind us of the critical role the individual plays in these relationships.

> *In order to adequately understand any concept, or acquiring any mastery of a skill or domain, a person has to make sense of things for himself or herself, irrespective of how much others know and how much a coach, mentor or teacher tries to help. We have also argued that although there is an indispensable social aspect to the construction of meaning, there's also an irreducible individual element.*[157]

Which brings us back to Arieta's second prerequisite of SELF, which is imagination. Creative imagination is the focus of Chapter 5. It is important to note that Arieta's two prerequisites—contingencies and imagination—work together. An enriched environment, which increases the formation and survival of new neurons, can produce a personal internal reflective world of imagination and creativity.[158]

The Importance of Balance

As we begin this discussion, note that balance *does not mean equal*. Each of us is unique—with different thoughts, beliefs and feelings, different desires—such that *the balance of elements in which you best experience life and the free flow of creativity is unique.*

Because we are complex adaptive systems, as are the organizations of which we are a part, *we are always in the process of becoming more* and our systems are not always in balance. Further, balance is often about more than just two opposite things, but can mean balancing many different things. However, nature herself tends to seek balance. For example, spiral galaxies and clusters of galaxies result from a balancing between gravity and the rotation of stars as they orbit the center of the galaxy or cluster. Individual stars sustain a balance between the hydrogen gas or radiation in the center of the star pushing outwards and gravity pulling inwards. A balance occurs between gravitational and atomic forces when matter has a density close to the density of single atoms. Planets, mountains, trees, people, insects, cells, and molecules are all composed of closely packed arrays of atoms. The density of these collections of atoms is therefore similar to the density of a single one of the atoms of which they are made. Despite their superficial diversity, they are linked by a single thread—the similarity of their densities—that issues from the fact that they represent states that can withstand the crushing inward force of gravity.

As can be seen, humanity can learn a great deal about balancing from Nature. Arthur Shelley, an Australian educator and businessman and co-author of this book, shares that perhaps humans have not evolved as far as we would like to think, and that we could learn from how nature responds. As he describes: "The natural balance that exists in nature is something rarely achieved in human systems ... nature usually rebalances herself. It is only when humans interfere that nature loses control and falls out of balance."[159]

As we co-evolve with our environment, we get information from others and give information to others, and that information comes largely through our senses. If our senses are not open or well connected, then we get and give bad information. When our senses are well developed, we increase the flow of information that is in turn used to create ideas. Balancing our senses means that we consider all incoming input and, using our mental faculties, make a conscious decision about which input is the most important when considering applying an idea in a specific situation and context … REMEMBER, ALL KNOWLEDGE IS CONTEXT SENSITIVE AND SITUATION DEPENDENT, which means that an idea that might work in one situation may not be appropriate for a different situation. Thus, environmental input must be considered. Since people all have different capabilities and reactions to change, for an idea to be effectively implemented the people who will be involved or affected by implementing an idea must be considered. Since our emotions are our human guidance system, those have to be considered. Since our feelings may be providing us an intuitive push, then those need to be considered. Etcetera.

As an individual, you can lighten and balance your senses. For example, beauty has the unique capability of unifying the senses with thought, that is, capturing the attention of all of your senses with the vibration of thought and feelings heading the same direction, feeling good about what you are seeing, doing, or thinking. The unification of senses with thought leads to greater levels of knowledge and creative energy as well as expanded consciousness. Another example is the use of yoga, which is the process of joining thought and the senses of the body together, thus bringing greater balance to the senses.

Balancing thought means creating in whole thought, engaging both the lower mental thinking of logic and cause-and-effect (events, activity) *and* the higher mental thinking of patterns and connections (concepts and theories), and finding the balance to ensure that whole thought is clearly understandable to others. A deeper discussion of lower and higher mental thinking is included in Chapter 4.

Mindfulness

When we have inner balance, the outer world can be firing away and we are still able to function coherently. One approach to achieving inner balance is meditation. Meditation practices have the ability to quiet the conscious mind, thus allowing greater access to the unconscious. More recently, mindfulness practices are being recognized as beneficial both personally and in the workplace. Mindfulness is "a state of consciousness in which attention is focused on present-moment phenomena occurring both externally and internally."[160] This is a receptive attention, that is, the notion of meta-awareness, being aware of being aware.

Mindfulness was initially developed by Buddhist monastics in order to produce a state of mind profoundly different than our usual mode of consciousness, one which would provide cognitive flexibility and creative insight.[161] Cognitive flexibility expands the range of choices as well as responses,[162] which provides greater freedom to address whatever arises triggered by external and internal information association. Consistent with the intent of creative insight, research published in 2015 by Kudesia described the potential of mindfulness as a third route for organizations to achieve creativity, that is, in addition to hiring talent and implementing policies and procedures to motivate employees to think creatively, engaging mindfulness training to provide a "distinctive intrapsychic path to enhanced workplace creativity."[163]

Formica sees mindfulness as coming in two general flavors or modes: one which is a state of unfocused thought, and the second when intent is set to achieve a specific task, an action-based mindfulness. When in the first mode, there is the opportunity to see things in different ways, making new associations and coming up with new ideas, which can also be facilitated by Knowledge Capacities (see Chapter 1 and Appendix A). In the second mode, there is a focus, eliminating internal and external extractions, allowing creative thought in an environment of silence. When we have the ability to operate in both modes, a bridge between incubation and illumination is created.[164]

As a form of meditation, mindfulness supports every part of the creative process. As Goh forwards, "The key to optimizing the creative process is balancing the brain networks."[165] First, it reduces the influence of habitual thinking and boosts divergent thinking which characterizes creativity in the exploration of multiple possible solutions, while simultaneously helping to eliminate distractions, enabling focus on the issue at hand during the preparation phase.[166] Second, it facilitates relaxation and empties the mind, which helps enable unconscious processing during the incubation phase. Third, it clears the mind such that we have heightened awareness, which assists illumination. Fourth, it helps sustain focus during the verification phase, providing an insight approach—recognition of a solution without a step-by-step factor analysis—and promoting attention during this convergent thinking process.

Hemispheric Balance

The philosopher and early scientist Pythagoras understood the importance of balance. Trying to discover a rational account of our existence, he contributed many important terms to our lexicon. For example, cosmos and theōria, from the Greek term theōros (translated "spectator"), which gave us the important concept of theory. Seeking to achieve a balance between the older mythical consciousness and the newer mental one (mathematics and science), Pythagoras felt that this meant "achieving a harmony within oneself that matched the cosmic harmony without, what he, or his followers, called 'the music of the spheres'."[167] And that brings us to a short discussion of hemispheric balance and hemispheric synchronization, using music (sound) to achieve a whole brain state.

Today pretty much everyone is familiar with the understanding that the human brain has two hemispheres, although the importance of this knowledge used to hold greater significance. The fascinating area of split-brain research began in the early 1960s when a team of surgeons at the California Institute of Technology—led by Nobel prizewinner Dr. Roger Sperry—attempted the first commissurotomy on a man suffering upwards of 30 epileptic seizures a day. A commissurotomy is a radical operation that involves severing the corpus callosum, a bundle of 200-250 million nerve fibers which interconnect the right and left cerebral hemispheres of the cortex. The intent of the surgery was to limit the patient's seizures to just one of the hemispheres, and then seek to re-train the seizure-free hemisphere. The results turned out better than was expected, and the team went on to perform 30 other commissurotomies. These surgeries became part of a study to determine the possible outcomes of radical intervention into the brain.[168]

As this study advanced, Sperry and his team began to notice a *strange doubling of streams of consciousness*. The surgically separated hemispheres were shown to perceive, learn and remember independently with each hemisphere cut off from the conscious experience of the other. For example, when angry the first patient would go for his wife's throat with his left hand (controlled by the right cerebral hemisphere) and try to save her with his right hand (controlled by the more logical left hemisphere). Another patient would unbutton her blouse with her left hand and button it back up in a prim fashion with her right hand. As these observations continued, scientists began to refer to the two halves of the brain as if they had two distinct personalities. We now know that in reality humans have two different brains in the same body and that each sees the world very differently, yet when one section of the brain is damaged other parts of the brain begin to take over those functions. When a commissurotomy was performed, the intercommunication between the two halves of the brain was eliminated.

The Left Hemisphere. To a large extent, the left hemisphere controls the right side of the body and is the main venue of education in today's classrooms. McGilchrist says that the major difference between the left and right hemispheres is how they attend to the environment.[169] The left hemisphere is dominant when you engage narrow, focused attention, processing the stimuli coming in through the senses in a *linear-sequential* manner. In other words, it takes incoming information and handles it in an orderly, step-by-step, detailed and focused manner. Commonly called the verbal brain because it processes 97 percent of our words—as well as handling many of our auditory inputs—the left brain is appropriate for much of spelling, reading, writing, and mathematics.[170]

Due to this emphasis on the linear-sequential focus, the left hemisphere prefers to process incoming information which is logical, analytical, objective, causal, and has a true-false or right-wrong context within our *cultural norms*. Because of the reliance on order and structure, it processes more slowly than the right hemisphere. In today's environment in both Western and Eastern cultures, we often spend more time in the domain of the left-hemisphere processing style to the detriment of the creativity of more right-brained approaches.

Let's interject a short exercise for individuals who feel they need to more fully engage their left hemisphere. The use of the word "feel" was purposeful, since this need would apply to those who tend to be more emotional in the process of thought and life.

* * * * *

EXERCISE 6: *Exercising Your Left Hemisphere*

Shifting ways to think such as those offered through Knowledge Capacities (Chapter 1 and Appendix A) exercises your left hemisphere. In this short exercise, we build on several ways to think suggested by Minsky[171] accompanied by our explications.

STEP (1) Identify an issue you would like to explore.

STEP (2) Select one approach (ways of thinking) from the list below and explore the independent and dependent variables, relationships among them, and patterns of behavior associated with that way of looking at the issue. Take notes, and if an idea emerges be sure and capture it in your Idea Book.

STEP (3) Select a second approach and explore that same issue from that different viewpoint, taking notes.

STEP (4) Select a third approach and do the same (and continue with different approaches should you choose to do so).

STEP (5) Compare your notes across the approaches you have chosen, exploring how these different ways of thinking have contributed to understanding the issue at hand, and perhaps emerging a potential insight or solution. *Ask*: Do I have a deeper understanding of the issue? Are there any patterns that have become visible? What have I learned from this exercise?

NOTE: When you look from different directions your mind is shifting from one thought focus to another, strengthening your ability to do so—offering different viewpoints from which to understand this issue and seek creative solutions—while simultaneously you are learning different ways to perceive future issues.

Some Different Ways to Think

Reasoning by Analogy. Connecting to a similar problem in the past, note the patterns of activity and relationships among activities, and apply those patterns to the new situation. Remember, knowledge is situation dependent and context sensitive. The learning is in understanding the *patterns and relationships* in one situation and being able to extrapolate those to another situation. When this pattern thinking occurs across different domains of knowledge, it enters into the realm of wisdom. (See the earlier discussion of and exercise for pattern thinking in Chapter 2.)

Dividing and Conquering. A larger problem may be made up of a number of smaller problems, which are easier to resolve. A corollary to this in complexity thinking is to simplify. While simplification can lead to only a partial solution, a solution to part of the problem can serve as a stepping-stone for resolving the larger problem.

Reformulating. Look at the issue through different lenses. Minsky suggests looking for more relevant information. As he examples, "We often do this by making a verbal description—and then 'understanding' it in some different way!"[172] Reformulating also plays a role in applying different Knowledge Capacities (Chapter 1).

Elevating and Demoting. When there are too many details bogging you down, try thinking about the situation in more general terms. Move from specifics to generalities (a higher concept) and look at the problem from that viewpoint. Conversely, if your problem is too vague, then try making it more concrete by adding detail.

Self-reflection. Address questions to your self. *Ask:* Why is this problem so hard? What might we be doing wrong? How might we make this easier? What can we do differently? Who might we ask to partner in solving this problem? So many of our answers reside within if we just take the time to dialogue with our self. (See the discussion under "Surfacing Tacit Knowledge" in Chapter 10.)

Logical contradiction. Take the opposite stance (this is a favorite, and is similar to the Knowledge Capacity of Reversal in Appendix A). As Minsky says, "Try to prove that your problem cannot be solved, and then look for a flaw in that argument."[173] What fun! A related approach is to set up a debate, which is an inducing resonance approach (see Chapter 10). NOTE: Paradoxical thinking, recognizing two contradictory propositions with apparently sound arguments, is a powerful thought stimulator and inducing resonance approach. For example, reflecting on the age-old question, "Which came first, the chicken or the egg?"

External Representations. Writing ideas down—making notes and/or creating records, or building a PowerPoint presentation—helps organize and keep track of your thoughts. The very act of creating diagrams and graphics limits and focuses thought, helping in understanding the relationships among elements of a problem. Even if you don't find a solution, you will better understand the problem and be able to better articulate it to others.

* * * * *

The Right Hemisphere. Prior to the exciting findings which emerged out of split-brain research, many people felt the right hemisphere was just there in case we needed it for backup when some brain damage occurred. This perception continued through the early days of split-brain research, with greater emphasis and respect given to the traits of the left hemisphere. This is not surprising. Since the Industrial Revolution—and increasingly as we moved into the 20th century—the focus on science and, specifically, technology has accelerated left-brain dominance. With this acceleration, trust in intuition has diminished, creating an imbalance between the two hemispheres *which were always meant to complement each other and work together.*

Let's briefly explore the significance of this imbalance. Science seeks to reduce reality, to abstract from it what can be usefully applied. While this is largely limited to matter and materialism, Lachman recognizes that matter itself is an abstraction since "It is not the stuff we encounter in the world, but our conceptual grasp of it. We have all seen material things—they surround us—but no one has ever seen matter."[174] Too much clarity can obscure what is truly important. For example, this hunt through science for the simplest formula—a theory of everything, which eliminates what George Stiner calls the "sovereignly useless"—can never express the richness of life,[175] such values as beauty, love, and freedom, things beyond utilitarian which are at the very core of what it is to be human. This parallels the same thinking that has finally been acknowledged in our business approaches, that efficiency cannot replace effectiveness, quantity cannot replace quality; without effectiveness efficiencies prove useless, without quality you are going to wind up with a lot of little value.

Most recent studies have found that the right hemisphere is longer, wider, and generally larger as well as heavier than the left with a greater dendritic overlap, which allows for greater interconnectivity as compared to the left brain. The right cerebral hemisphere processes information at speeds far greater than the left, up to 850 times faster. And whereas the major processing style of the left hemisphere revolves around linear-sequential inputs, the right hemisphere focuses more on detecting the big picture (the holistic gestalt) rather than individual facts and details. An analogy would be that the right hemisphere focuses on the forest rather than the individual trees.

While the right hemisphere possesses a limited amount of language, its richness revolves around nonverbal body cues and face recognition, as well as imagery, dreams and daydreams. Since much visual and spatial information from our internal and external environments is first processed here, it is often referred to as our visual brain.

For many of us vision is our most important sense. Machines that measure our brains such as functional MRIs illustrate that visual processing involves a rather large portion of the occipital lobes towards the back of both cerebral hemispheres. Conversely, a verbal thought tends to be localized to a space about the size of a quarter located above the ear in the left hemisphere only. Vision is so crucial that upwards of 70 percent of the neurons across the cortex are devoted to vision. A really intriguing aspect of this finding is that roughly two out of three of these neurons in the cortex (known as the intelligent brain, the part of the brain most recently developed in the course of evolution) are not focused on *external* vision but *devoted to inner vision, that is, imagination.*

It can be said that the major difference in the processing styles of the two hemispheres of the brain is that whereas the left brain processes thoughts that are logical, analytical and objective, the domain of the right brain is on information that is more emotional, impulsive, intuitive, and creative. Nature and nurture have wired in more than five times more connections from the older limbic brain (where much of our neurochemistry resides) into the right brain, which must then transfer and influence across the corpus callosum to produce a balanced perception. Because of its faster processing speed coupled with the emphasis on bodily and spatial balance, right hemisphere development is dominant in the areas of athletics, dance, body movement, art ,and music.[176]

* * * * *

EXERCISE 7: *Listening to Feelings*

Intuitive "nudges" often take the form of feelings conveyed through your body. However, unless there is pain involved, many people who are primarily working out of their left brain ignore these nudges. This exercise is geared toward becoming aware of what your body is telling you. It engages a "focusing" approach such that your conscious mind becomes more aware of what your body is trying to tell you.

As psychologist Ann Weiser Cornell says, "Our bodies carry knowledge about how we are living our lives, what we need, what we value and believe ... Focusing lets you form a trusting relationship with your body ... lets you listen to the whispers of your body before it has to shout."[177] In addition to supporting decision-making and creativity in terms of raising awareness to intuitive nudges as well as embodied tacit knowledge, this exercise can be used as a self-help skill to identify physical issues emerging in the body.

STEP (1) Find a comfortable place to sit or lie where you will not be disturbed. Close your eyes. Now take three or four deep breaths, in through the nose, out through the mouth, releasing your anxieties and any tenseness in your body as you release your breath. Feel your body become relaxed.

STEP (2) Continue feeling your body. Take a tour of your body, letting your thoughts roam through your body, reflecting on your head, arms, torso, legs, always feeling the energy that flows through your body. *Invite* something to be felt. *Ask*: "What wants my attention now?" Then listen to your body, *feel* your body.

STEP (3) When some part of your body catches your attention, focus on it. Say hello to it, then try to describe or name it. Putting it into words focuses it, and limits it. With interested curiosity get to know the feeling better. *Ask*: Is there an emotion connected with this feeling? When you name the emotion, *ask*: Is this the right word to describe it? Allow yourself to hear or feel your body's response to your questions.

STEP (4) Gently, taking your time, invite the feeling to tell you more. *Ask:* Is this feeling connected to a memory or a belief? Then, just put it aside or let it go. Don't deep dive into memory lane. The intent is to acknowledge that you are listening.

STEP (5) Go back to sensing your body. *Ask*: Is this a good place to stop focusing for now? If the answer is "no", repeat STEPS (2) through (4). If the answer is "yes", thank your body for this information, say you will be back, and slowly bring your focus back to the outside world. Open your eyes.

HINT: It is not necessary to wait until your body catches your attention through pain or physical distress to use "Focusing". All too often we only notice our bodies when something is wrong, yet our bodies are working day and night just for us, and pretty continuously sending us messages! Take a few minutes each day to thank every cell—all the healthy ones—for all they do for you: they are about you! It's a good idea to check in with your body daily. And once you raise awareness of your body, be sure and pay attention to those intuitive nudges!

* * * * *

McGilchrist argues that the ways the two "brains" (hemispheres) work have complemented each other throughout history, working through a system of checks and balances much like a democracy should. However, with the mental acceleration over the past two hundred years, awareness of the intuitive has diminished if not been dismissed outright. If this occurs, we're in for trouble.[178] Building on the thought of McGilchrist, as Lachman so eloquently phrases it,

> *If our left brain, fired with a passion for the new way of knowing, succeeds in evicting its neighbour, then the result will be some new kind of being that will be radically different from ourselves, or at least from how we are supposed to be. We would not have two brains if we did not need them and we would not need them if they did not work differently, with both approaches necessary for us to be 'fully human'.*[179]

Recognition of this looming issue has occurred from different directions. In a book written more than a century ago titled *From Religion to Philosophy*, classicist Francis Cornford charted the shift from mythic to the mental in terms of consciousness. Cornfield said that "driven by a deep-lying need to master the world by understanding it, science worked steadily toward its goal—a perfectly clear conceptual model of reality, adapted to explain all phenomena by the simplest formula that can be found …" And as he continues, "When we contemplate the finished result, we see that in banishing 'the vague', it has swept away everything in which another type of mind finds all the value and significance of the world."[180] And that "vague" includes such things as the beauty, freedom, and love we mentioned earlier, the very things that give our lives meaning, that make living worthwhile. In today's environment, these same questions are asked considering the emergence of Artificial Intelligence.

Hemispheric Synchronization

One approach to achieving inner balance between the two hemispheres of the brain is hemispheric synchronization, the use of sound coupled with a binaural beat to bring both hemispheres into coherence. Binaural beats were identified in 1839 by H.W. Dove, a German experimenter. In the human mind, binaural beats are detected with carrier tones (audio tones of slightly different frequencies, one to each ear) below approximately 1500 Hz.[181] The mind perceives the frequency differences of the sound coming into each ear, mixing the two sounds to produce a fluctuating rhythm and thereby creating a beat or difference frequency. Because each side of the body sends signals to the opposite hemisphere of the brain, both hemispheres must work together to "hear" the difference frequency. This perceived rhythm originates in the brainstem and is neurologically routed to the reticular formation,[182] then moves to the cortex where it can be measured as a frequency-following response.[183]

This inter-hemispheric communication is the setting for brain-wave coherence, which facilitates whole-brain cognition,[184] an integration of left- and right-brain functioning.[185] What can occur during hemispheric synchronization is a physiologically reduced state of arousal while maintaining conscious awareness,[186] and from this balanced state with both hemispheres of the brain engaged, *the capacity to reach the unconscious creative state through the window of consciousness.* This can be likened to being consciously awake in your sleep state.

At the turn of the century, advances in brain measurement techniques to measure electrical activity in the brain such as the EEG (electroencephalogram) enabled the measurement of brainwave states associated with creativity. It was discovered that the brainwave signature of flow was similar to brainwave signatures associated with heightened creativity, with brainwaves moving from beta to the line between alpha and theta during the flow state. This is similar to the hypnagogic state, a state which has been long associated with heightened creativity.[187] Further, research has shown that theta brainwaves which occur during the flow state improve creative performance.[188] It has also been shown that a readiness state for sudden creative insight happens during a theta brainwave state with intermittent gamma wave activity.[189] The flow state is more fully explored in Chapter 10.

A version of brainwave entrainment is Field Effect Audio Technology (FEAT), a trademarked product of musician and shaman Byron Metcalf, that is a complex and unique integrated system of isochronic and binaural beats with specific drum and percussion rhythms and patterns.[190] It makes sense that this was created by a shaman! The combined harmonics, spatial audio processing and auditory driving support a natural state of coherence and balance within us and our immediate surroundings—a phenomenon that Metcalf calls *field effect resonance.* What is fascinating about this field effect is that it builds on the drum and rattle resonances created by early man to achieve this same state. In other words, while the use of technology to assist brainwave entrainment is relatively new, the idea of creating isochronic and binaural beats for inner creative work has been around for thousands of years!

The Intelligent Social Change Journey

In the life experience, each of us is participating in a learning journey, what we call the Intelligent Social Change Journey (ISCJ). This is a developmental journey of the body, mind and heart, moving from the heaviness of cause-and-effect linear extrapolations, to the fluidity of co-evolving with our environment, to the lightness of breathing our thought and feelings into reality. These are phase changes, grounding in development of our mental faculties, each building on and expanding previous learning.

The ISCJ is very much a *social* journey. Change does not occur in isolation. The deeper our understanding in relationship to others, the easier it is to move into the future. The quality of sympathy is needed as we navigate the linear, cause-and-effect characteristics of Phase 1 of this three-phase journey. The quality of empathy is needed to navigate the co-evolving liquidity of Phase 2. The quality of compassion is needed to navigate the connected breath of the Phase 3 creative leap. See Figure 6.

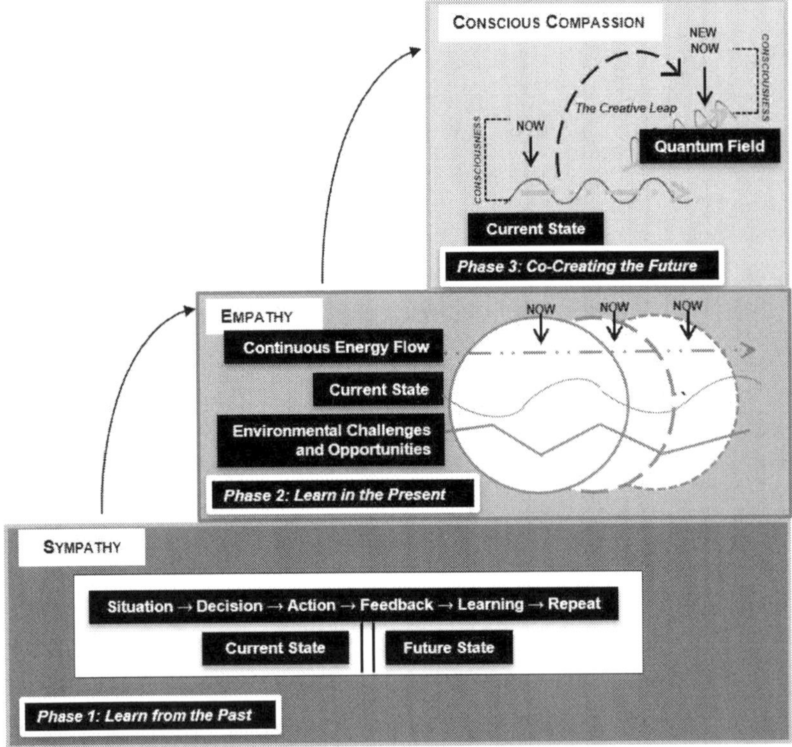

Figure 6. *The ISCJ Baseline Model. Each of the three phases, including a larger visual of each, will be introduced and detailed as we move through this little book.*

In the progression of learning to navigate change represented by the three phases of the ISCJ, we empower our "self", individuating and expanding. In the process, we become immersed in the human experience, a neuronal dance with the Universe, with each of us in the driver's seat selecting our partners and directing our dance steps.

Four critical growth elements during our journey, consistent with movement through the phases, are reflected in (1) expanded consciousness, (2) reduction of forces, (3) increased intelligent activity, and (4) greater creativity.

As introduced in Chapter 3, *consciousness* is considered a state of awareness and a private, selective, and continuous change process, a sequential set of ideas, thoughts, images, feelings and perceptions, and an understanding of the connections and relationships among them and our self. *Forces* occur when one type of energy affects another type of energy in a way such that they are moving in different directions, pressing against each other. Bounded (inward focused) and/or limited knowledge creates forces. *Intelligent activity* represents a state of interaction where intent, purpose, direction, values and expected outcomes are clearly understood and communicated among all parties, reflecting wisdom and achieving a higher truth.

Time and space play a significant role in the phase changes. Using Jung's psychological type classifications, feelings come from the past, sensations occur in the present, intuition is oriented to the future, and thinking embraces the past, present *and* future. Forecasting and visioning work is done at a point of change[191] when a balance is struck continuously between short-term and long-term survival. Salk describes this as a shift from Epoch A, dominated by ego and short-term considerations, to Epoch B, *where both being and ego co-exist.*[192] In the ISCJ, this shift occurs somewhere in Phase 2, with beingness advancing as we journey toward Phase 3.

<<<<<<<>>>>>>>

INSIGHT: **As Jung reminds us, feelings come from the past, sensations occur in the present, intuition is oriented to the future, and thinking embraces the past, present *and* future.**

<<<<<<<>>>>>>>

Phase 1: Learning from the Past

In Phase 1 of the Journey, *Learning from the Past*, we act on the physical and the physical changes; we "see" the changes with our sense of form, and therefore they are real. Causes have effects. Actions have consequences, both directly and indirectly, sometimes time delayed. For example, when you study, you get a good grade on a test; when you break a rule, you get punished. Phase 1 reinforces the characteristics of how we interact with the simplest aspects of our world. The elements are predictable and repeatable and make us feel comfortable because we know what to expect and how to prepare for them.

While these parts of the world do exist, our brain tends to automate the thinking around them and we do them with little conscious effort. The challenge with this is that they only remain predictable if all the causing influences remain constant ... and that just doesn't happen in the world of today!

The linear cause-and-effect phase of the ISCJ (Phase 1) calls for sympathy. Supporting and caring for the people involved in any change helps to mitigate the force of resistance, improving the opportunity for successful outcomes. Characteristics, which are words or short phrases representing ideas developed in this phase, include linear and sequential, repeatability, engaging past learning, starting from current state, and cause and effect relationships. See Table 1.

Nature of Knowledge	Points of Reflection	Cognitive Shifts
• A product of the past • Knowledge is context sensitive and situation dependent • Knowledge is partial and incomplete	• Reviewing the interactions and feedback • Determining cause-and-effect relationships; logic • Inward focus • Questioning of decisions and actions: What did I intend? What really happened? Why were there differences? What would I do the same? What would I do differently	• Recognition of the importance of feedback • Ability to recognize systems and the impact of external forces • Recognition and location of "me" in the larger picture (building conscious awareness) • Beginning pattern recognition and early concept development which supports creativity

Table 1. *Characteristics of Phase 1 of the ISCJ: Linear and sequential; repeatable; engaging past learning; starting from current state; cause-and-effect relationships.*

In this phase, the nature of knowledge is characterized as a product of the past and, remember, knowledge is context sensitive and situation dependent and always partial and incomplete. Reflection during this phase is on reviewing interactions and feedback, and determining cause-and-effect relationships. There is an inward focus, and a questioning of decisions and actions as reflected in the questions: What did I intend? What really happened? Why were there differences? What would I do the same? What would I do differently? In this phase, creativity is based on past events and learning.

The cognitive shifts that are underway during this phase include: (1) recognition of the importance of feedback; (2) the ability to recognize systems and the impact of external forces; (3) recognition and location of "me" in the larger picture (building conscious awareness); and (4) pattern recognition and concept development which, as developed, support creativity. These reflections are critical to enabling the phase change to co-evolving (moving from Phase 1 to Phase 2).

Phase 2: Learning in the Present

As we expand toward Phase 2 of the ISCJ, **we begin to more clearly recognize patterns**; they emerge from experiences that appear to repeat over and over. Recognition of patterns enables us to "see" (in our mind's eye) the relationship of events in terms of time and space, moving us out of an action and reaction mode into a position of co-evolving with our environment, and enabling us to better navigate a world full of diverse challenges and opportunities. It is at this stage that we move from understanding based on past cause-and-effect reactions to a focus on how things come together to produce new things both in the moment at hand and at a future point in time.

Learning in the Present (Phase 2) takes us to the next level of thinking and feeling about how we interact with our world, including the interesting area of human social interactions. In Phase 2 patterns grow into concepts, higher mental thought, and we begin the search for a higher level of truth. Although complex, the somewhat recognizable patterns enable us to explore and progress through uncertainty and the unknown, making life more interesting and enjoyable, and *engaging a higher level of creativity*.

Concepts (higher mental thinking)—which represent the structure of mental thought—answer the "why" while logic-based examples—which are an instant in time snapshot of a concept in form—comprise the "what" and "how". It is the human ability to perceive concepts that enables people to be mentally creative. Since concepts represent the relationships both within the example and with the environment, these patterns can be recreated without time structure, which can be referred to as creative imagination. When we are able to think in concepts as well as connecting those concepts with the examples (or form) of the thought, then we are creating "whole thought", which moves us into the realm of wisdom. (See Chapter 5 on creative imagination and wisdom.)

* * * * *

EXERCISE 8: *Thinking in Whole Thought*

Whole Thought coalesces higher knowledge processing of patterns, and processing of logic and cause-and-effect of events and activities from the past, to envision and create the future. The ability to think in whole thought can be developed through purposeful practice.

STEP (1) Starting from the lower mental thinking of logic (cause-and-effect), when an event occurs take an objective step backwards and try to identify the independent and dependent variables that are involved in this event and then map their relationships, that is, using arrows to denote how variables affect each other. The idea is to create a pattern, a form or model that can be used to imitate or repeat this event. Be sure and capture the context of the event so that the pattern can be more fully understood. If you have several similar events, this allows you to develop a pattern of patterns, giving you a higher "truth" regarding the relationships you are mapping out. *Consider*: Are there any models or theories to which these patterns relate?

STEP (2) Starting from the higher mental thinking of concepts (theories), choose a model within your area of interest/passion and search for events that fit into or demonstrate the application of that model. Do not be content with discovering a single event, but search for multiple events. If the model does not fit exactly, then shift the model to fit what you are discovering.

STEP (3) Repeat this exercise until you become adept at linking lower and higher mental thinking, achieving whole thought.

The better you can train your mind to make these connections—from events to concepts, and from concepts to events—the greater your ability to recognize pattens in situations and events occurring around you which enable your creative mind to see the larger relationships that can lead to opportunities and problem solutions.

* * * * *

To co-evolve with our environment requires us to develop a larger understanding of our self (values, beliefs, emotions, desires, etc.) as well as others, developing empathy, which occurs when most of the information entering through your five senses of form is being used to benefit others. Empathy provides a direct understanding of another individual, and a heightened awareness of the context of their lives and **their desires and needs in the moment at hand**. At this state, while not yet achieving the creative leap of the intuitional (represented in Phase 3), we are clearly developing higher mental faculties and instinctive knowledge of the workings of the Universe, which helps cultivate intuition and develop insights in service to our self and society.

Characteristics, which are words or short phrases representing ideas developed in this phase, include recognition of patterns; social interaction; identifying the needs and desires of others; and co-evolving with the environment through continuous learning, quick response, robustness, flexibility, adaptability and alignment.

<<<<<<<>>>>>>>

INSIGHT: **Empathy provides a direct understanding of another individual, and a heightened awareness of the context of their lives and their desires and needs in the moment at hand.**

<<<<<<<>>>>>>>

The nature of knowledge is characterized in terms of expanded cooperation and collaboration, and knowledge sharing and social learning. There is also the conscious *questioning of why*, and the *pursuit of truth*. Reflection includes a deepening of conceptual thinking and, through cooperation and collaboration, the ability to connect the power of diversity and individuation to the larger whole. There is an increasing outward focus, with the recognition of different world views and the exploration of information from different perspectives, expanded knowledge capacities, all of which expand the potential of creativity.

Cognitive shifts that are underway include: (1) the ability to recognize and apply patterns at all levels within a domain of knowledge to predict outcomes; (2) a growing understanding of complexity; (3) increased connectedness of choices, recognition of direction you are heading, and expanded meaning-making; and (4) an expanded ability to bisociate ideas resulting in increased creativity.

As a form of natural innovation, this expanded ability to bisociate ideas can make full use of what Andreas Wagner calls "sleeping beauties", which are genes waiting to be born into an environment where they will prove useful. Similarly, cultural innovations are "made possible by sophisticated brains and their neural circuits"[193] which may lay dormant for many millennia, waiting to be triggered by the environment. In the changing and complex environment of today, this highlights the "immense, yes, nearly limitless, potential of a brain to use the old for new purposes."[194] See Table 2.

Nature of Knowledge	Points of Reflection	Cognitive Shifts
• Expanded knowledge sharing and social learning • Engaging cooperation and collaboration • Questioning of why? • Pursuit of truth	• Deeper development of conceptual thinking (higher mental thought) • Through cooperation and collaboration ability to connect the power of diversity and individuation to the larger whole • Outward focus • Recognition of different world views and exploration of information from different perspectives • Expanded knowledge capacities	• The ability to recognize and apply patterns at all levels within a domain of knowledge to predict outcomes • A growing understanding of complexity • Increased connectedness of choices • Recognition of direction you are heading • Expanded meaning-making • Expanded ability to bisociate ideas resulting in increased creativity

Table 2. *Characteristics of Phase 2 of the ISCJ: Co-Evolving (requires empathy); recognition of patterns; identifying the needs and desires of others; co-evolving with environment through continuous learning, quick response, robustness, flexibility, adaptability, alignment.*

Phase 3: Co-Creating the Future

There is a freedom that occurs as we leave behind the thinking patterns of Phase 2 and open to the choices and discoveries of Phase 3. As we enter this phase, we are acquiring the ability to tap into the larger intuitional field that energetically connects all thought (see Chapter 7). This can only be accomplished when energy is focused outward in service to the larger whole, not constrained within, thus deepening our connection to others. Compassion deepens that connection. Note that each phase of the ISCJ calls for an increasing depth of connection to others, moving from sympathy to empathy to compassion, as we become more fully engaged in co-creating our reality. See Table 3.

Nature of Knowledge	Points of Reflection	Cognitive Shifts
• Recognition that with knowledge comes responsibility • Conscious pursuit of larger truth • Knowledge selectively used as a measure of effectiveness	• Valuing of creative ideas • Asking the larger questions: How does this idea serve humanity? Are there any negative consequences? • Openness to other's ideas • Questioning with humility: What if this idea is right? Are my beliefs or other mental models limiting my thought? Are hidden assumptions or feelings interfering with intelligent activity?	• A sense and knowing of Oneness • Development of both the lower (logic) and upper (conceptual) mental faculties, which work in concert with the emotional guidance system • Applies patterns across domains of knowledge for greater good (wisdom) • Recognition of self as a co-creator of reality • The ability to engage in intelligent activity • Developing the ability to tap into the intuitional plane at will

Table 3. *Characteristics of Phase 3 of the ISCJ: Creative Leap (requires compassion); creative imagination; recognition of global Oneness; mental in service to the intuitive; balancing senses; bringing together past, present and future; knowing; beauty; wisdom.*

Phase characteristics, which are words or short phrases representing ideas developed in this phase, include creative imagination; recognition of global Oneness; mental in service to the intuitive; balancing senses; bringing together time (the past, present and future); knowing; beauty; and wisdom. The nature of knowledge is characterized as a recognition that with knowledge comes responsibility. There is a conscious pursuit of larger truth, and knowledge is selectively used as a measure of effectiveness.

Reflection includes the *valuing of creative ideas* and asking the larger questions: How does this idea serve humanity? Are there any negative consequences? There is an openness to other's ideas, a questioning with humility: What if this idea is right? Are my beliefs or other mental models limiting my thoughts? Are hidden assumptions or feelings interfering with intelligent activity? (See Exercise 1 in Chapter 1.)

Cognitive shifts that are underway include: (1) a sense and knowing of Oneness; (2) development of both the lower (logic) and upper (conceptual) mental faculties which work in concert with the emotional guidance system; (3) *recognition of self as a co-creator of reality*; (4) the ability to engage in intelligent activity; and (5) a developing ability to tap into the intuitional plane at will, what is called *controlled intuition*. (See Chapter 12.)

In this very brief synopsis of the ISCJ—a journey in which all of us are participating—we are provided insight to the prerequisites of self for Innovative Creativity through reviewing the characteristics related to each phase of this developmental journey. These connections are not prescriptive, that is, an individual in Phase 1 may very well be developing characteristics generally related to Phase 2. However, generally these characteristics build on each other, expanding consciousness and, much like the progressive levels of consciousness, this expansion refocuses our thought and activity outwards in greater service.

Note that recognizing these phases provides an understanding of the challenges and impact of engaging with people not operating in the same phase. For example, people firmly embedded in Phase 1 of the ISCJ find it hard to understand the flow and intent of people in Phase 3. They think they are a "bit off with the fairies" and/or "not grounded". Similarly, people operating in Phase 3 struggle to engage Phase 1 people because they do not wish to oversimplify the complexities, but may need to since their level of dialogue is above the current capacity of Phase 1 participants.

As part of this learning journey, we recognize that emotions—present in all sentient complex adaptive systems—play a powerful role. Our emotional guidance system influences our perception of reality and how we respond to that perception, assigning values to options and alternatives, setting limits, without our even knowing it! Feelings—as will be addressed in the discussion of tacit knowledge in Chapter 9—also serve as intuitive nudges to bring ideas into our awareness. In short, our emotions are a building block of consciousness and a powerful force for creativity.

Chapter 5
Creative Imagination

The world is but a canvas to the imagination.
Henry David Thoreau

Imagery through the lens of the mind's eye offers a clue to the very nature of the creative process. "The ability to imagine, to conjure up images or visions of things different than our ordinary reality, has always been recognized as the hallmark of the innovative mind."[195] As previously introduced, vision is the dominant sense of perception in the human, a way of "knowing" the world that has been around longer than language. Indeed, imagery can be considered the language of the unconscious, and the "power of the unconscious is most directly evoked by the deliberate practice of imagery and visualization skills."[196]

Liu and Nopope-Brandon believe that there is no creativity or innovation without a "healthy and well-fed" imagination, and that imagination comes first.[197] We agree. So, what exactly is imagination? As with all important words emerging over time within a diverse humanity, there are differing opinions as to exactly WHAT imagination is. Still, various dictionaries seem to reference the forming of mental images or concepts which may or may not relate to external objects not present to the senses. A second interpretation goes on to add the relationship of these mental images or concepts to each other and to the thinker, which is very much an element of consciousness. Simultaneously, "creative" is touted as being imaginative, even going so far as saying that being creative is "intended to stimulate the imagination",[198] and indeed, it does! Thus, the imagination is a direct player in the creativity process.

Interestingly, while hunting for a definition of imagination, Lachman professed that

> *... we can't get 'under' imagination because the very act of trying to do so requires imagination itself. Memory, self-consciousness, thought, perception: all inform and are informed by imagination and are difficult, if not impossible, to pry apart from it or each other.*[199]

Lachman finally builds on the definition provided by Colin Wilson as he explored the evolutionary potential of imagination.[200] According to Wilson, imagination is "the ability to grasp realities that are not immediately present", that is, a deeper engagement with reality, "or even, in some strange way, to create it, or at least to collaborate in its creation."[201] Lachman describes this even further, and his rhetoric is well worth the read:

> *While it can be used for fantasy, illusion, make-believe, and escapism, the real work of imagination is to make contact with the strange world in which we live and to serve as both guide and inspiration for our development within it. It is the way we evolve. Imagination presents us with possible, potential realities that it is our job to actualize. It also presents us with a world that would not be complete without our help.*[202]

Thus, as Lachman purports, imagination is needed to *grasp reality* as well as *create the future reality.* It is that important. When Einstein was asked by journalist George Sylvester Viereck which he trusted more, his knowledge or his imagination, Einstein responded, "Imagination is more important than knowledge. Knowledge is limited. Imagination encircles the world."[203] As Lachman reflects, "the real work of imagination is to make contact with the strange world in which we live and to serve as both guide and inspiration for our development within it."[204] As introduced, it seems, quite literally, that imagination is the way we evolve, presenting us with potential and possible realities which then become our job to actualize.

Below is a short approach to exercising your imagination. As credited to Lucille Clifton, "We cannot create what we cannot imagine."[205]

* * * * *

EXERCISE 9: *Imagining*

In this exercise, use your imagination to engage an issue or problem. Relax. When we imagine we aren't taking any risks. As you are imagining, *ask:* How does it feel? Following are three specific ways to use your imagination (and feel free to *imagine* other ways that would be fun!)

STEP (1) *Wishful Thinking.* Imagine all the resources (including time) that you want. What would you do? If you can't imagine it, reformulate the problem, looking for more relevant information. Create a conversation with yourself and talk out loud. Try simulating actions inside your mental models.

STEP (2) *Impersonation.* Imagine you are someone else—a teacher, a scientist, a factory worker. *Ask:* What does this problem look like from this viewpoint? What actions would make sense? (Take notes, and if you discover a creative idea, be sure and capture it in your personal Idea Book.)

STEP (3) *Storytelling*. Imagine you are a storyteller in the future, telling the story about this problem and how it was solved. Take your time and enjoy the process. If you get stuck, imagine an adult or child asking a simple question, and then continue on until you get to the end, whatever you imagine that end to be.

Above all, have fun!

* * * * *

Symbolic Representation

Crawford forwards that imagination is a capacity of mind "to produce or reproduce several symbolic functions while in a state of consciousness, of awake-ness, without any deliberate effort to organize these functions."[206] This would exclude dreams or anything happening in the unconscious. We would beg to differ since *there are continuous contributions from the unconscious throughout the lived experience*, although we are not necessarily aware of those contributions. Further, an example of conscious and unconscious balance—a whole brain state—can be achieved through hemispheric synchronization (introduced in Chapter 4).

Crawford's use of "symbolic" in his definition is of interest. He believes that the characteristic of "being symbolic" is a primary feature distinguishing human psychological functions from other animals … and that it is the basis of creativity. Reflect on that for a moment. At different levels, animals have sentience, exhibiting cognitive process such as learning, memory and intelligence. They also learn to respond to stimuli, with responses depending on what is immediately given. A common example is the Pavlov experiment, where Pavlov's dog learned that when he responded to a buzz food would arrive. It didn't take long before he began to salivate in preparation for food whenever he heard the buzzer. So, the buzz was a sign that food was coming, but not a symbol.

Creative Imagination is different from other functions of the mind in that it uses many kinds of symbols in different contexts and proportions, "so that these new, different contexts and proportions themselves become symbols of things never before symbolized or else symbolized previously in different ways."[207] A symbol is "representative of something else, even when that 'something else' is completely absent."[208] An example is the name of a friend, which even when she is not around is a symbol of her. Similarly, words represent associations. For example, the word "beautiful" has a similar context even though what we each may consider beautiful may be entirely different (which it is)!

The Knowledge Capacity of Symbolic Representation (perceiving and representing) (Appendix A) takes advantage of the connection between symbols and creativity. The mind/brain does not store exact replicas of past events or memories. Rather, it stores invariant representations (symbols) that color the meaning or essence of incoming information.[209] There is a hierarchy of information where hierarchy represents "an order of some complexity in which the elements are distributed along the gradient of importance."[210] This hierarchy of information is analogous to the physical design of the neocortex, "a sheet of cells the size of a dinner napkin as thick as six business cards, where the connections between various regions give the whole thing a hierarchical structure."[211] There are six layers of hierarchical patterns in the architecture of the cortex. Documented for the sense of vision, it appears that the patterns at the lowest level of the cortex are fast changing and spatially specific (highly situation dependent and context sensitive) while the patterns at the highest level are slow changing and spatially invariant.[212] For example, values, theories, beliefs and assumptions created (over and over again) through past learning processes represent a higher level of invariant form, one that does not easily change, compared to lower-level patterns. Thus, once learned, the mind/brain can quickly associate with symbols which can represent large amounts of context yet be immediately understood and interpreted. For example, a cross or menorah carries with it all the myths it represents. "It is an outward sign of an inward belief."[213]

Symbols are everywhere we look. Mathematics is built on hypotheses and relationships, that is, patterns, assumptions and relationships. Letters represent sounds, notes represent tones, pictures represent thoughts and beliefs, shapes of signs on the highway represent the context of rules, and so on. We use symbols to organize our thoughts. For example, in human face-to-face interactions it has long been recognized that non-verbal's and voicing (tone, emphasis) can play a larger role in communication than the words that are exchanged. New patterns are emerging in social media that represent and convey these aspects of communication, helping provide the context and "feeling" for what is being said. As social media has matured, symbols such as emoji, icons used to express a concept or emotion, have become patterns of patterns, well understood by practicing social networkers and quickly conveying the message they are sending.

The question becomes, does the use of symbols limit or support creativity? The answer, of course, is that they have the potential to do both. For example, if a symbol represents a certain pattern or state and you automatically take that as a given, then it can be limiting. On the other hand, if a symbol or group of symbols enable you to look at higher-level patterns, then it can be expanding. By understanding the way our mind works—recognizing that the unconscious is continuously inserting its "voice" based on historic patterns—we have the ability to purposefully shift our thinking and potentially be open to new ideas.

Psychosynthesis effectively uses mental imagery for engaging imagination while still being directed by the intellect and will. The connection between the conscious and unconscious is used to learn how to shift gears, volleying between these two states to increase creativity. The value of this was presented in Chapter 3 as a neuroscience finding. Crampton, the Director of the Canadian Institute of Psychosynthesis, describes the use of imagery to create a dialogue between the conscious and unconscious. She notes that some of the broad range of available techniques work best when an experienced person serves as a guide, while others can be effectively used with or without assistance. The following short exercise builds on Crampton's description of the technique by this name. Note its similarity to the exercise in Chapter 2 called "Sleep on It".

* * * * *

EXERCISE 10: *Answers from the Unconscious*

In this exercise, you are going to ask a question of your unconscious. Crampton suggests using this approach to "acquire information, obtain guidance and gain better understanding of our inner processes."[214]

STEP (1) Formulate a question. Start small, that is, with a question you can get your mind around. For example, rather than asking "What is the answer to this issue?" you might wish to start by asking "What can I explore to find an answer to this issue?"

STEP (2) Address your question to your unconscious. Do not be afraid to say it out loud,

STEP (3) Allow the answer to emerge in the form of a mental image. Quite often the answer will spontaneously emerge, sometimes with surprising facility.

NOTE: It is important to not reject images which seem irrelevant. If you give these images sufficient attention, their significance may become clear. If a sequence of apparently unrelated images appears, the first one generally is the most meaningful.

* * * * *

The Power of Desire

A strong contributor to creative imagination emerging from the unconscious and not "produced or reproduced" in the conscious state is emotions and feelings. Creative imagination is tied directly to emotions and feelings and, in particular, to *desire*. As an expression of a feeling, to want or wish for something, desire is closely related to intention.[215]

Desire is a sustaining, motivating life force; indeed, an animating, continuously *expanding* life force which is unstoppable as long as we live and breathe, and which is viewed by Western philosophers as fundamental to human life. It often occurs without our conscious awareness—either rational or non-rational—a bedfellow driving our thoughts and actions. Heijen says desire is the reason that started creation, and which is—in its current sentient form—still driving it. Further,

> *... the notion of emotion as a later stage version of motion—with pain and pleasure from which we either run away from or get drawn to—can be seen as the sources of information by which sentient beings not only operate but also learn, and by which desire finds direction.*[216]

Supporting the powerful relationship between desire and imagination, especially when focused on "purposes beyond its own", Shaw wrote, "Imagination is the beginning of creation. You imagine what you desire; you will what you imagine; and at last you create what you will."[217]

Desire > Imagine > Will > Create

Desire, then, has a potential unlike other emotions. As Alexander Faulkner Shand, an English writer and barrister, recognized in 1920, "Every emotion, when its end is obstructed, tends to develop its impulse into desire, and so give rise to the prospective emotions" and thus "the system of every emotion potentially contains desire with its prospective emotions."[218] This stance has been forwarded through various other theories. For example, the Humean Theory of Motivation, which forwards there is a belief/desire pair behind all motivation, and the philosophical thesis that "all normative reasons must be grounded in desires."[219] So, desire is married to intent, which in the focus of the topic at hand would be a desire to find a solution to a problem or challenge or a desire to take advantage of an opportunity. When desire is very strong it is considered a passion (see Chapter 8 for a discussion of passion as a driver for creativity).

Before leaving this brief description of desire, it seems appropriate to share some wisdom from Kabir, a 15th century weaver, poet, philosopher, and mystic who is claimed by both Hindus and Muslims.[220] According to story and legend, Kabir forwarded that people were generally born with innumerable desires, far too many for anyone to pursue, with most of these being very superficial. Kabir considered these individuals the "poorest" of people and their lives "also the saddest, because they are the most superficial, dominated by too many desires that matter too little."[221] Those people who have "some desires" usually lead successful lives since they are able to focus on some of those. Then there are those who have only a few desires, and out of this group emerges the greats, whether scientists, musicians, poets, humanitarians or political leaders. These people have "tremendous passion to persevere and to succeed. Driven by a longing that is spread among only a few desires, passionate people often achieve great things."[222] Finally, we have those rare people who have only one desire, a focused passion. From these emerge the great mystics and spiritual leaders.

This message from the past is quite clear. Creativity and accomplishment follow your desire and passion, and the more focused your desire and passion, the greater the potential for creativity in that domain of knowledge.

A Caution

When an individual has a preference for structured thought, that is, a uniformity of ways of thinking and a similarity among activities and creations resulting from that thinking, then that thought is a balance of past and present, with the future largely missing. When this occurs, creative imagination is predicated on past experiences and learning—with rules and principles for creative thought emerging out of those experiences and learning—which limits Innovative Creativity.

Limits are also set when creative imagination is focused on the self since creativity can only be based on the past which is known to the self. This reflects the importance of Shaw's insight on the power of desire and imagination when focused on "purposes beyond its own". When an individual is focused on others in the Now—the second phase of the ISCJ human development journey, the stage of co-evolving, where empathy is developed—then the past and the present are engaged. Creative imagination and empathy expand consciousness. This makes sense considering the definition of consciousness includes awareness of our self *and* others, *and* the relationship of our self and others, and that empathy enables a deeper understanding of others *and* their relationship to us and to others. Thus,

Creative imagination + empathy + energy leads to Innovative Creativity

When the limits of the present are mentally and emotionally released and an individual is able to conceptually build on the patterns of the past to create whole thought, then creative imagination can leap into the future. While the idea of "whole thought" was introduced in the previous chapter, it is worth repeating here. When we are able to think in concepts as well as connect those concepts with the examples (or form) of the thought, and do the reverse as well, then we are thinking in "whole thought", which brings us to the door of wisdom. But first, let's explore the Capacities for Imaginative Learning developed by The Lincoln Center for the Performing Arts.

The Lincoln Center Capacities for Imaginative Learning

Founded in 1975, Lincoln Center Education (LCE)—also known as Lincoln Center Institute (LCI)—is the education division of the Lincoln Center for the Performing Arts. LCI created what they call the "Capacities for Imaginative Learning" to serve as a framework for their learning programs. While these are focused on art, they are applicable to every aspect of imaginative learning. As can be seen, the underlying theory is that close engagement with an object of study "unleashes a student's ability to think of and express new possibilities."[223] This is why deeply engaging in your domain of interest/passion is a prerequisite of creativity related to that domain.

These Capacities for Imaginative Learning are a good set to use when addressing an issue. With a few word shifts, these are:

- *Noticing deeply*—identifying and articulating layers of detail through continuous interaction with an object of study.
- *Embodying*—experiencing a work through our senses and emotions, and physically representing that experience.
- *Questioning*—asking "why" and "what if?" throughout your experience.
- *Making connections*—linking the patterns you notice to prior knowledge and experience (both your own and others').
- *Identifying patterns*—finding relationships among the details you notice, and grouping them into patterns (chunking).
- *Exhibiting empathy*—understanding and respecting the experience of others.
- *Living in ambiguity*—understanding that there is more than one valid point of view for each issue, and that finding answers requires patience and effort.

- *Creating meaning*—creating interpretations of what you encounter, and synthesizing them with the perspectives of others.
- *Taking action*—acting on the synthesis through a project or an action that expresses your learning.
- *Reflecting and assessing*—looking back on your learning to identify what challenges remain and to begin learning anew.[224]

Take a few minutes to reflect on these capacities as they pertain to creativity. These can serve you well in supporting the creative process.

Concept Formation

Concept formation serves as a launching pad for creative imagination. As introduced in Chapter 4, conceptual thinking is higher mental thought. In The Tao of Personal Leadership, Dreher writes,[225]

> *To succeed in any field, we must look to those skills that make us fully human: the ability to learn continuously throughout life, to communicate with others, to come up with creative new solutions, and to deepen our understanding, looking to the larger patterns within and around us.*[226]

When we are able to discover the larger patterns in life, we have moved into the higher mental thought of conceptual thinking. Pattern recognition and development of conceptual thinking is recognizing the relationships among *types of things* and the patterns of response and change because of those relationships. For example, adoption of a practice that was considered a "best practice" in one organization, does not mean the same change will occur when applied in another organization. Understanding the pattern related to the practice allows the transfer of the pattern and understanding of that success, enabling the shifts and changes necessary to achieve the desired results in a different situation and context.

Concepts are about the possible as well as the "what is", and here is where creative imagination comes into play, making it possible to envision a better world and get closer to our ideas through our personal thought. "It is through concepts that man's greatest psychological growth occurs. Concepts of concepts and symbols of symbols can continually be formed by creative people and used by the community of men."[227]

Arieti sees three distinct advantages of concepts: (1) they offer us a more or less complete description; (2) they permit us to organize since the different attributes (parts) appear logically interconnected; and (3) they permit us to predict since we can deduce what is going to happen to any member of the class covered by the concept.[228] Concepts as formulas facilitate rapid processing of large amounts of information coming in through all our senses on all three planes (physical, mental, and emotional). Rather than addressing each sense separately, these formulas help build a predictive approach to accurately determine the outcome of various actions and interactions. For example:

> *Within a specific domain of knowledge, when this action is taken within this situation and context, this is what is going to happen.*

OR, as a concept, a higher-order pattern:

> *Within a specific domain of knowledge, when this* **type** *of action is taken within this* **type** *of situation and context, this is the* **type** *of response that will occur.*

In the latter case, *type* refers to sameness in identity, although this may be a loose and popular identity,[229] something similar. Each example would represent a token of this type. This sameness in identity may mean that two things are different parts of some wider unity that includes both, or they are both different members of the same class of things, or they are different parts of a resemblance structure, or they fall under the same predicate or concept.[230]

Universals theory looks at resemblances of identity in terms of properties and relations. From these properties and their relationships, natural classes of things emerge. We add the term conditions to this description of universals, and defer to Armstrong's description that universals are the substance of the world, with substance something that is capable of independent existence.[231]

As demonstrated in the paragraphs above, we are using our conceptual thought to create changes in our interactions in a continuous loop of discovery: creating formulas from the examples we perceive, applying those formulas, discovering more examples through searching out similarities and differences in those formulas, and continuously shifting and changing the formulas to find a higher truth, discovering the nature in terms of heuristics. A concept that appears true may become a preconcept as more examples are explored or, if it does not include all the attributes which need to be defined, it may be a faulty construct. In this journey of discovery, we are using our mental faculties to discover new ideas and co-create the world within which we interact.

Earlier we introduced the "attribute" approach of creativity forwarded by Crawford, that is, identifying an attribute in something related to the focus of your search (problem, issue, opportunity) and adapting and applying that attribute to that focus.[232] This approach starts with a known thing, the selection of one of its attributes (usually the dominant one), changing it, and then proceeding to something new, or applying the attribute to another thing. Another approach is, following the collection of data around the subject of interest, to identify the association between these data based on space or time contiguity. Taken together, all the attributes that have been identified form the concept. Remember (and as no doubt you are getting tired of hearing over and over again in this book), knowledge is fragmented and piece-meal, partial and incomplete, context-sensitive and situation dependent, and ever changing. *It is the thinker who is creatively using the best knowledge at hand that makes the difference.*

Conceptual thinking provides the foundation for identifying a need and working backwards—from the larger pattern—*towards an unknown thing*. When a *need* for something to be created is recognized, this is an opportunity. While recognizing this need is certainly the starting point, the Innovative Creativity process is that of not only discovering a solution, but working out the developmental details and producing the concept. The starting point, as we have previously introduced, is drawing on past knowledge. For example, Henry Ford got the idea for a planetary transmission for the "Model T" car by combining the workings of an old Swiss watch and an old tractor differential gear. *The question becomes how to access your tacit knowledge*. (Several approaches are addressed in Chapter 10.)

You have to find some place to begin, and this may require you to diligently search in order to discover that upon which to build. Crawford's "attribute" transference offers a prescription for this search: (1) Know what you are seeking (specificity); (2) Through analysis, establish the dominant attribute of your prospective creation; and (3) Identify the elements of this prospective attribute. *Ask:* What else has this quality or attribute? As you hunt for examples (lower mental thought based on logic), the more examples you find, recognizing the patterns across those examples, the greater the potential to find a higher truth (the concept for which you are hunting). There may be several attributes you can identify, and now you explore these in more depth and how they interact together. The "answer" to your search will most likely come in small pieces that you will need to knit together, record, revise, and reintegrate. And somewhere along this process, an *Aha!* experience may very well occur, and the BIG IDEA emerge!

As can be seen, concept formation is an important part of Innovative Creativity, the place where all the attributes of an idea come together in relationship to each other, serving as a launching platform for your creative imagination.

Chapter 6
Creating in Wisdom

Wisdom bounces off of patterns and deepening connections to others and emerges from a passion for creating and learning. From the human viewpoint, wisdom is the highest part of mental thought. Representing *completeness and wholeness of thought*, which offers a strong foundation for creativity, wisdom occurs when activity matches the choices that are made and structured concepts are intelligently acted upon, thus *directly connecting wisdom to intelligent action*.

A large number of writers have considered wisdom as a part of intelligence.[233] For example, Paul Baltes and Jacqui Smith say that wisdom is "a highly developed body of factual and procedural knowledge and judgment dealing with what we call the 'fundamental pragmatics of life'."[234] And wisdom can be linked to the intelligence developed through experience: "Knowledge can be had by education, but wisdom, which is indispensable to true culture, can be secured only through experience and by men and women who are innately intelligent. Such a people are able to learn from experience; they may become truly wise."[235]

Wisdom is also in relationship with knowledge. They both have an information component and a process component dealing with the nature and structure of information, with *nature* representing the quality or constitution of information, and *structure* representing the process of building new information, or learning. Csikszentmihalyi and Nakamura refer to these two components as the *content* of wisdom (information) and the *capacity to think or act wisely*. Content would be context-sensitive and situation dependent,[236] which is consistent with the position that wisdom is grounded in life's rich experiences.[237] However, wisdom moves above and beyond specific circumstances as patterns develop. Wisdom "therefore is developed through the process of aging ... [and] seems to consist of the ability to move away from absolute truths, to be reflective, to make sound judgments related to our daily existence, whatever our circumstances."[238] Thus, patterns become more important than exact actions. Sometimes. As Oscar Wilde is credited with saying, "With age comes wisdom, but sometimes age comes alone."

In a beautiful flow of words and concepts, artist Joan Erikson says that a sense of the complexity of living is an attribute of wisdom. As she writes, a wise person embraces …

> *the sense of the complexity of living, of relationships, of all negotiations. There is certainly no immediate, discernible, and absolute right and wrong, just as light and dark are separated by innumerable shadings ... [the] interweaving of time and space, light and dark, and the complexity of human nature suggests that ... this wholeness of perception to be given particularly and realized, must of necessity be made up of a merging of the sensual, the logical and the aesthetic perceptions of the individual.*[239]

From qualitative research with Buddhist monks, clinical psychologist Heidi Levitt said that the monks tended toward a spiritual definition and believed that all people were capable of wisdom, regardless of their intellect. From a similar persuasion, Chögyam Trumpa, a Buddhist meditation master who coined the term "crazy wisdom", sees wisdom as a state of consciousness with the qualities of *spaciousness, friendliness, warmth, softness and joy.*[240] Similarly, Marion Woodman and Elinor Dickson see wisdom as the state of consciousness that *allows the spiritual Self to be active.*[241] Copthorne Macdonald—who is a social experimenter, inventor, engineer, ecologist, philosopher and independent scholar—describes this systemic thinking as "*acting with the well-being of the whole in mind.*"[242] That's the concept of the greater good.

Combining much of this thought, as a working definition, we turn to the definition provided by John Dalla Costa in *Working Wisdom*:

> *Wisdom is the combination of knowledge and experience, but it is more than just the sum of these parts. Wisdom involves the mind and the heart, logic and intuition, left brain and right brain, but it is more than either reason, or creativity, or both. Wisdom involves a sense of balance, an equilibrium derived from a strong, pervasive moral conviction ... the conviction and guidance provided by the obligations that flow from a profound sense of interdependence. In essence, wisdom grows through the learning of more knowledge, and the practiced experience of day-to-day life—both filtered through a code of moral conviction.*[243]

Similarly, as psychologist Robert Sternberg describes:

> *I view wisdom as the value-laden application of tacit knowledge not only for one's own benefit (as can be the case with successful intelligence) but*

also for the benefit of others, in order to attain a common good. The wise person realizes that what matters is not just knowledge, or the intellectual skills one applies to this knowledge, but how the knowledge is used."[244]

We concur with this description and repeat these core words: THE VALUE-LADEN APPLICATION OF TACIT KNOWLEDGE FOR THE BENEFIT OF OTHERS. With Innovative Creativity, we expand the responsibility for how our knowledge is used to include to *what end our creativity is used*. Let's look closer at the relationship between wisdom and intelligent activity.

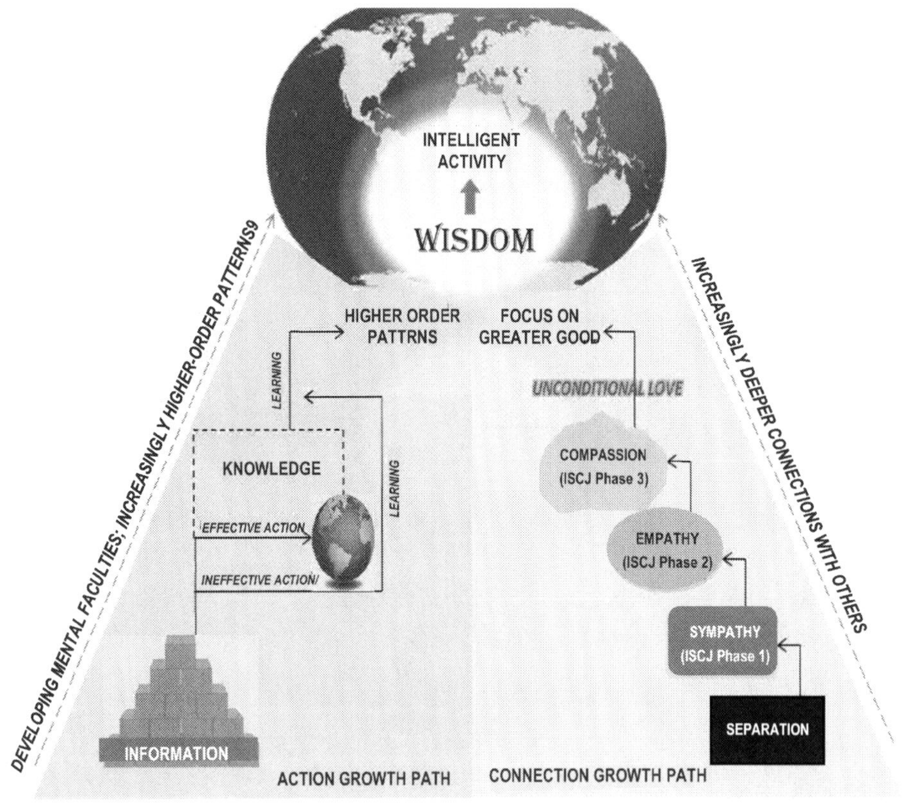

Figure 7. *Wisdom reflects the completeness and wholeness of thought.*

In the continuous search for higher order patterns, the concept of wisdom is clearly related to knowledge—and, in particular, to tacit knowledge, a multi-dimensional resource—and can also be related to the phenomenon of consciousness. More importantly, as with creativity, wisdom does not occur in isolation; it indeed appears to deal with the cognitive and emotional, personal and social, as well as the moral and religious aspects of life, very much based on the interconnectedness of people, which is developed in the co-evolving phase of the ISCJ developmental journey. See Figure 7.

This filtering through a code of moral conviction is critical. Knowledge and creativity acted upon without the actor taking responsibility for its use can be dangerous for both the actor and those who are affected by the innovation. In short, the human capacities of knowledge and creativity must be used wisely. As Peter Russel, the Canadian political scientist and author of *The Global Brain*, says, "Through knowledge we learn to act in our own better interests. … Wisdom reflects the values and criteria that we apply to our knowledge. Its essence is discernment. Discernment of right from wrong. Helpful from harmful. Truth from delusion."[245] Thus, wisdom—which is whole thought *engaging both concepts and the experiences in life that demonstrate those concepts*—is the value-laden application of tacit knowledge and creativity not only for one's own benefit, but also for the benefit of others.

The important role in creativity played by the wisdom each of us has developed is becoming clearer. First, we open our creative thoughts to larger possibilities when we think in terms of whole thought and the greater good. Second, we recognize that we as creators are *responsible for the way that which we create (innovation) is used*. Let's keep this in mind as we move toward controlled intuition on our Innovative Creativity journey.

Revisiting Creative Imagining

As we reflect upon the symbiotic relationship between wisdom and creative imagination, we recognize that wisdom is not a static repository of knowledge, but rather a dynamic catalyst for creative thinking. It is wisdom that enables the discernment of meaningful patterns amidst chaos and guides the imaginative process to yield insights that transcend mundane understanding.

The essence of wisdom lies in its ability to inform and shape our creative faculties, ensuring that our imaginative explorations are rooted in a deep awareness of life's complexities. This bond is articulated in our choices and actions, embodying a kind of intelligent creativity that references the past, comprehends the present, and aspires towards a future replete with innovation. In embracing wisdom, we honor the creative imagination not as an unfettered flight of fancy but as a purposeful and responsible endeavor that harmonizes our innermost visions with the external tapestry of communal existence.

As with knowledge, *with creative imagination comes responsibility*. With this focus on self-responsibility for creativity and knowledge, a note of caution as we begin to more fully appreciate the power of our imagination. Closely entangled with emotions, imagination alone—divorced from the critical, analytical mind—can easily move down what Goethe calls the path of "shadowy phantoms of vain imagination" or Paracelsus describes as an "exercise of thought without foundation in nature". As Coleridge recognizes, the integration of imagination and understanding produces a reason which enables us to "grasp the living reality of experience" and the "fragments of images and ideas inhabiting our minds".[246] As Lachman summarizes,

> *The idea is not for imagination to take the place of the analytical, quantitative mind ... The idea is for them to work together, or at least to recognize the need for each other, to see in each other one of our 'two permanent needs of human nature' and to work to accommodate both. Satisfying one need at the expense of the other does not work, whichever need is in question.*[247]

Barfield took this seriously, recognizing that imagination could be either good or bad, emphasizing that each individual needs to be responsible to and for their imagination. He forwards that this responsibility of the imagination requires a detached but engaged awareness.[248] This is the "passive potency" that Swedenborg speaks of, "an alert, self-possessed attention to detail and readiness to receive, with both ways of knowing available for work."[249] This is a state of wakefulness and purpose, the energetic home of Innovative Creativity.

This balanced state becomes even more important when we realize that *we are co-creators of our reality.* "[T]he imagination behind our perceiving the world is the same as the imagination that creates it."[250] And so, there are multiple realities. Just as each and every individual is unique, the realities we create individually and collectively are unique. Depending very much on our perception, different frames of reference are foundational to how and what our creative imagination creates. We will briefly explore the following perspectives: Literary, Living System, Consciousness, Scientific, and Spiritual. As in all human constructs provided to facilitate understanding, while these brief discussions are representative of these perspectives, they are not the perspectives themselves. As ever, the map is not the territory.[251]

Co-creating from a Literary Perspective

The relationships among thought, language and behavior have been explored throughout man's history. The power of knowledge in the form of writing is evident in early records describing the role of the *Overseer of All the King's*

Works in ancient Egypt. This Overseer, who directed the massive labor force required to build a pyramid, was a scribe. His palette and papyrus scroll were the symbols of his knowledge and of his authority, and bureaucratic lists and registers were the tools of political and economic power.[252] Literature was prized because of its influence over others, and brought fame to the scribe. In short, knowledge, demonstrated by writing, was considered an authority, whether it took the form of literature, a medical recipe or a list. Whatever was written (as symbols) was considered truth, or reality.

In 1784 Hugh Blair identified a clear, close alliance between thought and language, with the spoken/written word sometimes responsible for the clarification of thought, and the clarification of thought sometimes responsible for the improvement of the word. In Blair's words, *thought and language act and re-act upon each other mutually* and *by putting our sentiments into words, we always conceive them more distinctly*. How do I know what I mean until I hear what I am going to say? While this appears to be a truism for some, it is clear that Blair believes the conception of thought remains *prior in time and importance* to language.[253]

Later theorists (Brown, Black, Bloomfield, Skinner and Quine) regarded language as a major form of behavior, a significant entity in its own right. Language as behavior is very much in contrast with language as a subordinate feature in the process of communication. In 1982, a writing text contended that *the freedom to act upon the world and to construct reality is both the aim and the process of education*.[254] This implies that language is a powerful, if not unique, way of constructing reality and acting on the world. This is why a new word often emerges with a new idea. A number of well-known and well-published authors would agree. They describe the writing process—interacting with pen and paper or, in more recent years, keyboarding—as *their approach to creating the ideas they are writing out*.[255] Let's look at the thoughts of some well-known authors.

Francoise Sagan: "For *Bonjour Tristesse* all I started with was the idea of the character, the girl, but nothing really came of it until my pen was in hand. I have to start to write to have ideas …."

James Thurber: "I don't believe the writer should know too much where he's going. If he does, he runs into old man blueprint – old man propaganda."

Truman Capote: "But in the working-out, the writing-out, infinite surprises happen. Thank God, because the surprise, the twist, the phrase that comes at the right moment out of nowhere, is the unexpected dividend, that joyful little push that keeps a writer going."

William Faulkner: "Sometimes technique charges in and takes command of the dream before the writer himself can get his hands on it … It [*As I Lay Dying*] was simple in that all the material was already at hand."

Gertrude Stein: "It will come if it is there and you will let it come, and if you have anything you will get a sudden creative recognition. You won't know how it was, even what it is, but it will be creation if it came out of the pen and out of you and not out of an architectural drawing of the thing you are doing …"

In more prosaic terms, every act of writing is an act of creating, interacting with the medium in the environment to create symbols external to self, a release of the unconscious reality into public view. As Lakoff and Nunez note in their book, *Where Mathematics Comes From*, and as now a basic understanding:

> *Perhaps the most fundamental, and initially the most startling, result in cognitive science is that most of our thought is unconscious – that is, fundamentally inaccessible to our direct, conscious introspection. Most everyday thinking occurs too fast and at too low a level in the mind to be thus accessible. ... We all speak in a language that has a grammar, but we do not consciously put sentences together word by word, checking consciously that we are following the grammatical rules of our language. To us, it seems easy: We just talk, and listen, and draw inferences without effort. But what goes on in our minds behind the scenes is enormously complex and largely unavailable to us.*[256]

Since it is true that the large amount of our "thought" is unconscious, then we can agree with Blair that the conception of thought—occurring in the unconscious—remains prior in time and importance to language. Further, from the thoughts of authors Sagan, Thurber, Capote, Faulkner and Stein it is clear that the act of creation occurs with the pen in hand, and Lakoff and Nunez credit talking and listening to what we are saying. Thus, the literary approach to creating reality suggests that a potential method in support of Innovative Creativity is to place ourselves in the position of writing (today that would most likely imply sitting in front of a computer and keyboarding) or in a conversation with others around the specific topic/domain of interest (for example, interacting in a community of interest or practice).

Co-creating from the Living System Perspective

Autopoiesis is a term with Greek derivation that means self-production. The main argument of the theory is that living systems are created and reproduced in an autonomous, simultaneously open and closed self-referential manner. This means a porous boundary, where some things can come in and others are warded off. An example would be the intake and processing of food versus the rejection of foreign matter. Autopoiesis assumes everything the living system needs for self-production is already in the system.[257]

In epistemological terms, autopoietic systems are considered to contain their own knowledge since the system is the observer of external events. External events such as clouds, people, buildings, etc., are all part of the individual's experience and the interpretation and description of these events are the results of the *relationships* established between our previous experience and our perceptions. From an autopoietic viewpoint, it is impossible to step out of the individual and see ourselves as a unit in an environment because what the individual sees as the external environment is still part of his experience and by no means lies outside the interface that, in theory, separates the knower from the known.

If our reality cannot be separated between ourselves and the external world, then within our own minds what we perceive and create and believe *is* reality. Therefore, when we actively create new realities within ourselves, they become "the" reality upon which we act, anticipate and analyze. From this internal reality, and the forthcoming actions, comes behavior in the external world that then creates a perceived reality in the minds of others. Thus, the possibility of diffusion of our own individual reality to others becomes realized, and a significant external reality can be created through wide-spread commonality of interpretation.

Understanding that the reality we perceive as "real" is affected by our individual experiences and interpretations, and that the larger perceived external reality is a product of ourselves and others' perceptions also affected by others' experiences and interpretations, begs us to identify and understand our own limitations and stay open to the possible learning offered by others' thoughts. This is taking the approach of humility which is discussed in Chapter 1. (See also Exercise 1: Humility.)

Co-creating from the Consciousness Perspective

The permanency of form, or reality, is an illusion, since all consciousness is a process of change. Consciousness is a process in which thoughts, images and feelings are constantly evolving. Its major characteristics are unity, optimum complexity and selectivity. Unity is necessary to make the time flow of thoughts, images and feelings coherent. Optimum complexity allows the processing of divergent signals from within the individual and from the external environment. Selectivity limits the incoming signals to those that are essential to survival or interest. What this means is that when you receive incoming information from the senses, you take that information and mix it with your memories of thoughts, feelings and images related to that incoming information (the associative patterning process). The brain's ability to integrate these forms is what is called the remembered present.[258] The process we call consciousness is a continuous sequence of these remembered presents and the understanding of their connections and relationships to each other and our self.

Studies from consciousness would agree with autopoiesis in that when we receive external information, since we immediately compare it with what is already in our memory, it is the combination of these two, coupled with our own belief and value systems, that yields what we perceive as reality, an integrated mental scene. That means the individual mind participates in the creation of its own reality. The more we participate in learning experiences and are open to learning, the greater our ability to create a rich 'remembered present" and contribute to the perceived significant external reality.

Co-creating from a Scientific Perspective

From the viewpoint of Newtonian physics, scientific inquiry assumes the existence of an objective, external reality that can be studied, understood and tested through empirical methods. Although science recognizes the potential subjectivity of individual perceptions and observations, where possible, particularly in the domains of physics and chemistry, it has built into its methodology protection mechanisms that minimize or eliminate subjectivity in areas of concern to science. Through the process of creative construction of models and theories of objective reality, filtered by empirical testing and public dialogues and debate, the best estimate of objective reality is created. While this objective reality is not "the" objective reality, it is self-consistent and for each area of its applicability it has been highly effective, leading to great advances in technology and a deeper understanding of our world and our Universe.

Under these working assumptions, to some extent an individual's perception of reality can influence that reality predominantly through the psychological impact that belief has on the individual's actions. Through these actions, then, the external reality can be influenced, and therefore a self-fulfilling prophecy may be possible.[259]

While science recognizes that individuals have different subjective realities as explained by autopoiesis and numerous psychological studies, these differences in reality do not preclude understanding the objective reality in the hard sciences. However, there are significant open questions in several areas related to the observer's impact on that objective reality.

While Quantum physics is shifting all that was previously learned in science, there is still so little we understand, and many other fields of science have not yet taken into account what we *do* understand. This is not surprising since it challenges the big questions at the core of our very existence. As Carrol points out, although our understanding of Quantum mechanics at a fundamental level is not finished, "... there is nothing we know about it that necessarily invalidates determinism (the future follows uniquely from the present), realism (there is an objective real world), or physicalism (the world is purely physical)."[260] Change can be difficult regardless of the direction from which you look!

What we are beginning to understand is that the Quantum Field is a probability field, and, consistent with the treatment in this book, that *all that is possible exists*. Further, we know that there is a relationship of thought to this Field, and that consciousness emerges when enough thought is heading the same direction.[261] Much like the hierarchical structure of neuronal patterns in the human mind/brain, there are hierarchical relationships in the Quantum Field, with the qualities of self-organization and self-creation. Thus, consciousness itself creates more consciousness, and has the ability to, at the level of the hierarchy where it is focused, affect the direction of energy flows in the Field. When enough thought is focused in the same direction, a shift in the Field occurs.

From the viewpoint of cell biology and the discoveries related to the new field of Epigenetics—the study of the mechanisms by which the cell environment influences gene activity—we now know that we are not victims of our genes. It is the way genes are expressed that determine their strength in our lives, and that involves choice. As Lipton says, we now know that we are not frail bio-chemical machines controlled by genes, but rather "powerful creators of our lives and the world in which we live." Further, we have discovered that the cells of the body are controlled through receptor and effector proteins—a set of antennas, that appear on the outer membrane of the cell. Thus, consciousness is a simulation information field.[262] This has huge impact for the human as co-creator.

Co-creating from a Spiritual Perspective

Like the words in this book, the objects around us that make up our environment are symbols that transmit a reality with a learned, and agreed-upon, meaning. The true information is not in the object any more than thought is in words and letters, although there is no denying the potential impact of words and letters in the physical reality! Both words and objects are methods of expression. When you speak words, and though they may *express* more or less your feelings, *they are not your feelings*. There is a gap between our thought and our expression of thought. This gap is particularly visible when we consider how often each of us begins a sentence, and don't know exactly how it's going to end. As introduced in earlier discussion, we create the thought and the language as we go along. This same gap occurs between our thoughts, feelings and mental images and the creation of objects (in space) and events (in time).

Spirituality sees the continuous creation of our physical environment as a method of communication and expression, with the self in the role of co-creator. Feelings, thoughts and mental images are translated into physical reality, with feelings playing a significant role in this process. The intensity of a feeling, thought or mental image is an important element in determining subsequent physical materialization; feelings—often linked to thoughts and mental images—largely build that intensity. If your mind works with high intensity, and you think in vivid mental emotional images, these are swiftly formed into physical events. We form the fabric of our experience through our beliefs and expectations, which are not *about* reality, but *are reality itself*.[263] This is the power of intent discussed as a force in Chapter 8 and as a Knowing cognitive process in Appendix B.

Specific connection and openness to the larger field of the superconsciousness, whether that field is referred to as an information field, consciousness field, quantum field, or God field, is introduced in Chapter 1 and visualized in Figure 3. A discussion of spiritual tacit knowledge as a specific form of tacit knowledge is in Chapter 9. Tapping into this larger field is also the source of revealed intuition (Chapter 11).

Final Thoughts

Because we have addressed our roles as co-creators from a diversity of frameworks does not mean that each of these frameworks is separated from the other. Quite to the contrary. Humans are holistic, and energies emerging from all aspects of "being human"—physical, mental, emotional and spiritual—affect our creative imagination! Our preferences dictate our focus, but these frameworks interact, just as the energies within us interact to create an individual, and just as people in an organization interact to create a business, and just as organizations around the world interact to create a global economy.

Interestingly, just as our thoughts and feelings and perceptions encourage success, the ability to accomplish our goals, our misperceptions can threaten survival. As Lipton and Bhaerman acknowledge, "Almost all of us have unknowingly acquired limiting, self-sabotaging misperceptions that undermine our strength, health, and desires."[264]

Perceptions are beliefs, and the nature of our perceptions greatly influence our lives. For example, consider the placebo and nocebo effects. The placebo effect is a sense of benefit arising solely from the knowledge that treatment has been given;[265] the nocebo effect is a sense of illness or a toxic condition arising solely from the knowledge of exposure to same.[266] One research study on these effects dealt with Japanese children who were allergic to a poisonous plant. One leaf labeled as poisonous was rubbed on the children's forearm, and another leaf that looked the same but was labeled as non-poisonous was rubbed on the other forearm. As expected, the majority of the children developed a rash on the arm rubbed with the leaf labeled poisonous and had no reaction to the non-poisonous leaf. However, what the children did not know is that the two leaves had been purposefully mislabeled! The children had broken out in a rash because of *their perception* that the non-toxic leaf was poisonous.[267] *Ask*: What role does our creative imagination play in these two effects? Remember, our creative imagination can be good or bad, and we are responsible for that effect.

The answers to the nature of reality and our role in the creation of that reality are to be found through an inner journey into ourselves, through ourselves, and through the world we know. It is human creative imagination—imagination and creativity—that is constantly creating the reality in which we live.[268] Each and every one of us has observed or been a part of this great creativity, which always seems greater than our physical dimension with its perceived objective reality. This joy of creativity flows through us as effortless as our breath; and each of us uses this flow of creativity to create a unique reality, different from any other individual.

<<<<<<<>>>>>>>

INSIGHT: **The joy of creativity flows though us as effortless as our breath; and each of us uses this flow to create a unique reality, different from any other individual.**

<<<<<<<>>>>>>>

As we draw our exploration to a close, it becomes increasingly evident that co-creation, in its highest form, is the realization of wisdom in motion—it is the deliberate and ethical orchestration of knowledge, experience, and ingenuity towards the greater good. This integrative manifestation of wisdom within co-creation empowers us to construct realities that are not only reflections of our shared aspirations but also testaments to our commitment to act with foresight and moral responsibility. In recognizing our role as co-creators, we acknowledge the wisdom that informs our collective journey—an understanding that it is through the confluence of diverse perspectives, inspired by a shared vision, that we sculpt a future characterized by both profound depth and soaring creativity.

Chapter 7

We Live in a Field of Ideas!

Pretty much everyone who has given it much thought will agree that we live in some kind of an energy field, whether they prefer calling it (as we've previously noted) an information field, consciousness field, quantum field, God field, or any other of a myriad of descriptive terms. It is interesting that all these names focus on the field from *different perspectives of what it is to be human*. Lynne McTaggart avoids this naming dilemma by simply calling it *The Field* as described in a powerful book by that name. We will go along with her approach.[269]

We have long recognized that our Earth is surrounded by a *geomagnetic* field, which in turn has been called by dozens of names throughout history. For example, the French geologist/paleontologist Pierre Teilhard de Chardin called it a Noosphere, "a human sphere, a sphere of reflection, of conscious invention, of conscious soul".[270] Scientists with other electromagnetic theories have used terms such as Electric Fields of Life (Harold Saxton Burr); Orchestrated Reducation or Orch-OR (Hameroff and Penrose); Electromagnetic Information Field (E. Roy John); Akashic or A-Field (Ervin Lászlo); Conscious Mental Field (Benjamin Libet); Quantum Brain Dynamics (Jibu and Yasue); Conscious Electromagnetic Information Field (Johnjoe McFadden); Electromagnetic Consciousness Field (Michael Persinger); Electromagnetic Field (Susan Pockett); Electromagnetic Field Photon Theory (Hermes Romjin); Morphic Fields/Morphic Resonance (Rupert Sheldrake); and K*Space (William Tiller).

While that's a lot of different names, there is a clear connective thread in terms of energy, information, and consciousness. Let's explore these connections further.

Exploring from the Physical Perspective

Our human bodies—which are densified energy in form as matter—are literally complex energetic systems which are transformers of energy, not only continuously *receiving* energy from this Field, but also continuously *creating* energy and sending it into the Field. As physician Richard Gerber describes, "the biochemical molecules that make up the physical body are actually a form of vibrating energy."[271] As part of the Field (using this simple name), in every instant of life there is an exchange of energies underway. An important concept forwarded here is that of vibration, which will come up again in our conversation.

As far back as the middle of the nineteenth century, the English scientist Michael Faraday, who studied electromagnetism and has become well known today by electromagnetic-sensitive people for his "Faraday Cage"—believed that the space around the Field was the most important aspect of energy because of the influence of the force from each on the other. But in quantum language it is an *exchange of energy* that creates dynamic patterns in a continuous process of redistributing energy. "This constant exchange is an intrinsic property of particles, so that even real particles are nothing more than a little knot of energy which briefly emerges and disappears back into the underlying field."[272]

While Einstein's theory of relativity shows that empty space is literally bursting with activity, it was Max Planck who proved that particles and the empty space around them could not be separated (proven by a 1911 experiment by Planck, a founding father of quantum theory). This is at the root of symbiotic thinking (introduced in Chapter 1), which shows us that the very concept of "cause" *cannot* exist without the concept of "effect". *This deep relationship is not from causality, but from existence.* The very existence of a thing or idea requires the existence of something else. This pattern plays out in the discussion of time and space, noting that space cannot exist without objects, and objects exist because they are surrounded by space. And with symbiotic thinking, there is reason to expect that our individual ideas cannot exist without *a larger consciousness which seeks to incorporate these ideas.*

Exploring from the Mental Perspective

We begin by expanding our discussion of information. The life journey starts with information. In living systems, the distribution of atoms and molecules is non-random. Theoretical biologist Tom Stonier—who spent much of his life developing a theory of information, the results of which are published in three volumes—proposed that "organization is the physical expression of a system containing information."[273] Organization means the existence of a non-random pattern of particles and energy fields, or more generally, the sub-units comprising any system, such that

> *... the intricate organization of matter and energy which makes possible that phenomenon which we call life, is itself a product of the vast store of information contained within the system itself.*[274]

From this, we begin to understand that information is a basic property of the Universe—as Tom Stonier says, as fundamental as matter and energy—and a basic property of us. The Universe is literally organized in a hierarchy of information levels and, as we know, information is the fodder for knowledge and creativity, capacities that require information.

In the material world, organization can be observed in space and time as a physical phenomenon. Boltzmann, who was a thought leader in statistical mechanics, connected order/disorder changes in a system to visible changes in entropy,[275] which led Schrodinger to further explore the relationship of entropy and order in living systems.[276] This led to his reflection that "order" was the inverse of "disorder", with "entropy" the level of randomness in a system denoting a gradual decline into disorder. Stonier took this thought further, noting that describing information entropy as a state of a system was far more than a metaphor. He discovered that *changes in entropy were consistent with changes in a system's information content*. Further, he noted that "an increase in entropy measures an increase in the *absence* of information."[277]

Stonier saw many parallels between information and energy, seeing information as an intrinsic component in all physical systems, what could be defined as "potential energy". An example of potential energy often used in textbooks is a pencil, which sits on the desk or stays in a drawer until another force is applied to it (you picking it up and writing with it). Then, the force (energy) you have exerted in the writing is turned into information, that which is written on the paper. Consistent with this scenario, Stonier defined potential energy as "a state in which the *expenditure* of energy has resulted in an *increase* in the information content of the system."[278] Note that creative thought can also be defined as "potential energy" in terms of its potential contribution to innovation.

Stonier also described the exponential growth of information based on the recursive properties of information systems. As he says:

> *Organized systems exhibit resonances. Resonances lead to oscillations. Oscillations represent timed cycles during which changes may be introduced. Such changes may dampen or amplify the existing oscillations. Alternatively, they may create new resonances and excite new sets of*

oscillations. The more complex the system, the greater the likelihood of introducing changes into the system during any given cycle. Hence the exponential growth of information.[279]

This makes the relationship between information and entropy clear, which also plots the evolution of the universe. Where you have entropy approaching the infinite and information in a zero state, the Big Bang occurred (Creation). Then, as matter became more and more complex, moving toward biological systems, entropy moved toward the zero state. And here is where the phenomenon of intelligence (the emergence of consciousness) occurred, with systems capable of both organizing themselves *and* ordering their environment.

While we will not delve any deeper into Stonier's work—although we urge those who have the interest and energy to do so—it is important to our conversation to note that, just as energy and matter, energy and information are *interconvertible*. That means they can be exchanged one for the other, and that energy can be converted into either information *or* matter. Thus, the law of the conservation of energy can be expanded to read "in a closed system, what is conserved is the sum total of energy plus matter *plus* information", all available to be put into service to creativity.

Limiting the Field

Thought can be defined as a series (more than one) of choices connected by their direction.[280] Because a thought is more than one choice, it is often perceived as occurring over time. Thought, then, has a level of organization, which is information. Using the quantum frame of reference, we recognize that energy and matter are indefinite (continuously being redistributed) such that energy follows thought.[281] The material world is an effect, not a cause. Change occurs from the inside out, whether in our self, our local environment, or in the Field.

Thus, thoughts and images generated within ourselves have a profound creative and motivating power in human consciousness, with the heart-mind (that's thought and feelings related to that thought AND/OR feelings and the thought related to those feelings) *controlling energy and building form.* Besant and Leadbeater called these "energy complexes on the subtle levels of reality that are analogous to physical things. They are forms made of emotional-mental matter."[282] The word "subtle" refers to low intensity vibrations or frequencies, which can come from both the physical body (electromagnetic or quantum energies) or from the metaphysical (consciousness, thoughts and spiritual energies that transcend the physical).

These thought forms are sent out into the environment where they attract sympathetic vibrations, those vibrations that resonate with the thought and feelings being produced. While this idea of vibrational resonance is quite important to the creative process, this can be quite difficult to accept for those who suffer from the Cartesian dichotomy between matter and mind and desire to bring everything to the physical level. However, even using that frame of reference, we now understand from neuroscience the power of the mind/brain—as noted earlier, that our thoughts actually change the structure of the physical brain (as well as impacting all of our other human systems), and that the structure of the physical brain very much affects our thoughts.[283]

Scientists such as Bohm and Harold Puthoff explored the role of nature's information field in the "quantum vacuum". For example, Puthoff described an equilibrium that exists between matter and the energy field, which he refers to as the zero-point energy field.[284] One consequence of this connection is that we are—quite literally and physically—"in touch" with the rest of the universe, and that the modulation of such fields might just carry *meaningful* information, which insinuates purpose, much like the popular movie phrase, "The Force be with you".

This is the comprehensive concept of an *informed* universe, that is, a *meaningful* universe. Note that information serves as the raw material and it is only when the raw material is processed (in our case through the human mind) that it becomes a *message* which, upon receipt and processing by the recipient—and noting the context sensitivity of meaning—can become *meaning* to the processing individual.[285] This understanding sets the context for the discussion in Chapter 11 of revealed intuition, which is also exampled in our Chapter 14 case study which explores the power of revealed and unveiled knowledge in reconstructing local food systems in indigenous African tribes.

Ervin Laszlo describes this meaningful universe as the Akashic Field. In this Field, there is an informing of "everything by everything else", which is universal.[286] Remember, "universal" does NOT mean the "same", but rather isomorphic, which is having the same basic form. Perhaps a better way to think about this is as a resonance, where frequencies of sounds resonate with other sounds playing at the same frequency. When this occurs—when things are at the same frequency—they are said to be coherent. Coherence is a term which represents the degree of synchronization between coupling oscillating systems. In this Field, "things are directly 'in-formed' by the things that are most like them", yet there is also a coherence such that, less directly, other frequencies can also "in-form". This all happens at a staggering speed. As Laszlo explains, "Information conveyed through the A-field subtly tunes all things to all other things and accounts for the coherence [and the symmetry] we find in the cosmos, as well as in living nature."[287]

We are *active conscious participants* in this relationship with the Field, swimming in a vast ocean of energy which is full of entangled, continuously flowing sub-fields. *From a quantum perspective*, we now recognize this as a large probability field of thought, dynamically and continuously redistributing old patterns and creating new patterns. And, *our* thoughts and feelings and actions through a continuous exchange of energy are playing in this Field!

In 2005 Mountain Quest Institute reached out to 34 Knowledge Management Thought Leaders located across four continents to explore the aspects of KM that contributed to the passion expressed by these thought leaders. By definition, thought leaders are part of a social network, part of a collective whole, with both formal and informal, visible and invisible, networks with whom they exchange viewpoints and engage in discussions, using each other as sounding boards. This network can be described as partners, co-authors, spouses, friends, mentors, colleagues, associates, thought partners, people we trust, and other people who work in the field.

A concept forwarded by many of these thought leaders was that the ***ideas are already out there, just waiting to be recognized***, and we just need to be open to recognizing them and catching hold of them and have prepared ourselves for understanding and applying them. For example, Etienne Wenger, an educational theorist who developed the community of practice concept for organizations, says that ideas are, "In the air … you know what I mean? It's not like you invented things; you just sit and they're in the air. And you say, oh yes, that's right. But it was already in the air, you know?"

<<<<<<<>>>>>>>

INSIGHT: **The ideas are already out there, just waiting to be recognized.**

<<<<<<<>>>>>>>

One thought leader who, building on Lazlo's work, referred to this field of ideas in terms of the Akashic Records, says that along the way to becoming a thought leader he developed a holographic method to record interactions among people—and between people and computers in organizations—from spiritual models such as the Akashic Records. The Akashic Records represents the membrane of a higher frequency upon which every thought and every action is written, such that the past and the future as history can be read as a series of streams. For this thought leader, *the imagining and visioning of this capability* birthed a new process, and now AI is rapidly moving into this role.

The Shift to Idea Resonance

Human creativity is highly dependent on social interaction. Global connectivity and the internet have brought—and continue to bring about—new modes of social networking, demanding a shift in our perceptions, and facilitating a shift from relationship-based interactions to idea-based interactions, with affective attunement and trust developing through virtual relationships based on the *resonance of ideas*.

In the past, trust meant that you could rely on the integrity, ability or character of a person, thing, or process. Trust was built up over time. See Figure 8 below. However, in today's world, where everything happens quickly and often over the internet, virtual trust is not only trust among individuals and groups communicating virtually—and trust of the ideas being communicated, that is, idea resonance—but also a trust in the technology, the hardware and software used to communicate (security, reliability, accurate transmission, etc.) and the information being exchanged.

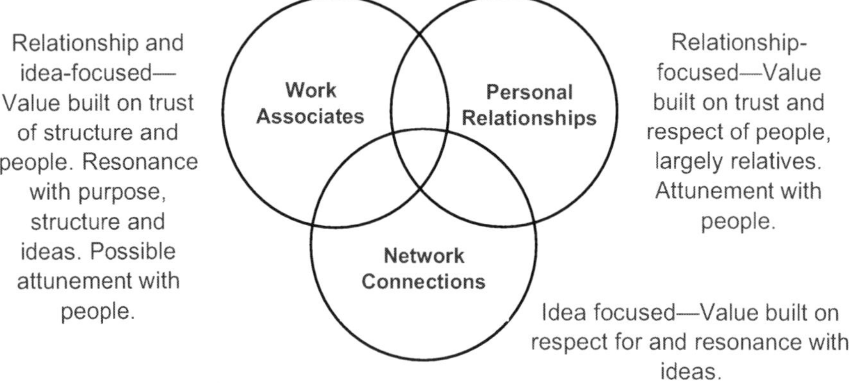

Figure 8. *The movement from relationship-focused value built on trust and respect of people with whom you have personal relations TO relationship and idea-focused value built on trust of structure (the workplace, partners) and people in that structure TO idea-focused value built on respect for, trust of, and* ***resonance with ideas.***

Since ideas spring from information, the trustworthiness of information is critical. Trust of information can be considered from a number of viewpoints: (1) its relevance to specific objectives; (2) its quality (accuracy); (3) its timeliness; and (4) its completeness. Of course, trusting information also means trusting the *source* of that information, whether it comes from a person, organization, database, webpage, book or social network. Since *trust is a feeling*, trust of your "self" (your feelings or intuition) is also paramount. Remember, feelings and emotions are different. Feelings are private, inwardly directed; while emotions are public, outwardly directed. While the *feeling* of trust may or may not be connected to emotions, it will undoubtedly *affect* emotions, especially when trust is broken.

* * * * *

EXERCISE 11: *Truth Searching*

Since truth deals with what is generally believed or considered "facts" in a particular context or focused on a particular situation, the search for truth is a search for examples of the *level of truth currently known*.

STEP (1) Clearly define the truth which you are affirming (Truth A).

STEP (2) Understand the context and/or situation clearly from which this truth is emerging (Situation/Event A). In this stage, it is important to engage both logical and conceptual thinking. Logic is lower mental thinking (cause-and-effect) and concepts (as patterns) are higher mental thinking. (See the discussion of the ISCJ in Chapter 4.)

STEP (3) Search for other situations or events that reflect similar patterns (Situations/Events B, C, etc.). For each situation or event, *ask*: Is Truth A also true in this situation or event?

STEP (4) Determine the *level of truth* of Truth A. If Truth A is true in every situation and/or event you have identified, then, for the present, you can be confident of its truth value in Situation A. If Truth A does not work in one or more of the events and/or situations you have identified, then reconsider the value of Truth A in Situation A.

STEP (5) For any event/situation identified where Truth A does not work, first ensure the event/situation has a similar pattern of activity. If so, then reflect on how Truth A might be changed in order to become true in both Situation A and in this new event/situation. Continue with this process until you discover a truth (a higher level truth) that works in all of the events/situations you have identified or can identify that reflect similar patterns to Situation/Event A.

NOTE: While your personal beliefs may be difficult to circumvent, your body will often indicate that which is true and that which is not true. A *cognitive dissonance* (which causes discomfort of some nature, such as a headache) can occur when considering two beliefs which are in conflict with each other. To help mitigate the possibility of cognitive biases and the injection of hidden assumptions, *vericate* your findings with others in your network. *Verication* is the process of consulting a trusted ally, that is, someone with expertise in the domain of knowledge in which you are truth search. There is considerable discovery power in engaging groups of minds in truth searching!

ADDITIONAL NOTE: Often, new ideas emerge from a negative insight, that is, recognition that the knowledge you have now is insufficient to explain a current situation. This requires discarding previous beliefs and theories in preference to a new or expanded conceptual truth. An example is Einstein's early paper on relativity, published at age 26 in 1905. In this paper, Einstein had to break away from the concept of absolute space and time so that he could accept the general principle of Maxwell's equations for electromagnetism, which are the symmetries that correspond to special relativity.[288]

* * * * *

Play with Your Ideas

As is probably now clear, at some level everyone who is living is creating. As we move through life, the free-flow of thought—the interaction among neuronal networks—randomly mixes patterns to create new ideas such that accidental associations can occur, which makes the point that creativity can happen by accident within an active mind that plays with ideas, connections, and their relationships. As forwarded, much of the co-creating process is happening in the unconscious, and this is occurring as humans interact with their environment and others in their environment.

There's nothing more joyful than creative thought, making that thought work for you, and then the recognition from others of the value of that thought! So, have fun. In your mind, try your idea out in different scenarios and explore its value in those scenarios. And COMMIT to your idea, following through with it, adapting it as needed to the environment in which it is emerging.

Would you buy a new suit without trying it on? Try your idea out and see how it fits, how it feels. The practical nature of your new idea, of what you are trying to do, is important. And, *share it with trusted others.* Innovative Creativity is more than having ideas, and even more than making those ideas work. It also involves having others resonate with your ideas, showing then the value of those ideas. And one way to do that is to *bring them in as partners in creating those ideas.* And quite often, this can make your idea even better.

In the Department of the Navy, we had a knowledge sharing model that reflects the seven levels of consciousness. In this model, we begin with a (1) closed structured concept, an idea that feels good, then (2) we share it with a trusted colleague or two to get their opinions, expanding our idea, making it even better, then (3) we take it to our team or community, or perhaps to management, and they agree it's a great idea and tweak it a bit to make it even better, so now we (4) update it interacting back and forth with our team or community, perhaps writing a white paper and developing a PowerPoint presentation, and now we're ready to (5) purposefully share it, putting it out there for the whole organization or even presenting it at a conference, open to questions, both praise and critique, and then that idea is so good that (6) we now have a depth of knowledge related to that idea, how to apply it, and we share that emerging knowledge with others, moving into the role of teaching and leading implementation, and then (7) it becomes part of the field, acknowledged by experts in your domain of knowledge, written about and purposefully shared, with others expanding it, jumping off that idea into further realms of thought and action. See Figure 9 below. [289]

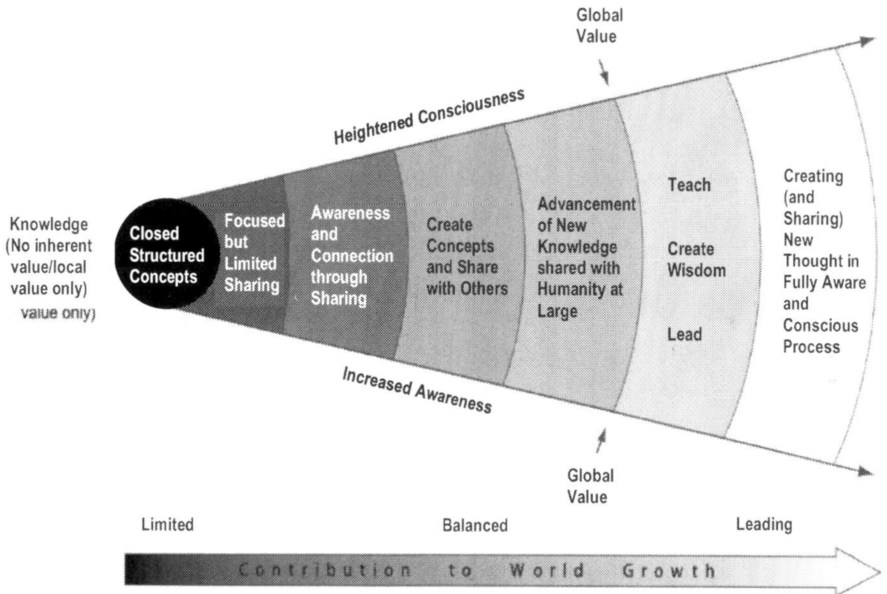

Figure 9. *The Growth of Knowledge and Sharing.*

We are Co-Creators

In Chapter 6 we talked about different ways humans co-create reality. We as a humanity are in a continuous cycle of co-creation such that every moment offers the opportunity for the emergence of new and exciting ideas, large and small. Note that in every aspect of creating and learning, there is a "co" element. This is because *ideas do not happen in isolation*. We are social creatures. This concept was introduced in Chapter 2, connected to learning in Chapter 4, connected to change in the latter part of Chapter 4, and connected to wisdom in Chapter 6. While this concept has been around for centuries, Cozolino believes that we are just waking up to this fact from a biological perspective. As he describes,

> *As a species, we are just waking up to the complexity of our own brains, to say nothing of how brains are linked together. We are just beginning to understand that we have evolved as social creatures and that all of our biologies are interwoven.*[290]

Recall the definition of knowledge as the capacity to take effective action (justified true belief). As inferred by the law of relativity (knowledge is context-sensitive and situation dependent), all knowledge is incomplete. When knowledge is focused inward, bounded and *not* shared, it has diminishing value as others continue to connect with the ever-changing and expanding reservoir of knowledge. An individual with bounded knowledge has ceased learning, with that knowledge over time losing any value it may have had in terms of taking effective action, and value in the creative process, and thus becoming a knowledge artefact as information. Further, there is a diminishing of consciousness and meaning that accompanies the cessation of learning. This is why new ideas are so important. We can't stand on the sidelines. As complex adaptive systems, when we cease creating, when we cease learning, we enter a downward spiral that is characterized by the loss of consciousness and the loss of meaning.

The greatest meaning of life comes with the expansion of co-creating, sharing knowledge that facilitates the creation of new ideas and potential innovation. Both consciously and unconsciously, as we interact with others, we develop a deeper understanding of others and ourselves and an appreciation for diversity, expanding the domain of potential ideas and creating collaborative advantage. Quite literally, we are able to gain the advantage of other's thinking at or above our personal level of thinking, while simultaneously creating in a way that is uniquely ours, concurrently individuated and one.

As introduced earlier, we recognize from neuroscience findings that the mind is an associative patterner, ever creating and recreating knowledge for the moment at hand. Simultaneously, we understand that creativity is the bisociation of two or more ideas to create a new idea or apply an idea in a new context. Thus, there is a multiplier effect of ideas as they are shared. The more we participate in cooperative and collaborative experiences, the more opportunity for the bisociation of ideas. See Figure 10.

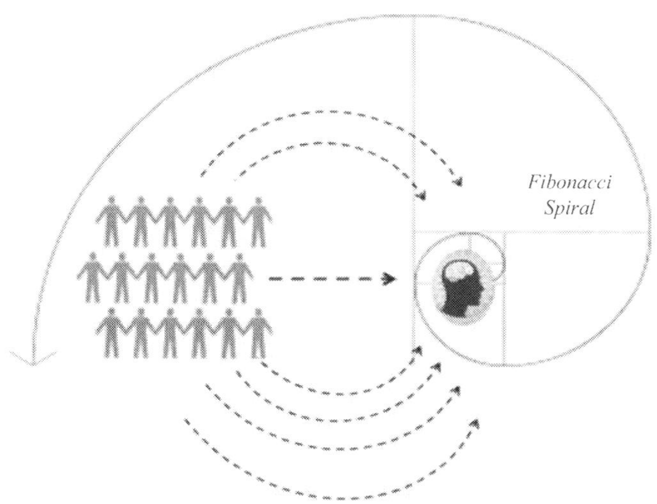

Figure 10. *There is a multiplier effect of ideas as they are shared, with all benefiting.*

As humans, we are action-oriented and knowledge-driven, and living in a continuous cycle of learning and expanding. It is the *context* of the activity or situation at hand (need, challenge, etc.) that triggers the putting things together in an unusual way to create (and recognize) something that may be new and potentially useful (innovation). We as a humanity are in a continuous cycle of knowledge creation such that every moment offers the opportunity for the emergence of new and exciting ideas, all waiting to be put in service to an interconnected world.[291] And conversations—with ourselves and with others—is where that can occur.

Conversations Really Matter

In our sea of difference, what is known to one is unknown to others, or perceived very differently. What seems real to one person can be totally unreal to another. Your truth may be considered an untruth by others, and vice versa. For example, one person's terrorist is another's war hero, an unfortunate reality that we collectively face in challenging times.

Creativity thrives on group interactions. Pragmatic reasons for this include (1) groups bring people together with different knowledge and skillsets representing a wide range of interests and ways of thinking; (2) differing points of view offer the opportunity for comparisons and broad and diverse ideas; and (3) groups tend to have more complex criteria when exploring and evaluating acceptable solutions, allowing a wider array of potential solutions to surface.[292]

Leonard and Swap offer that designing diversity into groups in terms of culture, disciplines, and thinking styles—even inviting "alien" visits and perspectives—and then managing that group effectively enhances creative output. For example, a relaxed timeline provides plenty of time for divergent thinking before converging on a solution or idea. The intent of this approach is to maximize creative abrasion, "re-channeling the tensions of conflicting points of view into new ideas and alternative options."[293]

When engaged in dialogue—equally sharing and listening—conversations can surface our beliefs, values and mental models as we verbalize our thoughts on a specific issue at hand. Sharing our experiences and stories and listening to the experiences and stories of others not only clarifies self-understanding and increases empathic appreciation of others but, because our mind is an associative patterner, *triggers new thoughts and connections*. Arthur Shelley, a capability development guru and originator of *The Organizational Zoo*, believes that a good way to start is using images designed to stimulate Conversations That Matter.[294] We've seen the effectiveness of this approach. These are a form of thought starters, which are all around us, and yet some people never notice or are afraid to value their own ideas. As Crawford emphatically states, "Ideas sparkle everywhere. Watch for them, particularly in your own mind."[295] And capture them in your personal Idea Book.

* * * * *

EXERCISE 12: *Co-Creating Conversations that Matter*

The process for facilitating co-creative converations that matter is quite simple.

STEP (1) Show the image or object in question (for example, see Figure 11), and

STEP (2) *Ask* a question. The questions can be changed depending on the desired oucomes. The question can be completely open-ended, such as: "Tell me what you think about this image?" Or, it can be somewhat leading to get a different focus, such as: "Where do you think our organization fits into this image and why?"

Best results come when you ask each person to write down a few quick bullet points. (You want them to capture their initial FEELING about the question before the thinking mind begins to over analyze ... that can wait for the wider conversation.)

STEP (3) Engaging intelligent rules of etiquette for dialogue, start the wider conversation. There is an amazing set of themes that come out of such conversations. Some people inherently see the pessimistic side of their situation and highlight barriers to progress. Some do the opposite and talk of the positives, perhaps even over-estimating the quality of what is being done. Some see the component parts of the organization, while others take a more holoistic or systems point of view. The key is to engage participants in *exploring the reasons behind the differences* to share why there are multiple perspectives. This is where the insights come from as ideas shared stimulate others to respond and new knowedge is co-created through this exchange.

* * * * *

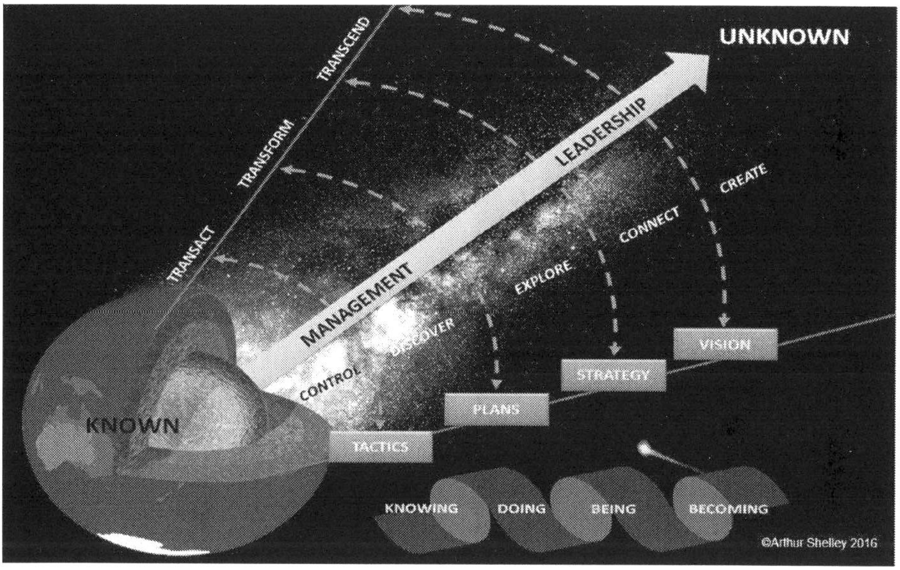

Figure 11. *Exploring the unknown to co-create more known.*

The specific image itself is not the critical factor, but meant to head the group in the direction where ideas are sought. Although Figure 11 has been deliberately designed to stimulate conversations and emerge ideas around strategic leadership, knowledge and relationships in visioning the future, it can be used for other conversations with great effect. Equally, other simpler artifacts can also trigger rich conversations. Combining a creative and out-of-context stimulant with a provocative question and open and inclusive facilitation generates optimal outcomes. All these elements leverage the diversity of views of engaged participants to create new knowledge and insights, which form the basis of new options. Synergies emerge from the connections between thoughts and ideas, and each component is critical to the richness and success of the interaction.

The key to remember about such interactions is that, as the facilitator, your aim is not to lead the participants to a predetermined outcome,but to co-create a set of options that did not exist before, and then intermix these to generate a range of options to co-create a future that does not yet exist. You are setting the field for new ideas. We offer a deeper conversation about the importance of facilitation later in this chapter.

Whether in dialogue, discussion, debate, or casual conversations, face-to-face or virtual, we can learn a great deal by talking and listening to ourselves and others. This helps keep learners mentally and physically safe in the sense that interaction with others may provide an atmosphere for relaxed yet challenging conversations, thereby supporting learning. From neuroscience we have discovered that language and social relationships actually build and shape the brain, expanding our individual capacity. When a sense of humility is present, the rich learning field of conversation can be fully engaged in the creative journey of Innovative Creativity.

Relationship Network Management

RNM is a self-empowering tool in social networking. Our everyday conversations lay the groundwork for the ideas that will emerge and the decisions we will make in the future. Therefore, since time is a scarce resource, it is critical to choose our interactions wisely; for example, ensuring that we are having interactions and conversations within our domains of interest, focus, and passion.

The relationship network is a matrix of people that consists of the sum of an individual's relationships: those individuals with whom you have interacted with in the past and continue to interact, and with whom you have a connection or significant association.[296] In short, all those with whom you have repeated and comfortable conversations based on interdependency, trust, openness, flow, and equitability, all of which overlap.

Relationship Network Management occurs when we recognize the potential of these relationships and use them to share and learn, creating and sustaining a conscious give and take movement, or flow, across the network. Active relationship networks crisscross the organization, increasing organizational awareness, providing redundancies, and, in turn, affecting organizational responsiveness in terms of agility and flexibility. An organization can react faster when information around key areas of concern is flowing freely.

An active relationship network provides a ***monitoring and scanning system*** for problems and opportunities. If a line of thinking gets off track, it is easy to correct the course through an open dialogue, where individuals share their thoughts and stories in a comfortable and trusted environment. Simultaneously, an increase in the exchange of ideas resulting from Relationship Network Management also ***increases the number of new ideas***. Remember, using our definition, creativity is an attribute that resides in all individuals. The greater the diversity of ideas, the more potential learning. The more an individual learns and understands, the more opportunity to build on that learning and understanding. The concept of "learning" includes the attribute of openness. Creativity can be limited by rigidity or the belief that there is only one answer to every question.

It is critical to choose your network wisely, remembering that at some point in the future, you will have an idea or make a decision based on a conversation you have today or had last year. Although you may or may not remember the specific conversation, the resonant content of that conversation is linked into your unconscious to associate with future thought. Thus, your everyday conversations—and reflections on those conversations—serve as grounding functions for creativity and innovation as well as future decisions and actions. Exercise 11 offers a simple five-step process for managing your relationship network. Appendix C provides a template in support of this process.

* * * * *

EXERCISE 13: *Relationship Network Management (RNM)*

There are five steps to managing your relationship network.

STEP (1) Recognize the value of your network. When we recognize the value of our relationship network, we can learn to consciously manage it, and provide the level of grounding needed to operate in the world of ideas.

STEP (2) Identify the domains of knowledge (areas of passion) that are important to you and what you want to achieve in life.

STEP (3) Identify the people with whom you regularly interact, both in your personal and professional life. Note how often you interact with them, the quality of the interaction, and whether they can depend on you and you on them to respond to questions with honest (and valued) opinions. *Ask*: What is at the root of this relationship? How do we complement each other? What do I learn from them? What do they learn from me? Is this relationships knowledge expanding? Consider the foundation of a successful relationship—interdependency, trust, openness, flow, and equability—and assure that each relationship exists within the bounds of these principles.

STEP (4) Carefully compare the list developed in Step (2) with your network and understanding developed in Step (3). Then, consciously choose to develop, expand, and actively sustain those positive relationships in terms of thoughts, feelings, and actions. Where gaps are identified, that is, where you have no exposure to the domains of knowledge (passion) which are important to you, prepare a plan that will bring that knowledge into your awareness and experience. For example, taking a college class related to that knowledge area will open the door to networking with people who have similar interests.

STEP (5) By choice, stay open to sharing your ideas and learning through your relationship network. (See the exercise on humility in Chapter 1.)

* * * * *

The Role of Facilitation in Creativity

We offer some final insights about facilitating creativity for innovation. Facilitation is a unique capability that is not as easy as it appears when exercised by an experienced practitioner.[297] The ability to facilitate the interactions and thinking of others in a neutral way is important to the creativity and innovation that is generated. A facilitator carefully guides participants to interact in ways that leverage the differences in perspectives to stimulate creativity. They are not advocating a specific path or solution, nor do they have specific outputs in mind. In one respect, a facilitator is like a conductor. They facilitate the overall pace and flow of interactions, skillfully engaging each participant at just the right moment to trigger optimal interactions. However, unlike an orchestra conductor, they are not following a pre-defined score. In this aspect, they act like the lead of a jazz band jamming in an improvised session, with each interacting with each other to produce a creative and innovative unique experience. *Every facilitation of Innovative Creativity is unique.* They vary because the participants, facilitator, feeling, and spirit of the interactions influence the product generated, and this cocreates a unique experience for all—participants and audience.

This complex mix of factors makes it impossible to define an exact recipe for creative facilitation. However, to help inexperienced facilitators build their competency and capability, there are few foundational pieces to be aware of and practice as you build your skills. Figure 12 highlights some important characteristics to guide your planning, facilitation of activities, and reflection after the activities.

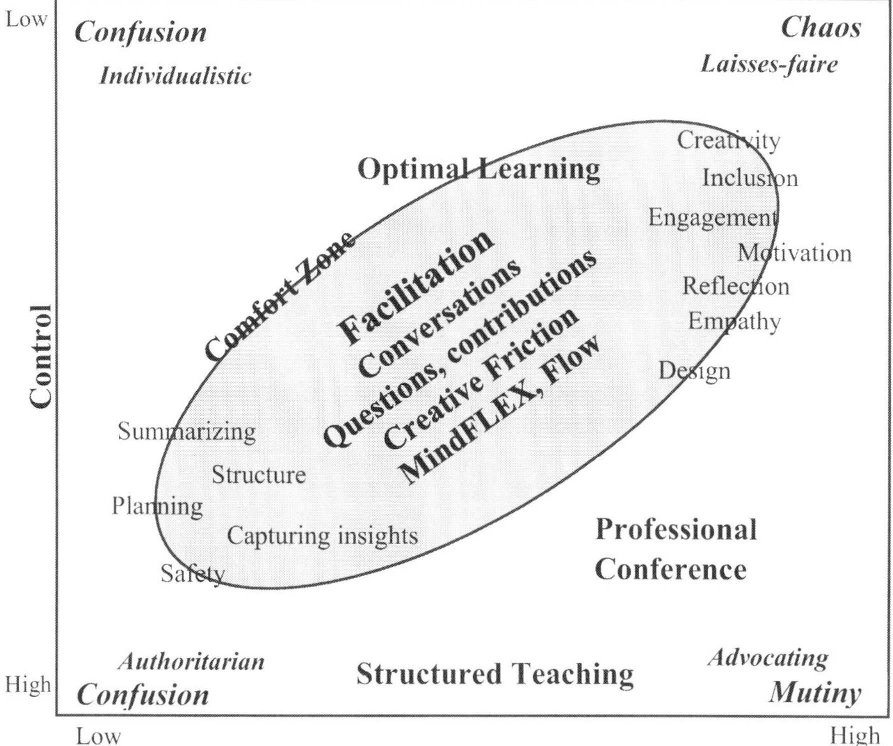

Figure 12. *Foundational aspects for effective Innovative Creativity facilitation.*

Facilitation generates more creative innovations when it effectively aligns the levels of socialization and control. Socialization (people openly engaging with each other to bounce ideas and provide constructive feedback) is required to generate the flow of ideas and trigger the connection between them. Done well, this can also generate unique ideas, often because the conversations around what is known highlights gaps to be explored. Control is required to ensure that when these unique ideas are generated, they are captured rather than lost. If interactions are all socialization and no control, there is a lot of fun, but no innovative ideas are generated. If interactions are tightly controlled with little socialization, the ideas do not emerge and the atmosphere of the interactions is so rigid that people are reluctant to openly engage. As a facilitator builds their experience, they will naturally adjust between these factors in smooth ways that are not apparent to the participants. Inexperienced facilitators will benefit from following the steps shown in Figure 13 until they develop their confidence to be more the jazz musician, which only comes through lots of practice, making a few errors along the way, and learning from those errors.

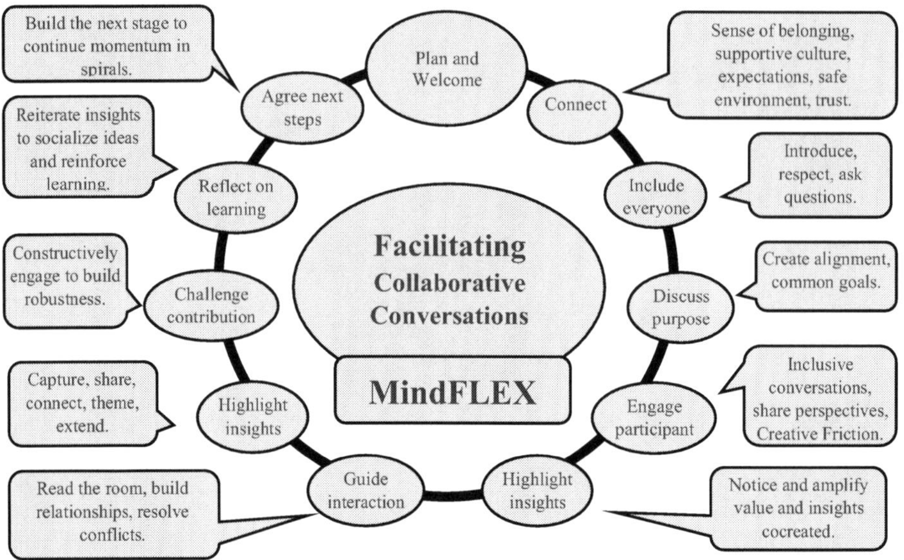

Figure 13. *A learning process to become an effective Innovative Creativity facilitator.*

One aspect of effective facilitation is understanding that optimal learning happens just outside the comfort zone of the learners. If participants remain inside their comfort zone, they are not sufficiently challenged to open their minds to reach into the intuitional plane (see Chapter 9). This requires a sensing of the room by the facilitator and in real time balancing the fear of being outside their comfort zone (causing disengagement) with the exhilaration of the higher learning experience of the intuitional plane. One way to create a safety margin for participants is to explain that they will benefit from stepping outside their comfort zone since this amplifies the learning and the creative outcomes. Encourage them to experiment, so that they can expand their comfort zone as part of learning how to more easily tap into their unconscious tacit knowledge. Figure 14 is a useful conversation starter to facilitate this dialogue. Talking about the concept before exposing them to the discomfort generates more engagement around areas that may not have been consciously explored without the "warning" conversation. As they experience stepping outside their comfort zone and experiencing the magic possibilities, confidence is built to explore further. Be sure to highlight that there are danger zones, and that working together will help ensure a psychologically safe environment. Perceptions of risk vary, and close monitoring of the activities is part of the role of professional facilitation.

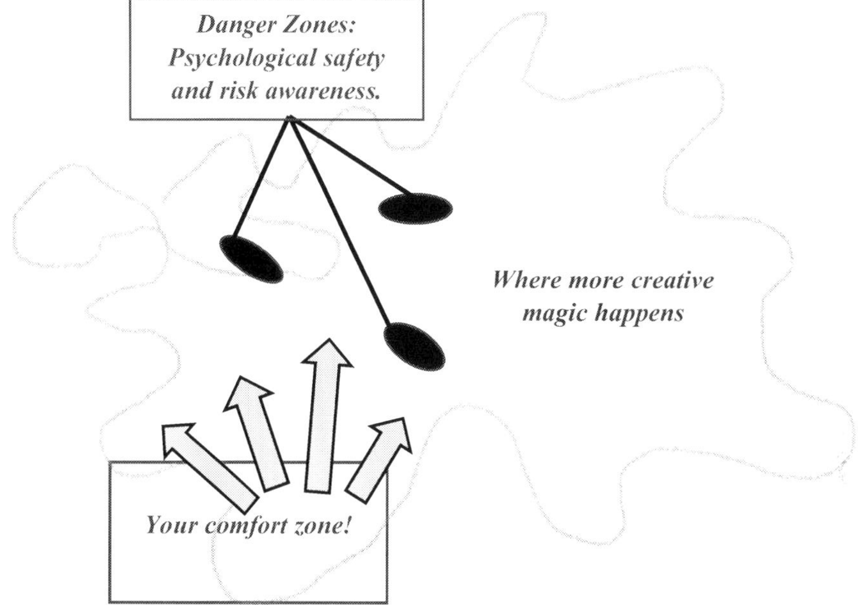

Figure 14. *Expanding the comfort zone is part of learning.*

Ideas are Contagious

We would like to add a few random thoughts that are pertinent to the subject at hand. First, *ideas are contagious*. This is the concept of memes, which are ideas that become enculturated, thoughts that resonate and linger, attaching themselves to other thoughts in a continuing cycle of regeneration. Memes evolve by natural selection in a process similar to that of genes in evolutionary biology. They are potent ideas that out-propagate other ideas in a process of self-replication.

Taking on a life of its own, a meme is a form of learning (an idea, instruction, behavior or piece of information) that is passed on by imitation. They spread themselves around indiscriminately without regard to whether they are useful, neutral, or positively harmful! And, over time, memes evolve as memes, building on other memes, re-appearing and re-associating patterns of thought, taking on new meaning. An example is the growth path of new technologies or new management strategies. The mind gravitates from one idea to another, seeing relationships among things, following patterns of thought. This especially occurs in the domains of knowledge in which you are concerned, where you have focused your energy, where you have prepared yourself for creative thought.

Second, despite certain cognitive losses, we now know that the engaged, mature brain—which refers to YOUR brain if you have read this book to this point—can engage new ideas and make effective decisions at more intuitive levels. As introduced earlier, this includes those of us who are a bit aged. Neuropsychologist Elkhonon Goldberg points out that the aging brain can accomplish mental feats that are different than younger brains. He makes the point that although older people forget names, facts, and words, they have the capability of remembering high-level patterns and meaningful insights that we often consider as deep intuition and as wisdom.[298] So, if we choose, the value of experience and individuation, and what each can contribute to the whole, continues to expand throughout our lives!

<<<<<<>>>>>>>

INSIGHT: **The value of experience and individuation, and what each can contribute to the whole, continues to expand throughout our lives.**

<<<<<<<>>>>>>>

Finally, when confronted with a problem or a challenge, the machinery of intuitive thought does the best it can. If the individual has relevant expertise, the situation will be recognized, and the intuitive and often innovative solution that comes to mind is likely to be correct. This is what happens in our example of a chess master looking at a complex position: the few moves that immediately occur to him are all strong. When the question is difficult and a skilled solution is not available, we often answer with an easier one instead, often without noticing the substitution.

Herbert Simon, a world class chess master coach, says that intuition is nothing more and nothing less than recognition.[299] Valid intuitions develop when experts have learned to recognize familiar elements in a new situation and to act in a manner that is appropriate to it. This is Earned Intuition (see Chapter 9.) So, when is intuition really the use of judgment?

The typical definition of judgment is the act or process of judging the formation of an opinion after consideration or deliberation.[300] In addition, it is the mental ability to perceive and distinguish relationships, or *the capacity to form an opinion by distinguishing and evaluating*. Perhaps these two concepts are more intertwined than we previously perceived them to be. It may just be that our judgment, which has emotion attached to it, emerges from intuition. Our unconscious is so much more than we have the ability to perceive. And thinking about all the thought that's floating around in the Field of which we are a part, there's certainly a lot of ideas out there waiting for us to tap into it.

Chapter 8
The Environmental Opportunity Space

In a turbulent environment—and this is the world we live in for the foreseeable future—there are holes that offer opportunities, emerging windows of choice in terms of space and time. These holes are filled with what we call environmental opportunity space (EOS). While you may not be able to pre-define this space, nor can you go there before it exists, through direction, intent, knowledge and knowing—four forces directly influencing the success of an individual or an organization—the EOS can be taken advantage of as it emerges. Intuition, judgment, and insight, all in support of Innovative Creativity, do not just happen in particular minds. They can be studied, developed, and practiced over time *within domains of interest and passion.*

This brings up a critical reminder. Creativity and knowledge cannot occur without information, and all of these are necessary for innovation. In that relationship, as introduced in Chapter 1, *knowledge is a trigger for creativity and an action-lever for innovation.*

As we know, knowledge is a product of learning. While as experiential learners the human is learning every day throughout life, for focused creativity and innovation within a domain of interest and passion, *preparation must occur within that specific domain of knowledge*, enough learning so that creative ideas can be understood and translated into useful application. This focusing is a seeding of sorts.

The Operating Threshold of Consciousness

At any given moment, each person and each organization functions from a very definable band or region of thinking, talking and acting, an attention space that has upper and lower thresholds. This is the space within which things make sense to us. Even if reality is hitting us in the face, we must still translate that through our personal lens! See Figure 15.

If a proposed new idea is above the upper threshold, it cannot be comprehended and has no perceived value. If a proposed new idea is below the lower threshold, it is so well-understood, so common to us, that it may be dismissed as unimportant. Pushing the edges of the threshold produces discomfort, and we seek to bring the environment and our values and beliefs back into balance. However, as we are able to integrate new experiences and knowledge into this space, understanding increases and, by definition, the threshold adjusts to accommodate this learning.

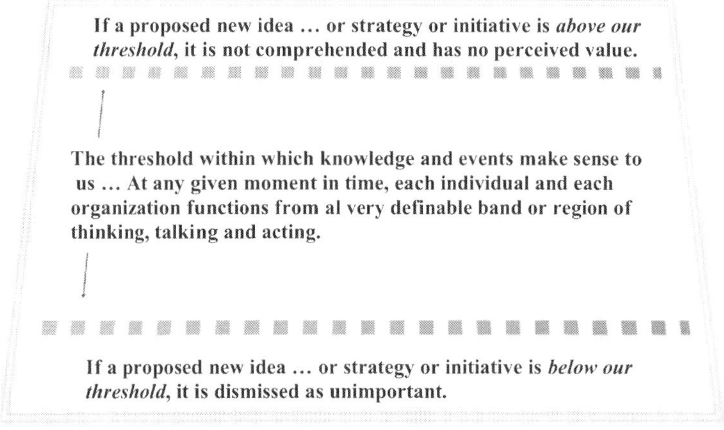

Figure 15: *The Threshold of Focus and Consciousness.*

Within each person's (or organization's or country's) threshold are deep pockets of focus, that is, areas that are of particular interest (or passion). The creative ideas that are triggered, whether by internal or external forces, will most likely relate to those areas. For example, a concert pianist may have a deep focus on a specific kind of music with a developed set of preferences and beliefs around the value of other music. A farm growing organic crops will have a bounded focus on specific methodologies, with a strong prejudice against insecticides, such that new ideas will spring from that belief and comfort zone. An IT organization may have deep knowledge that is bounded by a focus on non-Apple products (or vice versa), supporting a belief in the value of one over the other, and so new ideas will relate to that value set. A state or country with high elevation would have a focus on winter sports and would, most likely, value winter sports over other sports in terms of fitness, and so their Innovative Creativity would guide them in that direction. Conversely, the focus and beliefs of those living on a Caribbean Island would be quite different and creativity would follow a completely different focus!

<<<<<<<>>>>>>>

INSIGHT: **At any given moment, each person and each organization functions from a very definable band or region of thinking, talking and acting, an attention space that has upper and lower thresholds.**

<<<<<<<>>>>>>>

With the advent of the Internet came global connectivity such that people have greater access to an exponentially expanding amount of information, and this is further expanding with the emergence of AI available to a large part of the world population. Thought that is vibrating around the world collides with the expanding minds of thought leaders at all levels of the organization and society. This incoming thought (information) is now associated with all that is already known and brought into the situation and context of the moment. Out of this melee patterns appear and new thought emerges, and both individual and organizational thresholds for learning move higher and higher.

The point is that WE set ourselves up for success through focused learning in our area of interest and passion, where we CHOOSE to engage our creativity. Then, when those ideas are triggered, we know what to do with them, how to make them useful for ourselves and others. So, an important step to future creativity is preparing, engaging your mind consistently and deeply in the domain of knowledge in which you wish to creatively play. However, *this does not mean to stay solely in that domain*.

In his research, Csikszentmihalyi found that the "most significant insights ... are often characterized by a synthesis of information from multiple domains, which can be as far apart as chemistry is from social norms, or as close as neighboring branches of mathematics."[301] An insight, which is "an extended mental process" based on previous conscious preparation, can occur when a person is exposed to new information which provides a new way of looking at a problem or phenomenon.[302] A "significant insight" would be one that leads to an innovative new product.

Synthesis—an important human capability that we bring up throughout this text—is the ability to knit together information from disparate sources into a coherent whole. To achieve such a synthesis, Csikszentmihalyi says there are six things that must occur:[303]

(1) Thorough knowledge of one or more domains.

(2) Thorough immersion in a field that practices the domain.

(3) Attention on a problematic area of the domain.

(4) Idle time for incubation that allows insights to emerge.

(5) Ability to recognize an insight as one that helps resolve the problematic situation.

(6) Evaluation and elaboration of the insight in ways that are valuable to the field or domain.

Story Thinking

Another contribution to the emergence of new ideas is Story Thinking. William Shakespeare portrayed life as a play, and Carl Jung informed us that we are in a story whether we are aware of it or not. And indeed, we are living in a *story of our creation.*

Synthesis is at play in our everyday life as we tie our life together into a coherent story, a concept of self. Throughout the process of living, we are walking through a temporal sequence of how things are done, with one pattern evoking the next, with the recall of our memories following a pathway of association. Thus, we can say that *human memories are story-based.* Effective memories also have memory traces, which are labels that attach to previously stored memories. As we move through a variety of experiences, the individual singles out and accentuates what is significant and connects these events to historic events to *create a narrative unity*, what can be described as a fictionalized history. As Long forwards, "The person makes choices about the importance of persons and events, decides on their meanings … [which are[neither a lie nor 'the truth', but instead a work of imagination, evaluation and memory."[304]

Story Thinking moves beyond the value of storying as a communications and knowledge sharing approach to using the *structure of story* as an operational strategy. In his book by that name, John Lewis compares the story structure emerging from Aristotle's description of the natural story-telling pattern with 30 of the most common models related to change and through this comparison we find that often our institutional models break down because they do not align with our expectations of story.

In Aristotle's pattern of story there is a simple beginning, middle, and end. In the beginning there is a normalcy which is disrupted, followed by discovery of the real issues and the planning for how to deal with them. As in life, the plan has obstacles which have to be overcome, eventually achieving a resolution resulting in transformation. Emerging from this sequence, Story Thinking has a six-phase cycle: Automation, Disruption, Investigation, Ideation, Expectation, and Affirmation (ADIIEA). Expanding on this natural story cycle, Lewis describes the process as starting with a normal routine (Automation), encountering something out of the ordinary (Disruption), looking deeper into the situation (Investigation), coming up with some ideas (Ideation), and acting on a plan (Expectation), with results eventually recognized (Affirmation), which over time settles into a new routine (Automation) … and the cycle begins again.[305]

Innovation is a type of learning. As an enriching Innovative Creativity technique, the visualization of the story structure underlying creative activities accelerates the process of moving toward innovation. As seen in Figure 16, it includes creativity, but is a larger topic. While this process can certainly help focus us and move us toward a goal, you cannot tell someone how to innovate with prescriptive steps any more than you can demand someone to create knowledge. Innovation does not come from memorization or programming instruction. It is a matter of activating all of our innate learning processes. However, as Lewis forwards, there is no innovation without Story Thinking, whether it is done intuitively or shown explicitly.

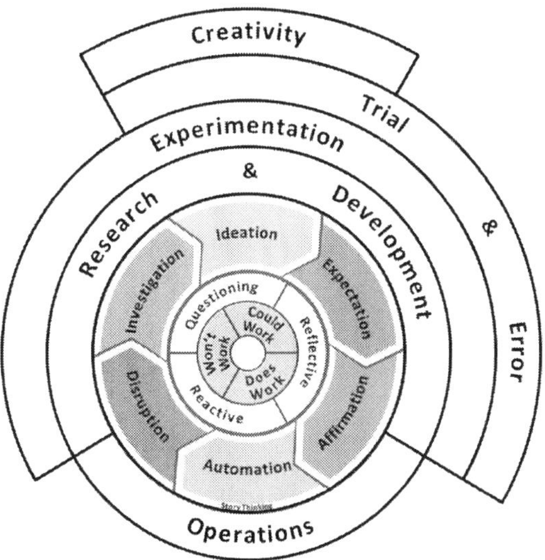

Figure 16. *The ADIIEA model in support of creativity and innovation (used with permission).*[306]

In a summary of the application of Story Thinking in an organization—whether focused on change, learning, leadership or innovation—Lewis stresses six key principles:[307]

- The mental model of work is a story, not a process. *Design* the work through agile navigation around the Story Thinking cycle.

• Seek the positive side of each story, and within each phase of the Story Thinking cycle.

• Provide transparency by keeping track of the options and choices made throughout the Story Thinking cycle.

• Move beyond causal sensemaking (IF/THEN) to look for symbiotic sensemaking (AND), that is, an existential relationship, with the very existence of a thing requiring the existence of something else (problem/opportunity).

• Continue lifelong learning even when it means shifting from a "knower" (stuck in the half-pipe of the Story Thinking cycle) to a "novice" in a new field of study.

• Develop your desire and ability to understand while simultaneously developing your desire and ability to influence others, seeking a balance and embracing *collaboration* instead of *competition* as influence.

The Value Role of Intention and Attention

Intention sets the direction and attention sustains the direction of your creative thought. Because of their importance to Innovative Creativity, these two terms deserve a deeper discussion. Intent is introduced as a force later in this chapter.

Intention is the source with which we are doing something, the act or instance of mentally and emotionally setting a specific course of action or result, a determination to direct our thought in a certain direction or act in some specific way. Intention can be directly related to the consciousness of an individual, with one definition of consciousness described as the "energized pool of intent from which all human experience springs."[308]

Searle believes that people have mental states, some conscious and some unconscious, which are intrinsically intentional. From this viewpoint, these are subjective states that are biologically based, both caused by the operation of the brain and realized in the structure of the brain, with consciousness and intentionality "as much a part of human biology as digestion or the circulation of the blood."[309] Intentionality is not a description of action, rather it is *in the structure of action*. We look to Searle's theory of intentionality for a baseline definition: "Intentionality is the property of many mental states and events by which they are directed at or about or of objects and states of affairs in the world."[310]

Thus, if you set an intention, it is an intention to *do something*. However, states such as those represented by beliefs, fears, hopes and desires insinuate intention, and they are *about something*. The relationship of intent and action has two schools of thought. The ideomotor model of human actions contends that human intentions are the starting point of the actions associated with those intentions.[311] Conversely, the sensory-motor model of human actions identifies sensory stimulation as the origination of actions. While there are strong arguments for both schools of thought, it is clear that intention has a powerful role in the creativity process in both models.

Attention can only occur in the NOW, and sustained attention is a series of NOWs. For example, the eyes work much like an old-time movie reel, with a fixation occurring approximately three times a second as the eyes make a small, quick movement (a saccade) and then stop. However, we perceive what we are seeing as a continuous flow of movement. Just as the eyes shift their focus from object to object, attention shifts driven by our thoughts and feelings. When these thoughts and feelings are focused, consistent, and accompanied by intelligent actions, we become the effective co-creators that is the human birthright.

At the unconscious level, human senses know how to process vast amounts of information effectively. The unconscious brain is always processing and there is a vast amount of new information coming in through our senses.[312] It is the frontal lobes that help an individual choose what to pay attention to and ask good questions about. As Amen describes, a more developed frontal lobe allows you to take better advantage of new knowledge, to know what to focus on, and to relate it to life experiences so that it has more useful value to you.[313] As Csikszentmihalyi confirms, strong interest, curiosity, or intrinsic motivation are the important individual characteristics that can drive a person or group to attend to a problem in a specific knowledge domain and move beyond generally accepted boundaries of knowledge.[314]

As can be seen, attention and intention are interrelated, and both are necessary to balance current priorities with future opportunities and guide your Innovative Creativity. Your thoughts (and actions) gravitate toward what you pay attention to; and what you intend requires your attention. Both can be the result of conscious choice. Thus, it is clear that in support of creativity, intention and attention—when built on expertise in a specific domain of knowledge—both set the direction and open the mind to explore solutions and opportunities.

Observation

Observation—the "key that unlocks the door of creation"[315]—is a tool of intention and attention which provides the foundation for identifying the environmental opportunity space. Creation begins with observation, and then the adaptation of what is observed, the recognition of patterns, to turn what is observed over in your mind and make something new. While an "observation" can certainly emerge from various interactions in a domain of focus, conscious focused observation is generally sparked by a theory or concept, idea, or specific situation. In a research setting, the postpositivist—whose deterministic philosophy holds that causes determine effects and who embraces a reductionist approach—explores "what is out there" through observation and measurement, with observation including but not limited to watching, listening, recording, reading, and/or touching.

The intent as part of the Innovative Creativity process is to raise awareness in your domain of knowledge—driven by passion and interest—of emerging research as related to new products, current trends, expressed and unexpressed needs, customer desires, and so forth. In the past, experts attended (and presented at) conferences and while this practice continues, largely with virtual attendance, it is today also possible to virtually follow thought leaders and have virtual access to their latest findings. Meanwhile, local data being collected by and emerging from your own organization can provide domain-specific documents which can be correlated to information from newspapers, minutes of meetings, official reports, etc., all of which can enable a creative observant individual to create patterns, in the present extrapolating behaviors from the past to predict opportunities in the future.

The advantages of observation are many. Direct observation of an issue or need avoids interpretation or bias which may be included in a communication about that same issue or need. Further, since observation provides direct access to what is occurring in the present, this skillset can be effective when used both formally and informally in the course of life as an individual focuses on a specific domain of interest. When a participant acts in a natural setting, behaviors are natural and the observer has the chance to see the total situation, potentially finding avenues forward that others have not observed. Note that *you are not searching for what you want to find, but for what there is to be found.*

When exploring an issue or opportunity, it is possible—when the context surrounding an issue or opportunity is better understood—to achieve *multiple perception points,* and there is almost always more context to discover. Remember, because knowledge is context sensitive and situation dependent the issue/opportunity you are exploring is entangled with a specific situation and contextual knowledge that *may provide deeper insight* into the issue/opportunity at hand. As Lachman advocates, "When the vague, implicit meanings are unpacked by an articulate mind attuned to them, and when the abstractions needed to conceptualize reality are informed by a wider, overall sense of context, then something that we might call genius, or at least insight, can occur."[316]

In qualitative observation, which involves capturing the behaviors and activities of people, field notes are taken in a structured or semi-structured way driven by the focus (open-ended questions regarding the issue or opportunity being researched). During these experiences, the researcher/observer may be a nonparticipant or fully a participant.[317] Either way, unusual aspects of an issue can be noticed during observation which can prove useful to triggering ideas.

The Drive of Passion

In Chapter 5 we introduced the power of desire, with desire linked to emotions and feelings, defined as a strong wanting or wishing for something and viewed by Western philosophers as fundamental to human life. There is no doubt that as a strong emotion passion is linked to desire, while in an historic sense as a verb it has been connected with suffering, pain and sorrow. Simultaneously, in today's literature, passion has been referred to as a gift of emotion[318] that causes us to take a precise interest in, and pay keen attention to,[319] specific aspects of our lives; to open us up to the larger picture;[320] and, even, to promote the greater good.[321] As Peter Senge so eloquently says, passion is directly connected to the "deep longing of human beings to make a difference", to contribute.[322] For purposes of our discussion we acknowledge that passion is a strong, sometimes difficult to control, emotion, a strong enthusiasm and, yes, a strong desire.

In the 2023 release of *INside INnovation: Looking from the Inside Out*, successful innovator Johan Cools links passion to right intention. As he says,

> *... any innovative effort should be founded on the right intention, and intention needs enough intensity. True passion is the ultimate sensation that drives creative efforts, and that counts even more if there is vision to contribute linked to it. The power of intention plays a very important role in its crystallization in the material world.*[323]

In his chapter titled "Crystallizing the Symphony of Passions" with reflections from Samara Hassoun, a lyric soprano from Minsk, Belarus, Cools points out that there is much more to innovation than pure brainpower and success. He provides the example of his current art project with Hassoun, the creation of an opera entitled "The Purple Camelia", what they refer to as a symphony of passions.

Passion is often linked to the concept of flow. This is understandable since the flow state is enabled by the strong emotion of passion. For example, in one model of flow passion is identified as a major attribute to creating the power of flow.

> *Flow is engendered by passion—passion for life, for knowledge, for a cause, for a relationship, for truth. Passion means caring deeply about something beyond ourselves. It means engaging with it at intense levels. It means letting go of self-protective caution to involve ourselves wholeheartedly with what we love.*[324]

This passion indeed "opens us up to a larger picture." Passion is the intensity of flow, the intense desire to be "active and engaged in the course of events" and the intense drive to know truth. "Not satisfied with surface explanations, we use every moment as an opportunity to break through to something new, to learn. We fully engage with what comes our way."[325] This is consistent with Cools' reference to the state of mind to create masterpieces as a

> ... *magical flow state which is characterized by heart rate coherence and lower alfa brainwaves. In such a state you feel intensively connected with the complete process and micro-environment of the creation itself. Then you become the brush and the canvas, the notes on the piano, or the pen and paper. Combined with intense feelings of passion, this coherent and connected state of mind enables the production of masterpieces.*[326]

In a discussion of people skills, Daniel Goleman, the foundational author of *Emotional Intelligence*, cited focus and passion as important elements of achieving group flow. "The demands of meeting a great goal inherently provide focus; the rest of life can seem not just mundane, but trivial by comparison. For the duration, the details of life are on hold."[327] Thus passion, driving the intensity of flow, elevates values and engages reality at all levels. Both as an individual and as a collective, passion acts as emotional super-fuel, propelling us into the flow to think and act in a focused domain of interest.

In the 2005 MQI research study referenced earlier, thought leaders in the field of Knowledge Management[328] linked passion directly to a higher order and the "creation of new ideas". As one thought leader explained, her passion fueled "continuous thought and a desire for clarity." Other thought leaders indicated that through their ideas they were making a contribution (as one described) to the "nourishment and cultivation of the future." Thus, passion around a field or domain of knowledge is a driver that sustains focus, learning, and activity in that domain, all of which support Innovative Creativity.

The Four Forces Behind Creativity

Forces are a part of our everyday world. A force occurs when one source of energy affects another source of energy, whether there are positive or negative results. The term "affects" can mean that one energy is pushing against, interfering with, or influencing another source of energy. For example, a high-jumper is repeatedly using his leg muscles to push off the Earth into the air while simultaneously pushing his whole body up against the force of gravity.

The process of creativity can cause forces to push against you, restrict you, and make life more difficult OR they can help us to grow and co-create with others, eventually becoming more knowledgeable and more conscious. When we deliberately create *against* an activity or force already in play and accomplish our objective, we produce maximum levels of force. Instead of just changing direction, we purposefully create something to destroy something already moving in a certain direction. For example, consider pushing an idea forward that requires the use of coal in an environmentally committed organization. As can be seen, to ensure minimal forces against a new idea, our ideas need to be consistent with the context in which they are situated.

In an intelligent complex adaptive system—referencing both the individual and the organization—there are four forces that directly influence success. These are the force of *knowledge*, the force of *intent*, the force of *direction*, and the force of *knowing*. The intent of the discussion below is to ensure that you are in the flow, that you are not pushing against, but working with, these forces as you engage your Innovative Creativity.

The Force of Knowledge. This is the fundamental force of the human and of the organizations of which we are a part, consisting of the creation, sharing, dissemination, leveraging, and application of knowledge. The strength of the force of knowledge is measured by capacity, competency, connectivity, flow and effectiveness. *Ask:* What is your knowledge capacity? Are you a learner? Do you understand the significance and importance of humility? What abilities do you (or your organization) have to create, leverage, and apply knowledge? In an organization, how do technology, structure, culture, and leadership support this force? How are you effectively bringing Artificial Intelligence and the power of quantum computing into your workplace? How do you ensure connectivity with your internal and external environments? How do the structure and culture of your organization facilitate flow in terms of data, information, and knowledge; in terms of people; and in terms of autotelic work, the optimal experience of flow, a state where people are so involved that nothing else seems to matter (see Chapter 10). How is innovation supported and rewarded?

The Force of Intent. As introduced earlier in this chapter, intention is mentally determining on some action or result. It includes the purpose and attitude toward the *effect* of one's action, the outcome, with purpose implying having a goal or the determination to achieve something and attitude encompassing loyalty and dedication. Intent focuses energy and knowledge at both the individual and organizational levels. As forces, knowledge is the "know how" and intent is the power to focus the knowledge and maintain the direction. The strength of the force of intent is measured by the desire, willingness, and energy of an individual or, at the organizational level, every member of the organization. *Ask*: Where is the focus of your attention? Are you excited about your focus? Is it an area you are passionate about? Are there any forces that are draining your energy? Are your ideas, decisions and actions consistent with the desired direction and your value set?

The Force of Direction. Direction, which should follow intent, serves as the compass as we move into an uncharted future. It both limits your activities within some action space surrounding the chosen direction and conserves energy by defining what areas you are *not* interested in. With any direction comes a purpose and a vision of what is required to make the journey. In that regard, direction acts on the reason for being and provides spirit and energy to move forward. In an organization, the strength of the force of direction is measured by organizational cohesion, the line of sight, and the connectedness of choices, that is, different decisions made at different parts of the organization all heading the organization in the same direction. At an individual level, *ask*: Does this direction follow my interest and passion? Am I spending my resources consistent with this desired direction? What happens if the environment changes?

Direction does not mean locking into a specific outcome. Since knowledge is context-sensitive and situation dependent and we live in what we call a CUCA world—a world of accelerating Change, rising Uncertainty, and increasing Complexity combined with the human response of Anxiety—it would be impossible to detail where we will be at some future point in time. However, we ARE complex ADAPTIVE systems such that we have the capability to adapt if we choose.

The concept of direction is consistent with the flow of energy in the quantum field. The greater the focus in a specific direction, that is, the more energy moving in a consistent direction, the greater the probability of what is in that direction occurring.

The same models applicable in organizational work can be applied to the individual. For example, the model below shows the setting of "intent" tightly set within values and, more loosely, with purpose in mind and, more tightly, focused on a specific vision and mission. While direction sustains a focus, the tactical level (actual actions taken) is not always what was imagined at the strategic level, yet stays within the boundaries of identified purpose and values.

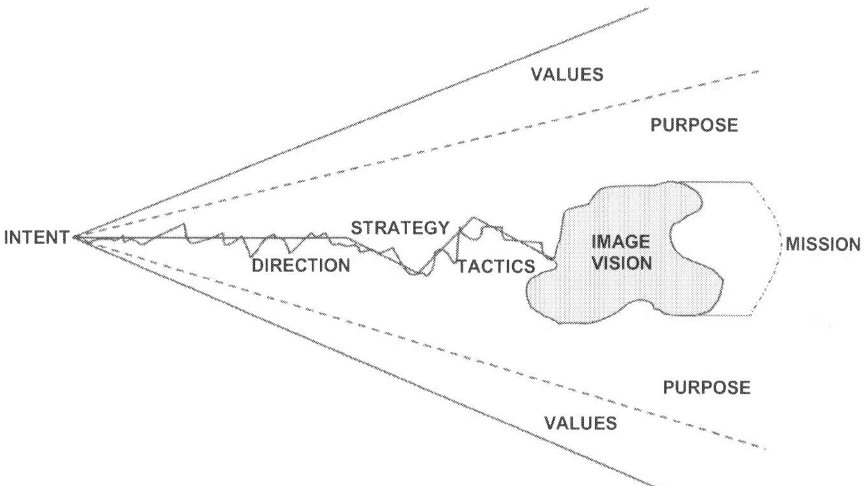

Figure 17: *Intent and Direction within the bounds of values and purpose.*

The Force of Knowing. Knowing, a sense (see Figure 3, the Knowledge and Knowing Loop, in Chapter 1), is a blending of the cognitive capabilities of observing and perceiving a situation, the cognitive processing that must occur to understand the external world and make maximum use of our intuition and experiences in finding creative solutions and taking advantage of opportunities, and the faculty for creating deep knowledge and acting on that knowledge. See Appendix B. Knowing can be elevated to the organizational level by using and combining the insights and experiences of individuals through dialogue and collaboration within teams, groups, and communities. Such efforts significantly improve the quality of understanding, responsiveness of actions, and the emergence of new ideas. These approaches also greatly expand the scope of complex situations that can be handled and the potential solution set because of increased access to diverse resources in terms of knowledge brought to bear. Knowing is the "tip of the Innovative Creativity sphere", the fog lights into the future, penetrating the haze of complexity by allowing workers to think beyond normal perception and dig into the meaning and hidden patterns in a complex world. The strength of knowing is measured by an individual's or organization's ability to perceive, interpret, and make sense of the environment, discover creative solutions, take advantage of environmental opportunity space when it occurs, and take actions. *Ask:* Is there the free flow of information in the focused domain of knowledge? Are the diversity of experiences and knowledge at all levels of the organization valued? Are lessons learned freely shared? Are new ideas listened to and explored? Do seasoned decision-makers trust their intuition and act accordingly?

Dynamic Balancing is the necessary real-time balancing—symmetrization, harmonization, equalization, co-ordination and integration—of forces or demands. While symmetrization is used to denote a mathematical process, in a larger sense it refers to the process of making something symmetrical, a quality of having mirror images opposite each other emerging from a common center line. In an organization, it is a sense of actions reflecting purpose and vision. Harmonization is bringing into harmony or agreement, adjusting differences and inconsistencies. In music it is the mixing of melodies and chords to create pleasing sounds. Reflect on what this means to an organization? Equalization is the act of making equal or uniform. Co-ordination is having two or more elements work together effectively, efficiently, and smoothly. Integration is the bringing together of parts, combining them to create a whole. Dependent on the context and situation at hand, *all of these are aspects of dynamic balancing*.

Since in a changing, complex, and uncertain environment, things rarely remain constant for very long, continuous learning is needed for continuous rebalancing, which means (1) huge amounts of creation; and (2) a huge amount of conscious balancing among these creations.[329]

The Correlation of Forces

Figure 18 represents a graphic display of the various aspects of the correlation of forces. This can be applied from an individual perspective or from an organizational perspective. At the top is represented the complex environment related to a specific domain of knowledge, and within that environment there are certain areas that represent opportunity spaces, depending on the direction the individual or organization is evolving and on the local capability of the individual or organization to identify these opportunities. The four major forces discussed above are represented by arrows.

Below the four forces (represented by the arrows) are interconnected circles that represent a set of particular success factors specific to the organization significant in driving the four major forces. The diagram shows general characteristics because each person (and each organization) embedded in a unique environment will, of course, have different critical success factors, with some more important than others. However, assuming every organization understands the importance of quality and hard work, a successful organization will include having a team approach, a systems approach, continuous learning, knowledge sharing, freedom and flexibility, and managing change, **all contributing to a focus on creativity and innovation**.

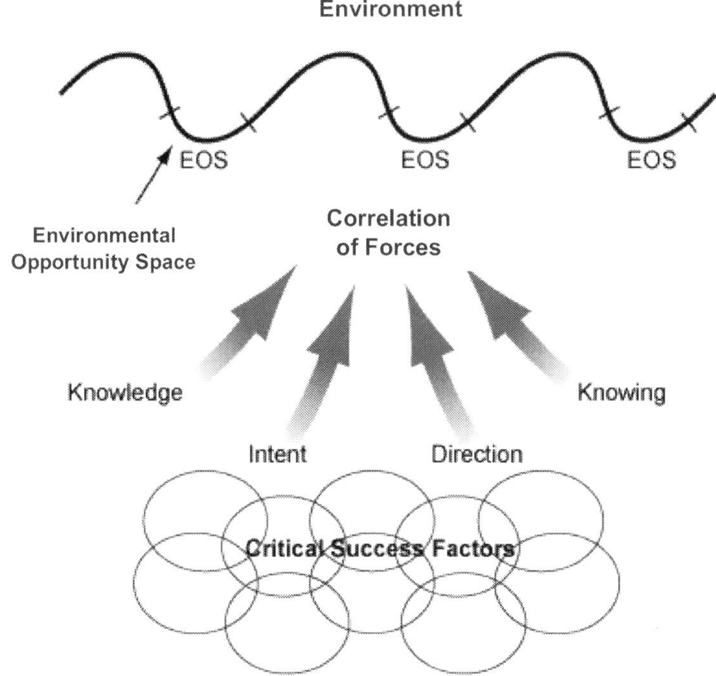

Figure 18. *The Correlation of Forces.*

Many of the critical success factors suggested here are mutually supportive. For example, when taken together freedom, flexibility, continuous learning, working in teams, and knowledge sharing form an interconnected system that generates trust and motivation along with new ideas. Meeting new challenges in a dynamic, uncertain, and complex environment REQUIRES the continuous insertion and implementation of new ideas, which emerge from within and without the organizational framework. Clearly, teams and communities are major catalysts in stimulation and integration of these ideas.

From an organizational perspective, the objective of a correlation of forces strategy is to create a specific organization with its unique environment in which the right set of critical success factors are managed. Each of the four forces (knowledge, intent, direction, and knowing) are maximized to support organizational goals and objectives through the actions of people at every level of the organization. In addition, these four forces can work together in a synergistic manner so they mutually support each other through facilitating the achievement of critical success factors in the day-to-day operations of collaborative leaders.

In summary, consider the four forces: knowledge, intent, direction, and knowing. Knowledge provides the competency to take the right actions. Intent provides the energy and consistency of movement. Direction sets the compass, gives meaning to the trip, and offers a vision of what to strive toward. Knowing provides a deeper understanding of the environment and how to deal with that environment over the long term. These forces are aligned when:

- Direction is set and understood.
- Intent moves the organization in the desired direction.
- Knowledge ensures actions follow intent and direction.
- Knowing improves knowledge, bolsters intent, and signals whether the actions and directions are on track.

Most opportunities and threats in the environment can be "sensed" by those emersed in that environment (through knowing) prior to actuality. Defining and understanding the environmental landscape is necessary before an individual or organization can set its direction and move forward. Success is then dependent on setting the intention to take advantage of that window, and creating, leveraging, and applying the right knowledge to do so. Deep domain knowledge enables an individual to continuously make sense of and track the window. Learning (open system) and knowledge provide the flexibility to keep up with (or ahead of) changes inside the window. Knowing creates the opportunity to see beyond the window. They all work together.

Chapter 9
Earned Intuition

So far, we've skirted around the concept of intuition. It's time to delve more deeply into this important concept, which is the ability, without any time delay, to determine the causes of any and all effects regardless of the complexity of those effects. Intuition is a higher awareness, a deeper understanding, very much supported by our five senses of form and our two inner senses focused from the heart and crown energy centers. If we go to the dictionary, it says that intuition is the act or faculty of knowing or sensing without the use of rational processes; an immediate cognition.[330] **This is the whisper within**. In the poet Ralph Waldo Emerson's famous words, *none of us will ever accomplish anything excellent or commanding except when he listens to this whisper which is heard by him alone.* This is a good starting point.

Looking at intuition from another perspective, organizational consultant Beth Crandall and her colleagues see insight as the result of searching for new relationships between concepts in one domain with those in another domain. This creates a recognition and understanding of a problem within the situation, including the how and why of the past and current behavior of the situation. She says this is often the *result of intuition, competence, and the identification of patterns, themes and cue sets.*[331] Insight may also provide patterns and relationships that will anticipate the future behavior of the situation.

Research cognitive psychologist Gary Klein proposes that intuition is "the way we translate our experiences into judgments and decisions. It is the ability to make decisions by using patterns to recognize what's going on in a situation and to recognize the typical action script with which to react."[332] That can be a little hard to understand, and it's kind of dry. In contrast, neuroscientist Antonio Damasio calls intuition "the mysterious mechanism by which we arrive at the solution of a problem without reasoning toward it."[333] That's intriguing!

Let's chew on those definitions and see if we can clarify these somewhat different perspectives. This requires looking at intuition through two different frames of reference, which, building on the concepts of earned knowledge and revelatory knowledge,[334] we will describe as *earned intuition* and *revealed intuition*. We begin with earned intuition.

Earned intuition is that part of intuition emerging from the unconscious (the subconscious) that is connected to our historic experiences and discoveries. This is largely *intuitive tacit knowledge,* a sense of knowing coming from inside that influences an individual's creativity, decisions, and actions. Yet the creator does not know from where this idea emerges, nor can the decision-maker or actor explain how or why the decision or action taken is the right one, but they "know" (or feel) that it is.

In order to focus on tacit knowledge—that storehouse of self-perceived "important" information gathered through our life experiences waiting to be put in service to your creativity—let's first develop a common understanding of what it is and what it is not. By the latter part of the 20th century, the push to understand knowledge and its value to organizations had spread across a number of disciplines with the result that the concepts of explicit, implicit and tacit knowledge began to emerge beyond the academic organizational literature and appear in the popular press. Our interpretation of each of these concepts is described briefly below.

Differentiating Explicit, Implicit, and Tacit

While there is some overlap in these terms, let's clarify the intent to enable a deeper conversation in the context of Innovative Creativity.

Explicit knowledge. Making explicit is the process of calling up information (patterns) and processes (patterns in time) from memory that can be described accurately in words and/or visuals (representations) such that another person can comprehend the knowledge that is expressed through this exchange of information. This has historically been called declarative knowledge.[335] Emotions can be expressed as explicit knowledge in terms of changes in body state since "Many of the changes in body state—those in skin color, body posture, and facial expression, for instance—are actually perceptible to an external observer."[336] Often these changes to the body state represent part of an explicit knowledge exchange.[337] Examples would be turning red with embarrassment or blushing in response to an insensitive remark.

Implicit knowledge is a more complicated concept, and a term not unanimously agreed-upon in the literature. This is understandable since even simple dictionary definitions—which are generally unbiased and powerful indicators of collective preference and understanding—show a considerable overlap between the terms "implicit" and "tacit," making it difficult to differentiate the two. We propose that a useful interpretation of *implicit knowledge* is knowledge stored in memory of which the individual is *not immediately aware.* While this information is *not readily accessible* (i.e., tacit) it may be pulled up when triggered (associated). Triggering might occur through questions, dialogue or reflective thought, or happen as a result of an external event. In other words, implicit knowledge is knowledge that the individual *does not know they have*, but is self-discoverable! However, once this knowledge is surfaced, the individual *may or may not* have the ability to adequately describe it such that another individual could create the same knowledge, and the "why and how" may remain tacit.

A number of published psychologists have used the term implicit interchangeably with the usage of tacit—which is the preferred term in the field of Knowledge Management—that is, with implicit representing knowledge that once acquired can be shown to affect behavior but is not available for conscious retrieval.[338] As described in the above discussion, what is forwarded here is that the concept of implicit knowledge serves a middle ground between that which can be made explicit and that which cannot easily (if at all) be made explicit (is tacit). By moving beyond the dualistic approach of explicit and tacit—that which can be declared versus that which can't be declared, and that which can be remembered versus that which can't be remembered—*we posit implicit as representing the knowledge spectrum between explicit and tacit.* Note that while explicit refers to easily available and expressed, some knowledge requires a higher stimulus for association to occur yet is not buried so deeply as to prevent access. This understanding opens the domain of implicit knowledge.

Calling them interactive components of cooperative processes, Reber agrees that there is no clear boundary between that which is explicit and that which is implicit (our tacit): "There is ... no reason for presuming that there exists a clean boundary between conscious and unconscious processes or a sharp division between implicit and explicit epistemic systems."[339] Reber describes the urge to treat explicit and implicit (our tacit) as altogether different processes, the "polarity fallacy". Similarly, Matthews says that the unconscious and conscious processes are engaged in what he likes to call a "synergistic" relationship.[340] What this means is that the boundary between the conscious and the unconscious is somewhat porous and flexible. Given that caveat, how do we describe tacit knowledge?

Tacit knowledge is the descriptive term for those connections among thoughts that cannot be pulled up in words, a knowing of *what* decision to make or *how* to do something that cannot be clearly voiced in a manner such that another person could extract and re-create that knowledge (understanding, meaning, etc.). An individual *may or may not* know they have tacit knowledge in relationship to something or someone. But even when it *is known*, the individual is unable to put it into words or visuals to convey that knowledge. In some situations, we all know things, or know what to do, yet may be unable to articulate *why* we know them, *why* they are true, or even exactly *what they are*. To "convey" is to cause something to be known or understood or, in this usage, to transfer information from which the receiver is able to create knowledge.

All knowledge starts as tacit knowledge, that is, the initial movement of knowledge is from its origins within individuals (in the unconscious) to an outward expression (howbeit driving effective action). What does that mean? Michael Polanyi, a professor of both chemistry and the social sciences, wrote in *The Tacit Dimension* that, "We start from the fact that we can know more than we can tell."[341] He called this pre-logical phase of knowing "tacit knowledge", that is, knowledge that cannot be articulated.[342]

Tacit and explicit knowledge can be thought of as residing in "places," specifically, the unconscious and conscious, respectively, although both Knowledge (Informing) and Knowledge (Proceeding)—whether tacit or explicit—are differentiated patterns spread throughout the neuronal system, which includes the volume of the brain and other parts of the central nervous system. On the other hand, implicit knowledge may reside in either the unconscious (prior to triggering, or tacit) or the conscious (when triggered, or explicit). See the continuum of awareness of knowledge source/content represented in Figure 19 and the discussion of tacit knowledge later in this chapter. Note that there is no clean break between these three characteristics of knowledge. This is a shifting continuum.

Knowledge (Proceeding) may be explicit, implicit or tacit. For anything except the simplest knowledge, the process we use to find, create and mix the information needed to take effective action is difficult, if at all possible, to communicate to someone else. Thus, the expertise involved in deciding what actions to take in many situations will be tacit. Team discussions, problem solving, and decision making, while helpful and necessary, must address the emotional, intuitive and embodied aspects as well as relevant data.

There are four tacit knowledges—embodied, affective, intuitive and spiritual—with, as a reminder, the term "tacit" representing that which is known or embedded within, but cannot be easily expressed. This means that tacit knowledges do not reside in the conscious mind. *Affective tacit knowledge,* which is connected to emotions and feelings, with emotions representing the external expression of some feelings, is attached to other types of knowledge. Feelings are often the conveyors of intuitive tacit knowledge. Each of these tacit knowledges is addressed below.

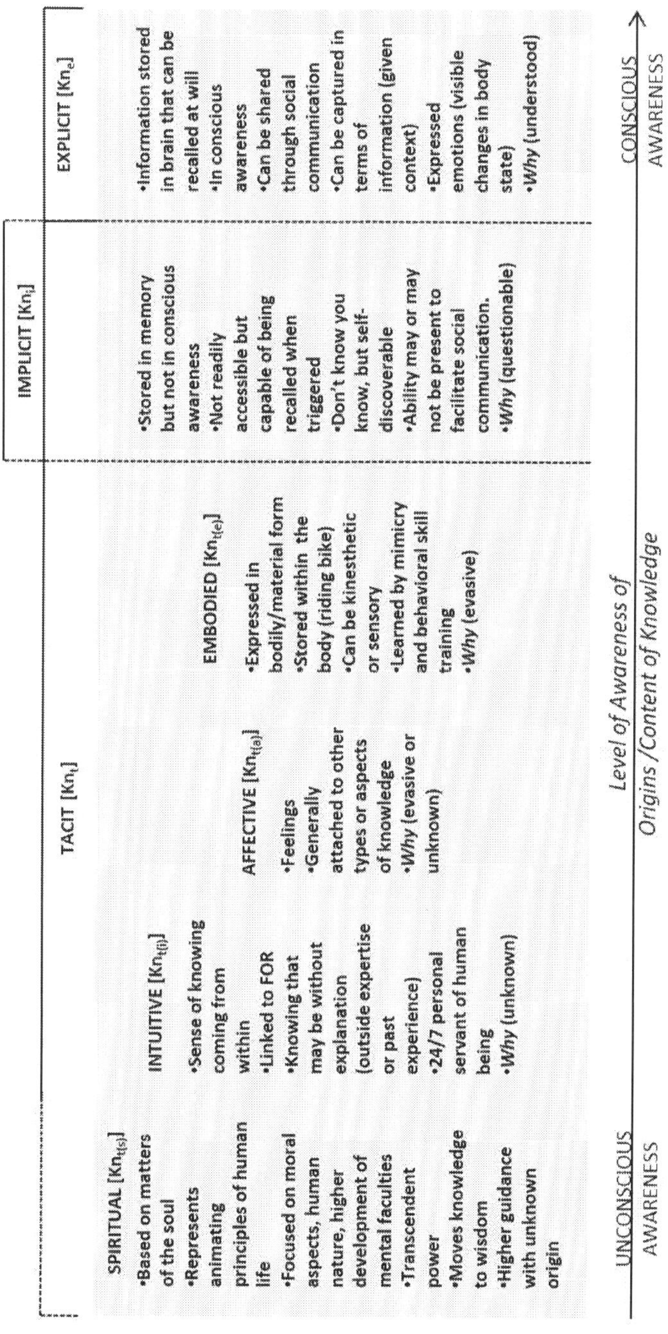

TACIT $[Kn_t]$				IMPLICIT $[Kn_i]$	EXPLICIT $[Kn_e]$
SPIRITUAL $[Kn_{t(s)}]$	INTUITIVE $[Kn_{t(i)}]$	AFFECTIVE $[Kn_{t(a)}]$	EMBODIED $[Kn_{t(e)}]$		
•Based on matters of the soul •Represents animating principles of human life •Focused on moral aspects, human nature, higher development of mental faculties •Transcendent power •Moves knowledge to wisdom •Higher guidance with unknown origin	•Sense of knowing coming from within •Linked to FOR •Knowing that may be without explanation (outside expertise or past experience) •24/7 personal servant of human being •*Why* (unknown)	•Feelings •Generally attached to other types or aspects of knowledge •*Why* (evasive or unknown)	•Expressed in bodily/material form •Stored within the body (riding bike) •Can be kinesthetic or sensory •Learned by mimicry and behavioral skill training •*Why* (evasive)	•Stored in memory but not in conscious awareness •Not readily accessible but capable of being recalled when triggered •Don't know you know, but self-discoverable •Ability may or may not be present to facilitate social communication. •*Why* (questionable)	•Information stored in brain that can be recalled at will •In conscious awareness •Can be shared through social communication •Can be captured in terms of information (given context) •Expressed emotions (visible changes in body state) •*Why* (understood)

UNCONSCIOUS AWARENESS → *Level of Awareness of Origins /Content of Knowledge* → CONSCIOUS AWARENESS

Figure 19. *Continuum of Awareness of Knowledge Source/Content.*

Embodied Tacit Knowledge

Embodied tacit knowledge, also referred to as *somatic knowledge*, can be represented in neuronal patterns stored within the body. It is both kinesthetic and sensory. *Kinesthetic* is related to the movement of the body and, while important to every individual every single day of our lives, is a primary focus for athletes, artists, dancers, kids, and assembly-line workers. A commonly used example is knowledge of riding a bicycle. *Sensory*, by definition, is related to the five human senses of form through which information enters the body (sight, smell, hearing, touch and taste). An example is the smell of burning metal from your car brakes while driving or the smell of hay in a barn. These smells can convey knowledge of whether the car brakes need replacing (get them checked immediately), or whether the hay is mildewing (dangerous to feed horses, but fine for cows). These responses would be overt, bringing to conscious awareness the need to take effective action and driving that action to occur.

Because embodied learning is often linked to experiential learning,[343] embodied tacit knowledge can generally be learned by mimicry and behavior skill training. While deliberate learning through study, dialogue or practice occurs at the conscious level, when significant or repeated over time such learning often becomes tacit knowledge. Further, as individuals develop competence in a specific area, more of their knowledge in that area becomes tacit, making it difficult or impossible for them to explain how they know what they know. The neuronal patterns representing that knowledge become embedded within long-term working memory where they become automatic when needed, but lost to consciousness.

Note that embodied tacit knowledge can be both preventative and developmental. For example, a physical response can warn *not* to do something or move an individual *to do something*. Both of these responses constitute the capacity to take effective action since *not taking an action is an action choice*.

Intuitive Tacit Knowledge

Intuitive tacit knowledge is the sense of knowing coming from inside an individual that may influence decisions and actions; yet the decision-maker or actor cannot explain *how* or *why* the action taken is the right one. As introduced above, Damasio calls intuition, "the mysterious mechanism by which we arrive at the solution of a problem *without* reasoning toward it."[344] The unconscious works around the clock with a processing capability many times greater than that at the conscious level. This is why as the world grows more complex, decision-makers depend more and more on their intuitive tacit knowledge. But in order to use it, decision-makers must first be able to tap into their unconscious (see Chapter 10).

Intuitive tacit knowledge can be both Knowledge (Informing) and/or Knowledge (Proceeding), and it may reside in either the potential aspect of taking effective action (knowing how) or the actual aspect of taking effective action (acting). A form of knowing, deep tacit knowledge (earned) is created over time within our minds (or hearts or guts) through experience, contemplation, and unconscious processing such that it becomes a natural part of our being—not just something consciously learned, stored, and retrieved.[345] In other words, earned intuitive tacit knowledge is the result of continuous learning through experience. To develop these intuitive skills requires making sure that your experiences are meaningful, that is, having specific objectives in mind such as how to size up situations quickly and develop a good sense of what will happen next.[346] It is also important to get immediate and accurate feedback directly related to the context within which a decision was made. Understanding the outcomes of actions and why something did or did not happen helps develop patterns in the unconscious (earned intuition). According to Klein, to build up expertise requires: (1) feedback on decisions and actions, (2) active engagement in getting and interpreting this feedback (not passively allowing someone else to judge them); and (3) repetitions, which provide the opportunity to practice making decisions and getting feedback.[347] It is this expertise that can enable your future ability to emerge creative solutions.

In Chapter 11 we focus on revealed intuition and in Chapter 12 we focus on controlled intuition, which both deal with another form of intuitive knowledge.

Affective Tacit Knowledge

Affective tacit knowledge is connected to emotions and feelings, with, as previously noted, emotions representing the external expression of some feelings. Feelings expressed as emotions become explicit.[348] Feelings that are not expressed—perhaps not even recognized—are those that fall into the area of affective tacit knowledge. From neuroscience research, information coming into the body moves through the amygdala, that part of the brain that is,

> *... important both for the acquisition and for the on-line processing of emotional stimuli ... [with] its processing encompassing both the elicitation of emotional responses in the body and changes in other cognitive processes, such as attention and memory.*[349]

As incoming information moves through the amygdala, an emotional "tag" is attached. If this information is perceived as life-threatening, then the amygdala takes control, making a decision and acting on that decision before conscious awareness of a threat! Haberlandt goes so far as to say that there is no such thing as a behavior or thought not impacted by emotions in some way.[350] Even simple responses to information signals can be linked to multiple emotional neurotransmitters. Thus, affective tacit knowledge is attached to other types or aspects of tacit knowledge. For example, when an individual thinks about recent occurrences like an argument or a favorite sports team losing in the Rose Bowl, feelings are aroused. Or, recall the internal responses to holding the hard copy of your first book, or your new born child. As Mulvihill states,

> *Because the neurotransmitters which carry messages of emotion are integrally linked with the information during both the initial processing and the linking with information from the different senses, it becomes clear that there is no thought, memory, or knowledge which is 'objective,' or 'detached' from the personal experience of knowing.*[351]

Feelings as a form of knowledge have different characteristics than language or ideas, but they may lead to effective action because they can influence actions by their existence and connections with consciousness. When feelings come into conscious awareness they can play an informing role in decision-making, providing insights in a non-linguistic manner (as a "nudge") and thereby influencing decisions and actions. For example, a feeling (such as fear or an upset stomach) may occur every time a particular action is started which could prevent the decision-maker from taking that action.[352]

Spiritual Tacit Knowledge

Spiritual tacit knowledge can be described in terms of knowledge based on matters of the soul. The soul represents the animating principles of human life in terms of thought and action, specifically focused on *its moral aspects, the emotional part of human nature, and higher development of the mental faculties*.[353] While there is a "knowing" related to spiritual tacit knowledge similar to intuition, this knowing does not include the experiential base of intuition, and it may or may not have emotional tags. The current state of the evolution of our understanding of spiritual knowledge is such that there are insufficient words to relate its transcendent power, or to define the role it plays in relationship to other tacit knowledges. Nonetheless, while this area represents a form of higher guidance with unknown origin, we consider it as the information exchange with the Field discussed in Chapter 7. Note that knowledge ABOUT things spiritual in nature can be earned tacit knowledge.

In a 2007 MQI research study, representative human characteristics spiritual in nature were identified that contribute to learning.[354] These characteristics were grouped into five general areas: *shifting frames of reference* (represented by the terms abundance, awareness, caring, compassion, connectedness, empathy, openness); *animating for learning* (represented by the terms aliveness, grace, harmony, joy, love, presence, wonder); *enriching relationships* (represented by the terms authenticity, consistency, morality, respect, tolerance, values); *priming for learning* (represented by the terms awareness, eagerness, expectancy, openness, presence, sensitivity, unfoldment, willingness); and *moving toward wisdom* (represented by the terms caring, connectedness, love, morality, respect, service).

The general area of *shifting frames of reference* was intertwined with learning, thinking and acting,[355] covering the external approach (looking from an outside frame of reference) and the internal approach (taking an empathetic perspective which moves the viewpoint from the objective to the subjective). Frames of reference can be focusing and/or limiting, allowing the mind to go deeper in a bounded direction. Shifting frames of reference potentially offers the opportunity to take a multidimensional approach to exploring the world around us, and facilitates creativity and innovation. The area of *animating for learning* speaks to the fundamental source of life—learning, the energy used for survival and growth, for adapting and creating. The area of *enriching relationships* is tied to competence theory,[356] which assumes that it is natural for people to strive for effective interactions with their world. This brings in the two dimensions of spirituality that exist beyond ourselves (other people and the larger energy system/ecosystem perceived as outside the human) with whom we can truly learn to grow in understanding.[357] *Priming for learning* attributes are considered as those that actively prepare and move an individual toward learning. Wisdom, the highest part of the knowledge spectrum, is considered as forwarding the goal of achieving the common or greater good.[358] (See Chapter 6.) Reflecting on this study, it would appear that spiritual knowledge would provide a transcendent frame of reference that puts things in relationship to a larger perspective while promoting self-knowledge and learning.

Zohar and Marshall describe spiritual tacit knowledge as,

> ... the intelligence with which we address and solve problems of meaning and value, ... place our actions and our lives in a wider-richer meaning-giving context, [and] ... can assess that one course of action or one life-path is more meaningful than another. [359]

It appears that **spiritual knowledge may be the guiding purpose, vision and values behind the creation and application of tacit knowledge.** It may also be the road to moving information to knowledge and knowledge to wisdom, i.e., purpose, vision and values are excellent guidelines.

In the context of this treatment, *spiritual tacit knowledge is considered the source of higher learning*, helping decision-makers create and implement knowledge that has greater meaning and value for the common good—wisdom. An example of spiritual tacit knowledge that is primarily Knowledge (Proceeding) is Csikszentmihalyi's concept of flow.[360] Spiritual tacit knowledge that is primarily Knowledge (Informing) is often referred to as the streaming or channeling of information that is outside an individual's personal experience or awareness, *a connection with and inflowing of ideas*. An example would be the numerous recorded instances in times of warfare where military personnel under fire have known what actions to take without detailed knowledge of the terrain or enemy troop movement.

Interconnections and Overlaps

Similar to the possible interactions among tacit, implicit and explicit knowledge, the four aspects of tacit knowledge can experience considerable interconnections and overlaps. For example, referring to a somatic learning model by Amann, Merriam says that "the spiritual aspect of somatic learning is meaning-making through music, art, imagery, symbols, and rituals and overlaps or intersects with the other three dimensions",[361] which are described as kinesthetic learning, sensory learning and affective learning. While organized differently than the knowledge model presented here, the Amann somatic learning model includes four elements—kinesthetic, sensory, affective and spiritual—as tacit knowledge.[362]

As a second example of overlap, affective and embodied somatic states can operate both inside and outside an individual's awareness or consciousness; however, when overlap occurs in the unconscious the results may surface as intuition. Conversely, affective and embodied somatic states are often accompanied by overt somatic markers; for example, a "gut feel." In contrast to somatic markers, intuition comes from the neural network of the reticular activating system. Instead of producing a body-state change (sematic marker), it inhibits the regulatory neural circuits located in the brain core, which can influence behaviors.[363]

It is important to realize that we as decision-makers are holistic in nature, that is, all of the tacit knowledges described above are playing a role in our experiential engagement of life, all of them are participating in your creation of new ideas. In an increasingly uncertain and complex environment, to take effective action requires a mix of explicit, implicit and, particularly, tacit knowledge. The growing criticality of gaining access to this knowledge magnifies the need to understand implicit knowledge and the four aspects of tacit knowledge (embodied, intuitive, affective and spiritual), and intentionally developing vehicles to bring that knowledge into play in the creative process, which is the topic of Chapter 10.

Chapter 10
Accessing Tacit Knowledge

It has only been in the past few decades that cognitive psychology and neuroscience have begun to seriously explore the unconscious mental life, with some of those findings shared in Chapter 3. This includes the recognition that conscious experience, thought, and action are influenced by unconscious concepts, memories, and other mental constructs inaccessible to conscious awareness and somehow independent of voluntary control.[364] At the same time, research in neuroscience is also digging deeper into the understanding of the emotions, working memory, and the unconscious processing that occur within the mind, and to some extent throughout the body.

As previously introduced, Polanyi felt that tacit knowledge consisted of *a range of conceptual and sensory information and images* that could be used to make sense of a situation or event in the context of a NOW experience and recognized need, enabling the bisociation of two separate conceptual patterns.[365] Two observations that have emerged in the discussion above are: (1) While the terms explicit, implicit and tacit may be useful in clarifying and understanding knowledge, these terms describe aspects of a fluctuating continuum (a range) rather than a rigid classification schema. (2) In the unconscious mind the association of incoming information with internal information is **a powerful form of continuous learning which lays the foundation for creativity, that is, recognition of related patterns**. Significant gains can be made in the effectiveness of Innovative Creativity through understanding and stimulating this process.[366] *So, how do we make best use of this process to sponsor creativity?* The search for an answer leads to thinking beyond what is described as ordinary consciousness towards what we will call **extraordinary consciousness.**

Ordinary consciousness represents the customary or typical state of consciousness, that which is common to everyday usage, or of the usual kind. Polanyi sees tacit knowledge as *not part* of one's ordinary consciousness;[367] thus, tacit knowledge resides in the unconscious. To access tacit knowledge an individual needs to move from ordinary consciousness to extraordinary consciousness, acquiring a greater sensitivity to information stored in the unconscious. This is the realm which can be considered special, exceptional, and outside of the usual or regular state of consciousness—having a heightened sensitivity to, awareness of, and connection with our unconscious mind together with its memory and thought processes. With extraordinary consciousness comes extraordinary creativity, that is, the ability to fully engage our creative potential.

So, again, how do we actually achieve this? The challenge is to **make better use of our tacit knowledge** through creating greater connections with the unconscious, building and expanding the resources stored in the unconscious, deepening areas of resonance, and sharing tacit resources among individuals. We propose a four-fold action model with nominal curves for building extraordinary consciousness within individuals that includes surfacing tacit knowledge, embedding tacit knowledge, sharing tacit knowledge, and inducing resonance (see Figure 15 below). Each of these approaches will be briefly addressed.

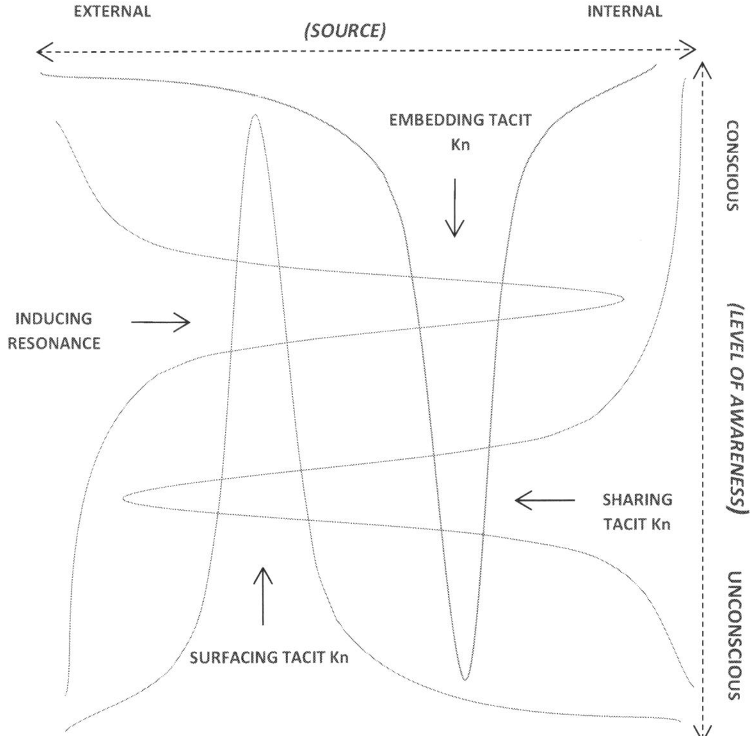

Figure 20. *Building Extraordinary Consciousness within an Individual.*

Surfacing Tacit Knowledge

The first approach toward building extraordinary consciousness is *surfacing tacit knowledge*. As individuals observe, experience, study, and learn throughout life they generate a huge amount of information and knowledge that becomes stored in their unconscious mind. Even though an individual may have difficulty pulling it up when needed, learning how to access our unconscious—and listen to it—can become a valuable learning resource. Surfacing tacit knowledge is focused on accessing the benefit of that which is tacit by moving knowledge from the unconscious to conscious awareness. In the case study provided in Chapter 14, surfacing tacit knowledge is described in terms of "unveiled" knowledge, knowledge emerging from the tribal elders.

Three ways that tacit knowledge can be surfaced are through external triggering, self-collaboration, and nurturing. As represented in Figure 20, the process of triggering is primarily externally driven with internal participation. For example, conversation, dialogue, questions, or an external situation with specific incoming information may trigger the surfacing of tacit knowledge needed to respond. The unconscious is aware of the flow of consciousness, available to affect decisions as incoming information is associated with internal information (the associative patterning process). In these cases, we would describe the knowledge surfaced from the unconscious as implicit, with externally-generated information mixing with tacit knowledge in order to create that surfaced implicit knowledge (see the earlier discussion on implicit knowledge.) Triggering is often the phenomenon that occurs in "sink or swim" situations, where an immediate decision must be made that will have significant consequences.

Triggering can also be achieved through sound. By listening to a special song in your life, you can draw out deep feelings and memories buried in your unconscious. Sound and its relationship to humans has been studied by philosophers throughout recorded history; extensive treatments appear in the work of Plato, Kant and Nietzsche. Through the last century scientists have delved into studies focused on acoustics (the science of sound itself), psychoacoustics (the study of how our minds perceive sound) and musical psychoacoustics (the discipline that involves every aspect of musical perception and performance). Sound (as do all patterns in the mind) has the ability to change and shape the physiological structure of the brain. Neuroscience has slowly begun to validate the capability of both internal thoughts and external incoming information (including sound) to affect the physical structure of the brain—its synaptic connection strength, its neuronal connections and the growth of additional neurons.[368]

Although collaboration is generally thought about as interactions among individuals and/or groups, there is another collaboration that is less understood. This is the process of individuals consciously collaborating with themselves. What this means is the conscious mind learning to communicate with, listen to, and trust its own unconscious. In order to build this trust, it is necessary for individuals to first recognize where their tacit knowledge is coming from. Recall that tacit knowledge is largely created from the continuous mixing of external information with internal information and stored in invariant form. This means that when you trust your unconscious you are trusting yourself, and the semantic complexing of all the experiences, learning, thoughts, and feelings throughout your life. Thus, the process of associating (learning) in your unconscious is related to life-long conscious learning experiences (see the section below on embedding tacit knowledge).

One way to collaborate with yourself is through creating an internal dialogue. For example, accepting the authenticity of and listening deeply to a continuous stream of conscious thought while following the tenets of dialogue. Those tenets would include: withholding quick judgment, not demanding quick answers, and exploring underlying assumptions,[369] *then* looking for collaborative meaning between what you *consciously think* and what you *feel*. A second approach is to ask yourself a lot of questions related to the task at hand. Even if you don't think you know the answers, reflect carefully on the questions, and be patient. Sleeping on a question will often yield an answer the following morning. (See Exercise 3 in Chapter 2.) Your unconscious mind processes information 24/7 and exists to help you survive. It is not a figment of your imagination, nor your enemy.

Although requiring time, openness, and commitment, there are a number of approaches readily available for those who choose to nurture their sensitivity to tacit knowledge through exploring their inner self. These include (as a representative set only) meditation, mindfulness, inner tasking, lucid dreaming, hemispheric synchronization, and flow. Other practices such as changing one's frame of reference and the use of other Knowledge Capacities also create new ways to view problems which often lead to new creative solutions. (See Exercise 6 in Chapter 4.)

Meditation practices have the ability to quiet the conscious mind, thus allowing greater access to the unconscious.[370] In a research study involving Tibetan Buddhists, it was found that their longtime contemplative practice produced gamma brainwaves, which occur during the creativity binding phase, when novel ideas are first generated.[371] In another study coming out of the University of North Carolina, it was found that four days of meditation practice resulted in significant improvements in creativity and cognitive flexibility as well as attention, memory, and vigilance.[372]

There is much literature available on a variety of specific meditation practices. For example, a study on "focused-attention meditation" and "open-monitoring meditation" showed specific effects[373] on creativity. The former induced a control state promoting divergent thinking, which allows many new ideas to be generated. In comparison, the latter minimized convergent thinking, which generates one possible solution to a specific problem.[374]

Of particular interest to our focus on creativity, "insight meditation" used in mindfulness practices guides attention to the observation of thoughts, feelings and sensations that are at a distance, apart from the meditator. This approach—providing an improved perspective and clearer insight than concentration meditation—supports enhanced awareness.

Mindfulness relates to purposeful and non-judgmental observation in the present moment[375] through self-regulated attention and orientation.[376] Specifically, it can be defined as "a state of consciousness in which attention is focused on present-moment phenomena occurring both externally and internally."[377] This is the receptive attention[378] which is associated with humility (see Exercise 1 in Chapter 1.) Recognizing their value in terms of productivity and creativity, over the past decade there has been an expansion of organization-based mindfulness programs.

Inner tasking is a wide-spread and often used approach to engaging your unconscious. Tell yourself, as you fall asleep at night, to work on a problem or question. The next morning when you wake up, but before you get up, lie in bed and listen to your own, quiet, passive thoughts. Frequently, but not always, the answer will appear, although it must be written down quickly before it is lost from the conscious mind. Like meditation, the efficacy of this approach takes time and practice to develop. While we have provided the example of tasking prior to sleep (Exercise 3 in Chapter 2), this tasking can occur in any quiet moment in the day, releasing it as you go about your daily process of living, then later in the day quieting the mind and listening, repeating the question at hand and listening.

Lucid dreaming, an existential learning experience, is a particularly powerful way to access tacit knowledge. The psychotherapist Kenneth Kelzer wrote of one of his lucid dreams:

> *In this dream I experienced a lucidity that was so vastly different and beyond the range of anything I had previously encountered. At this point I prefer to apply the concept of the spectrum of consciousness to the lucid*

dream and assert that within the lucid state a person may have access to a spectrum or range of psychic energy that is so vast, so broad and so unique as to defy classification.[379]

In lucid dreams you are aware that you are dreaming while you are asleep, that is, achieving the paradox of being conscious in the unconscious state (mind awake, body asleep). One way to do this is through **hemispheric synchronization**, introduced in Chapter 4 (bringing both hemispheres of the brain into coherence). This is accomplished by the use of sound coupled with a binaural beat.[380] In the human mind, binaural beats are detected with carrier tones (audio tones of slightly different frequencies, one to each ear) below approximately 1500 Hz.[381] The mind perceives the frequency differences of the sound coming into each ear, mixing the two sounds to produce a fluctuating rhythm and thereby creating a beat or difference frequency. Because each side of the body sends signals to the opposite hemisphere of the brain, both hemispheres must work together to "hear" the difference frequency. Thus, inter-hemispheric communication is the setting for brain-wave coherence which facilitates whole-brain cognition, assuming an elevated status in subjective experience.[382] As introduced, what can occur during hemispheric synchronization is a physiologically reduced state of arousal, quieting the body *while maintaining conscious awareness,*[383] providing a doorway into the unconscious and greater access to the larger consciousness field which can facilitate creativity and learning.

In a 2023 *National Geographic* article, Colino provided cognitive techniques, some performed during the day and others when you're falling asleep.[384] These included: (1) the reality testing technique where you pause regularly during the day to ask yourself whether you are in a dream or reality, and after establishing this pattern this cueing may repeat itself during the night; (2) Mnemonic Induction which is rehearsing a dream during the day while you visualize being lucid and tell yourself that the next time you are dreaming you will be aware in that state; (3) the Wake-Up-Back-Bed technique where you set your alarm clock after 5-6 hours of sleep, then stay awake for a half hour, and go back to bed with the intention of becoming lucid when you start dreaming; and (4) the Senses Initiated Lucid Dream which, similar to number (4), is where you wake up and shift your attention between sensations (physical, visual and auditory) before going back to sleep.

Similar to the "Sleep on It" approach (Exercise 3 in Chapter 2), keeping a journal in which you record your dreams can help facilitate dream recall.

Entering the Flow State

There is a flow to life. The idea of the flow experience can be found in a number of religions; for example, Christianity, Buddhism, and Taoism. When asked if every culture produced a religion, the anthropologist Mel Konner answered, "It's not God—they are seeking the rapture of life, to understand *what it means to be alive*."[385]

Flow is a current punctuated by our concept of time within which thoughts and actions (events) occur. Much like falling in love, when an individual finds their flow, life is forever changed. In the MQI Knowledge Management Thought Leader (KMTL) study,[386] one participant offered that through the creation of knowledge that we were creating both little drops of rain and, in some cases, monsoons. As he described,

> *If you think of knowledge broadly as all of the understanding that we as human beings have gained through experience, observation or study as the dictionary says, what we are doing either in the production of individual knowledge or in the development of this discipline that helps us to find and apply knowledge ... then it is as little drops of rain that start to flow down the hill that come together in little streams that eventually become big rivers flowing into the ocean. From that point of view, I think that we, whether as thought leaders or participants, are making that contribution. In some cases, it is little drops of rain, and in other cases it may be monsoons.*

This analogy points to the beginning of flow, to the thoughts and actions that come together to start the flow, some little and some large. Then, when other thoughts and actions are consistent with the flow, they expand and create a larger flow. Thoughts and actions that are inconsistent with the flow, heading upstream against the larger flow, must be quite strong to make any headway, and can easily be overcome by the larger flow or swept to the side, out of the current. Interestingly, this description sounds consistent with the flow of energy in a quantum probability field.

Seligman warns that there are no shortcuts to flow. All the cognitive and emotional resources that make up our thoughts and feelings are engaged in the concentrated attention that flow requires. As Seligman blatantly states,

> *... you need to deploy your highest strengths and talents to meet the world in flow. There are effortless shortcuts to feeling positive emotion ... you can masturbate, go shopping, take drugs, or watch television. Hence, the importance of identifying your highest strengths and learning to use them more often in order to go into flow.*[387]

Seligman's model of positive psychology, which engages the flow state, includes the elements of positive emotion, engagement, meaning, positive relationships, and accomplishment. From this brief introduction, it can be seen that flow is a behavior choice. In the mid-sixties, psychologists tended to explain the creative state of flow as a behavior related to extrinsic rewards. Maslow broke through this mindset, making a distinction in creative behavior between *process* and *product* orientation, which in turn led him to the idea of "peak experiences".[388] The motivation for these experiences was a personal desire for "self-actualization", the need to discover personal potential and limits through intense experience.

Through research with rats, Hebb had also forwarded his "optimal arousal hypothesis" which showed that rats did not respond exclusively to getting food or avoiding shocks, but appeared to be motivated by intrinsic drives such as novelty and curiosity.[389] While small steps of expanded learning continued to occur—for example, research on social motivation by deCharms and Muir,[390] followed by research led by Deci[391] and Lepper and his colleagues[392]—the rationale for a theory of intrinsic motivation had emerged. Enter Csikszentmihalyi, who today is the thought leader in terms of flow as the optimal experience. We will briefly address this body of work and its relationship to creativity.

Csikszentmihalyi focused on the quality of subjective experience, what made a behavior intrinsically rewarding. He wanted to know *how these rewards felt* and *why* they were rewarding, which led to his writing on flow as the optimal experience. In pursuit of answers, Csikszentmihalyi was able to observe people "in those moments when their lives reach peaks of involvement that produce intense feelings of enjoyment and creativity."[393] He describes this as the autotelic experience, an unanimity or order in consciousness that produces a desirable experiential state, "when a person's body or mind is stretched to its limits in a voluntary effort to accomplish something difficult and worthwhile."[394] In this state people are so involved with their work that nothing else seems to matter. Autotelic workers create their own experience of flow. They are often creative, curious, and lead vigorous lives, taking everything that comes along in their stride.

Using Csikszentmihalyi's concept of flow, the eight conditions that combine to create the flow experience are: Clear goals, quick feedback, a balance between opportunity and capacity, deepened concentration, being in the present, being in control, an altered sense of time, and the loss of ego. As Csikszentmihalyi notes, "I have given the name 'flow' to this common experience, because so many people have used the analogy of being carried away by an outside force, of moving effortlessly with the current of energy, at the moments of highest enjoyment."[395] Reflect back and try to recall a time when you were in the flow state. How did it feel?

There is considerable research that shows a direct link between the flow state and creativity. Csikszentmihalyi himself suggests that the creative process is intertwined with the characteristics of flow. He forwards that there are two reasons: (1) the effortless attention when in flow which enables the "flow-er" to focus for longer periods with less fatigue, and (2) complete focus while simultaneously enabling free association and implicit processes which can spur novel and relevant ideas. Thus, the state of flow itself facilitates creative thinking.[396]

Dietrich agrees. In foundational research on transient hypo frontality and flow, he explored creativity in terms of its neurological profile. This work led him to forward that "Flow represents a third mode of creativity, alongside the deliberate and spontaneous [technique and inspiration] modes of creative thinking."[397] Further, the increase in creativity appears to last *beyond* the flow experience itself. In a Harvard study, Amabile found that there was a spike in creativity that lasted for a number of days AFTER the flow experience. The study also affirmed that creative insights were consistently associated with the flow state.[398]

Whether you were able to recall a flow experience or not, each of us has experienced flow at times in our lives: playing a good tennis match, meeting a short deadline, or enjoying team camaraderie during an intense task. An individual or team is said to be in a state of flow when the activity at hand becomes so intense that the normal sense of time and space disappears, and all energy is invested in the task. In a team setting, individuals lose the sense of identity or separateness during the experience, then afterwards emerge from the experience with a stronger sense of self. While involved in this creative state, there is a sense of exhilaration and joy. As these optimal experiences are repeated, individuals develop a sense of experiencing their reason for being, coupled with a strong feeling of being in control.

Although the flow experience cannot easily be turned on and off, individuals and teams can develop the ability to experience flow and create environmental conditions that facilitate its onset. As developed and studied by Csikszentmihalyi, the conditions required for a team flow experience are:[399]

1. Tasks must have a good chance of being completed, yet not be too easy.
2. The team must be able to concentrate on what it is doing. Interruptions, distractions, and/or poor facilities prevent concentration.

3. The task should have clear goals, so that the team knows when it has succeeded. Immediate feedback should be provided to the team so that it can react and adjust its actions.

The phenomenon of flow results in individuals and teams creatively giving their best capabilities to the task at hand. Team members come away with feelings of accomplishment, joy, and well-being that positively influence their willingness to trust and openly communicate with other team members, enhancing collaboration and team performance. The bottom line for the organization is creative solutions to issues at hand and a high level of performance.

Note that while the larger phenomenon of the flow experience is not bounded, the description of flow as autotelic work *is* bounded, that is, with a specific task orientation—focused on a specific issue, problem, or opportunity—with specific boundary conditions cited to ensure success.

* * * * *

EXERCISE 14: *Discovering Flow*

STEP (1) Find a location that you love and where you can have a few quiet moments alone. This may be indoors or outdoors, perhaps sitting on the beach, or on a stone in a field, or in the corner of a library.

STEP (2) Reflect on an activity in which you repeatedly engage around which you have passion. This may be a physical or mental activity.

STEP (3) Using your creative imagination, slowly relive your perfect moment engaged in this activity. Let your body engage in active listening, moving, and smiling as appropriate for reliving the experience. Relish the detail, enjoy the feelings.

STEP (4) Repeat as necessary. When you have achieved a "floating" feeling, losing track of time and living in the moment, you are in the flow state.

STEP (5) Cultivate this experience such that you can choose to move into the flow state at will when you are looking for creative ideas with a specific focus. This ability becomes part of your Innovative Creativity toolkit.

* * * * *

An important aspect of the flow state is presencing, a core capacity needed to access the field of the future. This is going to sound a bit ironical since flow insinuates movement over time, and we're now talking about being present such that there is no awareness of past or future, only the instant at hand. To a large extent, presencing has very much to do with mindfulness, introduced earlier. Perhaps the most straightforward definitions of presencing are offered by Brown, Ryan and Creswell when they simply describe mindfulness as "being attentive to and aware of what is taking place in the present"[400] and as a "process of openly attending, with awareness, to one's present moment experience."[401] Innovative Creativity requires awareness; without awareness there would be nothing useful to create, nothing to improve. Digging a little deeper, Kabat-Zinn adds the elements of "on purpose" and "non-judgmental" and relinquishing personal attachment to the experience that is unfolding moment-by-moment.[402] Note that intent—based on purpose—is necessary for presencing, yet once intent is crystalized it needs to be released from the mind into the field. *An energy held onto is kept within the self and therefore not of use in creating something beyond self.*

Looking from the larger perspective, without presence we would *become* our environment. When we are conscious, we are present. But while presence and consciousness are interrelated, and presencing is core to consciousness, the idea of presence goes beyond an awareness of the NOW to include deep listening and the ability through awareness to move beyond the way we've done things in the past, bringing with it the freedom of choice. As Hawkins explains,

> *It is this accessibility of the past—the ability to jump back in time and slide forward again to the present—that gives us our sense of presence and awareness. If we couldn't replay our recent thoughts and experiences, then we would be unaware that we are alive.*[403]

Presencing, necessary for profound systemic changes,[404] is a core capability of the future, a way to access the living fields that connect us and that which is seeking to emerge.[405] See Chapter 7. The concept of connecting to "that which is seeking to emerge" is certainly consistent with the quantum field as a probability field containing all possibilities.

As part of presencing, Senge and his colleagues introduce seven capacities that are foundational to seeing, sensing, and realizing new possibilities: suspending [judgment], redirecting, letting go, letting come, crystalizing, prototyping, and institutionalizing.[406] Each of these capacities enables various activities which serve as a gateway to the next capacity. The idea of "letting come" is the process of allowing, whose importance cannot be overemphasized. We are often our own worst enemies. As we realize the power of the mind/brain in terms of thought and feelings in the process of creating (Chapter 6), we do not want to interject barriers to our desired progress forward. Similar to humility, presencing opens us to receiving and learning.

> *Over time, your appreciation for the question will become equivalent to your appreciation for the answer, and your appreciation for the problem will become equivalent to your appreciation for the solution. And in your newfound ease with what-is, you will find yourself in the state of allowing what you truly desire.*[407]

Csikszentmihalyi forwards that the organization of self becomes more complex when following the flow experience, which signifies growth. As Csikszentmihalyi explains,

> *Complexity is the result of two broad psychological processes: differentiation and integration. Differentiation implies a movement toward uniqueness, toward separating oneself from others. Integration refers to its opposite: a union with other people, with ideas and entities beyond the self. A complex self is one that succeeds in combining these opposite tendencies.*[408]

Thus, for self, the flow experience—as a consciousness state of deep concentration—is both differentiating and integrating, making the self more unique and simultaneously more connected to others, a state that appears to be primed for creativity.

Embedding Tacit Knowledge

The second approach toward building extraordinary consciousness is *embedding tacit knowledge*. Although information is continuously going into our unconscious, only "significant" things (significant to the individual) stay in memory—often without our conscious awareness. Said another way, **every experience and conversation is *embedding* potential knowledge in the unconscious** as it is associated with previously stored information, creating new patterns. Thinking about embedding as a process for improving our tacit knowledge can lead to new approaches to learning, and can be considered a preparatory state for future Innovative Creativity. In Figure 20, we see that embedding is both externally and internally driven, with knowledge moving from the conscious to the unconscious. Embedding knowledge in the unconscious can occur through exposure or immersion, by accident or by choice. Examples would include travel, regularly attending church on Sunday, or listening to opera and imitating what you've heard in the shower every day. Practice moves beyond exposure to include repeated participation in some skill or process, thus strengthening the patterns in the mind. For example, after many years of imitation (practice) look at what Paul Potts, Britain's Got Talent-discovered opera singer, accomplished![409]

Creating tacit knowledge occurs naturally and quietly as an individual lives through diverse experiences and becomes more proficient at some activity (such as public speaking) or cognitive competency (such as problem solving). As their scope of experience widens, the number of relevant neuronal patterns increases. As an individual becomes more proficient in a specific area through effortful practice, the number of neurons needed to perform the task decreases and the remaining pattern gradually becomes embedded in the unconscious, ergo it becomes tacit knowledge. When this happens, the reasons and context within which the knowledge was created often become hidden from consciousness (also tacit).

Recognizing the differences among the four aspects of tacit knowledge suggests specific ways to embed knowledge. Figure 21 offers representative examples of each type of tacit knowledge and suggestions for embedding each.

Embodied tacit knowledge requires new pattern embedding for change to occur. This might take the form of repetition in physical training or in mental thinking. For example, embodied tacit knowledge might be embedded through mimicry, practice, competence development, or visual imagery coupled with practice. An example of this would be when an athlete training to become a pole vaulter reviews a video of his perfect pole vault to increase his athletic ability. This is a result of the fact that when the pole vaulter performs his perfect vault, the patterns going through his brain while he is doing it are the same patterns that go through his brain when he is *watching* himself do it. When he is watching the video, he is repeating the desired brain patterns and this repetition strengthens these patterns in unconscious memory. When actually "doing" the pole vault, he cannot think about his action, nor try to control them. Doing so would degrade his performance because his conscious thoughts would interfere with his tacit ability.

In the late 1990's, neuroscience research identified what are referred to as mirror neurons. As Dobb's explains,

> *These neurons are scattered throughout key parts of the brain—the premotor cortex and centers for language, empathy and pain—and fire not only as we perform a certain action, but also when we watch someone else perform that action.*[410]

Similar to the pole vaulter example, when the goals of "others" in a video are understood and resonate with the watcher,[411] watching a video is a cognitive form of mimicry that transfers actions, behaviors and most likely other cultural norms. The movies we watch count. Given goal coherence, when we *see* something being enacted, our mind creates the same patterns that we would use to enact that "something" ourselves. As these patterns fade into long-term memory, they would represent tacit knowledge, both Knowledge (Informing) and Knowledge (Proceeding). While mirror neurons are a subject of current research, it would appear that they represent a mechanism for the transfer of tacit knowledge between individuals or throughout a culture.[412]

Intuitive tacit knowledge can be nurtured and developed through exposure, learning, and practice. Intuitive tacit knowledge might be embedded through experience, contemplation, developing a case history for learning purposes, developing a sensitivity to your own intuition, and effortful practice. Effortful study moves beyond practice to include identifying challenges just beyond an individual's competence and focusing on meeting those challenges one at a time.[413] The way people become experts involves *the chunking of ideas and concepts* and *creating understanding through the development of significant patterns* useful for solving problems and anticipating future behavior within their area of focus.

Figure 21. *Representative examples of tacit knowledges and suggestions for engaging each.*

A study of chess players concluded that "effortful practice" was the difference between people who played chess for many years while maintaining an average skill and those who became master players in shorter periods of time. The master players, or experts, examined the chessboard patterns over and over again, studying them, looking at nuances, trying small changes to perturb the outcome (sense and response), generally "playing with" and studying these *patterns*.[414] In other words, they use long-term working memory, pattern recognition, and chunking rather than logic as a means of understanding and decision-making. This indicates that by exerting mental effort and emotion while exploring complex situations, knowledge—often problem-solving expertise and what some call wisdom—becomes embedded in the unconscious mind.[415]

An important insight from this discussion is the recognition that when facing complex problems which do not allow reasoning or cause and effect analysis because of their complexity, the solution will most likely lie in studying patterns and chunking those patterns to enable a tacit capacity to anticipate and develop solutions. This was demonstrated in the movie *A Beautiful Mind* staring Russell Crowe as a brilliant mathematician on the brink of international acclaim who becomes entangled in a mysterious conspiracy.

Affective tacit knowledge requires nurturing and the development of emotional intelligence. Affective tacit knowledge might be embedded through digging deeply into a situation—building self-awareness and developing a sensitivity to your own emotions—and having intense emotional experiences. How much of an experience is kept as tacit depends upon the mode of incoming information and the emotional tag (unconsciously) embedded with it. The stronger the emotion attached to the experience, the longer it will be remembered, and the easier it will be to recall (even when you don't want to!). Subtle patterns that occur during any experience may slip quietly into our unconscious and become affective tacit knowledge.[416]

Spiritual tacit knowledge can be facilitated by encouraging holistic representation of the individual and respect for a higher purpose. Spiritual tacit knowledge might be embedded through dialogue, learning from practice and reflection, and developing a sensitivity to your own spirit, living with it over time and exploring your feelings regarding the larger aspects of values, purpose and meaning. Any individual or organization who demonstrates—and acts upon—their deep concerns for humanity and the planet is embedding spiritual tacit knowledge.

Sharing Tacit Knowledge

The third approach toward building extraordinary consciousness is *sharing tacit knowledge*. In our discussion above on surfacing tacit knowledge, it became clear that surfaced knowledge is new knowledge, a different shading of that which was in the unconscious. If knowledge can be described in words and visuals then this would be by definition explicit. Yet the subject of this paragraph is sharing tacit knowledge. **The key is that it is not necessary to make knowledge explicit in order to share it.**

In Figure 20, sharing tacit knowledge occurs both consciously and unconsciously, although the knowledge shared may remain tacit in nature. The power of this process has been recognized in organizations for years, and tapped into through the use of mentoring and shadowing programs to facilitate imitation and mimicry. More recently, it has become the focus of group learning, where communities and teams engage in dialogue focused on specific issues and, over time, develop a common frame of reference, language and understanding that can create solutions to future complex problems. These solutions may retain "tacitness" in terms of understanding the complexity of the issues where it is impossible to identify all the contributing factors, much less a cause-and-effect relationship among them. Hence these solutions would not be explainable in words and visuals to individuals outside the team or community. When this occurs, the team (having arrived at the decision based on their "tacit" knowledge) will often create a rational explanation to communicate to outside individuals why the decision makes sense.

Inducing Resonance

The fourth approach toward building extraordinary consciousness is *inducing resonance*. A 2008 MQI research study found that through exposure to diverse and specifically opposing concepts that are well-grounded, it is possible to create a resonance within the listener's mind that amplifies the meaning of the incoming information, increasing its emotional content and receptivity. While it is words that trigger this resonance, it is the current of the search for truth flowing under that linguistically-centered thought that amplifies feelings, bringing about the emergence of deeper perceptions and validating the recreation of externally-triggered knowledge in the listener.

Humans operate from a place of *yearning to know truth*. Truth—which is relative to a specific context and situation—is a living, dynamic awareness that expands our consciousness. It is the neocortex, as the organ of intelligence, that is very much concerned with updating its models of the world based on a continuous stream of incoming sensory input, ever creating new models.

Connections are not fixed. As we learn, connections are strengthened; as we forget (through non-use), they are weakened.

When we experience a positive reaction to someone's spoken words or written thoughts, we are experiencing a *resonance of thought*, with those ideas consistent with the rhythm of our natural frequency, that is, with our truth, beliefs, and values. Through exposure to diverse and specifically opposing concepts that are well-grounded, it is possible to create a resonance within the receiver's mind that amplifies the meaning of the incoming information, increasing its emotional content and receptivity.

In Figure 20, inducing resonance is a result of external stimuli resonating with internal information to bring tacit knowledge into conscious awareness. When resonance occurs, the incoming information is consistent with the frame of reference and belief systems within the receiving individual. This resonance amplifies feelings connected to the incoming information while also validating the re-creation of this external knowledge in the receiver. Further, this process results in the amplification and transformation of internal affective, embodied, intuitive or spiritual knowledge from tacit to implicit (or explicit). Since deep knowledge is now accessible at the conscious level, this process also creates a sense of ownership within the listener. The communicators are not telling the listener what to believe; rather, when the tacit knowledge of the receiver resonates with what the communicator is saying (and how it is said), a natural reinforcement and expansion of understanding occurs within the listener. This accelerates the creation of deeper tacit knowledge and a stronger affection associated with this area of focus.

An example of inducing resonance can be seen in the recent movie, *The Debaters*. We would even go so far as to say that the purpose of a debate is to transfer tacit knowledge. Well-researched and well-grounded external information is communicated (explicit knowledge) and tied to emotional tags (explicitly expressed). The beauty of this process is that this occurs on *both sides* of a question such that the active listener who has an interest in the area of the debate resonates with and is pulled into one side or the other. Since context is important to knowledge creation, an eloquent speaker will try to speak from the audience's frame of reference to tap into related tacit knowledge. She will come across as confident, likeable and positive to transfer embodied tacit knowledge, and may well refer to higher order purpose, etc. to connect with the listener's spiritual tacit knowledge. A strong example of this occurs in political debates. This also occurs in litigation, particularly in the closing arguments, where opposing sides of an issue use emotional tags to connect to the jurors and affect their judgment.

A second example of inducing resonance is paradoxical thinking. As we expand our understanding of the way the mind/brain works, we can now recognize that the mind is *primed to support* paradoxical thinking. A "paradox" is considered sets of inconsistent propositions with a "set" including an explicit contradiction or entailing one.[417] Alternatively, from other viewpoints, a paradox is considered an apparently unacceptable conclusion derived by apparently acceptable reasoning from apparently acceptable premises[418] or could be thought of as two contradictory propositions to which we are led by apparently sound arguments.[419] This means that two "ideas" or "positions" can both be right when looked at individually, yet when looked at as a set they do not agree, that is, they can't both be right since they oppose each other.

Whether from an individual viewpoint or in a group, when coupled with humility, paradoxical thinking can lead to highly creative thought. One approach to bringing paradoxical thinking into a larger context is to identify a paradox related to the specific domain of focus—when addressing an issue at hand or during a training session—and introducing that paradox in a warm-up session prior to addressing the larger issue. A second approach would be to introduce a selected (unrelated) paradox just before a meeting, then break for a few minutes, and spend 15-20 minutes at the start of the meeting soliciting thoughts from participants. Since paradoxes have been identified dating back to the early days of our Western Philosophers, and probably earlier, there are numerous texts that can serve as guides to identify paradoxes which have "taxed thinkers" from Zeno to Galileo and Lewis Carroll to Bertrand Russell."[420]

A Few Thoughts

Although it may be a mix of earned *and* revealed intuition—earned knowledge was discussed in Chapter 9 and revealed knowledge is discussed in Chapter 11—what we call intuitive tacit knowledge is *largely earned intuition.* As introduced in the previous chapter, deep tacit knowledge is created within our minds (and hearts and guts) over time through experience, contemplation, and unconscious processing such that it becomes a natural part of our being—not just something consciously learned, stored and retrieved. In other words, much of our intuitive tacit knowledge is the result of continuous learning through experience and our unconscious paying attention!

<<<<<<>>>>>>

INSIGHT: **Deep tacit knowledge is created within our minds, hearts and guts over time through experience, contemplation and unconscious processing such that it becomes a natural part of our being.**

<<<<<<>>>>>>

To develop intuitive skills requires making sure that your experiences are meaningful, that is, having specific objectives in mind such as how to size up situations quickly and develop a good sense of what will happen next. It is also important to get immediate and accurate feedback directly related to the context within which a decision was made. Understanding the outcomes of actions and why something did or did not happen helps develop patterns in the unconscious (intuition). According to Klein, a cognitive psychologist researcher, building up expertise requires: (1) feedback on decisions and actions, (2) active engagement in getting and interpreting this feedback (not passively allowing someone else to judge); and (3) repetitions, which provide the opportunity to practice making decisions and getting feedback.[421]

When we are focused at the conscious mental level, we are always exploring cause and effect and working backwards, which uses up time. Fortunately, this is not the case with unconscious processing, from which indicators in the form of intuition can emerge in the blink of an eye. Psychologist Frank Tallis says the activity underway in the unconscious is of profound importance since, "Virtually every aspect of mental life is connected in some way with mental events and processes that occur below the threshold of awareness."[422] As we seek deeper understanding, greater creativity, and the ability to apply that creativity, the conundrum is that the cognitive processes that give rise to intuitive knowledge cannot be examined directly because they are not conscious, so we don't know exactly what they are.[423] However, we are learning every day.

Diving within to our sense of knowing becomes a critical ability to successfully living in the changing, uncertain and complex environment of today, and to access what is needed to create a better world. In the MQI Knowledge Management Thought Leader Research Study, one thought leader shared that he listens to his "inner voice". *As part of intuition, both knowledge and knowing are a source of this inner voice*. (See Appendix B.) Tacit knowledge is largely within the storehouse of self, expanding and connecting within from the time we are in the womb, and is available to each of us.

Are we listening?

Chapter 11
Revealed Intuition

It all begins when the soul would have its way with you.
Ralph Waldo Emerson

Revealed intuition is supported by spiritual tacit knowledge from higher energy fields and can take many forms. Recall that spiritual knowledge is defined as knowledge based on matters of the soul. The soul represents the **animating principles of human life in terms of thought and action**, specifically focused on *its moral aspects, the emotional part of human nature, and higher development of the mental faculties*.[424]

While there is a "knowing" related to spiritual knowledge similar to intuition, as previously noted this knowing does not include the experiential base of earned intuition, and it may or may not have emotional tags. This area represents a form of higher guidance with unknown origin. In the context of this book, we have explored the energies related to the larger field—whether you call that a consciousness field, information field, quantum field, or God field. (See Chapter 7.) Thus, revealed intuition would be based on information passed from or through that field.

The concept of and various approaches to "seeking divine guidance" is very much a matter of personal belief and faith. This varies widely across different religions, with religion referring to a set of human behaviors and practices used to worship a superhuman power or God or gods. It originates from the Latin word *religio*, which denotes an obligation or bond, and in its early English usage it referred to life under monastic vows.

In the Christian tradition, people hear from God through prayer, reading the Holy Bible, and attending worship services, as well as experiencing prophecies and dreams. In Judaism God's messages are heard through the Torah, which are the first five books of the Hebrew Bible. They also receive messages through prayer, faith-based study, Prophet's words, and personal experiences. In the Islamic tradition, Muslims focus on revelations through the prophets, especially the final Prophet Muhammad, with these prophecies related through the Quran. Guidance is also provided through Hadiths, which are believed to be a record of Muhammad's words, teachings and actions. Dreams as divine revelation are emphasized ty Sufi Muslims.

Hindus are provided direction and guidance through the Vedas and Upanishads (sacred scriptures) as well as through priests and gurus. They also engage in meditation, yogic practices, and visions. Buddhists seek spiritual guidance through teachers, meditation, and mindfulness as well as reading sacred texts such as the Tripitaka. The Tripitaka includes the discourses of Buddha divided into sermons, monastic law, and metaphysics. Meditation and mindfulness, which are effective ways of surfacing tacit knowledge regardless of its origin (earned or revealed) were briefly introduced in Chapter 9.

Sikhs hear from *Waheguru* (God) through *Guru Granth Sahib* (the holy book) as well as through prayers and the hymns and teachings of their Gurus. In the Bahá'i faith, God communicates through manifestations and the wisdom of special individuals who have insight into divine will such as Abraham, Moses, Jesus, Muhammad, Buddha, and Bahá'u'llah (who is the founder of the Bahá'i faith).

As in several traditions related above, "seeking divine guidance" can be accompanied by ritual and physical activity. An example of this is the Sufi practice that is known in Arabic as the "Mevlevi Order", which was founded by Jalal ad-Din Muhammad Rumi, a Sufi mystic who was a 13th-century Persian poet, an Islamic scholar and a theologian in the Ottoman Empire. The "Sema ceremony" of the Mevlevi includes music, prayer and dance that involves spinning in place. This spinning with one hand pointed upwards to connect with God and the other hand pointed down toward the earth—which earned the Mevlevi the term "whirling dervishes" in the West—is a physically active meditation symbolizing the revolution around the sun of planets and celestial bodies and representing the individual spiritual journey through mind and love toward perfection.

In the Chapter 14 case study, "The Power of Revealed and Unveiled Knowledge Reconstructing Local Food Systems", the divination system of the African Shona culture, which includes ritual movements, is not mere faith, but a learned discipline based on an extensive body of knowledge involving natural and supernatural phenomena as well as visible and invisible dimensions of reality. See also Appendix D: Accessing Revealed Knowledge in African Cultures.

It is important to understand that **development of the mental faculties is in service to the intuitional**. For as far back as we can collectively remember, the human has been primarily focused on development of the mental faculties. In this rush (in evolutionary terms) for mental achievement, we have largely neglected our spiritual development, which facilitates entry into the higher energy realms (higher in terms of vibration and frequency). Energy follows thought. When our thought is focused on the perceived objects of our physical reality that surround us, it is difficult to tap into the energy flows within, much less tap into that which is beyond our current understanding. This unbalanced mental growth can lead to the arrogance often visible in a highly competitive global business environment.

<<<<<<<>>>>>>>

INSIGHT: **Spiritual development facilitates entry into the higher energy realms (frequencies).**

<<<<<<<>>>>>>>

While it may sound like a failing in current human history, that is not the intent. This rapid development of the mental offers considerable opportunity for the future of humanity, that is, *if* we are able to now bring the mental into balance on the physical and emotional planes, with the spiritual counterbalance woven throughout. This means bringing truth and compassion into our everyday lives as we cooperatively and collaboratively work together to achieve intelligent activity.[425]

There are several reasons this is true. First, no one can argue the technological advancements over the past 10,000 years that have led us to today, nor the incredible shifts underway today in every area of human endeavor. If used for the benefit of all, these advances offer the potential to take humanity to the next level in terms of the growth of both individual and collective consciousness.

Second, even when an individual is able to access the higher energy fields and have brief flashes of intuition, without development of the mental faculties in a related domain of knowledge or the wisdom involved in translating a concept across domains of knowledge, it is difficult, if not impossible, to effectively *act* on that intuitive flash. Further, these flashes happen sporadically, and the large amount of insight gleaned from the experience is difficult to grasp without preparation, and quickly forgotten. A colleague and friend with whom I've had a number of conversations related to the importance of developing the mental faculties in support of the intuitive, called during the polishing of this chapter to say that at lunch in a Chinese restaurant she had just received a fortune that read, "Intuition and knowledge walk hand in hand." Well said!

At the simplest level of intuition, almost everyone has experienced the intuitive nudge. A nudge can be either earned or revealed intuition, or a combination of both! For example, since the unconscious receives information from both the environment and higher energy fields of which the conscious mind may not be aware, an enhanced awareness of the unconscious may show itself through a sense that something is right or wrong (sensing), or a good or bad feeling about a situation (feeling). This happens when you have a "knowing" that you need to talk to your sibling and the phone rings immediately afterwards with a call from your sibling. This happens when you "feel" that something is wrong, and within minutes you discover what that "something" is. This sensing or feeling (nudge) helps guide our reactions to future experiences. As neuroscientist Candice Pert has noted, the emotional system works through the generation and transmission of chemicals throughout the body, which in turn impact neuronal activity.[426] These chemical changes represent the emotional tag of the amygdala.

Revealed intuition from higher energy fields can take many forms. In the book, *Thinking Fast and Slow*, author Daniel Kahneman relates a story about firefighters fighting a kitchen fire. All of a sudden, the commander said "let's get out of here" without realizing why. And immediately after the firefighters escaped, the floor collapsed. Only after the fact did the commander realize that the fire had been unusually quiet and that his ears had been unusually hot. Together, those impressions prompted what he called a sixth sense of danger. He had no idea what was wrong. It turned out that the heart of the fire had not been in the kitchen, but in the basement beneath where the firefighters had stood.[427]

Another example is a tune playing over and over again in your head, with either the melody having personal significance or the words conveying a message. Or, when a word or number keeps coming into your reality through different communications vehicles. A few years back, when one of the author's partner David was getting into a car on his way to lunch, he recalls feeling a warmth when his hand touched the door handle, and he had a knowing that there was going to be an accident. A few minutes later when sitting at a stop sign, a fatal motorcycle accident occurred right in front of the car at that intersection. In *Blink*, journalist and best-selling author Malcolm Gladwell shares a story about Getty Museum art experts knowing that the *kouros* was a fake.[428] The experts said that it was the feeling of thousands of humming birds popping in and out of their minds, accompanied by an immense rush of previous thoughts that led them to predict the statue's forgery.

Synchronicity

Synchronicities are another avenue of revealed intuition. This is such an interesting concept that we're going to spend a few minutes exploring it. Synchronicities, which are almost always beneficial, while not a prerequisite for creativity *can play an important role in the creative process*. For example, Lachman recognizes synchronicities as "a kind of nudge or gentle push to move in the right direction, or an acknowledgement that I am already doing so." And he adds, "… they tend to happen more when we are optimistic and positive minded,"[429] which demonstrates how the mind can affect reality.

Synchronicities can be thought of as coincidences of events that seem related, yet with no obvious connection one to the other. The term synchronicity was first used in the sense of a *meaningful occurrence happening in time* in the work of the psychologist Carl Jung. In the first chapter of Carl's work titled "Synchronicity: An Acausal Connecting Principle," he notes that "modern physics has shown natural laws to be statistical truths and the principle of causality to be only relatively valid, so that at the microphysical [i.e., subatomic] level there can occur events which are acausal." [430]

Jung also questioned whether acausal events could be demonstrated at the macrophysical level. "Acausal" means that there is no cause-and-effect relationship in the present or past. However, there is the possibility of some *future* input values affecting the current result. Evidence in support of Jung's theory was provided by Rhine in experiments that revealed statistically significant correlations between events even though there was no causal relationships between those events. Jung saw the synchronicity principle—that a meaningful coincidence is connected by simultaneity and meaning—as "the absolute rule in all cases where an inner event occurs simultaneously with an outside one."[431] The conclusion by Jung was that *time and space become relative under certain conditions, and events appear to be transcended.*

An early researcher looking into the nature of life's coincidences was Paul Kammerer, an Australian biologist who investigated coincidences and the unexplained clustering of events. Over a number of years at the turn of the century, Paul collected data and looked for clusters in time through careful statistical analysis. From this work, he hypothesized that random events fall together into clusters just as asteroids drift together in space under the influence of gravity.[432]

In his book, which speaks to synchronicity as the *bridge between matter and mind*, holistic physicist Francis David Peat suggests that synchronicity "arises out of the underlying patterns of the Universe rather than through a causality of pushes and pulls that we normally associate with events in nature."[433] This reflects the acausal principle of Jung, which suggests that there are inherited characteristics in the brain prefigured by evolution linking the individual with the history of the species. Never before a part of the consciousness of the individual, the collective unconscious "is that portion of the psyche which can be differentiated from the personal unconscious by the fact that its existence is not dependent upon personal experience."[434]

This is also the causal connection proposed in the Pauli principle. Wolfgang Pauli, a physicist and early contributor to the field of quantum mechanics, is best known for his exclusion principle, which complements Werner Heisenberg's quantum mechanics. Pauli argued that at the quantum level nature engages in an abstract dance—with electrons, protons, neutrons and neutrinos engaging in an antisymmetric dance and mesons and photons of light engaging in a symmetric dance, keeping particles of the same energy apart from each other. This is not the result of force or any specific act of causality, "rather it arises out of the ... abstract movement of the particles as a whole."[435]

Certainly, a causal explanation can be argued for all events and behaviors, and biological connections can be made as well. So, while causality certainly has a role to play, *it is only part of the picture*. For example, in the 18th century, David Hume concluded that causality could not be placed on a strictly logical footing, that is, because A follows B in one instance or in all similar instances of which we are aware, this does not mean that A will *always* follow B. He called this belief in causality a habit of the mind based on repeated historical precedent. "We have no other notion of cause and effect, but that of certain objects, which have been always conjoined together ... We cannot penetrate into the reason of the conjunction."[436]

While agreeing that when forces are well defined and time flows freely the concept of causality does not present problems, this is not the case as complexity increases. "As science probes deeper into the universe of internal flows and dynamic unfoldings, of subtle influences and intersecting time scales, then causal chains can no longer be analyzed and reduced to linear connections of individual events so that the very concept of causality begins to lose its power."[437]

Since mental events are not dependent on causality, this is where synchronicities can bridge the gap between matter and mind. Indeed, the human mind is an associative patterner, continuously creating knowledge for the moment at hand, triggered by internal and external stimuli yet not necessarily part of a linear chain of causality. We as humans are engaged in a continuous process of unfolding patterns.

<<<<<<<>>>>>>>

INSIGHT: **While causality certainly has a role to play, it is only part of the picture. This is where synchronicities can bridge the gap between mind and matter.**

<<<<<<<>>>>>>>

From complexity theory we understand that emergence is a global property of a complex system that results from the interactions and relationships among its agents, and between the agents and their environment. In this case, the agents we're thinking about are people. Systems can also generate responses that are not proportional to the action taken. We say a system possesses nonlinearity when a small action may generate a very large outcome, or a large action may have very little effect on the system. Further, meaningful patterns can emerge from an instable and chaotic system. These unpredicted, unexpected, unplanned events or coincidences often trigger new ideas and perspectives which fuel creativity.

When coupled with interoperability (the ability to work together) and orchestration of means (the ability to act in concert in a timely manner), self-synchronization, whether applied to an individual or a larger group, is consistent with the definition of intelligent activity. Self-synchronization is the self-arrangement of actions in time, space, and purpose to produce maximum relative effect at a decisive place and time. For example, the tenets in order to achieve self-synchronized forces and actions in Network Centric Warfare are defined as: (1) a clear and consistent understanding of command intent; (2) high quality information and shared situational awareness; (3) competence at all levels of the force; and (4) trust in the information, subordinates, superiors, peers, and equipment.[438] In other words, *self-synchronization is dependent on measures that guide but do not dictate details*.

From another frame of reference, American systems scientist Peter Senge and his colleagues say that perhaps "synchronicity is simply what it feels like, from our personal vantage point, to be part of a field knowing itself and to be taking action informed by the whole."[439] And in this informing, there are strong emotional resonances that occur, which can stimulate creativity. Rupert Sheldrake, cell biologist and physiologist, asserts that this is not extraordinary, but rather that synchronicity is a natural feature of a living system.[440] From the viewpoint of experience over our collective years of life, we agree.

<<<<<<<>>>>>>>

INSIGHT: **Synchronicity is a natural feature of a living system.**

<<<<<<<>>>>>>>

Intuition is strengthened by synchronicity, which helps make connections between seemingly unrelated things, introducing a perspective and level of depth that may not have otherwise been possible. While intuition can certainly take the form of a day vision, a dream, or actually hearing a voice that conveys information you need or an idea for you to pursue, the information obtained through these more complete forms are more appropriately called revelatory knowledge. Note that revealed intuition, a form of knowing that has no traceable roots, can never be validated initially and must be self-authenticating. "It can only prove its worth over time based on the lasting quality and the integrity of its message."[441] As with experiential knowledge, it will evolve over time as an individual increases his understanding and expands his consciousness.

Mirror Neurons

Another form of revealed intuition can be explained through our growing understanding of mirror neurons, a more recently discovered phenomenon in the brain relating to the ease and speed with which we understand simple actions. While mirror neurons were previously introduced, we're going to dig a bit deeper. Research on experiments with Macaque monkeys that began in the early 1990s indicated that the activation of subsets of neurons in brain-motor areas appeared to *represent actions*. The initial experiments had one monkey grasp an object (an orange) while the experimenters monitored what went on inside an observer monkey's brain. Over the past 10 years many variations of this have verified that *an observer's neurons fire (or mirror) the actor's neurons*. Testing has moved from monkeys to great apes to humans. Non-invasive measurement techniques have enabled the experiments on humans to be greatly expanded.

These measurements have included mirror neurons in humans located in the frontal lobe and in the parietal lobe, which include the Broca's area, a key area for human language.[442] Using fMRI, emotional mirrors have been discovered by "feeling disgust activated in similar parts of the brain when human volunteers experienced the emotion while smelling a disgusting odor or when the same subjects watched a film clip of someone else disgusted."[443]

As semantic scholar Giacomo Rizzolatti describes, "Subsets of neurons in human and monkey brains respond when an individual performs certain actions and also when the subject observes others performing the same movements."[444] In other words, *the same neurons fire in the brain of an observer as fire in the individual performing an action*. These neurons provide an internal experience that replicates another's experience, thereby experiencing another individual's act, intentions, and/or emotions. These researchers also found that the mirror neuron system responded to the intentional component of an action as well as the action itself.

Exploring this idea further, Marco Iacoboni, behavioral scientist and psychiatrist, proposes that mirror neurons facilitate the direct and immediate comprehension of another's behavior without going through complex cognitive processes. This makes the learning process more efficient because it can instantly transfer not only visuals but emotions and intentions as well. And since the mind is an associative patterner, this new learning is associated with past learning and experiences, widening and deepening the potential for bisociation of separate conceptual patterns fueling the emergence of Innovative Creativity.

Mirror neurons also serve as a means of learning through imitation, which is "a very important means by which we learn and transmit skills, language and culture."[445] Often, a significant part of learning requires good social communication, which includes parity and direct comprehension. Parity indicates that the meaning within the message is similar for both the sender and the receiver. Direct comprehension means that no previous agreement between individuals is needed for them to understand each other. From the neuroscience perspective, both of these aspects of communication seem to be inherent in the neural organization of individuals.[446]

The question becomes how this phenomenon impacts revealed intuition. One answer is that it serves to explain how actionable tacit knowledge can be transferred between individuals, and the potential of mimicry with no idea of where such knowledge came from. Note that the capacity to re-create feelings, perspectives, and empathy with people by reliving their experiences can greatly aid us in cooperative and collaborative endeavors.

Specific neuroscience findings from MQI research related to mirror neurons that could potentially influence experiential learning as revealed knowledge include: (1) cognitive mimicry that transfers active behavior and other cultural norms; (2) rapid transfer of information that bypasses cognition; (3) neurons create the same patterns when we see something as when we do it; (4) what we see we become ready to do; and (5) mirror neurons facilitate neural resonance between observed actions and executing actions.[447] Recognizing that no two people are, or ever will be, identical, it follows that levels of sensitivity to the energies of others and energies of the field, as well as the processing of those energies through the senses, are different.

Earned and Revealed Can Work Together

While for the sake of discussion and developing understanding we have addressed earned intuition and revealed intuition as separate things, since intuition is by its very nature primarily tacit, it is difficult to differentiate the two in terms of their source. Further, the two have the potential to work together.

Our intuitive tacit knowledge—along with our embodied, affective and spiritual tacit knowledge—is working for us 24/7, energetically on call when triggered by an internal or external stimulus, including needs, desires, opportunities, and what often appears as random bisociations. While intuitive tacit knowledge is described as a *sense* of knowing coming from inside an individual that may influence decisions and actions, remember, the decision-maker or actor cannot explain how or why the action taken is the right one.

<<<<<<<>>>>>>>

INSIGHT: **Our intuitive tacit knowledge is working for us 24/7, energetically on call when triggered by an internal or external stimulus.**

<<<<<<<>>>>>>>

Neuroscientist Antonio Damasio's description of intuition as "the mysterious mechanism by which we arrive at the solution of a problem without *reasoning* toward it"[448] used the term "mechanism". But today we understand intuition isn't really a "mechanism" but the *living* mind/brain. The unconscious works around the clock with a processing capability many times greater than the processing that occurs at the conscious level. But in order to use it fully, *we must first be able to recognize its messaging system.*

As has been forwarded, the sense of knowing can occur not only by tapping into the tacit knowledges acquired and connected during the life experience, but also by tapping into the larger field of which we are a part and, consistent with our earlier discussion, connecting with ideas with which we resonate. We expand on this below.

From the viewpoint of the human, we now bring into the conversation a fourth plane that is available to those who develop extraordinary creativity. While we will refer to this fourth plane as the intuitional plane, through connection to the superconscious it offers connectivity to higher intuitive thought, which includes expanded spiritual thought. See Figure 17.

Note that spiritual energy is available through all the planes regularly utilized by the human, that is, the physical, emotional and mental planes (we move, we feel, we think). Recall that "spiritual" tacit knowledge is described in terms of knowledge based on matters of the soul, with "soul" representing the animating principles of human life in terms of thought and action, specifically focused on its moral aspects, the emotional part of human nature, and higher development of the mental faculties. As we navigate the challenges of these planes, the spiritual is always available as a counterbalance so that we stay on track in our search for higher truths and expanded consciousness.

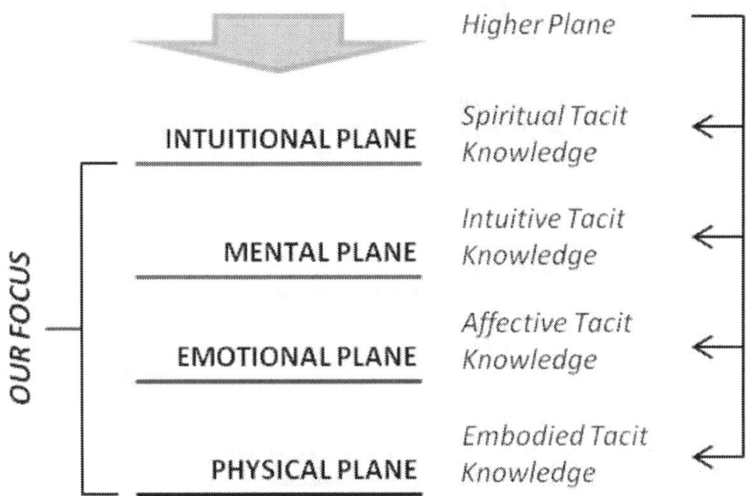

Figure 22. *From a mental plane focus we can access intuitive tacit knowledge embedded in the subconscious and that which is accessible through the larger field of the superconscious, which is spiritual in nature.*

We now move into a third related topic regarding intuition, that of "controlled intuition".

Chapter 12
Controlled Intuition

The good news is that in the human journey of growth there are unending possibilities, and one of those possibilities is controlled intuition, *the ability to tap at will into the intuitional plane at will.* You can turn intuitive thought on and off, just as you can turn conscious mental thought on and off, although admittedly *that* can prove difficult.

The first step to turning on intuitional thought is to **know that it can be done** and recognizing that *we are the master of our thoughts*. Second, is to **set the intent, then quiet the mind, and listen to our self.** Quieting the mind can be in the form of meditation, brain wave entrainment and re-wiring, biofeedback, sensory perception exercises, conscious dreaming, reciting a mantra, paying more attention to synchronicities, entering the flow state, or through deep breathing. (See Exercise 4 in Chapter 3: *Quieting the Mind*.)

<<<<<<<>>>>>>>

INSIGHT: **In the human journey of growth there are unending possibilities, and one of those possibilities is the ability to tap at will into the intuitional plane.**

<<<<<<<>>>>>>>

One tool that is quite easy to use, especially when it is difficult to quiet the mind with meditation, is to REDIRECT the mind with a mantra or song that is uplifting and shifts us into the vibration of love or reverence. There are two reasons this approach is so effective. First, the best process for "letting go" is inattention by diverting the flow of your thought, and *the very best way to avoid attending to some memory is to have a stronger, more significant memory replace it.* Second, music and the human mind have a unique relationship, with neuroscience findings showing that "all of us have a biologic guarantee of musicianship, the capacity to respond to and participate in the music of our environment."[449]

* * * * *

EXERCISE 15: *Redirecting the Mind*

This is a tool for stopping a negative thought pattern's neural firing in the moment and redirecting it to a more positive one.

STEP (1) Identify a mantra or song that is uplifting and shifts you into the vibration of love or reverence. If you have a religious belief (for example, as a Christian) this could be the Lord's Prayer or a church hymn that lifts your spirit and is easily remembered. For example, one author's partner David discovered that he always whistled the tune "Amazing Grace" in times of stress. The words that run through his head as he whistles are: "Amazing grace! How sweet the sound, that saved a wretch like me! I once was lost, but now am found, was blind, but now I see." One or two verses of whistling and he literally felt stress relief! Regardless of an individual's belief set, the concept of living in grace—with grace representing beauty, kindness and mercy—enables the perception of a positive learning experience. Eastern mantras such as the *Ohm Mani Padme Hum* serve this purpose, as does the heart sutra mantra of *Gate' Gate' Paragate Parasam Gate' Bodhi Svaha*. Just about every spiritual tradition has good options to draw from. And if an individual is more secular in nature, since we seem to be hard-wired for music, there are most likely favorite songs to be found in memory that catch hold of the mind and uplift.

STEP (2) Whenever you catch your thoughts or emotions spinning in a negative direction, make a ritual out of repeating the mantra, prayer or song to yourself over and over as many times and as often as needed until you feel your state of being shift into a more positive state.

NOTE: Even if you have not been aware of it, you may discover that you have unconsciously been using this tool throughout your life!

* * * * *

While the brain may have palpable limits, human consciousness is not bound by the body. The best way to start enhancement of the mind/brain is different for different people. However, a common limitation is the focus on the "how" instead of the what and why. When we limit ourselves by thinking about those things for which we can see a clear path from here to there (the "how") then we are *building our future on patterns of the past.* The "past" in this context includes what we have previously experienced and what we already "know" such that we are not allowing the future to emerge anew in the now, which is necessary in the continuously changing and challenging world of today. In the quantum field, the only limits are those we set upon ourselves, howbeit the necessity that we stay within the sphere of our values and are heading the direction we desire and choose to head.

In order to dismiss the negative limits we set for ourselves, we must first be aware that we are doing so. Start with awareness of when you are automatically negating an intuitive thought that surfaces in your mind. Next is making the conscious decision to catch yourself in such an act of negating "irrational thoughts" and suspending your doubt/disbelief in order to give those thoughts a try, so long as there is no harm to yourself or others in following the thought. This process helps you to start validating your intuitive thoughts and begin to trust them more. It also breaks the pattern of automatically negating what seems illogical.

Note that when we talk about controlled intuition, the "control" here refers to the ability to connect to the intuitional plane at will. This does not insinuate controlling the *content* of that thought. Most people assume that in order to create you have to control what you create. This need to control is an illusion, and, in this context, *the need to create is not dependent upon the need to control*.

<<<<<<<>>>>>>>

INSIGHT: **Controlled intuition refers to the ability to connect to the intuitional plane at will; it does not insinuate controlling the content of that thought.**

<<<<<<<>>>>>>>

Prerequisites for Controlled Intuition

There are several prerequisites for developing controlled intuition. How to begin has been the subject of the above paragraphs, that is, clearing the mind, and opening and becoming comfortable with the inner realms of consciousness, a field of which you are a part. This is not always as easy as it sounds. We have programmed ourselves to focus on a perceived external physical reality, which is the world in which we are experiencing life—interacting, learning and expanding. While the inner realms have always been available to us, it is now as a humanity in the times we find ourselves in that we are ready to become the fullness of who we are. It is time to rediscover the inner realms, and open and strengthen our connections to the field of consciousness.

There are several other pre-requisites. First, you must have developed—and use—your lower mental mind in a balanced way. This balance refers to how your learning is acted upon in service to others, the larger ecosystem of humanity, and the world at large.

<<<<<<<>>>>>>>

INSIGHT: **A first step toward controlled intuition is rediscovering the fullness of who we are, and opening and strengthening our connections to the field of consciousness.**

<<<<<<<>>>>>>>

Second, you must have developed your upper mental mind, that is, *developed conceptual thinking* and be *ever seeking a higher level of truth* in your thinking. Recall that lower mental thinking is based on logic and cause-and-effect relationships. When we have lived experience, we begin to recognize patterns, and that is when we begin to expand. When we use both lower and higher mental thought, the pragmatic and the conceptual, fully recognizing their relationships, not only is there deeper understanding but there is greater potential for Innovative Creativity. Remember, the mental faculties are in service to the intuitional.

Third, you must have deepened your connections with others. This occurs as we learn to co-evolve with our environment, which requires a deeper understanding of ourselves as well as developing an empathy for others, understanding why and how they feel and act. As we continue expanding, we begin to recognize the higher ecosystem of which we are a part, regardless of how each of us describes that ecosystem. With this recognition of interconnectedness, of Oneness, empathy expands to compassion. If these four aspects sound familiar, they are the same conditions that move us toward wisdom, manifesting in intelligent activity! This is no coincidence.

Now, bring together the focus from your emotional plane, which tells you how you *feel* about a situation, and the mental plane, which tells you what you and others *think* about a situation, and helps you think in structured, causal logic and, as you expand your faculties, in concepts. Think of your mind as providing the gas for your thought, pulling information from the brain, a magnificent storage and information processing device.[450] The intent is to know the past, present, and future, and determine the causes of things you are thinking about, that is, *why* something is happening, and *what* you want to happen next.

When an individual *can think through all three planes*—physical, emotional and mental—making sure that they are in balance, that is, neither physical nor mental wants or emotions separately driving thought—*that individual can develop controlled intuition.*

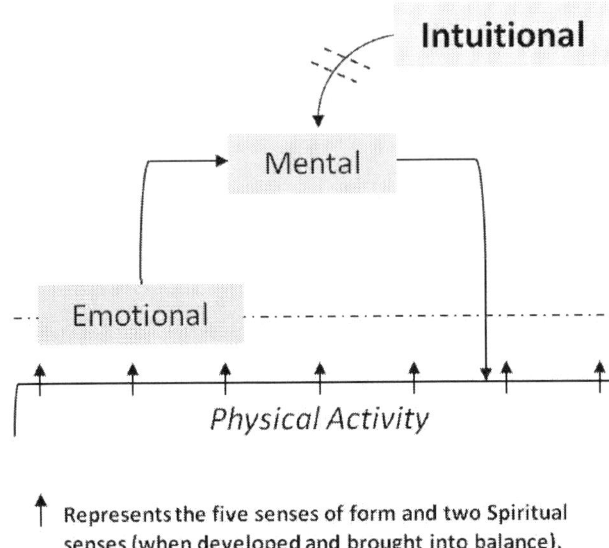

Figure 23. *When the mental mind is used in a balanced way in service to others so that they may serve others (sending energy outwards), controlled intuition becomes available.*

While the prerequisites are essential, there are other, more complex ways of tapping into the intuitional plane. One of these, the *I Ching*, also called *The Book of Change* and considered a fundamental text of the Chinese culture, is arguably one of the oldest recorded works in existence. It represents "a way of knowing common to both magical or pre-technological cultures and to the world we contact each night in dreams."[451]

The *I Ching*

While some historians date its origins back as far as 5,000 years, the most widely-accepted origin connects the *I Ching* with Fu His, a Chinese emperor circa 2582 BC. Fu His contemplated "the shapes of heaven, the patterns of the Earth, bird and animal markings and the movements of his body and soul."[452] Through close association with and observation of the tortoise, he discovered a perfect mathematical model emerging from the broken and unbroken lines of the tortoise shell. These observations led to development of eight trigrams that he used to symbolize the eight natural elements: *Heaven, Earth, Water, Fire, Thunder, Mountains, Wind, and Lakes*. Other teachers contributed their thought, with the trigrams eventually yielding 64 hexagrams. These symbols were passed from generation to generation as a tool for addressing difficult situations, especially those situations emotionally charged, where rational knowledge does not work and yet we must make decisions and act on those decisions.

The *I Ching* approach *helps us create an imaginative space*, an opening to tap into our own unconscious. Coming to light through a particular situation with a specific context, the symbols help us experience the situation differently in order to understand the inner forces at play and how they are affecting us and shaping the situation. Note that the *I Ching* is built on the understanding that knowledge is situation dependent and context sensitive. Further, consistent with our understanding of knowledge, the *I Ching* does not advocate a passive approach to life, rather, it is about *action and reaction*, the essence of continual change.[453] The *I Ching* supports the search for Truth (a larger truth), zooming in on the possible outcomes of decisions and actions. The world of *I Ching* is simultaneously an intellectual world with its own logic and boundaries *and* a mystical experience. While the system itself is based on mental development of mathematical formulas emerging from nature, the result of the *I Ching* process is an intuitive clarity called *shen ming* or *the light of the gods.*[454]

Interestingly, some of the greatest Western philosophers have honored the potential of the *I Ching*. For example, Confucius once said, "If some years were added to my life, I would give fifty to the study of the *Yi* (*I Ching*) and might then escape falling into great errors."[455] And, as Carl Jung described, "The *I Ching* does not offer itself with proofs and results; it does not vault itself, nor is it easy to approach. Like a part of nature, it waits until it is discovered."[456] For those interested in exploring this tool of change, this door to ideas, a short but excellent treatment of application is provided by translator Steven Karcher. As Karcher begins his explanation, "The modern world thinks that change is objective and predictable. We use statistics and norms to describe it, and pretend it is the same for everyone. The old world saw things differently … This symbolic approach can help you deal with the changes in your life."[457]

The Wisdom of Lao Tzu

A second ancient text, the *Tao Te Ching*, a book of around 5,000 words written over 2500 years ago, is perhaps the most translated classic next to the Bible. It has been explored and embraced by physicists, psychologists and business leaders for its potential to influence society. Lao Tzu is represented as a gifted scholar who lived in China during the Chou Dynasty and worked as the Custodian of the Imperial Archives. The Chou Dynasty was an era where hostile political actions and counter-actions spiraled out of control, much like today. It was Yin His, then Keeper of the Gate, later to become the Emperor of China, and, as noted above, today remembered as originator of the *I Ching*, who encouraged Lao Tzu to write down what he had learned for the enlightenment of those who were in a position to guide others, that is, princes, politicians, employers, and educators.[458]

Writing for these leaders, Lao Tzu urges them to discover themselves through fully sensing the world around them and reflecting deeply to develop their personal intuitive power. This personal power, or *Te*, is built up through an awareness and knowledge of the physical laws "as they operate both in the Universe and in the minds of others (*Tao*)."[459] Without using force, this power is then used to create and direct events *through attitude instead of action*, leading by guiding rather than ordering or directing, and managing people by letting them act on you instead of you acting on them.

<<<<<<<>>>>>>>

INSIGHT: **Without using force, this power is used to create and direct events through attitude instead of action, leading by guiding rather than ordering or directing, and managing people by letting them act on you instead of you acting on them.**

<<<<<<<>>>>>>>

As can be seen, Lao Tzu believed in methods that did not create resistance (force) or lead to counter-reactions. He believed that through observing the laws of nature we could understand the way matter and energy function in the Universe and *become one with that approach to creation*. As is translated: "[Lao Tzu] realized that excessive force in a particular direction tends to trigger the growth of an opposing force, and that therefore the use of force cannot be the basis for establishing a strong and lasting social foundation … He realized that the physical laws of the Universe directly affect the ways that individuals tend to behave and societies tend to evolve, and that to comprehend these laws could give a leader the power (*Te*) to bring harmony to the world."[460] Excessive force exerted in a specific direction triggers opposing forces. This is a lesson we are still learning today. (See the Conscious Look Book on *Engaging Forces*.[461])

Lao Tzu challenges us as thought leaders and creators to develop an intellectual independence, that is, to *trust our own perceptions and rely on our inspirations and instincts* (our intuition), and to influence others using nature as our pattern. As Lao Tuz puts it:

> Evolved Individuals hold to the *Tao*,
> And regard the world as their Pattern.

They do not display themselves;
Therefore, they are illuminated.
They do not define themselves;
Therefore, they are distinguished.
They do not make claims;
Therefore, they are credited.
They do not boast;
Therefore, they advance.

Since, indeed, they do not compete,
The world cannot compete with them.[462]

When individuals are (a) focused on a conceptual thought, (b) trying to determine the level of truth in that concept in service to a greater good, and (c) interacting with others who are operating at a similar level of consciousness to do so, they are opening to the uncontrolled flooding of dozens to thousands or more concepts revolving around the area of focus. *The process is both instantaneous and effortless*.

In both your personal experience and group events, note when several of the prerequisites for developing controlled intuition discussed above are present. As a group continues to work together, open to and sharing the new thoughts of each, the flooding of new ideas continues. When this occurs, *lock in the feelings that accompany this experience*. Given similar circumstances and intent, the memory of these feelings can help trigger a reoccurrence of this experience, moving you into the realm of controlled intuition.

As you participate repeatedly in this process, *creating more whole thought* (concepts with a high level of truth linking events and concepts) and sharing and using what is intuited to the benefit of others, the mental senses increase such that you have a greater capability to understand the concepts that are flooding in. As you reach the point of controlled intuition, that is, tapping into the intuitional plane at will, choosing new thought instantly without effort, you are able to process the incoming information at a rate of speed which helps to unify your senses.[463] As this becomes part of your nature, you more easily identify truth, with your thinking aligning with higher and higher levels of truth.

Chapter 13
The Creative Leap

As part of the Intelligent Social Change Journey, understanding and applying the three prerequisites of self in preparation for controlled intuition has begun the process of preparing us to make a creative leap, which changes our direction and the frequency of our energy flows. As a reiteration, these prerequisites of self include: (1) rediscovering the fullness of who we are, and opening and strengthening our connections to the field of consciousness; (2) achieving balanced lower mental thought, focused on service to others; (3) developing higher mental thought, conceptual thinking and the search for truth; and (4) deepening our connections with others. With this preparation, there is the opportunity to expand our creative capacity, and that is the subject of this chapter.

It should be clear by now that experience and learning (the creation of knowledge) provide the fodder for human creativity. Nonetheless, there are a number of specific ways to expand our creative capacity. While these have been teased throughout this book, we will focus and briefly discuss four of these: freedom of thought and self-expression; embracing the mythic worldview; bringing the past and future together to illuminate the present; and knowledge sharing, that is, streaming our thoughts outward.

Freedom of Thought and Self-Expression

Freedom and choice are synonymous. An example is the emergent concept of neo-management control, which posits that management through individual freedom is a defining element of the 21st century workforce.[464] This is because of the growing recognition of *the value of innovation, which emerges from creativity and self-expression.* We specifically focus here on freedom of thought, which enables the diversity necessary for continuously expanding our world. An extensive treatment of the freedoms related to the creation of knowledge and tied to creativity and innovation can be found in the book by

Alex Bennet and Robert Turner: *Reblooming the Knowledge Movement: The Democratization of Organizations*.[465]

When discussing this concept with her partner, one of the authors asked: How do you know your thinking is free? Even with the awareness that we have mental models, and even if we periodically engage in self-reflection, self-knowledge is difficult to achieve. We all have limits in terms of mental models and personal paradigms, and certain things that we believe which seem to surface again and again, sometimes making it difficult to accept new ideas.

Perhaps the greatest tool we have in this regard is openness to learning, an openness provided through humility. *The simple and profound conscious choice of humility provides an opportunity to ensure freedom of thought*. As introduced in Chapter 1, in taking this approach, you assume the ideas of the "other" are right and reflect on these ideas from that perspective, seeking truth. When contrasted with ego ("I am right; you are wrong") and arrogance ("I am right; you are wrong; and I don't care what you think"), it is clear that utilizing the tool of humility moves the individual beyond embedded mindsets, providing an opening for learning from others. This benefit occurs for us as well as the others with whom we share. Openness to the thoughts of others allows us to be freer in *our* thinking, thus increasing our contribution to the diversity of thought and increasing the potential for the bisociation of ideas.

<<<<<<<>>>>>>>

INSIGHT: **The simple and profound conscious choice of humility provides an opportunity to ensure freedom of thought.**

<<<<<<<>>>>>>>

Embracing the Mythic Worldview

The mythic worldview, a way of appreciating life and creation as a connected whole, is rooted in nature, beauty, and community. Somewhat ironically, mythical thought helps us logically understand reality based on symbolism and patterns emerging from myths, the metaphorical use of narrative. This approach to thinking heavily diverges from the scientific approach, which is based on empirical evidence in an attempt to develop universal explanations of events. Conversely, mythical thought, which has had a strong influence on society in the past, continues to convey cultural values and provide inspiration for creative thinking.

This worldview—which sees a unity encompassing the universe and all life—originated throughout Mesoamerica with three major themes: (1) the creation of the world for people, (2) development of the world, and (3) renewal of its resources, thus focusing on relationships among people, the planet on which they live, and the larger cosmos.

While attention to the mythic worldview of reality diminished with the accelerated mental development spurred on by the focus on science and an exponential expansion of technological development, which has come up several times in this book, the importance of mythical thinking to the creative mind is beginning to be recognized. As leadership educator Michael Jones so eloquently describes:

> *Our current worldviews are mostly formed through the lenses of politics and power, strategy and structure, human assets and development. But there is a fresh lens emerging, a narrative of aliveness that taps into the ancient wisdom of our mythic imagination. As this new narrative—which is rooted in nature, art and community—begins to inspire our thoughts and ideas, our world may be truly transformed.*[466]

The mythic reality is a combination of beliefs in free will and a monistic view of the universe. The behaviors of someone with this world view might seem unreal, yet monistic free will is necessary to understand the creation and evolution of systems as well as the behavior of great leaders in nearly every field of human endeavor. It is the mythic world view that is the creator of symbols and ideas which are *not limited by what is already present*.[467] We briefly explore this worldview through the eyes of representative authors who have embraced and explored the mythic world view.

From Will McWhinney: "If I were to speak from the mythic view, I would say (to myself): 'All the world is my creation; you, my readers, are my creation; I people the world, I create its phenomena, and I assign it in time and locate it in space—which themselves are given meaning by my thought.'"[468] In other words, causality is will and intentionality, and I am totally responsible for the world I have created and in which I exist.

From Francis Bradley: "I cannot transcend experience and experience is *my* experience. From this it follows that nothing beyond myself exists; for what is experienced is the [self's] state."[469] Personal experience and creation are "indistinguishable"; everything exists because we give it meaning through volition. That which is, is what I have created.

From Lawrence LeShan: "Nothing is arbitrary; nothing occurs by chance. Everything has meaning and is charged with implications and power. Things, however, may look arbitrary because it can be hard to trace the connections between the various parts of a unity as these connections, from the sensory viewpoint, range over objective and subjective, past and future, things and symbols, until they come to that one arbitrary act of will underlying the whole thing that neither needs explaining nor is explainable."[470]

From James Carse: "The mythic reality is a world of story in which we assign and play a role, both created and to be created. Part factual and part fiction, whole civilizations arise from stories—and can rise from nothing else … Myths, told for their own sake, are not stories that have meanings, **but stories that give meanings**" [emphasis added].[471] Carse describes the mythic as an infinite play with no scripted conclusion, and the infinite player in this reality is neither old nor young, for time doesn't pass and each moment of time is another beginning, living in eternal birth. Work is not to fill time, but to put time into play, with freedom a function of time and the future full of possibility.[472]

The tale of *Don Quixote* written by Unamuno reflects the power of the mythic worldview. As Unamuno writes,

> *His mind bloomed in the most far-fetched and beautiful fantasies, and he believed to be fact what was merely beautiful. He believed it with such a lively faith, with the faith which engenders works, that he decided to put into practice what his folly suggested, and by sheer belief in it he made it true.*[473]

And again, as the tale nears its end, Unamuno reminds us of the importance of belief and will in this way of being.

> *That's the way, My Lord Don Quoixote, that is the way of naked courage, insisting aloud and in the sight of all, defending one's claims with one's life; that is the way of creating any and all truth. The more one believes in a thing, the truer it is believed, and it is not intelligence, but will, which imposes the truth.*[474]

As can be seen, the mythic reality is the realm of free-will, without limitation, while embracing that we are all part of a larger quantum field, that is, *Oneness with individuated volition*. Interestingly, the power of myth in the planning process has long been acknowledged. Planning is a learning process with two parts: the creation of myths about social realities and the process of emergence.[475] Our creative imagination plays a large role in this.

Bringing the Past and Future Together to Illuminate the Present

As McWhinney forwards, in the mythic world view the phenomena that is created is assigned in time and located in space.[476] There is a direct relationship between maturity and the unit of time consciousness in any given intellect. Whether the time unit being considered is a day, a year, or a longer period, inevitably it becomes the criterion by which the conscious self evaluates the circumstances of life, and by which the conceiving intellect measures and evaluates its temporal existence.[477] To become mature is to live more intensely in the present while at the same time *escaping the limitations of the present*. Founded on past experience, the plans of maturity are coming into being in the present in such a manner as to *enhance the value of the future*.

<<<<<<<>>>>>>>

INSIGHT: **Time is the criterion by which the conscious self evaluates the circumstances of life, and by which the conceiving intellect measures and evaluates its temporal existence.**

<<<<<<<>>>>>>>

We look to *Urantia* to help us better understand this concept: *The maturity of the developing self brings the past and future together to illuminate the true meaning of the present*.[478] For example, an entrepreneur combines the knowledge and capabilities he has gained from the past with the vision he has of the future to make meaningful decisions in the present. *As the self matures, it reaches further and further back into the past for experience, while its wisdom seeks to penetrate deeper and deeper into the unknown future.* As the conceiving self (you as you engage your creative mind) extends this reach ever further into both the past and the future, so does judgment become less and less dependent on the momentary present. In this way, the decision-action loop begins to escape the fetters of the moving present—perceived roadblocks in the present due to current perceived limitations—and takes on aspects of past-future significance. As introduced earlier, one way of perceiving this is to focus on the "what" and "why" (which represent a future desired state and experience from the past) and let go of the "how" such that your decisions are not impacted by perceived limitations of the present.

<<<<<<<>>>>>>>

INSIGHT: **As creative self extends its reach ever further into both the past and future, so does judgment become less and less dependent on the momentary present**.

<<<<<<<>>>>>>>

This process enables the individual to see the wholeness of events spanning time. For example, when the time unit of immaturity concentrates meaning-value into the present moment, it divorces the present of its true relationship to that which is not-present, that is, the past-future. When the time unit of maturity is proportioned, it reveals the co-ordinate relationship of past-present-future such that the self begins to gain insight into the wholeness of events, even to the point that the individual "begins to view the landscape of time from the panoramic perspective of broadened horizons, begins perhaps to suspect the non-beginning, non-ending eternal continuum, the fragments of which are called time."[479]

If you didn't understand this the first time you read it, go back and read it again. This is a REALLY important point. It's only when we can let go of our limitations perceived in the present (for example, the "how" we're going to do something) that we can direct the power of our thought to that which we desire of the future, that unique and creative idea that may just make a LARGE difference in the world!

Knowledge Sharing, Streaming Our Thoughts Outward

Streaming our thoughts outward can be described in terms of knowledge sharing, cooperation and collaboration, or social knowledge, and, as a result, our own learning and expanding. This was introduced in Chapter 7; see also Figure 8. We now understand from neuroscience findings that the mind is an associative patterner, recreating knowledge for the moment at hand. Simultaneously, we understand that creativity is the bisociation of two or more ideas to create a new idea or apply an idea in a new context. Thus, *there is a multiplier effect of ideas as they are shared*. The more we share and participate in cooperative and collaborative experiences, the more opportunity for the bisociation of ideas.

Forwarded in *Reblooming the Knowledge Movement*,[480] as the necessity for knowledge sharing in organizations became more fully recognized, along with that recognition came awareness of knowledge withholding, hoarding, and hiding as non-sharing behaviors. Yang, Ribière and Bennet convey—based on the findings of dozens of organizational research studies from 2014 through 2019—that this behavior

> … not only results in harmed interpersonal relationships, reduced individual creative performance, and decreased innovative work behavior, but also jeopardizes team viability, team creativity, and project team performance, while encouraging organizational deviance.[481]

Organizational culture plays a prominent role in mitigating knowledge hiding since employees generally tend to comply with organizational norms and expectations. Building a positive and open environment leads to collaboration and knowledge sharing, which helps remove the organizational foundation of knowledge hiding, thus limiting it.[482]

As a humanity, we are action-oriented and knowledge-driven. To wax eloquent, and influenced because MQI is situated in the middle of the beautiful Allegheny Mountains of West Virginia: *Just as a winding stream in the bowels of the mountains curves and dips through ravines and high valleys, so, too, with knowledge*. In a continuous journey towards intelligent activity, context-sensitive and situation-dependent knowledge, imperfect and incomplete, experientially engages a changing landscape in a continuous cycle of learning and expanding.

It is the context of the activity or situation at hand (need, challenge, etc.) that triggers the putting things together in an unusual way to recognize a possibility and create something that may be new and potentially useful (innovation). *We as a humanity are in a continuous cycle of knowledge creation such that every moment offers the opportunity for the emergence of new and exciting ideas, all waiting to be put in service to an interconnected world*.

When knowledge is focused inward, that is, *not* shared, it has diminishing value as others continue to connect with the ever-changing and expanding reservoir of knowledge emerging a continuous stream of new ideas. An individual with bounded knowledge has ceased learning, with, over time, that knowledge losing any value it may have had in terms of taking effective action, and thus reverting to information. This process is accompanied by a diminishing of consciousness and meaning. Physicist Niles MacFlouer emphasizes that **we can't stand on the sidelines. The greatest meaning of life comes with co-creating**.[483] When we cease co-creating, when we cease learning, we enter a downward spiral that is characterized by the loss of consciousness, the loss of meaning, and, eventually, the loss of life.

Taking the Leap

The creative leap is the result of creative imagination grounded in the bisociation of multiple points (ideas/concepts) of knowledge and knowing comprising more than half the field of thought. Now, *that* is a mouthful! Let's explore this concept a bit further. The creative leap is a combination of *conscious choice*, with connected thoughts heading the same direction, and *unconscious participation* (which would include feelings), with the leap occurring in the NOW state yet not constrained by, nor necessarily even connected to, a perceived current reality.[484] This disconnection means that the creative leap is potentially beyond current context-sensitivity and situation-dependence. This new condition *may* produce an entirely new context and situation, or be something *entirely new in a similar context and situation*. IT IS NOT DIRECTLY CONNECTED TO THE CURRENT NOW.

While the creative leap occurs through interaction with the intuitional plane, and therefore *may* be an outcome of controlled intuition, it is not controlled intuition. Remember that intuition is defined as the ability to determine the causes of any and all effects, a higher awareness, a deeper understanding, an immediate cognition. And "controlled intuition" is described as the ability to tap into the intuitional plane at will. In terms of relationship, the creative leap is that which *may* occur when you tap into the intuitional plane, whether by conscious choice or not. See Figure 26 below.

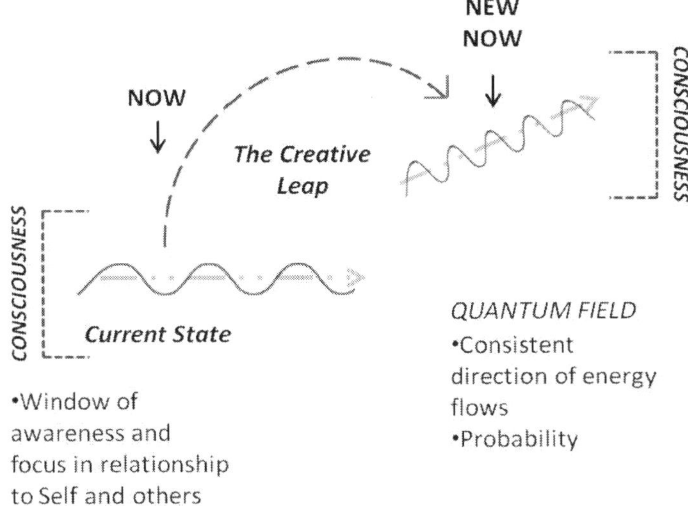

***CHARACTERISTICS**: Creative imagination;* Recognition of global Oneness; Mental in service to the intuitive; Balancing senses; Bringing together past, present and future; Knowing; Beauty; Wisdom

Figure 24. *The creative leap comes in the final phase of the Intelligent Social Change Journey (See Chapter 4)*

However, that said and remembering that development of the mental faculties is in service to the intuitive, this includes *both* controlled intuition and the creative leap. This is not a new idea. Tim Brown, the CEO and President of IDEO, historically ranked independently as one of the ten most innovative companies and the designer of such innovations as the first mouse for Apple and Palm V, understands that *intuitive leaps follow along the path of mental development*. As he says in the opening description of his book, we don't simply realize solutions; *we design them*:

> ***The myth of innovation is that brilliant ideas leap fully formed from the minds of geniuses.*** [Emphasis added] *In reality, most innovations are borne from rigor and discipline. Breakthrough ideas—whether for a new bicycle, an advertising campaign, a treatment plan for diabetes, or a program aimed at tackling the national obesity epidemic—emerge not by chance, but by studying and embracing the immediate challenges we encounter every day in our offices and homes, laboratories and hospitals, classrooms and conference rooms, and in all the spaces in between.*[485]

The visual depiction of design thinking printed on the inside cover of Tim Brown's book, *Change by Design*, is worth the purchase of the book. Embracing a human-centered approach, it graphically connects the new social contract, converting need into demand, inspiration, observation, and empathy (all of which have been introduced in this book); deep-diving and surfacing (volleying between the conscious and unconscious); thinking with our hands; building an experience culture, and so much more. The bottom line of his message is that design thinking combines the creation of elegant objects and beautifying the world around us with necessity and utility, constraint, and possibility and demand. Design thinkers combine rigorous observations of the use of spaces and objects and the services that use them, discover patterns within complexity and chaos, synthesize ideas from diverse fragments, and convert issues and problems into opportunities.[486]

Brown links design thinking to intuition. As he describes, "It is not only human-centered; it is deeply human in and of itself. Design thinking relies on our ability to be intuitive, to recognize patterns, to construct ideas that have emotional meaning as well as functionality, to express ourselves in media other than words or symbols."[487] We would also link it to the ability to synthesize and development of pattern thinking.

From the Quantum Perspective, the creative leap occurs as expanding consciousness achieves a consistency of focus, with energies in the quantum field flowing in the same direction. Thus, the creative leap "might simply be a sudden coalescence of coherence in The Field",[488] that is, *increased* thought heading the same direction. Recall that consciousness is defined as a process—a sequential set of ideas, thoughts, images, feelings and perceptions and an understanding of the connections and relationships among them that represent the sum total of who we are, what we believe, how we act and the things we do, thus fully engaging all the senses. The quantum field is a probability field; the greater the focus in a specific direction, that is, the more energy moving in a consistent direction, the greater the probability of what is in that direction occurring, yet until the instant of that leap all possibilities exist.

When we explore the past and future in the co-evolving NOW, an important aspect of our creative imagination which emerges from patterns of the past is our *assumption of continuity*. The developing mental mind is pulled into this assumption because it is consistent with mathematics, objective and logical. But this is thinking that is superseded. "Quantum physics, from its very inception, has beaten the doctrine of continuity to a pulp."[489]

Quite different than the concept of continuity, a fascinating characteristic of the quantum field is the capacity for instant change from one state to another. From the quantum viewpoint, something can go from point A to point B at the subatomic level *without ever having been anywhere in between*. This is the concept of the quantum leap—where an electron orbiting one atom jumps to another atom—that was introduced by Nobel Prize-winning physicist Niels Bohr, and the basis for what we call the creative leap. Recognizing the quantum field as a probability field, this instantaneous shift or change is unpredictable. Thus, much like intuition, the starting point of the creative leap can be described and known but the ending point of the creative leap is unknown, although it will be *in the direction of thought and energy in the field.*

The Planck constant,[490] or quantum constant, is a measure of the degree to which energy is indefinite within time or space, a measure of the effect that thought has on energy. The greater the thought, the less controlled by gravity, and the greater the potential for a creative leap to occur in the field. As soon as a field becomes greater than it is not, it is automatically re-invented. We can now begin to understand how development of the mental faculties serves the potential for a creative leap, *both in terms of direction and strength*.

Creating is a Natural State of Being

The creative leap occurs in concert with a continuous loop of creative thought moving through the four stages of creativity: preparation, incubation, illumination and verification.[491] Because we live in a changing, uncertain and complex environment, it is often difficult to trace back to the triggers or ideas that spur our creative thought, nor is it necessary to do so as we share our ideas and the next idea comes to mind.

You as a human have been participating in and preparing yourself for creativity since your inception. *Creation is an element of your natural state of being*. When creating for the benefit of others, you are sharing a part of yourself, willing to give to and serve others so they can do the same. In this mode of creation, *there are no forces pushing against you.* You are free to create. Thus, everything becomes effortless and you, and others, become more creative.

<<<<<<<>>>>>>>

INSIGHT: **When creating for the benefit of others, you are sharing a part of yourself with no forces pushing against you**.

<<<<<<<>>>>>>>

If something is forceful it is lacking in creativity. A forced field is missing the element of interactive choices, the ability within a field to produce a consistency of choices (or "will") that allows co-creation. When two or more people are working together and sharing thoughts in service to the other, or others, forces are diminished. We now have identified an important step in Wallas' preparation phase, that is, *the reduction of forces.* This is consistent with the deepening of connections with others. (See the MQI conscious look book *Possibilities that are YOU! Volume 3: Engaging Forces*.)[492]

One way to reduce forces in the midst of the creative process is through honoring mistakes. We briefly present this as a tool.

* * * * *

EXERCISE 16: *Honoring Mistakes*

Use mistakes as learning experiences. Pushing ourselves beyond our limitations opens us up to making mistakes. While few people choose to make mistakes, these mistakes nonetheless provide learning experiences, and are a way to develop humility. Here's a three-step approach to success:

STEP (1) Be as creative as possible, creating in the most effective, efficient and practical way while remaining humble. Do your research, consult with others as needed, and engage your best decision-making practices. Simultaneously, be aware that the more you create, the greater the potential that mistakes will be made. Remember that inaction, never following your creative thought, will never achieve your full capability.

STEP (2) When mistakes occur, be the first to admit/acknowledge your mistakes, and show gratitude to those who show you your mistakes.

STEP (3) After acknowledging the mistakes, try to learn from them and improve on them.

And, SIMULTANEOUSLY:

STEP (4) Do the best you can to help others to be as creative as possible. Try to help them see more creative ways.

STEP (5) When others make a mistake, help them improve without being critical of them.

STEP (6) Show gratitude to everyone who displays the behaviors described in STEPS (4) and (5) above.

* * * * *

Entering Phase 3 of the Intelligent Social Change Journey

While quantum awareness seeped into human consciousness well over a hundred years ago, the last 20 years have ushered in an explosion of quantum research and literature, *with much creative imagination at play*. Despite this flood, most people still think along the lines of slow evolution, that things are gradually developed and that big changes require big efforts. Yet even a shallow understanding of quantum field theory allows us to dismiss this learned, often culturally implanted, belief and lifestyle.

Almost everyone living today has started to "jump" in response to their thought (intent and focus/attention), if not "leap", and these jumps are moving us in unexpected directions. *The creative leap is a part of the human experience.* For example, reflect on the nexus of the pre-adolescent years and the hormonal rush introducing the physical and psychological transition into puberty. It happened in the instant; you were one thing, then you were another; all of a sudden you were different. And this amazing change is what is happening today in small things and in large things to the human race.

In her book *Jump Time*, Jean Houston, scholar, teacher and co-director of the Foundation for Mind Research, introduces the concept *jump time* as the precursor to an upcoming quantum leap for each citizen of the Earth. As she describes, we live in an amazing time "that demands that we 'Jump!' to a new dispensation of humanity."[493]

As introduced and exampled in various television shows and movies, a jump, or leap, is not gradual; you are sensing two different ways of being in the instant, the past and future, and then they are one and the future becomes the present. Thinking takes a jump (leap), from nothing to everything suddenly, and then things are different. Surprises that completely change your lives are hovering probabilities right around the corner. For example, as Alex shares,

> *I was adopted by an older couple and have lived for many years with no living parents or siblings or known extended family, although I often*

"wished" for and imagined what it might be like to have an adult sibling with whom to interact. Then, with 2016 in full swing, a 15 months younger full sister actually discovered me! Yep, we've done the DNA, and sure enough! I never even knew she existed. In these latter years, we've rapidly integrated into each other's lives, forever changing the past, present and future ... and the journey of discovery continues.

<<<<<<<>>>>>>>

INSIGHT: **A leap is not gradual; you are sensing two different ways of being in the instant, the past and future, and then there is one and the future becomes the present.**

<<<<<<<>>>>>>>

The creation of the five-book series, *The Profundity and Bifurcation of Change* published by MQIPress flowed through the creative stages of preparation, incubation, illumination and verification, with the growth and expansion of the "Intelligent Social Change Journey" supported by cognitive theory, social theory, systems and complexity theory, leadership theory, and learnings from neuroscience, psychology, cell biology and spirituality, among other fields. The preparation phase was consciously started a number of years previously, although no doubt the seeds of change were planted far earlier. The incubation phase went on for several years while other projects were focused on and created. When illumination finally came, it came quickly as a creative leap and in the form of unexpected, entangled messages, with all 36 of the original chapters "jumping around" and largely writing themselves! And then came the verification phase, where, through conversation and dialogue and focused attention, the authors ensured, aided by several committed readers, a consistency of the message and integrated examples. Ironically, the whole birthing process for all five books spanned nine months.

It is important to remember that the creative leap *can only occur when thought is focused outward and in service to others*. As you tap into the larger flow of ideas, you become extraordinarily creative, and, having achieved balanced senses, are able to move beyond the mental world into intuitional thought, the stream of creativity, when you choose to do so.

Through thought we create ourselves and the abilities we have. Energy following thought is becoming more intelligent. As we tap into the intuitional plane, we enter a new way of thinking, and creating leads to creating, which when shared becomes knowledge for others, who in turn create and share, who in turn create and share, *returned tenfold.* And the world expands. This is the growth of beauty of thought, with ever-increasing levels of truth unfolding, connecting thought to thought and field to field. In this process, creation is an ever-expanding spiral, allowing life to become more conscious and creative in new ways. *The creation of thought is the creative force of the Universe.*

Chapter 14: A Case Study

The Power of Revealed and Unveiled Knowledge in Reconstructing Local Food Systems

with Charles Dhewa

Authors' Note: This chapter is built on the research of Charles Dhewa while working with African communities. The concept of "unveiling" knowledge refers to bringing knowledge into conscious awareness and is inclusive of Earned Intuition (as introduced in Chapter 9) being shared with others. In this research, Revealed Intuition as knowledge also plays a key role. Concepts related to Innovative Creativity, discussed in detail in previous chapters, are included in brackets throughout the text. A summary of these concepts is in Chapter 15. See Appendix D for additional approaches to accessing revealed knowledge in African cultures.

In many indigenous African communities, including the Shona of Zimbabwe, knowledge has a very strong spiritual dimension through which the spiritual realm participates in the lives of the living [SPIRITUAL TACIT KNOWLEDGE] by directly informing them through dreams, signs, divination and other mystical means [REVEALED INTUITION]. This is an extension of shared belief systems and the binding force of tradition. No matter how formally-educated, many Africans consult the spiritual realm through spirit media and harmony with natural forests, among other channels through which knowledge is unveiled [MYTHIC WORLD VIEW]. In the African sense, knowledge is not only oral but also spiritual and fluid literature.

Several African communities still make sense of the world through reincarnation, spirit mediumship, extra-sensory perception and possession. These are often marginalized by western imported forms of knowledge that came to Africa as part of the colonial experience. Ignoring such knowledge explains why most development interventions have failed to make a difference in many African communities in spite of billions of dollars spent on development initiatives.

Unveiled Knowledge as an Epistemic Resource

At the time some global scholars and thought leaders are advocating for epistemic justice by addressing epistemic injustice, unveiled knowledge is gaining currency as a very powerful epistemic resource [A BALANCED STORY OF SELF] that can enable marginalized communities to reconstruct their values and food systems following decades of infiltration from external knowledge systems. Originally conceptualised by the philosopher Miranda Fricker,[494] epistemic injustice comprises unfair treatment in knowledge-related and communicative practices in which the voices, experiences and problems of marginalised individuals, communities and societies are not being taken seriously.

In spite of sustained infiltration by western knowledge systems, African communities have continued to rely on their own unique epistemic resources. For instance, among the Shona and other African communities, **secrecy plays a critical role in controlling and sharing specialised knowledge** which could be about rain-making rituals or identifying medicinal plants and other extraordinary knowledges that lie beyond the familiar everyday world. Such knowledge is controlled by a privileged group of elders through secrecy. It is through secrecy that much secular and ritual experience, including traditional forms of education through values and identity are conveyed to the young generation as a way of advancing the survival of the community, clan or tribe [SECRECY AS A DRIVER FOR KNOWLEDGE SHARING].

While the West may associate secrecy with sinister, negative connotations of espionage, of subversive or self-serving illegal political groups, in Africa secrecy is viewed as a necessary part of social reality and a defining element of certain systems of knowledge. There is a close connection between highly valued knowledge and the degree of public disclosure. Expertise is qualified by possession of specialised forms of knowledge, skilled performance, the recognition of status, and the politics of exclusion [DEVELOP MENTAL FACULTIES IN CHOSEN DOMAIN(S) OF KNOWLEDGE].

Access to various forms of knowledge considered invaluable and esoteric is regulated through ritual and initiation practices [THE ABILITY TO VOLLEY BETWEEN THE CONSCIOUS AND UNCONSCIOUS]. This knowledge includes access to special geographical sites which only those with privileged positions conferred by tribal seniority and ritual enjoy [AN ENRICHED ENVIRONMENT]. Specialist and exclusive knowledge such as that of medicine, magic and ritual is the preserve of a selected few in society. It is believed those privileged individuals are called into such practice directly by the spirits or initiated into the practice through ritual training under the guidance of mediums and tribal elders publicly recognised as custodians of sacred spaces [SEEKING AN AFFECTIVELY ATTUNED OTHER TO LEARN].

The Shona are also aware of the fact that **knowledge can be dangerous if it falls into wrong hands since it can be used for personal gain and to the detriment of others** [WITH KNOWLEDGE COMES RESPONSIBILITY]. Therefore, the liberal disclosure of knowledge is considered irresponsible and punishable by the spirits hence the strict control of knowledge in terms of who gets access to what knowledge is very important. Where knowledge is of absolutely crucial importance to the survival of the community or kingdom and the wellbeing of its caretakers, secrecy is paramount and precautions against reckless revelation are uppermost.

It is through a process of deliberate exclusion that some indigenous knowledge systems remain powerful, protected and highly sought after, making its holders highly invaluable. In fact, secrecy in indigenous African communities is a form of patenting valuable knowledge from unscrupulous abuse or exploitation. If there was no secrecy, much of the indigenous knowledge on preserving nature and traditional medicine [ENRICHED ENVIRONMENT/ONENESS/ONENESS/CONNECTIONS AMONG THE ECOSYSTEM OF WHICH WE ARE A PART] would by now be extinct due to more than a century of colonial exploitation. Up to this day, particular individuals – whether by blood line or descent – are renowned for specific trades such as traditional healing while others are selected through some of form of 'calling' to serve the community by providing moral and spiritual guidance [ENABLING THE OUTWARD FLOW OF THOUGHTS].

The Divination Process to Access Revealed Knowledge

In both the East and the West, one of the fundamental practices through which knowledge is revealed is divination which has a long history in many societies including ancient Greek mythology on wisdom and foresight. Divination is a seeking of knowledge in an attempt to foretell the future, the direction of things. It can be thought of as the imagination tapping into the unconscious side of a situation, perceiving forces and then creating ways to deal with those forces. It "involves a combination of analysis and intuition that normal thinking usually keeps apart. This process values imagination and creativity [ENGAGE YOUR CREATIVE IMAGINATION]. It shifts the way you make decisions."[495]

As a means of obtaining knowledge, divination draws from the repository of cultural insight and meaning production which exists in a particular society. Every divinatory tradition constitutes a specific hermeneutic horizon in which questions of existential concern are addressed. In other words, divination and the knowledge that follows from it are integral to the life and function of the communities in which it is practiced. The practice of divination – and the search for meaning which ensues – is anchored in the general metaphysical outlook which defines that particular society. As a procedure, **divination is a major source of revealed knowledge** – specialized knowledge gained by means of techniques like spiritual possession that tap into the power of the invisible world to reveal knowledge to human beings through visions and dreams. [See Chapter 11 and Appendix D.]

In Shona culture, divination is not mere faith but a learned discipline based on an extensive body of knowledge which involves natural [ONENESS/CONNECTIONS AMONG THE ECOSYSTEMS OF WHICH WE ARE A PART/ENRICHED ENVIRONMENT] and supernatural [OPENING AND STRENGTHENING THE NATURAL CONNECTION TO THE FIELD OF CONSCIOUSNESS/FLOW] phenomena as well as visible and invisible dimensions of reality. Among the Shona, divination is a means by which people seek to transcend the limitations of human sensory knowledge by reaching out for intervention or direction [REVEALED KNOWLEDGE] from the realm of the invisible beings. Divination may take many forms but the most popular image of a diviner is that of an individual who throws divining dices or bones called *hakata* in Shona. These bones or dices are regarded as a means of communicating, instruments through which messages from the invisible world can be decoded. For the Shona, *hakata* constitute a means of communicating with the spirits in that they literally write down the answers being sought for the diviner to see. As primary investigative tools, *hakata* are therefore special instruments. However, the diviners remain completely blind and cannot be expected to 'see' [DELVE INTO THE QUIET MIND AND LISTEN] until they have been prepared for contact with the spirit world through special rituals.

Divination operates through the repeated throwing of the *hakata* to produce certain patterns believed to be visual commentary from the spirits which the diviner is then able to interpret in terms of its relevance to the problem being dealt with. To check the validity of the message received, the diviners have to cast their divining bones a number of times to confirm the outcome. On the other hand, those seeking advice from the diviner are also encouraged to visit more than one diviner to ascertain the facts and to satisfy themselves on the findings. This is the procedure available to ascertain truth [DEVELOPING

HIGHER MENTAL THOUGHT (THE SEARCH FOR TRUTH)] and a part of the verification process.

According to Mr Tavhirenhau Matoro, divination systems are dynamic systems of knowledge upon which the proper ordering of social action is based (Figure 20). The search for deep understanding and the attempt to get to hidden knowledge is itself philosophic since it calls for reflective and interpretive endeavours about life and action [NURTURE AN OPEN MIND]. Divination processes are marked by established procedures for arriving at truth [DEVELOPING HIGHER MENTAL THOUGHT (THE SEARCH FOR TRUTH)], and if truth is to be taken in its pragmatic sense, then divination can be a contending source of knowledge as part of solutions to practical problems [INNOVATIVE CREATIVITY].

Figure 20. *One of the great Shona Diviners in Gokwe North District of Zimbabwe: Mr Tavhirenhau Matoro.*

While African divination systems are a genuine form of knowing, elders remain critical as part of the total repositories of African systems of knowledge. That is, the elders are part of a community dialogue [DEEPEN CONNECTIONS TO OTHERS/ENRICHED ENVIRONMENT] to lead in answering questions such as:

What has happened to local food systems and traditional practice over the past decades?

Reconstructing Food Systems and Values through Unveiled Knowledge

Unless someone invests in surfacing dominant knowledge systems [GROWING EARNED INTUITION; DEVELOPING MENTAL FACULTIES IN CHOSEN DOMAIN(S) OF KNOWLEDGE], some knowledge may never become unveiled. Working with farming communities and local food markets, the author has witnessed the prevalence of unveiled knowledge, a combination of tacit and "secret" knowledge which has remained unrecognized by those who can benefit from it for decades. For example, one of the most enduring contemporary questions dominating discussions on African food systems with African elders is: ***At what point did communities start losing indigenous food and related local knowledge systems?***

The author used diverse approaches to unveil knowledge in answering the above fundamental question in the Chimanimani and Masvingo districts of Zimbabwe, which are dominated by the Shona people. In these communities, old people are blaming young people for shunning indigenous food but young people are also blaming elders for not sufficiently introducing them to indigenous food. It appears there is a generation where colonization of indigenous food gained ground [SEEKING OUT ENRICHED ENVIRONMENTS]. According to participants in dialogue sessions that sought to access unveiled knowledge [DEEPENING CONNECTIONS TO OTHERS], the role of women in protecting indigenous food systems remains critical.

Post-harvest and value addition is provided by women as they continue to play a critical role in preserving the knowledge system. Besides enhancing social cohesion, the pride of a woman in building a rural home remains a critical part of identity and resilience. However, with increasing urbanization and women moving to formal employment, most young women who should be receiving knowledge from their mothers-in-law and grand-mothers are no longer available to receive that knowledge. This preparation [GROWING EARNED INTUITION; DEVELOPING MENTAL FACULTIES IN CHOSEN DOMAIN(S) OF KNOWLEDGE] is essential to enable creative and innovative solutions to very real food system issues. Sadly, many grandmothers are dying with their knowledge still to be unveiled to the younger generation. While documentation is good, there is a limit to which it can replace human interaction and transmission of values [THE HUMAN SEEKS OUT AN AFFECTIVELY ATTUNED OTHER TO LEARN] as well as intrinsic state of the art knowledge.

Emergent Issues

Unfortunately, academic institutions are not closing critical knowledge gaps through building solid pathways for knowledge exchange. Awareness of the colonial influence on indigenous food systems is still high in most communities in Masvingo and Manicaland districts where local people lament that the way indigenous food knowledge is documented or discussed associates it with poverty. If you are seen eating dried vegetables (*mufushwa)* people *think* you are poor. Communities are aware that colonization was too powerful and they are now struggling with external food systems whose production and post-harvest handling knowledge communities lack. For instance, knowledge about the fall army worm and other pests is limited, which prevents potentially finding new innovative solutions to this perennial problem.

Another big issue being witnessed and lamented by rural elders is the increasing consumption and infiltration of foreign foods in service centers through corporates. Small and Medium Enterprises (SMEs) like rural general dealer shops are said to be opening avenues for corporates by testing and developing markets for corporate processed products. For instance, many SMEs at growth points and rural business centers now cook doughnuts, potato chips and other commodities that are changing tastes for rural consumers. This is triggering the demand for fast foods that are then pushed by corporates. Barter trade is becoming a major transaction mode that benefits corporates who specialize in processed food. Through Agro-dealers, commodities like maize are aggregated using barter-related purchasing and procurement pathways. Agro-dealers exchange cooking oil, sugar, flour and other processed foods with maize which is then delivered to the Grain Marketing Board (GMB) from where some processing companies procure maize. However, the same method is not being used to mobilize indigenous food like small grains, indigenous chickens, brown rice, indigenous vegetables, sweet potatoes and many others.

Elders in Chimanimani and Masvingo districts including diviners also blamed the education system for undermining indigenous food and related knowledge by not inserting indigenous knowledge systems (IKS) in the curriculum. The only way young people acquire IKS is through pass on since it is not embedded in books or practiced in food and nutrition programs supported by the government and/or non-governmental organizations. Communities feel the government is not helping to document, package and utilize IKS for easy practical application. Loss of IKS leads to loss of indigenous food systems and medicinal practices. Where some farmers are weeding crops, they now remove natural vegetables before the seed matures and that is destroying the natural seed system for indigenous vegetables. Others remove indigenous vegetables from the land due to lack of knowledge.

Knowledge on different indigenous food is also being lost due to limited intentional support from the government. For example, in the past, Chimanimani communities used baobab as a source of porridge and other products like coffee, oil and peanut butter while fresh baobab leaves were a vegetable which was good for community resilience. Due to neglect and deforestation, communities no longer have young baobab trees and seed is not being given time to regenerate. The communities are losing related knowledge and worse so they are not being supported to invest in propagating indigenous fruit trees and other foods. [CONSIDER INTENT, THEN RELEASE]

Framework and Process for Unveiling Local Knowledge

The methodology for documenting unveiled knowledge within the food baskets was contextualized through dialogue with people who really understand their food systems including how food production zones are related to food baskets and markets [DEVELOPING MENTAL FACULTIES IN CHOSEN DOMAIN(S) OF KNOWLEDGE]. A food basket in a particular community or district indicates commodities consumed in that community or district. The other thread was identifying commodities produced in surplus for the market in each community or district because some local households expand their food baskets using food from distant markets. Food can travel directly from one district to the other, for instance, Chimanimani to Masvingo.

In unveiling existing knowledge [EARNED KNOWLEDGE/EARNED INTUITION], documenting the food basket was not just listing commodities in the districts but mapping and conducting supply chain analysis to show the intricacy and relationships between production zones and markets. When this process reveals niche markets for particular commodities like fruits from Chimanimani, it became possible to do a comparative analysis showing types and amounts of food from outside the community or district. Differences in food baskets between districts eventually revealed supply corridors that build food baskets at different supply chain nodes.

The mass market has become part of the food basket mapping because markets are good at revealing the seasonal nature of food baskets including socio-economic and political factors influencing the structure of the food basket. The market can answer questions like what is the relationship between food and non-food enterprises and how do these affect indigenous food? What is the food basket like during the festive season? All these can only be analysed from the market because the market interacts with farmers, consumers and traders at one place.

More importantly, as a knowledge system, the food basket is an activity designed to feed into other activities [DEVELOPING HIGHER MENTAL THOUGHT (CONCEPTUAL THINKING)]. Monitoring the food basket in each district can also enrich the community with fresh knowledge [ACHIEVING WHOLE THOUGHT] in several ways including answering questions like what is happening to the food basket during the festive season? Since much of the production in most districts is controlled by rainfall, what is happening to supplies from particular districts during the rainfall season? What is the food basket in April during the harvesting season? What about in winter? What about during school holidays? To what extent is exposure to processed industrial food a threat to local indigenous food?

When these questions are adequately answered, initiatives can then be introduced to prevent infiltration of industrial food in rural communities if the food basket shows which commodities are going to which district and which ones are coming from which district or markets into Chimanimani or Masvingo, for example. Such intelligence can be used to promote African substitutes for exotic fruits that are getting into rural communities from outside. The capture of markets by local and external food can also be seen through markets, for instance, what has been pushing demand for sweet potatoes and small grains in cities over the past 10 years? Is it the increase in the price of bread or knowledge about eating health and wellness?

Using Dialogue and Stream of Consciousness to Reveal Knowledge on Food Baskets

As an entry point to unveiling knowledge, correctly targeting key informants is critical when assessing knowledge about community food systems. Also important is creative contextualization of a topic or theme [CREATIVE IMAGINATION] to link with what people have always wished to say if somebody had asked them. Engaging communities in a conversation they have never been asked about [THINKING EQUALLY ON ALL PLANES: PHYSICAL, MENTAL AND EMOTIONAL] makes them see the need for their knowledge to be documented. For instance, from discussions about their local food system, communities in Chimanimani and Masvingo realized they were losing their historical and current food systems which could be saved by documentation.

The dialogue [DEEPENING CONNECTIONS TO OTHERS] commenced with posing simple questions like, out of more than 40 commodities in your community, which commodities comprise a household's food basket? From brainstorming as a group, they could see that white maize meal *(sadza)* is dominating out of 12 grains while in the vegetables section, exotic Covo and

Rape are displacing indigenous vegetables. These are issues they may not notice unless an outsider asks them.

Creative dialoguing [STRENGTHENING CONNECTION TO THE FIELD OF CONSCIOUSNESS/FLOW] was used as a central approach to unveiling indigenous knowledge on indigenous food systems through streams of consciousness because of the way such knowledge is differently packaged, preserved and shared within communities. Instead of using digital tools and software like Open Data Kit, indigenous knowledge on indigenous food was captured in ways that enabled communities to remember how they used to grow food over the past years, places they used to grow and other details that are part of their stream of consciousness [RECOGNIZING ONENESS/CONNECTIONS AMONG THE ECOSYSTEM OF WHICH WE ARE A PART]. That is why the documentation process resorted to open dialogue through creative facilitation that built local people's confidence as contributors to their own knowledge building processes. [See "The role of facilitation in creativity at the end of Chapter 7.]

In this approach, dialogue was about getting people to bring out what they know – a story of a particular community [REDISCOVER THE FULLNESS OF WHO YOU ARE; A BALANCED STORY OF SELF AND COMMUNITY]. A story starts from the mind – tell us the story about small grains. Do you remember what was happening with production, uses, recipes and consumption patterns decades ago? All this forms a real-life story. The dialoguing process was like a sport where the ball is passed from one participant to the other. Historical and life experiences that were shared showed that some participants have visited some communities, some have been to cities, others never went anywhere. Some shared how and where they tasted new food [DEVELOPING PRESENCE; BRINGING THE PAST AND FUTURE TOGETHER TO ILLUMINATE THE PRESENT]. That background and the whole narrative knitted and revealed a deep story about food systems.

Different contexts also enriched the dialogue as some issues in Chimanimani were different from those in Masvingo [HONORING DIVERSITY OF THOUGHT]. This is contrary to the straight-jacket questionnaire method which does not have room for people to dialogue in relation to their context. Behind every answer is a reason which you cannot get from frequency of assertion such as yes/no responses, satisfied/less satisfied. Through an open dialogue [NURTURE AN OPEN MIND (HUMILITY)], the documentation process generated findings, results and further dialogue about the emerging results. Bringing together as many people as possible, each dialogue created its own pathway connecting gender, natural resources, mechanization and other aspects which shaped the story into a meandering river of unveiled knowledge

[ACHIEVING WHOLE THOUGHT (CONNECTING CONCEPTS AND LIFE EXAMPLES); UPPER AND LOWER MENTAL THOUGHT BALANCED].

During the dialogue process, some people who had not had an opportunity to discuss an issue were so eager to express issues they have never been asked [PERMITTING FREEDOM OF THOUGHT AND SELF-EXPRESSION]. The dialogue caused some to remember what they ate during their youth days or the food they took to school when they were young. Remembering and unveiling something made them feel proud. Others were forced to remember their grandmothers, in the process re-creating the whole food system – taking the whole dialogue to how food was grown and prepared 30 years ago. That became the foundation for building new trends together with the community such that at the end there was a whole picture with fewer gaps - showing the ins and outs of the local food system [DEVELOPING PRESENCE; BRINGING THE PAST AND FUTURE TOGETHER TO ILLUMINATE THE PRESENT].

Ultimately, the whole community in the dialogue [KNOWLEDGE SHARING, COOPERATION AND COLLABORATION; DEEPENING CONNECTION TO OTHERS] reached the Ahaa! moment of truths and transformation [TRUTH AS HIGHER MENTAL THOUGHT] – "This is where we are now". The trend showed people acknowledging [NURTURING AN OPEN MIND; HUMILITY] what they have lost. The dialogue sessions became like bringing people together [DEEPENING CONNECTIONS TO OTHERS] to use the unveiled knowledge to build a road map based on their memory and then reflect new opportunities [CREATIVE IMAGINATION] leading to questions like – should we continue with this path and pace or we need to take a step back and re-strategize around our food system?

Dialoguing also enabled the communities to realize they are rich with water, natural resources and intangible assets like culture and tradition [RECOGNIZING ONENESS; CONNECTIONS AMONG THE ECOSYSTEM OF WHICH WE ARE A PART]. That realization was a good foundation and vantage point enabling them to see if they are gaining or losing value as a community. The process also awakened them [SURFACING TACIT KNOWLEDGE] to the fact that at one time they had 50 indigenous vegetable varieties whose seed they controlled. These vegetables also had medicinal and nutritional properties that people could not explain scientifically. However, the community now has less than 10 indigenous vegetables. From eight indigenous fruits, they now rely on three exotic fruits. The nutrition basket has become narrow and expensive such that communities declare themselves poor when they lack money to buy external food like rice and sugar. The definition of poverty is now around money but when food was diverse, poverty was not defined by money. The communities realized words like ***vulnerable*** and ***poor*** used in the development speak are insulting.

Vulnerable to what when people are in their community and are surrounded by natural resources and relatives? [THINKING EQUALLY ON ALL THREE PLANES (PHYSICAL, MENTAL AND EMOTIONAL)]

The dialogue sessions confirmed community consensus and consciousness to the point of realizing how much they need alternatives to food aid. *While we appreciate external seed, we are not happy that we are not consulted the way we would prefer to make our choices.* As people respond in dialogue, they are sharing their experiences [DEVELOPING PRESENCE; BRINGING THE PAST AND FUTURE TOGETHER TO ILLUMINATE THE PRESENT]. A natural de-rolling takes place during dialogue. When women are talking about what affects them around food, it does not matter whether the chief is there because they are not attacking anyone but addressing an issue [BUILDING ON PREREQUISITES OF SELF]. It becomes a platform for women to voice their concerns to the community and bringing issues to the attention of leaders, making leadership more conscious of what is being lost. In a way, they are asking what are you doing as leaders about these issues?

We are losing our food systems to rampant religious practices. We are losing our indigenous knowledge because the academic system is not good at capturing indigenous food systems [ACHIEVING WHOLE THOUGHT; CONNECTING CONCEPTS AND LIFE EXAMPLES]. Such dialogue is a way of speeding up conversation within the community – as people go home, they share with their peers who were not there and within a week the whole community knows the whole issue [DEEPENING CONNECTIONS TO OTHERS]. It is another way of raising awareness, unveiling dormant knowledge [SURFACING TACIT KNOWLEDGE] and building ownership of discussions and decisions on community food systems. The choice of elders above 60 years set solid criteria because this age group is the one with abundant undocumented knowledge [TACIT KNOWLEDGE] yet to be unveiled.

Conversing with community elders was like picking diverse pages thrown away from a single book – page 3 picked in one village, another village has page 17 and so on until the entire memory of the whole community is brought together into one book in the form of unveiled community knowledge [REDISCOVERING THE FULLNESS OF WHO YOU ARE; A BALANCED STORY OF SELF AND COMMUNITY]. **This would not be possible without facilitated dialogue**. When communities are empowered to regularly convene these dialogues on their own, it is a rich way of reclaiming local tradition and reviving harmonious society through food systems dialogue and unveiled knowledge. Although dialogue processes may not insist on tradition because some religious practices have built strong roots, the community needs harmony that can only come through dialogue [FOCUS ON THE JOY OF THE WHAT AND WHY OF YOUR DESIRE].

Utilization of unveiled collective knowledge in production and the market can start from dialogue. If the problem is shortage of labour, communities can decide to revive the *nhimbe* concept which is about collectively working together for the common good. If the challenge is about marketing, they can decide to embrace collective market search.

Conducting this process calls for good listening [NURTURING AN OPEN MIND (HUMILITY)] and the ability to relate with the subject. The facilitator should have experienced some of the issues including references like how cattle were herded and small grains were threshed using cattle in the past decades. In such a dialogue, the facilitator may just introduce a theme around food, nudge old people to recall and within one to two hours a lot of information starts flowing as elders remember things and their memory becomes very active [DEVELOPING PRESENCE; BRINGING THE PAST AND FUTURE TOGETHER TO ILLUMINATE THE PRESENT]. As the conversation evolves, some of the participants can shout names of vegetables to support the memory of the one narrating and revealing the local food story [REDISCOVERING THE FULLNESS OF WHO YOU ARE; A BALANCED STORY OF SELF AND COMMUNITY]. The facilitator can even say, "Women you are good with vegetables, may you get into a group and list all the vegetables you know?" As they present, ask which types of vegetables are still being consumed? Next – how are vegetables prepared? The whole dialogue naturally evolves into an incredible humane and fluid knowledge platform.

Reviving and Preserving the Micro Climate through Unveiled Knowledge

Community dialogues have evolved into reconstructive dialogues and documentation processes to ensure African food systems and intellectual heritages are conferred with the immortality that other food systems and knowledge systems enjoy across the world. Communities in Chimanimani and Masvingo have woken up to the fact that when food systems and natural resources are reconstructed, future generations will not only be able to dialogue with this heritage but to **innovate with it** as well. The best way of dealing with the colonial misfortune and its painful reality is not just to dwell on its ills on African tradition and food systems, but to articulate knowledge systems and intellectual heritage embedded in African communities as part of reconstructing indigenous values, culture, knowledge and identity [FOCUSING ON THE JOY OF THE WHAT AND WHY OF YOUR DESIRE].

In the spirit of reconstructing local natural ecosystems, some of the communities have started promoting agroecology principles and Indigenous Knowledge Systems (IKS) through preserving local forests [RECOGNIZING ONENESS/CONNECTIONS AMONG THE ECOSYSTEM OF WHICH WE ARE A PART]. Surrounding communities and people from distant areas have been coming to learn about how to re-generate and protect their local natural habitat through a strong initiative for knowledge exchange [KNOWLEDGE SHARING, COOPERATION AND COLLABORATION] which is inspiring many people to become environmental stewards. These communities go back and restore or revive their natural habitats through activities like gulley reclamation and replanting vegetation. Sports like soccer games and other forms of entertainment are used as platforms for awareness raising and sensitization on the importance of protecting the environment and building climate consciousness [RECOGNIZING ONENESS; CONNECTIONS AMONG THE ECOSYSTEM OF WHICH WE ARE A PART]. Reclaiming the environment, gullies and planting different types of grasses that hold the soil together is not only averting land degradation but also preserving IKS.

A new micro climate has been created in one community of Chimanimani district called Chaseyama which is now characterized by a cool environment that preserves moisture in the community especially after some rainfall. Being close to mountains, relief rainfall patterns are now giving new life to the micro climate of the community. The spiritual dimension is also playing a key role in building a new natural region similar to natural region 2 characterized by reliable relief rainfall patterns [THINKING EQUALLY ON ALL FOUR PLANES: THE PHYSICAL, MENTAL, EMOTIONAL AND SPIRITUAL]. Transforming natural region four or five to two or three is a significant achievement.

And the potential for innovative creativity to expand …

There is no doubt that more benefits can extend to other parts of the country if the government is to adopt this community model and upscale it to the national level. All communities can be capacitated and inspired to reclaim and protect their micro climates for purposes of preserving local food systems like fruits, honey and wildlife. Many rural communities have natural features and land marks that are good for certain wild life that should be preserved through agroecology principles. For instance, river banks can easily be preserved against siltation and gullies reclaimed to combat soil erosion.

Embracing agroecology principles would also see government re-designing irrigation systems in ways that revive and strengthen the preservation micro climates, rivers and weirs rather than channelling water long distances to field crops through canals that by-pass natural forests which are an integral component of wildlife. When designed from an agroecological perspective, irrigation systems should mimic natural rivers or streams. Water flowing from dams to irrigation schemes would be directed to navigate communities the way roads meander through communities. That can ensue some of the water flows to pastures and forests for the benefit of wild life, natural fruits and forests. Such an approach can give irrigation systems a fitting agroecology face that mirrors a natural ecosystem as opposed to only supporting monocropping of a few industrial foods. People are beginning to realize that when 1000 hectares of land are put under monocropping, a bigger part of the natural ecosystem is destroyed for the benefit.

Embracing agroecology principles is also beginning to influence the way boreholes are sited. In several communities, there is increasing awareness to the fact that boreholes may be a good source of water but many of them may draw all underground water and cause communities to be too dry in the long-term. Even if rainfall is received, it may take a long time for underground water withdrawn through boreholes to be replenished into underground sources. Agroecology principles recognize natural methods of preserving water like weirs, streams and river banks that enable different types of vegetation to grow as well as restore pastures for livestock and wildlife. Swampy areas and big water pools (*Madziva)* should be protected for their spiritual role because they are said to be the home of mermaids. Natural plants like reeds and small islands (*Zvitsuwa)* should also be preserved unlike the current situation where some are desecrated by religious groups who baptize their members in water bodies that are considered sacred by some community members.

From an agroecology principles perspective, climate change mitigation is not just about food crops but also livestock, wild life and spiritual beliefs as a source of livelihood. Rainfall benefits the entire ecosystem comprising natural water sources, livestock pastures and natural forests on which wildlife depends. Human-wildlife conflict is increasing due to the way most food systems including irrigation schemes are set up not consider benefits from wildlife. Some of the challenges were exacerbated by the colonial notion of building National Parks. It seems national parks were designed to exclude predators like baboons, monkeys, wild pigs and other small animals that crawl or burrow. These animals have been left to co-exist with local communities. However, conventional industrial agriculture and food systems have destroyed the natural habitat for these predators by cutting trees and grasses as well as re-purposing land.

In addition, due to limitations of energy and materials for building infrastructure, communities have continued to rely on firewood and use of grasses and poles for building houses. Most rural communities still have natural features suitable for habitation by wild life, for example mountain places, hills and streams that are found in rural communities and game reserves. If communities are involved in managing wild life, they will become their own watch dogs, the same way communities now manage forests through traditional leaders such that anyone found cutting a tree is prosecuted. It is important to look at other animals that live in harmony with communities, for example crawling small animals which can easily become community assets. Communities can provide information on the types of wild animals that can co-exist with communities – Antelope (*mhembwe*), Hare (*tsuro*) and others. In fact, communities have their own security system which can prohibit wild animals from being hunted to extinction if properly empowered like what has been done with the preservation of forests.

With enough support, academic institutions and researchers can be empowering communities to convert natural resources into products and services for socio-economic growth. Government departments could invest in converting natural resources into commercial products rather than exporting food products in a raw state which has no commercial value.

Final Thoughts

Crucial to the growth of knowledge today is the need for openness and willingness to accept whatever is positive from the experiences offered by the world's varied cultures. As we assess the validity of traditional forms of knowledge it is important to remember that there is more than one philosophical and epistemological trajectory open to humankind. Different types of knowledge and forms of knowing enrich rather than impoverish humankind.

Today's burgeoning Christian faiths across Africa, which in part owe their origin to the resilience and strength of African metaphysics, have become in themselves champions of revealed knowledge. Owing to their claim to know and to be able to reveal the nature and source of occult forces in people's lives, the Christian churches, particularly the Pentecostal ones, have become an important force not only in the renewed quest for revealed knowledge but in its widespread acceptance.

One of the reasons for the extraordinary popularity of the Pentecostal church in Africa is its claim to be able to reveal the occult forces behind money, power and goods. In light of this it is clear that Christianity has not displaced traditional metaphysical thinking, including beliefs about the occult, but has instead created a platform on which they make perfect sense. In this way it has become one of the strongest contenders for revealed knowledge in modern society with its ever-growing set of diviners and charismatic prophets. The main question is whether this phenomenon should be ignored or acknowledged as a competing source of what people regard as valuable knowledge. Although its logic remains shrouded in controversy there is little doubt that **this divinatory practice and the revealed knowledge it yields is solving practical problems of life** as testimonies demonstrate.

Besides documenting and unveiling indigenous knowledge, dialoguing is another way of capacitating communities to conduct their own dialogues in a structured manner. Such knowledge cannot be collected by conventional enumerators through questionnaires, which ask for answers not explanations. Given the way communities have participated in research projects by being asked questions, after cycles of participation they should be able to provide data to national processes regularly with no need for some enumerators to come and ask questions.

Continuing the Unveiling ...

While this case study provides a good example of the innovative creativity approach, there is still much unveiling to be accomplished. Who will drive the turning point toward indigenous food? Is it children, government, consumers who don't have the knowledge or farmers with favoured climates? Such initiatives best succeed as national programs led by chiefs who can mobilize their leadership. If leaders can recognize they are going the wrong way, that can be the beginning of a solution. For example, why not push the price of maize when small grains are in abundance so that people can buy commodities that will be in abundance, unlike depending on imports? Why should maize be imported when small grains are abundant? Needed technology could be provided by government and development agencies. Currently, remittances are only coming for local people to buy food produced by big farmers in developed countries, yet there is still some food identity within people's blood. Instead of children being laughed at when they take indigenous fruit like *Matohwe* to school, it could be considered a source of pride.

Let's expand for a few paragraphs on the innovative creativity that has emerged from revealed and unveiled knowledge and the dialogue around that knowledge. A key starting point can be **building evidence for supporting and protecting community ecosystems in line with agroecology principles**. This implies a strong advocacy strategy including challenging unmonitored negative impacts of industrial agriculture production practices that are disrupting agroecology principles such as soil health, external inputs reduction, community participation, land governance, unfairness against dominance of industrial practices, animal health and others. Advocacy could be built around agroecology principles by putting in place systems for generating evidence showing how communities are being impacted by systems that undermine agroecology. That way, it becomes easy to explain food sovereignty as communities tackle food and nutrition security by managing our natural ecosystems.

Unveiled knowledge is beginning to show communities that Indigenous Knowledge Systems can also provide several substitutes if properly recognized. For example, in some regions where manure-driven horticulture is being promoted, communities have lost livestock such that manure is not available for use. What are the substitutes? This is where researchers could work hard to bring substitutes. When substitutes are needed, to what extent is government willing to support communities to develop alternatives? There is also a strong case for taking AE principles to diverse communities so that these principles become a monitoring, evaluation and learning framework that can answer the following questions, among others:

- How are communities and farmers practicing AE co-creating knowledge with other actors?
- How are they connecting with markets in order to generate economic value?
- How are they accounting for food diversity?

Answering these questions will ultimately lead to an investment framework based on AE principles which enables communities to protect their resources against external investors interested in extracting traditional resources, social values, culture and food systems. AE principles can also be used to challenge models introduced into communities by development agencies, private sector and government programs that tend to have a narrow focus on external commodities at the expense of diverse local commodities.

Contextualizing AE principles can also be achieved through dialoguing each principle with communities to ensure the principles are integrated into the local status quo. Eventually, AE principles can be used as a standard to which each intervention can hold. Some of the questions to be answered using AE principles include: As private contractors promote tobacco or cotton, how are you conscious of AE principles? Answering such critical questions will assist in laying the foundation for community self-evaluation or cross-learning framework. Effectiveness and cost-efficiency could be built into the framework to answer questions like:

- How sustainable are interventions by NGOs and private contractors from an AE principles framework?
- How effective is *murakwani* or manure from an economic diversification perspective? Can farmers earn enough income from using these organic resources to be able to sustain economic livelihoods using AE principle 13 which speaks about soil health? Can farmers really use manure to eliminate use of fertilizer? Can farmers use AE to sufficiently deal with pests and diseases that characterize a changing climate?
- Who is benefitting from promoting chemicals and hybrid seed? How can communities have more than five chemicals controlling one pest when there should just be one chemical? No one is protecting consumers and farmers from commercialization of inputs which is all designed to suppress indigenous knowledge systems. Why are universities not researching imported chemical solutions and blending them with IKS to come up with contextual solutions? How can communities valuate agricultural economic drivers for farmers to be able to get a fair deal when exchanging with industrial or processed products? Where 2kg of sugar costs USD2 - how can farmers trade their Bambara nuts with sugar fairly? The challenge is that farmers do not have bench marks for costing compared to companies which process industrial foods who calculate value using cost of inputs like ingredients, water, energy, labour and other elements. Companies calculate profit from sugar, flour and others but cannot calculate the value of sweet potato which farmers sell to buy sugar.

Another emerging idea relates to **the value of using indigenous knowledge as intellectual property rights for communities**. Where does the intellectual property that is being commercialized around indigenous food systems originate? For example, the knowledge on processing baobab fruit has been taken from communities who have been doing it for decades. Some food processing companies have literally stolen that recipe and commercialized it, yet nobody has acknowledged or tracked the role of communities that started processing baobab fruit many years ago. These communities already had milk from their cows or goats and baobab powder was readily available. Why have these communities not been supported to commercialize their products and knowledge?

Further, unveiled knowledge is enabling communities to realize that using industrial inputs and products makes it difficult for African countries to adequately value their natural resources like soil, water and natural climates. What is the opportunity cost of undermining local micro climates using industrial products? Answering such questions can reveal that there are more benefits in bringing together ecology and organic. Agroecology means agriculture and ecology but there is no practice. What type of practice can you do in the ecology? Organic becomes a practice in the ecology although in an ecology one can still practice inorganic agriculture or industrial agriculture like emphasizing productivity without looking at the cost of natural resources.

Currently, 90% of African returns support production in countries where African countries source inputs. Promoting organic production is re-investing within communities contributing to resilience and get rid of dependence on foreign currency. African food systems do not need an external life support systems from industrial inputs. The natural habitat is the life support system for local food systems. African research institutions could conduct thorough research on local natural inputs including natural grasses and tree leaves. If grasses can be grown to support cattle production, why not identify grasses that can enhance natural soil fertility? There is the need to totally change irrigation schemes towards organic natural production. Some communities still have intact environments that support organic production. Why not support Mwenezi as a natural economic zone for small grains and groundnuts which do not need gypsum?

Knowledge on different indigenous food is also being lost. Continuing the innovative creativity approach, **the idea of affirmative and inclusive programs emerges**. Communities are finding their voices to demand that the market should not just be about growing maize or wheat for the Grain Marketing Board. The communities need affirmative programs for indigenous food which has been orphaned for years so that it catches up with modern food. This might mean government procurement saying that unless indigenous food is prioritized, we will not import food. Decisions to import could be informed by the availability of indigenous food in the country.

Community elders are the key knowledge holders, knowledge that is often tacit in nature, but available to be triggered. If a new curriculum is introduced with a bigger component of indigenous knowledge systems, community elders would be the professors for developing that IKS curriculum. Communities need a university of IKS from primary education all the way to higher education. Currently, knowing too much about IKS and being known to have that type of knowledge is considered spiritual and therefore stigmatized by many. If you have too much knowledge to be able to talk about indigenous food systems in public you may be considered demonic or possessed by the evil spirits, which can compromise sources of livelihoods. While seven days beer would keep the money circulating in communities, they have now been penetrated by opaque beer producers who contract farmers, providing them little money which they then come back to take through opaque beer.

Development agencies are **looking at communities as receivers of knowledge, not contributors of their own knowledge**. They don't ride on IKS, which provides resilience for centuries. Working collectively in nutrition gardens is good but why do individuals opt for their own individual garden at the river rather than where there are solar and water tanks? The criteria to select beneficiaries does not consider social criteria through which communities build their communities through new ecosystems. Trying to build communities using external criteria is a dead end. This is where we see leakages and distraction of indigenous knowledge systems.

There are certainly other issues to address in this important area of focus to these African communities, but enough has been exampled above to demonstrate the value of the innovative creativity approach to very real day-to-day problems. The ideas emerging through revealed and unveiled knowledge – and the dialogue among communities bringing their stories from the past and their dreams and desires for the future to address the present – emerge endless possibilities for process and product innovation.

In the next chapter we will attempt to connect the dots, bringing together core ideas presented throughout the book, many of which presented in our case study, in an overarching model. As is brought up throughout this text, we simultaneously recognize that there is not one model that will serve all, although the higher-order patterns the model exudes may well serve most.

Chapter 15
Connecting the Dots

We've talked about a lot of things across 14 chapters, and touched many different fields of thought related to Innovative Creativity. How do all these things connect? What steps can I take to fully engage Innovative Creativity? The reality is that there is not a simple answer to these questions because, as forwarded throughout this text, no two people are alike. YOU are unique. Your creativity is unique. We are each at a different starting point and have different ways we learn, different approaches to accessing our tacit knowledge, different methods of tapping into our unconscious or reaching the flow state, different capabilities and capacities, and, well, we're just different in so very many ways. And yet, we are all human with an incredible streak of creativity weaving in and out of our everyday lives and, sometimes, bringing forth something we recognize as really useful and special.

The creative process fulfils the human longing and search for new objects, experiences, and existential ways of thinking. This longing—with both conscious and unconscious motivation—can often be observed during the process, and sometimes as part of the product of that process, particularly prevalent in aesthetic creativity.

And creativity is about connecting the dots, by definition, bringing two or more ideas together to achieve something new. This is what happened to emerge so many of mankind's firsts. For example, Johannes Guttenberg discovering a connection between a wine press and coin punch to bring about the printing press; Karl Benz connecting engines and wheels to invent the first "horseless carriage"; Alexander Graham Bell connecting the human voice to electrically transmittable vibrations leading to development of the telephone; and Ruth Wakefield connecting cookies and chocolate chunks to create the chocolate chip cookie. And the list goes on and on. So, an important part of YOUR creativity is connecting the dots between YOUR knowledge and the focus of your interest and passion.

Figure 21 provides a visual review of elements in preparation for the creative leap, including prerequisites of self, expanding our creative capacity, and developing controlled intuition. When the field is prepared, a phase change occurs in the Intelligent Social Change Journey, expanding from the co-evolving phase (Phase II) and moving toward the creative leap (Phase III). The creative leap, then, instantaneous and not constrained by a perceived current reality, is the result of *creative imagination grounded in the bisociation of multiple points (ideas/concepts) of knowledge and knowing comprising more than half the field of thought.*

Now, let's take a step backwards in time and connect the dots in terms of Preparing, Focusing, Accessing and Freeing. The entangled activities supporting these areas are (not necessarily occurring in this order): Prerequisites of SELF, Expanding Creative Capacity, Developing Controlled Intuition, and The Creative Leap. While you can reread this book for details, we're going to stress a few highlights.

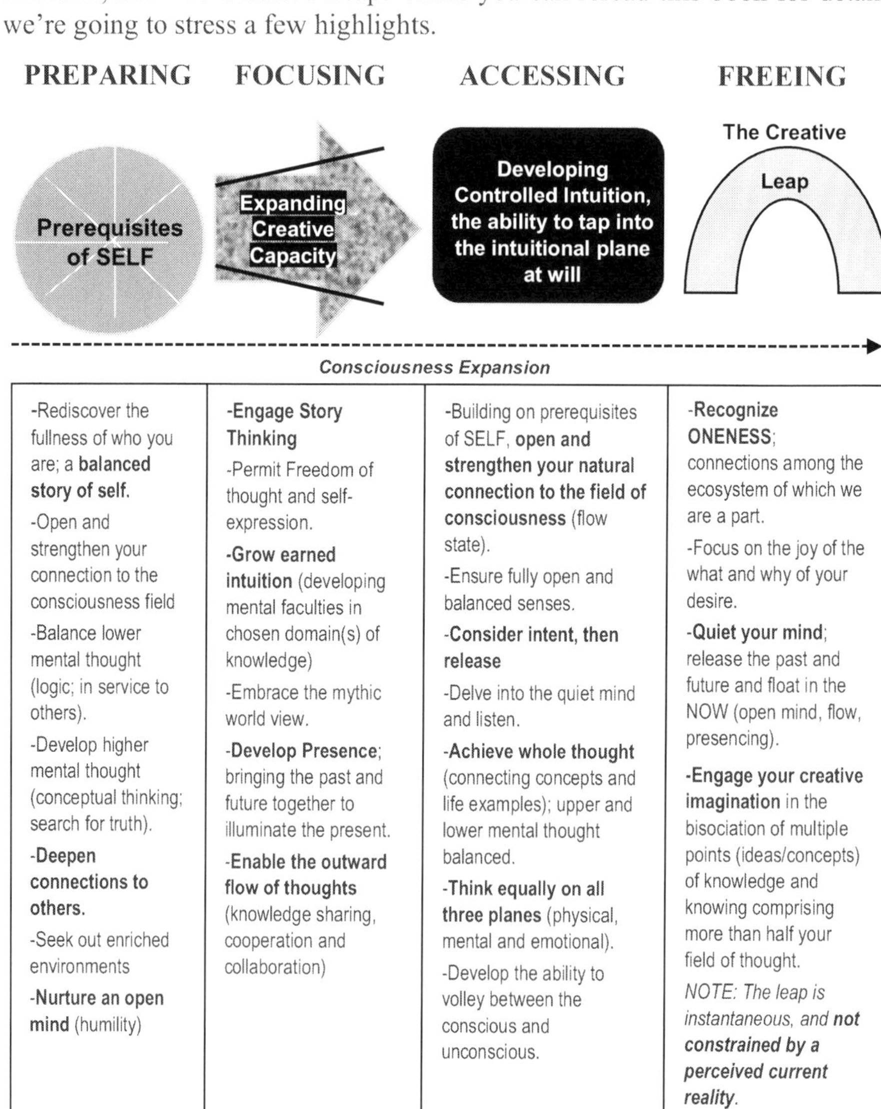

PREPARING	FOCUSING	ACCESSING	FREEING
-Rediscover the fullness of who you are; a **balanced story of self.** -Open and strengthen your connection to the consciousness field -Balance lower mental thought (logic; in service to others). -Develop higher mental thought (conceptual thinking; search for truth). -**Deepen connections to others.** -Seek out enriched environments -**Nurture an open mind** (humility)	-**Engage Story Thinking** -Permit Freedom of thought and self-expression. -**Grow earned intuition** (developing mental faculties in chosen domain(s) of knowledge) -Embrace the mythic world view. -**Develop Presence**; bringing the past and future together to illuminate the present. -**Enable the outward flow of thoughts** (knowledge sharing, cooperation and collaboration)	-Building on prerequisites of SELF, **open and strengthen your natural connection to the field of consciousness** (flow state). -Ensure fully open and balanced senses. -**Consider intent, then release** -Delve into the quiet mind and listen. -**Achieve whole thought** (connecting concepts and life examples); upper and lower mental thought balanced. -**Think equally on all three planes** (physical, mental and emotional). -Develop the ability to volley between the conscious and unconscious.	-**Recognize ONENESS**; connections among the ecosystem of which we are a part. -Focus on the joy of the what and why of your desire. -**Quiet your mind**; release the past and future and float in the NOW (open mind, flow, presencing). -**Engage your creative imagination** in the bisociation of multiple points (ideas/concepts) of knowledge and knowing comprising more than half your field of thought. *NOTE: The leap is instantaneous, and **not constrained by a perceived current reality**.*

Figure 26. *Facilitating the Creative Leap (a quick review).*

First, you have prepared the field, that is, through education and experience you have focused your attention in a domain of knowledge—with attention attracting and bringing related information into consciousness—and learned and continue to learn. In this instant, the mental work has been done in terms of learning in, and focusing on, the knowledge domain of interest. We know that this has been repeated numerous times in this text; and this has occurred because mental preparation is critical to your personal creative success. Over the years of engagement in this field, your historic learning has moved into your subconscious, ever expanding, waiting there to be triggered as needed. Your conscious mind continues focusing on the incoming information in the moment at hand, associating (complexing) it with what is known, and creating knowledge which drives the decisions you make and actions you take in the NOW and the continuing cycle of NOWs.

Remember, the mental faculties are in service to the intuitive. We can use our minds to create the conditions for creativity. When intuition occurs in your domain of experience and knowledge, it is to a large extent earned intuition. Creative juices follow the earned intuition track for several reasons. Largely because this is our area of interest (and passion), it is where we focus our attention and set our intention.

Second, this is the viewpoint from which we *discover patterns* and have developed a *higher level of conceptual thinking* and *discernment of truth.* Similarly, a major finding of Robert Sternberg, a polymath of psychology, was that creativity has a tendency to be domain-specific.[496] This does not mean that creative thought is limited to a specific domain. Quite to the contrary. As you develop expertise in a domain of knowledge, you are able to recognize patterns and extrapolate those across from one situation to another. As you shift frames of reference, you begin to see similar patterns in other domains of knowledge. When this is coupled with intent for the greater good, you have moved into the condition of wisdom.

Creating in wisdom was explored in Chapter 6. We're going to include a few more words about wisdom here, and wanted to share the diversity of opinion regarding the relationship of wisdom and creativity. For example, Sternberg says that they are two entirely different ways of thinking, with creativity requiring a brashness and wisdom requiring balance.[497] Conversely, Galenson says that wisdom can be the *source* of creativity.[498] He goes on to explain that creativity can be viewed in two ways: as *conceptual creativity*, which can be brash, and *experimental creativity*, which is balanced, noting that the latter is directly related to both age and wisdom. Archetypal examples of Old Masters who exhibited the latter include Darwin, Cezanne and Hitchcock. Robert Frost, who wrote his famous poem "Stopping by the Woods on a Snowy

Evening" at the age of 48, forwarded that young people can have insight and a flash here and there, but older poets can provide a clarification of life that "begins in delight and ends in wisdom."[499]

Our polymath Sternberg used a WICS model in teaching at Yale. WICS represents Wisdom, Intelligence, and Creativity Synthesized.[500] Creativity helps to form a vision of where to go and cope with change along the way, intelligence is needed to discern good ideas and convince others of their value, and wisdom is required to ensure the common and greater good over the short and long term. This is a good model and consistent with the definitions and usage of these terms in this book.

Third, an important secret addressed in Chapter 4 is balance, that is, bringing the physical, mental and emotional planes into balance, and looking for *whole thought* that triggers the intuitional mind. Recall that **whole thought** is the ability to integrate lower mental thought (logic) and higher mental thought (concepts). This means that you recognize the patterns and relationships (concepts/theories) among and beyond the cause-and-effect connections of logical events AND that you have the ability to understand concepts and theories such that you can apply them (as events) when it makes sense and you choose to do so. This understanding of a higher truth in terms of relationships and knowledge flows enables the ability to transfer successes from one situation to another, and, as you polish this skillset, from one domain of knowledge to another domain of knowledge.

In this context, whole thought is inclusive, not only engaging both events and concepts, but also thinking through the physical, mental and emotional planes; considering the past, present and future; and taking into account short and long-term outcomes for the common and greater good. This requires full consciousness, interacting at a full level of sensing while simultaneously balancing the senses.

While meditation is a practice we forwarded as an example to help facilitate this state, all too often the thought that emerges is selfish, focused on the individual, thus not capable of moving beyond self to tap into the larger field of ideas. More recently, organizations have recognized the power of mindfulness in support of creativity. For example, Google, Target, Aetna, Intel and General Mills offer mindfulness programs for employees. Google Thailand has designed a space for mindfulness meditation and provides a daily break for this practice. Mindfulness improves focus and clarity, while helping people be fully present in the NOW moment.

This capability becomes stronger when collaboratively working with others, becoming a unified One, creating together while not losing individual uniqueness and consciousness. As forwarded in this text and reflected in the definition of intelligent activity,[501] when a group is intelligently working together there are no forces hindering creativity and the application of that creativity, or innovation. This requires humility, opening ourselves to others' thoughts and ideas, and, for the moment, not locked into our own thought, and open to the possibility that others' thoughts are right. Taking this approach provides the opportunity for listening, reflecting, learning and expanding, and the group is working together in a search for truth, *which is the hallmark of scientific thinking*.

Fourth, a word about emotions, your internal guidance system. In the past, people would try to separate from their emotions in order to fully engage their creative imagination, then try to tap into their intuition to create an imaginative picture. Once an idea emerged, the individual might meditate to help fill in the pieces, often engaging various types of yoga to build a unified mental structure that would lead to something different.[502] Today, recognizing the value of bisociation, we prepare our minds by looking at the world through multiple frames of reference, interacting intelligently with others, and reaching for a place where creative ideas emerge, all activities in which emotions have a role to play.

<<<<<<<>>>>>>>

INSIGHT: **To fully engage our creative imagination, we prepare our minds by looking at the world through multiple frames of reference, interacting intelligently with others, and accessing that place within where creative ideas emerge**.

<<<<<<<>>>>>>>

Note that **all thought is not equal.** Thought carries motive. MacFlouer says that minds have the ability to affect the speed and direction of energy through *emotive energy*, that is, energy that has motive to it.[503] Motive is the substance within living things. For us to live, energy must flow through us. *The basic goal of humans, as well as of any living organism, is to achieve and maintain a balanced internal energy flow despite environmental disruptions*. All of our thoughts have an energy strength. Recalling our earlier discussion, in order to thrive creativity requires outward focused thought through knowledge sharing, cooperation and collaboration. The *motive behind thought*, which can be focused inward or outward, is embedded in the thought. If the motive is based on personal desire that is only self-serving, that thought will be met with forces. Thus, motive is very much an element in the ability to tap into the intuitional plane. Thinking about self does not expand self and causes you to stay in the same place.

Negative emotions can also create barriers. For example, fear closes off the ability to learn, moving an individual into a lower level of thinking and reducing consciousness. Further, while an individual who carries fear *may* tap into the intuitional plane, what is received or perceived would be distorted through the lens of fear.

<<<<<<<>>>>>>>

INSIGHT: **The motive behind thought, which can be focused inward or outward, is embedded in your thoughts. If the motive is based on personal desire that is only self-serving, that thought will be met with forces.**

<<<<<<<>>>>>>>

Fifth, honor the diversity of the human, the Universe, and your SELF. Take the opportunity to interact in diverse groups—diverse in terms of culture, domains of knowledge, and ways of thinking. The interaction is exhilarating, stretching your mind. Then, a "spark" occurs, some little thing that is different and from which—when complexed with other "sparks" that have been through the course of life associated with other historic learning—a new pattern is forthcoming, flowing through your conscious mind, catching your attention. You SEE it, you FEEL it, you KNOW it, and become excited with the knowing. Bursting with that knowing, you share it, with affirmation and expansion occurring in the sharing.

* * * * * * *

Creating with innovation in mind points your creative juices in a positive direction that can make a difference in the world. Recognizing that while H-Creativity is certainly valuable to the knowledge domain of focus and does fan the ego and validate the effort, EVERY shift is valuable—no matter how small or large—that heads us in the direction of discovering a higher truth and using that truth to benefit humanity. And, since the information transfer in the Field is two-way, you are both receiving and contributing such that all your learning will at some level benefit a future emerging SELF.

You have been given the capacities of knowledge and creativity, which, as presented in this text, can be expanded and used innovatively. How you choose to use these capacities is up to you.

Afterword

Still connecting the dots, an AFTERWORD is a wonderful thing! It provides the opportunity to forget about all the references and supporting everything you are writing and just, well, speak from the heart!

Are you interested in Innovative Creativity? By now there can be no question that a critical first step is to prepare yourself in your domain of passion, that is, where your interests and thoughts and feelings direct you. No matter how many creative ideas may come to mind, if you don't know what to do with them, how to act on them, then those ideas will dissipate into the nether without coming to fruition.

A second important learning is that YOU as a healthy human are naturally gifted with creativity. YOU are co-creating your life even as you read this! Everything you do for the first time is creative to you, and, frankly, YOU are the focus this time around, so all those creative acts are learning experiences. Remember, just as knowledge is effectively applying information, innovation is effectively (usefully) applying creativity. Both are your birthright.

A third important learning is that innovation is a team sport. While that is quite simply put, it is actually all about the amazing entanglement of minds and energies. We are social beings, and physical mechanisms have developed in our brain to enable us to learn through social interactions. The free flow of ideas across and among open minds stimulates new ideas; in other words, creative thought begets creative thought in a never-ending spiral should we choose to listen to others with humility. Within and without, accidental associations can create new patterns, which can lead to locking onto a new useful idea and bringing it into physical reality.

And if I could add one more important learning it would be that creativity is a choice. YOU are an amazing, unique individual with world-changing (at all levels) potential. Moving humanity forward—creating a better world—REQUIRES this diversity. So, no matter how small a contribution, EVERY CONTRIBUTION COUNTS. As the world explodes with indecision, promulgating feelings of vulnerability, it is time for each of us and all of us to embrace our values and abilities and choose to contribute. Your Innovative Creativity, my friend, can make a difference.

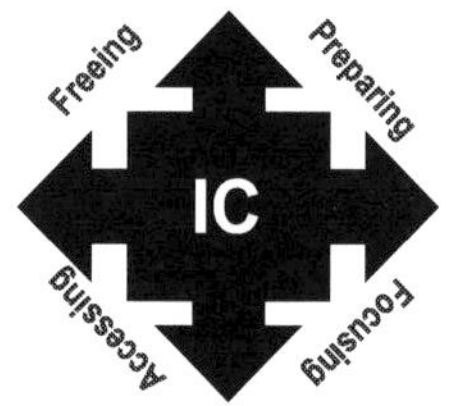
Freeing
Preparing
IC
Accessing
Focusing

Appendix A

Examples of Knowledge Capacities

Learning How to Learn (perceiving and representing)

Every individual is unique. Each person has a unique DNA, unique early development history, and adult life experiences and challenges different from all other humans. This uniqueness means that each of us learns differently and, to maximize that learning, we must understand ourselves, how we think and feel about specific subjects and situations, and how we best learn. For example, people who are more visual learners prefer learning through books, movies or databases; those who are more auditory prefer learning through storytelling and dialogue; those who are kinesthetic prefer learning through hands-on approaches such as role-playing.

A first step is to observe ourselves as we learn and assess our efficacy in different learning situations, noting what works well and what doesn't work well. We can also try adding different techniques that aid learning such as journaling, creating songs and stories, or asking others (and ourselves) key questions, then trying to answer those questions, recognizing the importance of emotions and repetitiveness in remembering and understanding. For skills that require body movements, then similar body movements must be included in the learning process. For skills that require mental agility, then mental games or simulations might be involved. In other words, the best way to learn is to understand your preferences and ensure that the learning process is consistent with the skill or knowledge you want to learn.

Undoubtedly, *the most important factor in learning is the desire to learn*, to understand the meaning, ramifications and potential impact of ideas, situations or events. In the present and future increasingly CUCA (change, uncertainty, complexity, anxiety) world, learning—that is, the creation and application of knowledge, the capacity to take effective action—is no longer just an advantage. It is a necessity. Because of individual uniqueness, each of us must learn how best we learn..

There is a relationship between your own learning style preferences and the way you share. Effective facilitation and communication require tailoring learning techniques to the preferred learning styles of your target audience. Applying multiple learning and communication styles enables you to reach target audiences with multiple preferences. Further, exposing multiple learning styles to the larger audience helps expand individual learning capacities, enriching the learning experience.

Shifting Frames of Reference (looking and seeing)

When we find ourselves in confusing situations, ambiguities or paradoxes where we don't know or understand what's happening, it is wise to recognize the limited mental capacity of a single viewpoint or frame of reference. Confusion, paradoxes and riddles are not made by external reality or the situation; they are created by our own limitations in thinking, language and perspective or viewpoint.

The patterns in the mind have strong associations built up through both experience and the developmental structure of the brain. For example, as children we learn to recognize the visual image of a "dog" and with experience associate that visual image with the word "dog". As our experience grows, we identify and learn to recognize attributes of the visual image of "dog" such as large, small, black, brown, head, tail, poodle, akita, etc. The way we store those in the brain are as associations with the pattern known as "dog" to us, perhaps connected to the particular characteristics of a beloved childhood pet. Thus, when we think of a dog, we immediately associate other attributes to that thought.

Shifting Frames of Reference is the ability to see/perceive situations and their context through different lenses; for example, understanding an organization from the viewpoints of its executives, workforce, customers, etc. The ability to shift frames of reference is enhanced by a diversity of experiences available to networked and interactive knowledge workers. Individuals who are subjected to a wide range of ideas and perspectives through social media are going to be much more attuned to differences, while at the same time becoming engaged through dialogue. This participation with lots of people and interaction with differences helps develop a healthy self-image, and comfortable connections with different situations and people that build a feeling of "capability." Through these interactions, knowledge workers are actively doing things which in and of themselves demonstrate their capability of interacting with the world. Through this broad set of reference experiences individuals can identify those disciplines or dimensions that they are excited about, and capable and competent to develop and grow from. This process can result in better decisions and choices that match their personal needs.

Frames of reference can be both expanding (as introduced above), and focusing and/or limiting, allowing the individual to go deeper in a bounded direction. Learning to consciously shift our frames of reference offers the self the opportunity to take a multidimensional approach in exploring the world around us. As introduced above, one approach is by looking at an issue from the viewpoint of different stakeholders. For example, if you are looking at an organization problem, you might ask the following questions: How would our customers see this problem? How would other employees see this problem? How would senior management see this problem? How would the bank see this problem? As another example, when exploring a system's issue, you might look at it from the inside out as well as the outside in, and then try to understand how you might see it differently from looking at it from the boundaries. Another example is learning to debate both sides of an issue. Morgan creatively described several metaphors in *Images of Organization* (for example as a machine or an ecosystem) that enabled people to consider oblique perspectives of the organization to inform decision making more comprehensively.[504] Still another approach is to look at an issue first as simple, then as complicated, then as complex, and then as chaotic, each yielding a different potential decision set. A unique capability that develops as the self becomes proficient at shifting frames of reference is the ability to extend our visual and auditory sensing perception capabilities by analogy to other time dimensions. For example, having the ability to "see" and "hear" some point in the future that is the result of a decision made today.

An excellent example of shifting frames of reference is the use of Dihedral Group Theory. Thought processes of entrepreneurs like Steve Jobs follow six distinct shifts in perspective which directly correspond to the six permutations of what is known in mathematics as a Dihedral (3) Group. Each of the six models changes the relationship of subject/verb/object, offering the opportunity to discover hidden connections and unique insights, giving rise to faster innovation and potentially more significant breakthroughs. This meaning-making approach also helps individuals understand their personal focus, that is, where their awareness is centered. Mathematician Tom McCabe's legendary work on algorithm complexity has led to an even more impactful mathematical breakthrough. He has discovered a connection between mathematical group theory and consciousness, directly connecting the mathematical group Dihedral order 6 with different perspectives of our thoughts.[754]

Reversal (looking and seeing)

One of the fun ways to shift our frame of reference is Reversal, that is, the ability to see/perceive situations and their context by turning something inside out, or generally reversing the order of things, whether front and back, or top and bottom, or side to side, or back to front. There are lots of ways to think about this.

For example, during a big Acquisition Reform movement in the U.S. Department of the Navy, part of which was the shift to performance-based standards, there was the need to eliminate thousands of standards that had crept into various contracting vehicles over the years. Given one year and a pot of money to accomplish this task, the DON started down the same path as the other services, holding a mini-trial for each standard, where one-by-one it had to be "proved" that a standard was not needed. The task was an impossible one; there was always some contractor or contracting officer who felt that each standard was absolutely essential. As the weeks went by, with maybe 5 or 6 standards eliminated out of several thousand needing to be addressed, it was clear this approach was doomed to failure. Embracing the Knowledge Capacity of Reversal, all of the standards were eliminated, and mini-trials were held for those around which contractors and contracting officers had enough energy to bring back to the board and support their reinstatement. This was a game changer; when all was said and done, a couple of hundred standards were important enough to invest the energy necessary to have them reinstated.

Comprehending Diversity (perceiving and representing)

From an internal perspective, quick responses require a diversity of responses from which to draw. Since there is not much time to effectively respond in a CUCA environment, it makes sense to explore and develop a variety of potential responses prior to their need. An example is the use of scenario building, a foresight methodology that has been well-developed and tested in government, business and education. Scenarios are a form of story that can be used to consider possible, plausible, probable and preferable outcomes. Possible outcomes (what might happen) are based on future knowledge; plausible outcomes (what could happen) are based on current knowledge; probable outcomes (what will most likely happen) are based on current trends; and preferable outcomes (what you want to happen) are based on value judgments. For a well-connected knowledge worker, building scenarios can be both fruitful and fun. When facing surprises, scenarios can help in understanding new situations or at least foster a faster response by comparing the surprise with a related scenario.

From an external perspective, Comprehending Diversity means developing a competency in identifying and comprehending a wide variety of situations. For example, if you know nothing about complexity you won't be able to differentiate a complex system from a complicated system, each of which requires different sets of decisions and actions to achieve goals.

A first step is to recognize what you are looking at: the existence of diversity, the situation, and its context. Key questions: Is it diverse? Does it have many aspects that are in play or that may come into play? A second step is to comprehend it. *Vericate*, that is, consult a trusted ally, someone who understands the systems at play. Develop knowledge about a situation to comprehend it within the context of the situation. Move through the value chain of the individual change model to develop knowledge about the diversity, that is, awareness, understanding, meaning, insight, intuition, judgment, creativity, and anticipating the outcome of your decisions and actions.

Orchestrating Drive (acting and being)

There are many wives' tales and beliefs about our personal energy. One is that we just have so much energy in a life, and we just sit down and die when it is spent. Another says the more you give away the more you have. Regardless of whether we refer to this energy as spark, subtle energy (metaphysics), prana (Hindu), chi (Chinese), libido (Freud), orgone energy (Reich), or any other of the numerous other descriptive terms, every individual possesses a life force or, as described by Henri Bergson, a French philosopher, the élan vital, a source of efficient causation and evolution in nature. What we have learned about this energy—both by observation, and confirmed more recently through neuroscience findings—is its relationship to feelings. As Candace Pert, a research professor of physiology and biophysics at Georgetown University Medical Center, asserts, "… this mysterious energy is actually the free-flow of information carried by the biochemicals of emotion, the neuropeptides and their receptors." [505]

While the expression of any strong emotion requires some energy output, the expression of negative emotions generally represents a larger expenditure of energy, and the expression of positive emotions generally represents a generator of energy. For example, consider the crowds following a close-tied football game. While all may be physically tired from the experience, those who supported the loosing team are generally depressed with low energy and drag home; those who supported the winning team are generally buoyant, and may well go out and celebrate.

By understanding—and using—the emotions as a personal guidance system and motivator, knowledge workers can orchestrate their energy output. For example, by interacting, working with, and writing about ideas that have personal resonance, a knowledge worker is generating energy while expending energy, thus extending their ability to contribute and influence. See the discussion on the power of desire in Chapter 5.

Symbolic Representation (perceiving and representing)

Representations in terms of words and visuals are the tools of trade for facilitating common understanding. The mind/brain does not store exact replicas of past events or memories. Rather, it stores invariant representations that color the meaning or essence of incoming information.[506] There is a hierarchy of information where hierarchy represents "an order of some complexity, in which the elements are distributed along the gradient of importance."[507] This hierarchy of information is analogous to the physical design of the neocortex, "a sheet of cells the size of a dinner napkin as thick as six business cards, where the connections between various regions give the whole thing a hierarchical structure."[508] There are six layers of hierarchical patterns in the architecture of the cortex. As documented for the sense of vision, it appears that the patterns at the lowest level of the cortex are fast changing and spatially specific (highly situation dependent and context sensitive) while the patterns at the highest level are slow changing and spatially invariant.[509] For example, values, theories, beliefs, and assumptions created (repeatedly) through past learning processes represent a higher level of invariant form, one that does not easily change, compared to lower-level patterns.[510]

Thus, once learned, the mind/brain can quickly associate with symbols which can represent large amounts of context yet be immediately understood and interpreted. For example, a cross or menorah carries with it all the myths it represents. "It is an outward sign of an inward belief."[511] As self, symbols are everywhere we look. Mathematics is built on hypotheses and relationships, that is, patterns, assumptions and relationships. Letters represent sounds, notes represent tones, pictures represent thoughts and beliefs, shapes of signs on the highway represent the context of rules, and so on. A whole field of endeavor, *Semiotics*, has emerged around the study of signs.

We use symbols to organize our thoughts. For example, in human face-to-face interactions it has long been recognized that non-verbals and voicing (tone, emphasis) can play a larger role in communication than the words that are exchanged. New patterns are emerging in social media that represent and convey these aspects of communication, helping provide the context and "feeling" for what is being said. In electronic communication, symbols, or emogi, are small icons used to express a concept or emotion. For example, whether on Twitter or email, ":)" immediately conveys a smiley face, so much so that when these keystrokes are entered in MSWord followed by a space, they are immediately translated into ☺. As social media has matured, these symbols have become patterns of patterns, well understood by practicing social networkers and quickly conveying the message they are sending.

Appendix B

Knowing

NOTE from authors: We explore knowing from a more pragmatic viewpoint inclusive of brief exercises to expand our external sensing capabilities. To this end, a Knowing Framework developed for the U.S. Department of the Navy is utilized. For purposes of this discussion, Knowing is poetically defined as **seeing beyond images, hearing beyond words, sensing beyond appearances, and feeling beyond emotions**. *In this treatment, it is considered a sense that emerges from our collective tacit knowledge.*

Every decision and the actions that decision drives is a learning experience that builds on its predecessors by broadening the sources of knowledge creation and the capacity to create knowledge in different ways. For example, as an individual engages in more and more conversations across the Internet in search of meaning, thought connections occur that cause an expansion of shallow knowledge. As we are aware, *knowledge begets knowledge*. In a global interactive environment, the more that is understood, the more that can be created and understood. This is how our personal learning system works. Over time, as we tap into our internal resources, *knowledge enables knowing, and knowing inspires the creation of knowledge.*

The concept of "knowing" is not easy to define, since the word and concept are used in so many different ways. We consider Knowing as a *sense* that is supported by our tacit knowledge. In this appendix, we provide a Knowing Framework[512] that focuses on methods to increase individual sensory capabilities. This Framework specifically refers to our five external senses and to the increase of the ability to consciously integrate these sensory inputs *with our tacit knowledge*, that knowledge created by past learning experiences that is *entangled with* the flow of spiritual tacit knowledge continuously available to each of us. In other words, knowing—**driven by the unconscious as an integrated unit**—is the *sense* gained from experience that resides in the *subconscious* part of the mind, *and* the energetic connection our mind enjoys with the *superconscious*.

The subconscious and superconscious are both part of our unconscious resources, with the subconscious directly supporting the embodied mind/brain and the superconscious focused on tacit resources involving larger moral aspects, the emotional part of human nature, and the higher development of our mental faculties. When engaged by an intelligent mind which has moved beyond logic into conscious processing based on trust and recognition of the connectedness and interdependence of humanity, these resources are immeasurable.

In the figure below [which is also Figure 3 in Chapter 1], the superconscious is described with the terms spiritual learning, higher guidance, values and morality, and love. It is also characterized as "pre-personality" to emphasize that there are no personal translators such as beliefs and mental models attached to this form of knowing. The flow of information from the superconscious is very much focused on the moment at hand and does not bring with it any awareness patterns that could cloud the decision-makers full field of perception.

In contrast, the memories stored in the subconscious are very much a part of the personality of the decision-maker, and may be heavily influenced by an individual's perceptions and feelings at the time they were formed. Embodied tacit knowledge would be based on the physical preferences of personality expression while affective tacit knowledge would be based on the feelings connected with the personality of the decision-maker. For example, if there was a traumatic event that occurred in childhood that produced a feeling of "helplessness," later in life there might be neuronal patterns that are triggered that reproduce this feeling when the adult encounters a similar situation. While these feelings may have been appropriate for the child, they would rarely be of service to a seasoned, intelligent decision-maker.

Descriptive terms for the subconscious include life learning, memory, associative patterning, and material intellect. The subconscious in an autonomic system serving a life-support function. We must recognize that **the human *subconscious* is in service to the conscious mind**. It is not intended to dominate decision-making. The subconscious expands as it integrates and connects (complexes) all that we put into it through our five external-connected senses. *It is at the conscious mind level that we develop our intellect and make choices that serve as the framework for our subconscious processing.*

The figure below is a nominal graphic showing the continuous feedback loops between knowledge and knowing. Thinking about (potential) and experiencing (actual) effective action (knowledge) supports development of embodied, intuitive and affective tacit knowledges. When we recognize and use our sense of knowing—regardless of its origin—we are tapping into our tacit knowledge to inform our decisions and actions. These decisions and actions, and the feedback from taking those actions in turn expand our knowledge base, much of which over time will become future tacit resources. Since our internal sense of knowing draws collectively from all areas of our tacit knowledge, the more we open to this inner sense, respond accordingly, and observe and reflect on feedback, the more our inner resources move beyond limited perceptions which may be connected to embedded childhood memories.

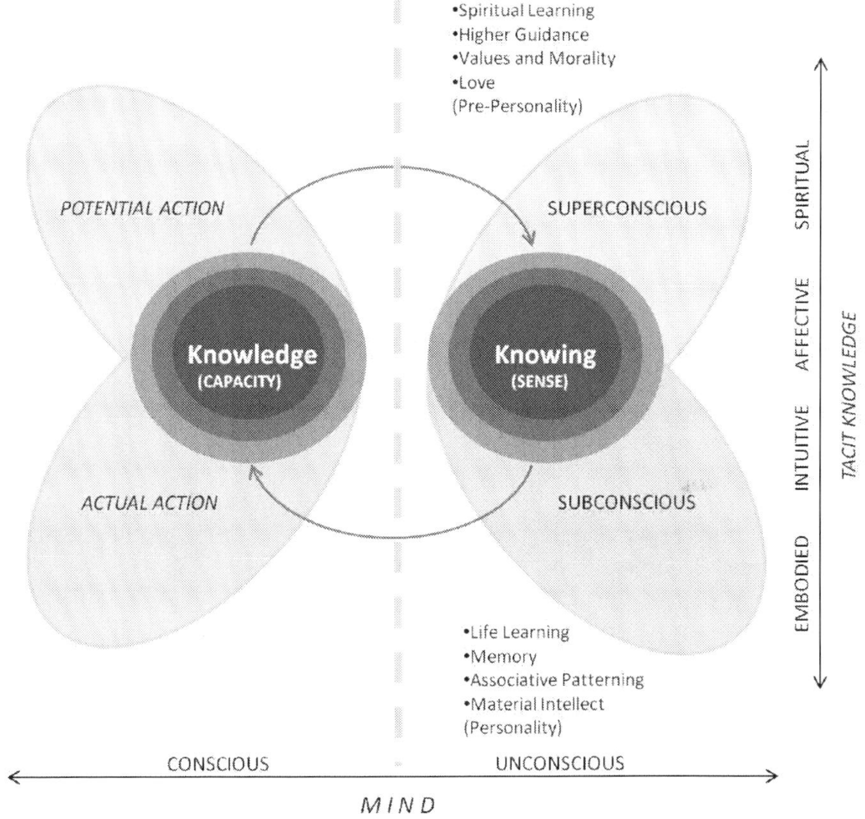

Figure 21. *The Eternal Loop of Knowledge and Knowing*

Critical Areas of Knowing

The Knowing Framework encompasses three critical areas. The first is "knowing our self," learning to love and trust ourselves. This includes deep reflection on our self in terms of beliefs, values, dreams and purpose for being, and appreciation for the unique beings that we are. It includes understanding of our goals, objectives, strengths and weaknesses in thought and action, and internal defenses and limitations. By knowing ourselves we learn to work within and around our limitations and to support our strengths, thus ensuring that the data, information, and knowledge informing our system is properly identified and interpreted. Further, knowing our self means recognizing that we are a social being, part of the large ecosystem we call Gaia and inextricably connected to other social beings around the world, which brings us to the second critical element: knowing others.

We live in a connected world, spending most of our waking life with other people, and often continuing that interaction in our dreams! There is amazing diversity in the world, so much to learn and share with others. Whether in love or at war, people are always in relationships and must grapple with the sense of "other" in accordance with their beliefs, values and dreams.

The third critical area is that of "knowing" the situation in as objective and realistic a manner as possible, understanding the situation, problem, or challenge in context. In the military this is called situational awareness and includes areas such as culture, goals and objectives, thinking patterns, internal inconsistencies, capabilities, strategies and tactics, and political motivations. The current dynamics of our environment, the multiple forces involved, the complexity of relationships, the many aspects of events that are governed by human emotion, and the unprecedented amount of available data and information make situational awareness a challenging but essential phenomenon in many aspects of our daily lives.

As we move away from predictable patterns susceptible to logic, decision-makers must become increasingly reliant on their "gut" instinct, an internal sense of knowing combined with high situational awareness. Knowing then becomes key to decision-making. The mental skills honed in knowing help decision-makers identify, interpret, make decisions, and take appropriate action in response to current situational assessments.

This construct of knowing can be elevated to the organizational level by using and combining the insights and experiences of individuals through dialogue and collaboration within teams, groups, and communities, both face-to-face and virtual. Such efforts significantly improve the quality of understanding and responsiveness of actions of the organization. They also greatly expand the scope of complex situations that can be handled through knowing because of the greater resources brought to bear—all of this significantly supported by technological interoperability.

Organizational knowing is an aspect of *organizational intelligence*, the capacity of an organization as a whole to gather information, generate knowledge, innovate, and to take effective action. This capacity is the foundation for effective response in a fast-changing and complex world. Increasing our sensory and mental processes contributes to the "positioning" understood by the great strategist Sun Tzu in the year 500 B.C. when he wrote his famous dictum for victory: *Position yourself so there is no battle.*[513] Today, in our world of organizations and complex challenges, we could say "Position ourselves so there is no confusion."

By exploring our sense of knowing, we expand our understanding of ourselves, improve our awareness of the external world, learn how to tap into internal resources, and increase our skills to affect internal and external change. The Knowing Framework provides ideas for developing deep knowledge within the self and sharing that knowledge with others to create new perceptions and levels of understanding. Since each situation and each individual is unique, this Framework does not provide specific answers. Rather, it suggests questions and paths to follow to find those answers.

Principles of Knowing

In response to a changing environment, the Knowing Framework presented below in its expanded form was first developed at the turn of the century for the U.S. Department of the Navy. There are a number of recognized basic truths that drove its development. These truths became the principles upon which the Knowing Framework is based.

(1) Making decisions in an increasingly complex environment requires new ways of thinking.

(2) All the information in the world is useless if the decision-maker who needs it cannot process it and connect it to their own internal values, knowledge, and wisdom.

(3) We don't know all that we know. Each of us has knowledge far beyond that which is in our conscious mind. Put another way, we know more than we know we know. (Much of our experience and knowledge resides in the unconscious mind.)

(4) By exercising our mental and sensory capabilities we can increase those capabilities.

(5) Support capabilities of organizational knowing include organizational learning, knowledge centricity, common values and language, coherent vision, whole-brain learning, openness of communications, effective collaboration, and the free flow of ideas.

The concept of knowing focuses on the cognitive capabilities of observing and perceiving a situation; the cognitive processing that must occur to understand the external world and make maximum use of our internal cognitive capabilities; and the mechanism for creating deep knowledge and acting on that knowledge via the self as an agent of change. Each of these core areas will be discussed below in more detail.

The Cognitive Capabilities

The cognitive capabilities include observing, collecting and interpreting data and information, and building knowledge relative to the situation. The six areas we will address are: listening, noticing, scanning, sensing, patterning, and integrating. These areas represent means by which we perceive the external world and begin to make sense of it.

Listening

The first area, listening, sets the stage for the other five cognitive capabilities. Listening involves more than hearing; it is a sensing greater than sound. It is a neurological cognitive process involving stimuli received by the auditory system. The linguist Roland Barthes distinguished the difference between hearing and listening when he says: "Hearing is a physiological phenomenon; listening is a psychological act." What this means is that there is a choice involved in listening in terms of the listener choosing to interpret sound waves to potentially create understanding and meaning.[514] There are three levels of listening: alerting, deciphering and understanding. Alerting is picking up on environmental sound cues. Deciphering is relating the sound cues to meaning. Understanding is focused on the impact of the sound on another person. Active listening is intentionally focusing on who is speaking in order to take full advantage of verbal and non-verbal cues.

In developing active listening, imagine how you can use all your senses to focus on what is being said. One way to do this is to role-play, imagining you are in their shoes and feeling the words. Active listening means fully participating, acknowledging the thoughts you are hearing with your body, encouraging the train of thought, actively asking questions when the timing is appropriate. The childhood game of pass the word is an example of a fun way to improve listening skills. A group sits in a circle and whispers a message one to the next until it comes back to the originator. A variation on this theme is Chinese Whispers where a group makes a line and starts a different message from each end, crossing somewhere in the middle and making it to the opposite end before sharing the messages back with the originators. Another good group exercise is a "your turn" exercise, where one individual begins speaking, and another person picks up the topic, and so forth. Not knowing whether you are next in line to speak develops some good listening skills.

The bottom line is that what we don't hear cannot trigger our knowing. Awareness of our environment is not enough. We must listen to the flow of sound and search out meaning, understanding, and implications.

Noticing

The second area, noticing, represents the ability to observe around us and recognize, i.e., identify those things that are relevant to our immediate or future needs. We are all familiar with the phenomenon of buying a new car and for the next six months recognizing the large number of similar cars that are on the streets. This is an example of a cognitive process of which we are frequently unaware. We notice those things that are recently in our memory or of emotional or intellectual importance to us. We miss many aspects of our environment if we are not focusing directly on them. Thus, the art of noticing can be considered the art of "knowing" which areas of the environment are important and relevant to us at the moment, and focusing in on those elements and the relationships among those elements. It is also embedding a recall capability of those things not necessarily of immediate importance but representing closely related context factors. *This noticing is a first step in building deep knowledge, developing a thorough understanding and a systems context awareness of those areas of anticipated interest.* This is the start of becoming an expert in a given field of endeavor, or situation.

A classic example of mental exercises aimed at developing latent noticing skills is repetitive observation and recall. For example, think about a room that you are often in, perhaps a colleague's office or a friend's living room. Try to write down everything you can remember about this room. You will discover that despite the fact you've been in this room often, you can't remember exactly where furniture is located, or what's in the corners or on the walls. When you've completed this exercise, visit the room and write down everything you see, everything you've missed. What pictures are on the walls? Do you like them? What personal things in the room tell you something about your colleague or friend? How does the layout of furniture help define the room? (These kinds of questions build relationships with feelings and other thinking patterns.) Write a detailed map and remember it. A few days later repeat this exercise from the beginning. If you make any mistakes, go back to the room again, and as many times as it takes to get it right. Don't let yourself off the hook. You're telling yourself that when details are important you know how to bring them into your memory. As your ability to recall improves, repeat this exercise focusing on a street, a building, or a city you visit often.

Scanning

The third area, scanning, represents the ability to review and survey a large amount of data and information and selectively identify those areas that may be relevant. Because of the exponential increase in data and information, this ability becomes more and more important as time progresses. In a very real sense, scanning represents the ability to reduce the complexity of a situation or environment by objectively filtering out the irrelevant aspects, or environmental noise. By developing your own system of environmental "speed reading," scanning can provide early indicators of change.

Scanning exercises push the mind to pick up details and, more importantly, patterns of data and information, *in a short timeframe*. This is an important skill that law enforcement officers and investigators nurture. For example, when you visit an office or room that you've never been in before, take a quick look around and record your first strong impressions. What feelings are you getting? Count stuff. Look at patterns, look at contrasts, look at colors. Try to pick up everything in one or two glances around the room. Make a mental snapshot of the room and spend a few minutes impressing it in your memory. As you leave, remember the mental picture you've made of the room, the way you feel. Impress upon yourself the importance of remembering this. This picture can last for days, or years, despite the shortness of your visit. Your memory can literally retain an integrated *gestalt* of the room. Realize that what you can recall is only a small part of what went into your mind.

Sensing

The fourth area, sensing, represents the ability to take inputs from the external world through our five external senses and ensure the translation of those inputs into our mind to represent as accurate a transduction process (the transfer of energy from one form to another) as possible. The human ability to collect information through our external sensors is limited because of our physiological limitations. For example, we only see a very small part of the electromagnetic spectrum in terms of light, yet with technology we can tremendously expand the sensing capability. As humans we often take our senses for granted, yet they are highly-sensitized complex detection systems that cause immediate response without conscious thought! An example most everyone has experienced or observed is a mother's sensitivity to any discomfort of her young child. The relevance to "knowing" is, recognizing the importance of our sensory inputs, to learn how to fine tune these inputs to the highest possible level, then use discernment and discretion to interpret them.

Exercise examples cited above to increase noticing, scanning, and patterning skills will also enhance the sense of sight, which is far more than just looking at things. It includes locating yourself in position to things. For example, when you're away from city lights look up on a starry night and explore your way around the heavens. Try to identify the main constellations. By knowing their relative position, you know where you are, what month it is, and can even approximate the time of day. The stars provide context for positioning yourself on the Earth.

Here are a few exercise examples for other senses. Hearing relates to comprehension. Sit on a park bench, close your eyes and relax, quieting your mind. Start by listening to what is going on around you—conversations of passersby, cars on a nearby causeway, the birds chattering, the wind rustling leaves, water trickling down a nearby drain. Now stretch beyond these nearby sounds. Imagine you have the hearing of a panther, only multidirectional, because you can move your ears every direction and search for sounds. Focus on a faint sound in the distance, then ask your auditory systems to bring it closer. Drag that sound toward you mentally. It gets louder. If you cup one hand behind one ear and cup the other hand in front of the opposite ear, you can actually improve your hearing, focusing on noises from the back with one ear and noises from the front with the other. How does that change what you are hearing?

Next time you are in a conversation with someone, focus your eyes and concentrate on the tip of their nose or the point of their chin. Listen carefully to every word they say, to the pause between their words, to their breathing and sighs, the rise and fall of their voice. Search for the inflections and subtle feelings being communicated behind what is actually being said. When people are talking, much of the meaning behind the information they impart is in their feelings. The words they say are only a representation, a descriptive code that communicates thought, interacting electrical pulses and flows influenced by an emotion or subtle feeling. By listening in this way, with your visual focus not distracting your auditory focus, you can build greater understanding of the subtleties behind the words.

There are many games that accentuate the sense of touch. An old favorite is blind man's bluff; more current is the use of blindfolding and walking through the woods used in outdoor management programs. Try this at home by spending three or four hours blindfolded, going about your regular home activities. At first, you'll stumble and bump, maybe even become frustrated. But as you continue, your ability to manage your movements and meet your needs using your sense of touch will quickly improve. You will be able to move about your home alone with relatively little effort, and you'll know where things are, especially things that are alive, such as plants and pets. You will develop the ability to *feel* their energy. Exercises such as these force your unconscious mind to create, re-create, and surface the imagined physical world. It activates the mind to bring out into the open its sensitivity to the physical context in which we live.

Patterning

The fifth area, patterning, represents the ability to review, study, and interpret large amounts of data/events/information and identify causal or correlative connections that are relatively stable over time or space and may represent patterns driven by underlying phenomena. These hidden drivers can become crucial to understanding the situation or market behaviors. This would also include an understanding of rhythm and randomness, flows and trends. Recall the importance of structure, relationships, and culture in creating emergent phenomena (patterns) and in influencing complex systems.

A well-known example of the use of patterning is that of professional card players and successful gamblers, who have trained themselves to repeatedly recall complicated patterns found in randomly drawn cards. To learn this skill, and improve your patterning skills, take a deck of cards and quickly flip through the deck three or four at a time. During this process, make a mental picture of the cards that are in your hand, pause, then turn over three or four more. After doing this several times, recall the mental picture of the first set of cards. What were they? Then try to recall the second set, then the third.

The secret is not to try and remember the actual cards, but to close your eyes and recall the *mental picture* of the cards. Patterns will emerge. After practicing for a while, you will discover your ability to recall the patterns—as well as your ability to recall larger numbers of patterns—will steadily increase. As you increase the number of groups of cards you can recall, and increase the number of cards within each group, you are increasing your ability to recall complex patterns.

Study many patterns found in nature, art, science, and other areas of human endeavor. These patterns will provide you with a "mental reference library" that your mind can use to detect patterns in new situations. Chess experts win games on pattern recognition and pattern creation, not on individual piece placement.

Integrating

The last area in the cognitive capabilities is integration. This represents the top-level capacity to take large amounts of data and information and pull them together to create meaning; what is frequently called sense-making. This capability—to pull together the major aspects of a complex situation and create patterns, relationships, models, and meaning that represent reality—is what enables us to make decisions. This capability also applies to the ability to integrate internal organization capabilities and systems.

While we have used the word "integrating" to describe this capability, recall that the human mind is an associative patterner that is continuously complexing (mixing) incoming information from the external environment with that which is stored in memory. Thus, while the decision-maker has an awareness of integrating, the unconscious is doing much of the work and providing nudges in terms of feelings and speculative thought. Our unconscious is forever our partner, working 24/7 for us.

These five ways of observing represent the front line of cognitive capabilities needed to assist all of us in creative and accurate situational awareness and building a valid understanding of situations. To support these cognitive capabilities, we then need processes that transform these observations and this first-level knowledge into a deeper level of comprehension and understanding.

The Cognitive Processes

Internal cognitive processes that support the cognitive capabilities discussed above include visualizing, intuiting, valuing, choosing, and setting intent. These five internal cognitive processes greatly improve our power to understand the external world and to make maximum use of our internal thinking capabilities, transforming our observations into understanding.

Visualizing

The first of these processes, visualizing, represents the methodology of focusing attention on a given area and through imagination and logic creating an internal vision and scenario for success. In developing a successful vision, one must frequently take several different perspectives of the situation, play with a number of assumptions underlying these perspectives, and through a playful and imaginative trial-and-error, come up with potential visions. This process is more creative than logical, more intuitive than rational, and wherever possible should be challenged, filtered, and constructed in collaboration with other competent individuals. Often this is done between two trusting colleagues or perhaps with a small team. While there is never absolute assurance that visualizing accurately represents reality—nor would you want it to do so in a CUCA environment—there are probabilities or degrees of success that can be recognized and developed.

Intuiting

The second supporting area is that of intuiting. By this we mean the art of making maximum use of our own intuition developed through experience, trial-and-error, and deliberate internal questioning and application. There are standard processes available for training oneself to surface intuition. (See Chapter 10.) Recognize that intuition is typically understood as being the ability to access our unconscious mind and thereby make effective use of its very large storeroom of observations, experiences, and information. In our framework, intuition is one of the four ways tacit knowledge expresses.

Empathy represents another aspect of intuition. Empathy is interpreted as the ability to take oneself out of oneself and put oneself into another person's world. In other words, as the old Native American saying goes, "Until you walk a mile in his moccasins, you will never understand the person." The ability to empathize permits us to translate our personal perspective into that of another, thereby understanding their interpretation of the situation and intuiting their actions. A tool that can be used to trigger ideas and dig deeper into one's intuitive capability, bringing out additional insights, is "mind mapping." Mind mapping visually display and recognizes relationships from discrete and diverse pieces of information and data.[515]

Valuing

Valuing represents the capacity to observe situations and recognize the values that underly their various aspects and concomitantly be fully aware of your own values and beliefs. A major part of valuing is the ability to align your vision, mission, and goals to focus attention on the immediate situation at hand. A second aspect represents the ability to identify the relevant but unknown aspects of a situation or competitor's behavior. Of course, the problem of unknown unknowns always exists in a turbulent environment and, while logically they are impossible to identify because by definition they are unknown, there are techniques available that help one reduce the area of known unknowns and hence reduce the probability of them adversely affecting the organization.

A third aspect of valuing is that of meaning, that is, understanding the important aspects of the situation and being able to prioritize them to anticipate potential consequences. Meaning is contingent upon the goals and aspirations of the individual. It also relies on the history of both the individual's experience and the context of the situation. Determining the meaning of a situation allows us to understand its impact on our own objectives and those of our organization. Knowing the meaning of something lets us prioritize our actions and estimate the resources we may need to deal with it.

Choosing

The fourth supporting area is that of choosing. Choosing involves making judgments, that is, conclusions and interpretations developed through the use of rules-of-thumb, facts, knowledge, experiences, emotions and intuition. While not necessarily widely recognized, judgments are used far more than logic or rational thinking in making decisions. This is because all but the simplest decisions occur in a context in which there is insufficient, noisy, or perhaps too much information to make rational conclusions. Judgment makes maximum use of heuristics, meta-knowing, and verication. Verication is the process by which we can improve the probability of making good choices by working with trusted others and using *their* experience and knowing to validate and improve the level of our judgmental effectiveness. Again, this could be done via a trusted colleague or through effective team creativity and decision-making.

Heuristics represent the rules-of-thumb developed over time and through experience in a given field. They are shortcuts to thinking that are applicable to specific situations. Their value is speed of conclusions and their usefulness rests on consistency of the environment and repeatability of situations. Thus, they are both powerful and dangerous. Dangerous because the situation or environment, when changing, may quickly invalidate former reliable heuristics and historically create the phenomenon of always solving the last problem; yet powerful because they represent efficient and rapid ways of making decisions where the situation is known and the heuristics apply.

Meta-knowing is knowing about knowing, that is, understanding how we know things and how we go about knowing things. With this knowledge, one can more effectively go about learning and knowing in new situations as they evolve over time. Such power and flexibility greatly improves the quality of our choices. Meta-knowing is closely tied to our natural internal processes of learning and behaving as well as knowing how to make the most effective use of available external data, information, and knowledge and intuit that which is not available. An interesting aspect of meta-knowing is the way that certain errors in judgment are common to many people. Just being aware of these mistakes can reduce their occurrence. For example, we tend to give much more weight to specific, concrete information than to conceptual or abstract information.[516]

Setting Intent

Intent is a powerful internal process that can be harnessed by every human. Intention is the source with which we are doing something, the act or instance of mentally setting some course of action or result, a determination to act in some specific way. It can take the form of a declaration (often in the form of action), an assertion, a prayer, a cry for help, a wish, visualization, a thought, or an affirmation. Perhaps the most in-depth and focused experimentation on the effects of human intention on the properties of materials and what we call physical reality has been that pursued for the past 40 years by Dr. William Tiller of Stanford University. Tiller has proven through repeated experimentation that it is possible to significantly change the properties (ph) of water by holding a clear intention to do so. His mind-shifting and potentially world-changing results began with using intent to change the acid/alkaline balance in purified water. The ramifications of this experiment have the potential to impact every aspect of human life.

What Tiller has discovered is that there are two unique levels of physical reality. The "normal level" of substance is the electric/atom/molecule level, what most of us think of and perceive as the only physical reality. However, a second level of substance exists that is the magnetic information level. While these two levels always interpenetrate each other, under "normal" conditions they do not interact; they are "uncoupled." Intention changes this condition, causing these two levels to interact, or move into a "coupled" state. Where humans are concerned, Tiller says that what an individual intends for himself with a strong sustained desire is what that individual will eventually become.[517]

While informed by Spiritual, the Embodied, Intuitive and Affective tacit knowledges are *local expressions of knowledge*, that is, directly related to our expression in physical reality in a specific situation and context. Connecting Tiller's model of intention with our model of tacit knowledge, it begins to become clear that effective intent relates to an alignment of the conscious mind with the tacit components of the mind and body, that is Embodied, Intuitive, and Affective tacit knowledge. We have to *know* it, *feel* it, and *believe* it to achieve the coupling of the electric/atom/molecule level and magnetic information level of physical reality.

As we use our power of intent to co-create our future, it is necessary to focus from outcome to intention, not worrying about what gets done but staying focused on what you are doing and how you "feel" about what you are doing. Are we in alignment with the direction our decisions are taking us? If not, back to the drawing board—that's looking closer at you, the decision-maker, and ensuring that your vision is clear and your intent is aligned with that vision.

In summary, the five internal cognitive processes—visualizing, intuiting, valuing, choosing and setting intent—work with the six cognitive capabilities—listening, noticing, scanning, patterning, sensing, and integrating—to process data and information and create knowledge within the context of the environment and the situation. However, this knowledge must always be suspect because of our own self-limitations, internal inconsistencies, historical biases, and emotional distortions, all of which are discussed in the third area of knowing: The Self as an Agent of Change.

The Self as an Agent of Change

This third area of the Knowing Framework is the mechanism for creating deep knowledge, a level of understanding consistent with the external world and our internal framework. As the unconscious continuously associates information, the self as an agent of change takes the emergent deep knowledge and uses it for the dual purpose of our personal learning and growth, and for making changes in the external world.

Recall that deep knowledge consists of beliefs, facts, truths, assumptions, and understanding of an area that is so thoroughly embedded in the mind that we are often not consciously aware of the knowledge. To create deep knowledge an individual has to "live" with it, continuously interacting, thinking, learning, and experiencing that part of the world until the knowledge truly becomes a natural part of the inner being. An example would be a person who has a good knowledge of a foreign language and can speak it fluently; a person with deep knowledge would be able to *think* in the language without any internal translation and would not need their native language to understand that internal thinking.

In the discussion of self as an agent of change, there are ten elements that will be presented. Five of these elements are internal: know thyself, mental models, emotional intelligence, learning and forgetting, and mental defenses; and five of these elements are external: modeling behaviors, knowledge sharing, dialogue, storytelling, and the art of persuasion

Internal Elements

Alexander Pope, in his essay on man originally published in 1732, noted that: "Know then thyself, presume not God to scan; the proper study of mankind is man." We often think we know ourselves, but we rarely do. To really understand our own biases, perceptions, capabilities, etc., each of us must look inside and, as objectively as possible, ask ourselves, who are we, what are our limitations, what are our strengths, and what jewels and baggage do we carry from our years of experience. Rarely do we *take ourselves out of ourselves and look at ourselves*. But without an objective understanding of our own values, beliefs, and biases, we are continually in danger of misunderstanding the interpretations we apply to the external world. Our motives, expectations, decisions, and beliefs are frequently driven by internal forces of which we are completely unaware. For example, our emotional state plays a strong role in determining how we make decisions and what we decide.

The first step in knowing ourselves is awareness of the fact that we cannot assume we are what our conscious mind thinks we are. Two examples that most of us have experienced come to mind. The first is that we frequently do not know what we think until we hear what we say. The second example is the recognition that every act of writing is an act of creativity. And our biases, prejudices, and even brilliant ideas frequently remain unknown to us until pointed out by others or through conversations. Consciousness is our window to the world, but it is clouded by an internal history, experiences, feelings, memories, and desires.

After awareness comes the need to constantly monitor ourselves for undesirable traits or biases in our thinking, feeling, and processing. Seeking observations from others and carefully analyzing our individual experiences are both useful in understanding ourselves. We all have limitations and strengths, and even agendas hidden from our conscious mind that we must be aware of and build upon or control.

Part of knowing ourselves is the understanding of what mental models we have formed in specific areas of the external world. Mental models are the models we use to represent our own picture of reality. They are built up over time and through experience and represent our beliefs, assumptions, and ways of interpreting the outside world. They are efficient in that they allow us to react quickly to changing conditions and make rapid decisions based upon our presupposed model. Concomitantly, they are dangerous if the model is inaccurate or misleading.

Because we exist in a rapidly changing environment, many of our models quickly become outdated. We then must recognize the importance of continuously reviewing our perceptions and assumptions of the external world and questioning our own mental models to ensure they are consistent with reality.[518] Since this is done continuously in our subconscious, we must always question ourselves as to our real, versus stated, motives, goals and feelings. *Only then can we know who we are, only then can we change to who we want to be.*

The art of knowing not only includes understanding our own mental models, but the ability to recognize and deal with the mental models of others. Mental models frequently serve as drivers for our actions as well as our interpretations. When creating deep knowledge or taking action, the use of small groups, dialogue, etc. to normalize mental models with respected colleagues provides somewhat of a safeguard against the use of incomplete or erroneous mental models.

A subtle but powerful factor underlying mental models is the role of emotions in influencing our perception of reality. This has been extensively explored by Daniel Goleman in his seminal book *Emotional Intelligence*.[519] Emotional intelligence is the ability to sense, understand, and effectively apply the power and acumen of emotions as a source of human energy, information, connection, and influence. It includes self-control, zeal and persistence, and the ability to motivate oneself. To understand emotional intelligence, we study how emotions affect behavior, influence decisions, motivate people to action, and impact their ability to interrelate. Emotions play a much larger role in our lives than previously understood, including a strong role in decision-making. For years it was widely held that rationality was the way of the executive. Now it is becoming clear that the rational and the emotional parts of the mind must be used together to get the best performance in organizations.

Much of emotional life is unconscious. Awareness of emotions occurs when the emotions enter the frontal cortex. As affective tacit knowledge, emotions in the subconscious play a powerful role in how we perceive and act, and hence in our decision-making. Feelings come from the limbic part of the brain and often come forth before the related experiences occur. *They represent a signal* that a given potential action may be wrong, or right, or that an external event may be dangerous. Emotions assign values to options or alternatives, sometimes without our knowing it. There is growing evidence that fundamental ethical stances in life stem from underlying emotional capacities. These stances create the basic belief system, the values, and often the underlying assumptions that we use to see the world—our mental model. From this short treatment of the concept, it is clear that emotional intelligence is interwoven across the ten elements of the self as an agent of change.[520]

Creating the deep knowledge of knowing through the effective use of emotional intelligence opens the door to two other equally important factors: learning and forgetting. Learning and letting go—in terms of "filing" away or putting away on the bookshelf—are critical elements of the self as an agent of change because they are the primary processes through which we change and grow. They are also the prerequisite for continuous learning, so essential for developing competencies representing all of the processes and capabilities discussed previously. Because the environment is highly dynamic and will continue to become more complex, continuous learning will be more and more essential and critical in keeping up with the world.

Since humans have limited processing capability and the mind is easily overloaded and tends to cling to its past experiences and knowledge, "letting go" becomes as important as learning. Letting go is the art of being able to let go of what was known and true in the past. Being able to recognize the limitations and inappropriateness of past assumptions, beliefs, and knowledge is essential before creating new mental models and for understanding ourselves as we grow. It is *one of the hardest acts of the human mind* because it threatens our self-image and may shake even our core belief systems.

The biggest barrier to learning and letting go arises from our own individual ability to develop invisible defenses against changing our beliefs. These self-imposed mental defenses have been eloquently described by Chris Argyris.[521] The essence of his conclusion is that the mind creates built-in defense mechanisms to support belief systems and experience. These defense mechanisms are invisible to the individual and may be quite difficult to expose in a real-world situation. They are a widespread example of not knowing what we know, thus representing invisible barriers to change. Several authors have estimated that information and knowledge double approximately every nine months. If this estimate is even close, the problems of saturation will continue to make our ability to acquire deep knowledge even more challenging. We must learn how to filter data and information through vision, values, experiences, goals, and purposes using an open mind, intuition and judgment as our tools. This discernment and discretion within the deepest level of our minds provides a proactive aspect of filtering, thereby setting up purposeful mental defenses that reduce complexity and provide conditional safeguards to an otherwise open system. This is a fundamental way in which the self can simplify a situation by eliminating extraneous and undesirable information and knowledge coming from the external world.

The above discussion has identified a number of factors that can help us achieve an appropriate balance between change and our resistance to change. This is an important attribute: not all change is for the best, yet rigidity begets antiquity. This balance is situational and comes only from experience, learning, and a deep sense of knowing when to change and when not to change the self.

This section has addressed the self as an agent of change through internal recognition of certain factors that can influence self-change. Another aspect of change is the ability of the self to influence or change the external world. This is the active part of knowing. Once the self has attained deep knowledge and understanding of the situation and external environment, this must be shared with others, accompanied by the right actions to achieve success. We live in a connected world.

External Elements

The challenge becomes that of translating knowledge into behavior, thus creating the ability to model that behavior and influence others toward taking requisite actions. Role-modeling has always been a prime responsibility of leadership in the government as well as the civilian world. Having deep knowledge of the situation the individual must then translate that into personal behavior that becomes a role model for others to follow and become motivated and knowledgeable about how to act. Effective role-modeling does not require the learner to have the same deep knowledge as the role model, yet the actions and behaviors that result may reflect the equivalent deep knowledge and over time creates deep knowledge in the learner—but only in specific situations. This is how you share the effectiveness from learning and thereby transfer implicit knowledge.

Wherever possible, of course, it is preferable to develop and share as much knowledge as possible so that others can act independently and develop their own internally and situation-driven behavior. This is the reason Knowledge Management and communities of practice and interest require management attention. Since most deep knowledge is tacit, knowledge sharing can become a real challenge.

A third technique for orchestrating external change is through the use of dialogue. Dialogue is a process described by David Bohm[522] to create a situation in which a group participates as coequals in inquiring and learning about some specific topic. In essence, the group creates a common understanding and shared perception of a given situation or topic. Dialogue is frequently viewed as the collaborative sharing and development of understanding. It can include both inquiry and discussions, but all participants must suspend judgment and not seek specific outcomes and answers. The process stresses the examination of underlying assumptions and listening deeply to the self and others to develop a collective meaning. This collective meaning is perhaps the best way in which a common understanding of a situation may be developed as a group and understood by others.

Another way of creating change and sharing understanding is through the effective use of the time-honored process of storytelling. Storytelling is a valuable tool in helping to build a common understanding of our current situation in anticipating possible futures and preparing to act on those possible futures. Stories tap into a Universal Consciousness that is natural to all human communities. Repetition of common story forms carries a subliminal message, a subtext that can help convey a deep level of complex meaning. Since common values enable consistent action, Story in this sense provides a framework that aids decision-making under conditions of uncertainty.

Modeling behavior, knowledge sharing, dialogue, and storytelling are all forms of building understanding and knowledge. Persuasion, our fifth technique, serves to communicate and share understanding with others who have a specific conviction or belief and/or to get them to act upon it. To change the external environment, we need to be persuasive and to communicate the importance and need for others to take appropriate action. The question arises: When you have deep knowledge, what aspects of this can be used to effectively influence other's behavior? Since deep knowledge is tacit knowledge, we must learn how to transfer this to explicit knowledge. Nonaka and Tageuchi[523] have done seminal work in this area. Persuasion, as seen from the perspective of the self, gets us back to the importance of using all of our fundamental values, such as personal example, integrity, honesty, and openness to help transfer our knowing to others.

As can be seen in the discussion above, **all four forms of tacit knowledge inform knowing**. The Knowing Framework seeks to engage our senses and hone our internal processing mechanisms to take full advantage of our minds/brains/bodies. By bringing our focus on knowing, we have the opportunity to move through relational, experiential, and cultural barriers that somewhere along the course of our lives have been constructed, and sometimes self-imposed. This, however, is not the case for many of the young decision-makers moving into the workplace.

Appendix C

Relationship Network Management Template

A sample chart is provided on the next page with the following columns:

a. Name and Relationship
b. Length of Relationship
c. Related Expertise and Knowledge
d. Access
e. Willingness to Share
f. Follow-through
g. Your Feelings
h. **Your** Contribution
NOTES AND ACTIONS

A process for using the chart:

(1) On a separate sheet of paper, list the critical knowledge and skill areas which are needed to achieve your goals and create innovative health solutions. Put that aside.

(2) On the same chart, fill out columns a and b (listing the individuals with whom you interact and the groups in which you participate). Examples of "Relationship" would be: friend, colleague, mentor, manager, etc. Assess columns c through h in terms of a strength scale from 1-10, with 1 being weak and 10 being strong. "Your Feelings" would be rated in terms of respect, trustworthiness and ability to interact. "Contribution" refers to the level or value of knowledge you contribute to the relationship. Positive learning relationships would be those rated above the midpoint (5). Under "NOTES AND ACTIONS" write anything you think may be important to the relationship; for example, "Need to interact more often."

(3) From this simple chart, assess your gaps, that is, circle any number less than 5, and—comparing with your list of knowledge and skill areas—determine the relationships that need to be expanded or relationships that need to be added. For example, if your numbers are low and a specific individual or team is important to accomplishing your goals, then actions must be taken to build/expand that relationship and increase the assessment numbers. (Refer to the RNM key success factors.) Add the action you plan to take under "NOTES AND ACTIONS".

a. Name and Relationship	b. Length of Relationship	c. Related Expertise and Kn	d. Access	e. Willingness to share	f. Follow-through	g. Your Feelings	h. Your contribution	NOTES AND ACTIONS

Table 4. The Relationship Network Management Assessment Chart.

Appendix D

Accessing Revealed Knowledge in African Cultures

[NOTE: This appendix is based on detailed discussion and examples in *African Divination Systems: Ways of Knowing*,[524] several other referenced academic studies, the on-the-ground research of Charles Dhewa, and a ChatGPT generic exchange.]

Divination is an ancient tradition in African cultures. Peek forwards that "An understanding pervades African societies that the true reasons for all events can be known",[525] thus knowledge is in continuous demand. Since historically it has been difficult to gain sufficient knowledge for relevant decision-making, divination practices filled this gap. Douglas describes this search for knowledge differently. As he conveys,

> *Any culture which admits the use of oracles and divination is committed to a distinction between appearances and reality. The oracle offers a way of reaching behind appearances to another source of knowledge.*[526]

Lévi-Strauss describes divination as a "thirst for objective knowledge"[527] and the Sisala of Ghana[528] and others affirm that that which is beyond the human realm is the source of true knowledge.

As the custodians of knowledge and cultural heritage and a source of wisdom central to various aspects of life—including spirituality, healing, problem-solving, and decision-making—diviners play a significant role in the everyday happenings of African societies. Diviners often tap into their intuitive and spiritual abilities to provide insights, guidance, and solutions to individuals or communities seeking advice. They possess a deep understanding of mythology, symbolism, rituals, and ancestral wisdom, which are all sources of inspiration and creativity.

Divination is often performed within specific rituals or ceremonies, involving offerings, prayers, chants, dances, storytelling, and creative artistic expressions. These rituals create a sacred space and help establish a spiritual connection between the diviner, the seeker, and the spiritual realm. Various symbols, objects, or natural elements play a significant role in these rituals, and include cowrie shells, bones, animal parts, seeds, divination boards, dice, or patterns formed by objects. The diviner interprets the symbolism and patterns to extract message and insights. For example, The Nyole people of Uganda practice divination using a wooden board with symbols called a *Tonga*.[529] Seeds or small objects are placed on the board, and the diviner interprets the messages based on the patterns formed by these objects. The Tonga is used to seek guidance, diagnose illness, or find lost objects. Somewhat similar but with variations, the Lobi people of Burkina Fasco use divination called *Tongo*, which involves the use of various objects like stones, shells, or bones.[530] The diviner interprets the patterns formed by these objects to reveal information about the past, present, and future, as well as to identify the causes of misfortune.

While other forms of knowledge such as oral histories, communal wisdom, and formal education play crucial roles in Africa societies, in many African tribes the knowledge gained from divination is highly valued and considered significant. The symbolism, narratives, and metaphors present in divination systems can inspire artists, writers, and performers to create works reflecting the cultural ethos and traditional African beliefs.

Below we briefly touch on the reasons why divination knowledge is esteemed, including its role in spiritual guidance, cultural and traditional significance, holistic worldview, value in problem-solving and conflict resolution, and oral tradition and authority.

Spiritual Guidance

In terms of spiritual guidance, divination is believed to connect individuals with the spiritual realm, including ancestors, deities, or nature spirits. The knowledge obtained through divination is seen as guidance from these higher powers, who are believed to possess wisdom, foresight, and the ability to influence events. This spiritual aspect contributes to the perceived value and legitimacy of divination knowledge. For example, the Dogon people practice divination through the use of wooden divination dice known as *Bini*. The dice are thrown onto a square divination cloth, and the diviner interprets the resulting patterns to gain insight into various life issues, healing, and spiritual matters.

Many African divination practices involve **communication with ancestral spirits** or seeking guidance from the wisdom of ancestors. This is not surprising since in most African tribe's elders are valued or their experience and stories. Ancestors are considered highly influential and wise beings who have passed on and are believed to be able to guide and protect their living descendants. They are believed not only to hold knowledge and experience, but also to have the ability to influence the present and the future. Diviners are seen as intermediaries who can communicate with and receive messages from the ancestors. For example, the Batammaliba practice a form of divination called

Bwana, which involves using cowrie shells and interpreting the patterns they form when thrown.[531] The diviner, known as a *Tengwin*, communicates with ancestral spirits to gain insights and guidance. The Temne people of Sierra Leone use a divination system known as *Fambul Tok*.[532] It involves consulting a secret society, which communicates with ancestral spirits through rituals and ceremonies. The diviners within the society interpret the messages conveyed by the spirits.

In addition to acting as intermediaries with ancestors, some African tribes believe that diviners have a direct connection to **specific deities or nature spirits**. These deities or spirits are often associated with natural elements such as rivers, mountains, or animals. For example, the Pagibeti people believe that the universe communicates messages through various signs and symbols found in nature such as the behavior of animals, the sound of thunder, or the formation of clouds.[533] These signs are interpreted by skilled individuals within the community. The Zande people located in the Sudan and D.R. Congo have a unique form of divination known as the *Poison Oracle*. It involves placing poison on a special prepared mat and asking questions. The movement of a white or brown beetle on the mat is interpreted by a diviner, who provides answers based on the beetle's behavior.

In certain African belief systems, diviners are considered to have a connection to overarching divine forces or **cosmic energies**. These forces or energies are seen as the source of ultimate wisdom and power. Diviners may channel or access these forces, enabling them to interpret the messages and provide guidance based on this divine connection.

Some diviners are believed to have **personal spirit guides** who assist them in their divination work. These spirit guides are often thought to be benevolent and knowledgeable beings who act as intermediaries between the human realm and the spiritual realm. Diviners may enter trance states or altered states of consciousness to communicate with, gain insights, and receive guidance from these spirit guides. Altered states of consciousness can be achieved through chanting, rhythmic drumming, dancing, or the sue of herbal substances. For example, in Kenya divination is commonly performed through *oracular speech*.[534] Diviners, known as witch doctors or herbalists, communicate with spiritual entities through altered states of consciousness induced by meditation, chants, or the use of herbal substances. The information received is then interpreted and provided to the seeker.

Cultural and Traditional Significance

In terms of **cultural and traditional significance**, divination practices are embedded in the cultural and traditional frameworks of various African tribes. They are part of the broader belief systems and rituals that have been passed down through generations. Therefore, the knowledge gained from divination holds cultural importance and is upheld as a respected tradition.

Elders and diviners are often seen as having complementary roles in the community. Elders, with their life experience and wisdom (earned knowledge/intuition), are respected for their knowledge and guidance based on their own experiences and accumulated wisdom. Diviners, on the other hand, are valued for their ability to access spiritual insights beyond the realm of personal experience (revealed knowledge/intuition). Interestingly, this revealed knowledge is often perceived as coming from ancestors (elders) who have passed. Recognizing that all knowledge is situation-dependent and context-sensitive, the balance between seeking the knowledge of elders and diviners varies dependent on the issue being addressed. For practical and community-related matters, the advice and knowledge of elders may be given more weight. Their experience and understanding of social dynamics, customs, and traditions applicable to the situation at hand may be highly regarded. However, in matters of spiritual guidance or uncovering hidden causes of challenges, diviners may be consulted, as their connection to the spiritual realms in addition to ancestors may be deemed essential.

In Zulu, South Africa, *Sangomas* are traditional healers and diviners.[535] They use various methods including throwing bones or shells, dream interpretation, and communicating with ancestral spirits. Sangoma divination is focused on healing, spiritual guidance, and resolving personal and communal issues. The traditional divination in Yoruba, Nigeria, is a highly complex system called Ifa Divination. It involves the use of a divination tray, palm or kola nuts, and a set of 256 *odus* (verses). The diviner, known as a *Babalawo*, interprets the patterns formed by the nuts and the verses to provide guidance and solutions to the seeker.

Holistic Worldview

In terms of **holistic worldview**, many African tribes maintain a holistic understanding of existence, where physical, emotional, and spiritual aspects are interconnected. Divination is seen as a means of understanding and navigating this interconnected reality. The knowledge obtained through divination is valued for its ability to provide insights into various aspects of life, including personal matters, communal issues, health concerns, and future events.

Many African practices deal do include some level of prediction. For example, the Mambila people (Mambila, Cameroon) use a divination system called *Tsohon-Karkafi*. It involves pouring a powdered substance onto a special mat and interpreting the patterns formed. The diviner deciphers those patterns to predict future events, identify causes of misfortune, or provide guidance. Some practices move beyond prediction to "destiny". For example, the Dagara people in Dagara, Burkina Faso, have a divination practice called Song Lines, which involves the use of cowry shells. The shells are thrown on the ground, and the diviner interprets the patterns they form to understand the individual's destiny and offer guidance on various aspects of life.

Problem-Solving and Conflict Resolution

In terms of **problem-solving and conflict resolution**, divination is often sought when individuals encounter challenges, uncertainty, or conflicts. The divination process is believed to help identify the root causes of problems, offer solutions, and guide decision-making. The practical utility of divination knowledge in resolving personal or communal issues enhances its perceived value.

Decision-making in African tribes often involves a communal and inclusive process. Peek says that divination systems "temporarily shift decision making into a liminal realm by emphatically participating in opposing cognitive modes" and that this defining feature of divination is what makes it both unique and effective.[536] Elders, diviners, and other community members may come together to discuss and deliberate on various matters. Both the perspectives of elders and diviners may be considered in reaching a consensus or making decision. Collaborative decision-making ensures that a range of perspectives, including traditional wisdom and spiritual insights, are taken into account.

When problem-solving, the Yaka people in the Northern Yaka of Zaire practice mediumistic divination.[537] A diviner called a Nganga communicates with ancestral spirits or deities on behalf of individuals seeking guidance. The Nganga enters a trance-like state and provides answers and solutions to problems.

Oral Tradition and Authority

In terms of **oral tradition and authority**, divination practices are frequently passed down through oral tradition, and diviners undergo long periods of training and initiation. This lineage and the authority of the diviners contribute to the esteem place upon the knowledge gained. Diviners are respected members of the community and are often regarded as spiritual advisors or healers, further enhancing the perceived value of their insights.

There is a direct correlation between the values placed on elders with experience and stories and diviners who have access to higher energies. Both are typically respected figures within African communities. They are seen as sources of wisdom, guidance, and community support. The trust placed in their knowledge and insights is crucial for striking a balance between their respective roles, with elders brining a sense of continuity and cultural knowledge and diviners valued for their spiritual connections and ability to access broader energies. Mutual respect and recognition of each other's roles contribute to a harmonious balance.

Many African divination practices are orally transmitted, passed down through generations within specific families or secret societies. This secrecy occurs in the Chapter 14 case study. Diviners often undergo long periods of training and initiation to acquire the necessary skills and knowledge. Secrecy is maintained around specific practices to preserve the sacredness and effectiveness of the divination process.

Endnotes

[1] Berman, S., & Korsten, P. (2010). *Capitalizing on complexity: Insights from the global chief executive officer (CEO) study.* IBM Institute for Business Value.
[2] Crawford, R.P. (1954). *The techniques of creative thinking: How to use your ideas to achieve success.* Hawthorn Books, Inc., p. 57.
[3] Ibid.
[4] Ibid, p. 59.
[5] Ibid., p. 23.
[6] McCabe, T. J. (2017). *Expanded consciousness: The many dimensions of our thoughts.* Self-published.
[7] Crawford, p. 149.
[8] (http://quoteinvestigator.com/2013/01/01/einstein-imagination/
[9] See The Mona Lisa Code at https://monalisacode.com .
[10] Peterson, B. (2022). *Grand Experience Leonardo da Vinci, 500 Years of Genius*, A Legends of Art and Innovations Publication at Biltmore, North Carolina.
[11] Hutchins, R.M. (1952). *Great Books of the Western World.* William Benton Publisher.
[12] Ibid, 16.
[13] Ibid, 56.
[14] Ibid, 82.
[15] Drucker, P. F. (1967). *The effective executive.* Harper & Row.
[16] Bennet, D., Bennet, A., Turner, R. (2022). *Unleashing the human mind: A consilience approach to managing self.* MQIPress, p. 1.
[17] Wilson, E.O. (1998). *Consilience: The unity of knowledge.* Alfred A. Knopf.
[18] Gardner, H. (1993). *Creating minds: An anatomy of creativity seen through the lives of Freud, Einstein, Picasso, Stravinsky, Eliot, Graham, and Gandhi.* Basic Books.
[19] Bennet, A. (2018). *Possibilities that are YOU! Volume 20: The humanness of humility.* MQIPress.
[20] See a discussion of creativity and contribution as operational values in the Millennial generation: Avedisian, J., & Bennet, A. (2010). Values as knowledge: A new frame of reference for a new generation of knowledge workers. *On the Horizon, 18*(3), pp. 255-265.
[21] Gell-Mann, M. (1994). *The quark and the jaguar: Adventures in the simple and the complex.* W.H. Freeman & Company.
[22] Checkland, P. (1999). Systems thinking, systems practice: Include a 30-year retrospective. John Wiley and Sons, Inc. Also, Bennet, A., & Bennet, D. (2018). *Decision-making in the new reality: Complexity, knowledge and knowing.* MQIPress.
[23] Stonier, T. (1997). *Information and meaning: An evolutionary perspective.* Springer-Verlag, p. 25.
[24] Stonier, T. (1990). *Information and the internal structure of the universe.* Springer-Verlag, p. 13.
[25] Bennet, A., Bennet, D. & Avedisian, J. (2018). *The course of knowledge: A 21st century theory.* MQIPress.
[26] Weisbert, R.W. (1999). Creativity and knowledge: A challenge to theories. In R.J. Sternberg (Ed.), *Handbook of creativity* (226-250). Cambridge University Press, p. 226.

[27] Ibid.
[28] Machlup, F. (1962). *The production and distribution of knowledge in the United States*. Princeton University Press, p. 179.
[29] Ryle, G. (1949). *The concept of mind.*
[30] Kolb, D.A. (1984). *Experiential learning: Experience as the source of learning and development*. Prentice Hall.
[31] Bohm, D. (1980). *Wholeness and the implicate order*. Routledge & Kegal Paul, p. 64.
[32] Bennet, Bennet, & Avedisian, *The course of knowledge: A 21st century theory*. Also, Edelman, G.M., & Tononi, G. (2001). *A universe of consciousness: How matter becomes imagination*. Basic Books.
[33] Marchese, T.JU. (1998). The new conversations about learning: Insights from neuroscience and anthropology, cognitive science and workplace studies. www.newhorizons.org/lifelong/higher)ed/marchese.htm
[34] Marton, F., & Booth, S. (1997). *Learning and awareness*. Lawrence Erlbaum Associates.
[35] Moon, J.A. (2004). *A handbook of reflective and experiential learning: Theory and practice*. RoutledgeFalmer, p. 23.
[36] This model was developed for and first published in Bennet, A., Bennet, D., & Lewis, J. (2018). *Leading with the future in mind: Knowledge and emergent leadership*. MQIPress.
[37] See Bennet, D., Bennet, A., & Turner, R. (2018). *Expanding the self: The intelligent complex adaptive learning system*. MQIPress. Also, Bennet, Bennet, & Turner, *Unleashing the human mind: A consilience approach to managing self*. .
[38] Bennet, A. (2018). *Possibilities that are YOU!: Volume 10: Knowing*. MQIPress.
[39] Bennet, A., & Bennet, D. (2008). The knowledge and knowing of spiritual learning. *VINE: The Journal of Information and Knowledge Management Systems, 37*(2), 150-168.
[40] http://quoteinvestigator.com/2013/01/01/einstein-imagination/
[41] Arieti, S. (1976). *Creativity: The magic synthesis by Silvano Arieti*. Good Reads.
[42] Ibid., p. 5.
[43] Ross, P.E. (2006, August). The expert mind. *Scientific American*, 64-71.
[44] Csikszentmihalyi, M. (1996). *Flow and the psychology of discovery and invention*. Harper Collins.
[45] Goswami, A. (2014). *Quantum creativity: Think quantum, be creative*. Hay House, Inc.
[46] Sheldrake, R. (1989). *The presence of the past: Morphic resonance and the habits of nature*. Vintage Books.
[47] Quoted from Warmington and Rouse (1984). *Great dialogues of Plato*, p. 18.
[48] Csikszentmihalyi, M. (1996). *Creativity: Flow and the psychology of discovery and invention*. HarperCollins Publishers, p. 23.
[4]9 Gardner (1993).
[50] Ibid., p. 36.
[51] Ibid, p. 37.
[52] Feldman, D.H. (1999). The development of creativity. In R. J. Sternberg (Ed.), *Handbook of creativity*, 169-186. Cambridge University Press, pp. 171-172.

[53] Note that using the term knowledge when defined as the capacity (potential or actual) to take effective action can be applied to Artificial Intelligence IF the idea of "effective action" is defined as input to the system. For example, in terms of Tesla, "effective action" might be defined as delivering the passenger safely to his/her destination. When that occurs, it can be assumed that the system had the "knowledge" of how to accomplish that task effectively.
[54] (Gardner, 1993)
[55] Andreasen, N. (2005). *The creating brain: The neuroscience of genius.* The Dana Foundation.
[56] Gell-Mann.
[57] Crawford, p. 39.
[58] "Knowledging" represents a conscious learning choice in a specific situation and context. It is the focused link (activity) between seeking expertise as a response to an issue or opportunity and knowledge creation, highly situation dependent and context sensitive. See Bennet, A., & Turner, R. (2023). *Reblooming the Knowledge Movement: The Democratization of Organizations.* MQIPress.
[59] Kandel, E.R. (2006). *In search of memory: The emergence of a new science of mind.* W.W. Norton & Company.
[60] Hawkins, J. (2021). *A thousand brains: A new theory of intelligence.* Basic Books.
[61] Senge, P. (1990). *The fifth discipline: The art and practice of a learning organization* (2nd ed.). Doubleday Currency.
[62] Bennet, D. (2023). Systems and complexity thinking. In Bennet, A., & Turner, R., *Reblooming the knowledge movement: The democratization of organizations*, pp. 456-486. MQIPress.
[63] Amen, D.G. (2005). *Making a good brain great.* Harmony Books.
[64] Boden, M. (1991). The creative mind, myths & Mysticism. Basic Books.
[65] Kipling, R. (1985). Working-tools. In B. Ghiselin (Ed.), *The creative process: A symposium.* Berkeley, CA, University of California Press, 161-163. (Original article published in 1937).
[66] de Bono, E. (1992). *Serious creativity: Using the power of lateral thinking to create new ideas.* HarperCollins.
[67] Freud, S. (1926). *Collected papers*, Vol. 4. Hogarth Press.
[68] Guilford, J.P. (1950). Creativity. *American Psychologist, 5*, 444-454.
[69] Torrance, E.P. (1974). *Torrance tests of creative thinking.* Personnel Press.
[70] Finke, R.A., Ward, T.B., and Smith, S.M. (1992). *Creative cognition: Theory, research, and applications.* MIT Press.
[71] Amabile, T.M. (1983). *The social psychology of creativity.* Springer.
[72] Eysenck, H.J. (1993). Creativity and personality: A theoretical perspective. *Psychological Inquiry, 4*, 147-178.
[73] Campbell, D.T. (1960). Blind variation and selective retention in creative thought and other knowledge processes. *Psychological Review, 67*, 380-400.
[74] Perkins, D.N. (1995). *Outsmarting IQ: The emerging science of learnable intelligence.* Free Press.
[75] Simonton, D.K. (1999). Talent and its development: An emergenic and epigenetic mode. *Psychological Review, 106*, 435-457.
[76] Csikszentmihalyi, M., & Csikszentmihalyi, I.S. (Eds.) (1988). *Optimal experience: Psychological studies of flow in consciousness.* Cambridge University Press.

[77] Amabile, T.M. (1996). *Creativity in context.* Westview.
[78] Gruber, H.E. (1989). The evolving systems approach to creative work. In D.B. Wallace, & H.E. Gruber (Eds.), *Creative people at work: Twelve cognitive case studies*. Oxford University Press, 3-24.
[79] Sternberg, R.J. (2003). *Wisdom, intelligence, and creativity synthesized.* Cambridge University Press, p. 125.
[80] Ibid., 188.
[81] The Intelligent Complex Adaptive Learning System (ICALS) theory is based on over a decade of research experiential learning through the expanding lens of neuroscience. See Bennet, Bennet, & Turner, *Unleashing the human mind: A consilience approach to managing self.*
[82] Hobson, J.A. (1999). *Consciousness*. Scientific American Library. Also, Christos, G. (2003). *Memory and dreams: The creative human mind.* Rutgers University Press.
[83] Stonier (1997).
[84] Andreasen.
[85] Csikszentmihalyi, *Creativity: Flow and the psychology of discovery and invention*, p. 26.
[86] Andreasen.
[87] Ibid., p. 159.
[88] Ibid.
[89] Ibid., p. 77.
[90] Arieti, p. 31.
[91] Csikszentmihalyi (1996), p. 76.
[92] Ibid.
[93] Grudin, R. (1984). The ethics of inspiration. In Rizzoli, *The phenomenon of CHANGE*. Cooper-Hewitt Museum, The Smithsonian Institution's National Museum of Design, p. 15.
[94] Amen, p. 37.
[95] Green, R.D. (2016) Conversation from Huffington Post. http://www.huffingtonpost.com/r-kay-green/giving-back)b)3298691.html
[96] Carroll, S. (2016). *The big picture: On the origins of life, meaning, and the universe itself.* Dutton, p. 319.
[97] Searle, J.R. (2000). Consciousness, free action, and the brain. *Journal of Consciousness Studies*, 7(10), p.4.
[98] May, R. (1970). *The courage to create*. Bantam.
[99] Hobson.
[100] Andreasen, p. 64.
[101] Christos, p. 74.
[102] Hawkins, J. (2021).
[103] Christos, pp. 74-75.
[104] Ibid., p. 36.
[105] Tallis, F. (2002). *Hidden minds: A history of the unconscious*. Arcade.
[106] Poincaré, H. (2001). *The Value of Science: Essential Writings of Henri Poincaré*. Random House (Modern Library Science).
[107] Christos, p. 90.
[108] Andreasen, p. 43.
[109] Amen, p. 37.

[110] Koestler, A. (1975). *The act of creation*. Macmillan, p. 206.
[111] Begley, S. (2007*). Train your mind change your brain: How a new science reveals our extraordinary potential to transform ourselves*. Ballantine Books, p. 69.
[112] Andreasen, p. 164.
[113] Pinker, S. (2007). *The stuff of thought: Language as window into human nature.* Viking.
[114] Bennet, A., & Bennet, D. (2008). The human knowledge system: Music and brain coherence. *VINE: The Journal of Information and Knowledge Management Systems, 38*(3), 277-295.
[115] Poincaré
[116] Ibid.
[117] Tchaikovsky, M. (1906). *The life and letters of Peter Ilich Tchaikovsky*. John Lane Company.
[118]Rossman, J. (1931). *The psychology of the inventor: A study of the patentee.* Inventors Publishing.
[119] Ibid., p. 57.
[120] Osborn, A.F. (1953). *Your creative power*. Scribner.
[121] Ibid., pp. 13-21.
[122] Isakson, S.G., & Parnes, S.J. (1985). Curriculum planning for creative thinking and problem solving. *Journal of Creative Behavior* 19, 1-29.
[123] Ibid., pp. 27-29.
[124] Taylor, I.A. (1959). The nature of the creative process. In P. Smith (Ed.), *Creativity*. Hastings House.
[125] Stein, M.I. (1967, 1974). *Stimulating creativity*. Academic Press.
[126] Koestler (1975).
[127] Poincaré, p. 389.
[128] Ibid.
[129] Jeffrey, S. (2008). *Creativity revealed: Discovering the source of inspiration.* Creative Crayon Publishers.
[130] Andreasen.
[131] Gell-Mann, p. 264.
[132] Lovejoy, A.O. (1976) The great chain of being. Harvard University Press.
[133] Murphy, M. (1992). The future of the body. Tarcher. Also, Wade, J. (1996) Changes of mind: A holonomic theory of the evolution of consciousness. SUNY Press.
[134] Wilber, K. (2000) Integral psychology: Consciousness, spirit, psychology, therapy. Shambhala Publications.
[135] Hawkins, D.R. (2002). *Power vs force: The hidden determinants of human behavior*. Hay House.
[136] Ibid., p. 70.
[137] Bennet, Bennet and Turner.
[138] Byrnes, J.P. (2001). *Minds, brains, and learning: Understanding the psychological and educational relevance of neuroscientific research*. The Guilford Press.
[139] Begley (2007).
[140] Bennet, Bennet and Turner.
[141] Crandall, B., Klein, G., & Hoffman, R.R. (2006). *Working minds: A practitioner's guide to cognitive task analysis*. The MIT Press.

[142] Ibid.
[143] Christos.
[144] Ibid.
[145] Begley, p. 214.
[146] The Monroe Institute (TMI) furthers the experience and exploration of consciousness, expanded awareness, and discovery of self through technology and education. See www.monroeinstitute.org/
[147] Andreasen.
[148] LeDoux, J. (1996). *The emotional brain: The mysterious underpinnings of emotional life.* Touchstone.
[149] Bennet, A., Bennet, D., Shelley, A., Bullard, T., & Lewis, J. (2020). *The profundity and bifurcation of change part III: Learning in the present*. MQIPress.
[150] Hawkins, J. (2021).
[151] Urantia, 111:4.9.
[152] Arieta.
[153] Johnson, S. (2006). The neuroscience of the mentor-learner relationships. In S. Johnson & K. Taylor (Eds.), *The neuroscience of adult learning: New direction for adult and continuing education* (pp. 63-70). Jossey-Bass, p. 65.
[154] Cozolino, L.J. (2006). *The neuroscience of human relationships: Attachment and developing social brain.* W.W. Norton, p. 291.
[155] Taylor, K. (2006). Brain function and adult learning: Implications for practice. In S. Johnson & K. Taylor (Eds.), *The neuroscience of adult learning: New directions for adult and continuing education* (pp. 71-86). Jossey-Bass, p. 82.
[156] Cozolino, L., & Spokay, S. (2006). Neuroscience and adult learning. In S. Johnson & K. Taylor (Eds.), *The neuroscience of adult learning: New directions for adult and continuing education* (pp. 71-86). Jossey-Bass, p. 14.
[157] Caine, G., & Caine, R.N. (2006). Meaningful learning and the executive functions of the brain. In S. Johnson & K. Taylor (Eds.), *The neuroscience of adult learning: New directions for adult and continuing education* (pp. 71-86). Jossey-Bass, p. 54.
[158] Bennet, Bennet & Turner.
[159] Shelley, A. (2007). *Organizational zoo: A survival guide to work place behavior.* Asian Publishing, xiii.
[160] Dane, E. (2011). Paying attention to mindfulness and its effects on task performance in the workplace. *Journal of Management, 37*(4), pp. 997-1018.
[161] Bodhi, B. (1984). *The noble eightfold path: Way to the end of suffering*. Pariyatti.
[162] Moore, A., & Malinowski, P. (2009). Meditation, mindfulness and cognitive flexibility. *Consciousness and Cognition, 18*(1), 176-186.
[163] Kudesia, R. S. (July 05, 2015). Mindfulness in the workplace. In J. Reb & P. W. B. Atkins (Eds.), *Mindfulness in Organizations: Foundations, Research, and Applications*, pp. 190-212.
[164] Formica, M. J. (March 6, 2015). *Mindfulness and cultivating creativity*. Find a Therapist. See also Enlightened Living.
[165] Goh, C. (May 16, 2016). How to apply mindfulness to the creative process. *Mindful: healthy mind, healthy life.*
[166] Capurso, V., Fabbro, F., & Crescentini, C. (2014). Mindful creativity: the influence of mindfulness meditation on creative thinking. Frontiers in Psychology.
[167] Lachman, G. (2017, 2022). *Lost knowledge of the imagination*. Floris Books, p. 25.

[168] See https://embryo.asu.edu/pages/roger-sperrys-split-brain-experiments-1959-1968
[169] McGilchrist, Iain (2009). *The master and his emissary*. Yale University Press.
[170] Bullard, B., and Bennet, A. (2013, 2020). *Remembrance: Pathways to expanded learning with music and meta-music®*. MQIPress.
[171] Minsky, M. (2006). *The emotion machine: Commonsense thinking, artificial intelligence, and the future of the human mind.* Simon and Schuster.
[172] Ibid., p. 227.
[173] Ibid., p. 228.
[174] Lachman, p. 23, seeing this as a variation on Dr. Johnson's refutation of Bishop Berkeley, saying that "You may … pick up a stone and say 'Here is matter.' If you do, I will answer, 'No, it is a stone.' Show me matter that is not stone, or tree, or cloud, or lake—matter, that is, that is not some 'thing' but simply itself. That, I say, you cannot do.", p. 142.
[175] Steiner, G. (1978) *Has truth a future?* BBC Publications, p. 16.
[176] Bullard & Bennet.
[177] Cornell, A.W. (1990). *The power of focusing: A practical guide to emotional self-healing*. MJF Books, front cover.
[178] McGilchrist.
[179] Lachman, p. 21.
[180] Cornford, F. (1991). *From religion to philosophy*. Princeton University Press, p. xiv.
[181] Oster, G. (1973). Auditory beats in the brain. *Scientific American, 229*, 94-102.
[182] Swann, R., Bosanko, S., Cohen, R., Midgley, R., & Seed, K.M. (1982). *The brain—A user's manual*. G.P. Putnam & Sons.
[183] Hink, R.F., Kodera, K., Yamada, O., Kaga, K., & Suzuki, J. (1980). Binaural interaction of a beating frequency following response. *Audiology, 19*, 36-43.
[184] Ritchey, D. (2003). *The H.I.S.S. of the A.S.P.: Understanding the anomalously sensitive person.* Headline Books.
[185] Carroll, G.D. (1986). *Brain hemisphere synchronization and musical learning*, reprint of paper published by University of North Carolina at Greensboro, N.C.
[186] Atwater, F.H. (2004). *The Hemi-Sync process*. The Monroe Institute. Also, Fischer, R. l (1971). A cartography of ecstatic and meditative states. *Science, 174*(12), 897-904. Also, Delmonte, M.M. (1984). Electrocortical activity and related phenomena associated with meditation practice: A literature review. *International Journal of Neuroscience, 24*, 217-231. Also, Goleman, G.M. (1988). *Meditative mind: The varieties of meditative experience.* G.P. Putnam. Also, Jeving, R., Wallace, R.K., & Beidenbach, M. (1992). The physiology of meditation: A review. *Neuroscience and Behavioral Reviews, 16*, 415-424. Also, Mavromatis, A. (1991). *Hypnagogia.* Routledge. Also, West, M.A. (1980). Meditation and the EEG. *Psychological Medicine, 10*, 69-375.
[187] Gruzelier, J. (2008). A theory of alpha/theta neurofeedback, creative performance enhancement, long distance functional connectivity and psychological integration. Cognitive Processing *10*(81), pp. 101-109.
[188] Roberts, G. (2006). *Free your mind: A scientific approach to unleashing creativity.* [Blog] independent.co.uk
[189] Martindale, C., & Mines, D. (1975). Creativity and cortical activation during creative, intellectual and EEG feedback tests. *Biological Psychology 3*(2), pp. 91-100.

Also, Kaufman, J., & Sternberg, R. (2011). *The Cambridge handbook of creativity.* Cambridge University Press.
[190]Metcalf, B. (2016). Field Effect Audio Technology™ (F.E.A.T.™) FAQ shared with author by Metcalf on 11/05/2016.
[191] McHale, J. (1977). Futures problems or problems in futures studies. In H.A. Linstone & W.H.C. Simmonds (Eds.), Futures research: New *directions*. Addison-Wesley Publishing Company, Inc.
[192] Salk, J. (1973). The survival of the wisest. Harper & Row.
[193] Wagner, A. (2023). Sleeping beauties: the mystery of dormant innovations in nature and culture. One World, p. 9.
[194] Ibid., p. 10.
[195] Harman, W., & Rheingold, H. (1984). Higher creativity: Liberating the unconscious for breakthrough insights. Jeremy P. Tarcher/Putnam, p. 82.
[196] Ibid., p. 84.
[197] Liu, E., & Noppe-Brandon, S. (2009). *Imagination first: Unlocking the power of possibility*. Jossey-Bass, p. 20.
[198] *Shorter Oxford English Dictionary* 5th ed, vol 1, p. 551.
[199] Lachman, p. 30.
[200] Wilson, C. (1965). *Beyond the Outsider*. Houghton Mifflin Co.
[201] Lachman , p. 31.
[202] Ibid., p.
[203] See http://quoteinvestigator.com/20113/01/01/einstein-imagination/
[204] Lachman, p. 31.
[205] Attributed to Lucille Clifton, poet, teacher, and children's book author.
[206] Crawford, p. 37.
[207] Ibid. p. 39.
[208] Ibid., p. 38.
[209] Hawkins, J., & Blakeslee, S. (2004). *On intelligence: How a new understanding of the brain will lead to the creation of truly intelligent machines*. Times Books, p. 137.
[210] Kuntz, P.G. (1968). The concept of order. University of Washington Press, p, 162.
[211] Hawkins and Blakeslee, p. 109.
[212] Hawkins and Blakeslee.
[213] James, J. (1996). *Thinking in the future tense: A workout for the mind.* Touchstone, p. 78.
[214] Crampton, M. (1975). Answers from the unconscious. *Synthesis 1*(2), 140-141.
[215] Bennet, A., Bennet, D., Shelley, A., Bullard, T., & Lewis. J. (2020). *The profundity and bifurcation of change part II: Learning from the past.* MQIPress.
[216] Heijnen, R.D. (2022). Desire—Life as a drama based game or the thermodynamics of everything. In S.B. Schafer & A. Bennet (Eds.), *The handbook of global media's preternatural influence on global technological singularity, culture and government* (pp. 214-242). IGI Global, p. 215.
[217] Shaw, B. (1934). The compete plays of Bernard Shaw. Odhams Press, p. 858.
[218] Shand. A.F. (1920). The foundation of character (2nd ed.). Macmillan, p. 519.
[219] Holton, R. (n.d.). Belief/desire psychology, the Humean theory of motivation & emotions. *Moral Psychology, 24*(120), p. 1.

[220] Vaudeville, C. (2017). *A weaver named Kabir: Selected verses with a detailed biographical and historical introduction*. Motilal Banarsidass Publishers.
[221] Guengerich, G. (2015). *The four stages of desire: From everything to one thing: Why we should stop wanting everything and focus on what matters most*. Blog posting.
[222] Ibid.
[223] Liu and Noppe-Brandon, p. 37.
[224] Ibid., p. 37-38.
[225] Dreher, D. (1995). *The Tao of personal leadership*. HarperBusiness.
[226]Templeton, Sir John (2002). *Wisdom from world religions: Pathways toward heaven on earth*. Templeton Foundation Press, p. 256.
[227] Arieti, p. 93.
[228] Ibid., pp. 88-89.
[229] Butler, J. (1906). *The analogy of religion, natural & revealed*. J.M. Dent & Company.
[230] Armstrong, D.M. (1989). *Universals: An opinionated introduction*. Westview Press.
[231] Ibid.
[232] Crawford.
[233] Smith, J., Dixon, R.A., & Baltes, P.B. (1987). Age differences in response to life planning problems: A research analog for the study of wisdom, related knowledge (unpublished manuscript). Also, Dittmann-Kohli, F., & Baltes, P.B. (1990). Toward a neofunctionalist concept of adult intellectual development: Wisdom as a prototypical case of intellectual growth. In C. Alexander & E. Langer (Eds.), *Beyond formal operations: Alternative endpoints to human development*. Oxford University Press.
[234] Baltes, P.B., & Smith, J. (1990). The psychology of wisdom and its ontogenesis. In R.J. Sternbert (Ed.), Wisdom: Its nature, origins and development, Cambridge University Press, 87-120.
[235] *Urantia* 1.
[236] Clayton, V., & Birren, J.E. (1980). The development of wisdom across the lifespan: A reexamination of an ancient topic. In P.B. Baltes & O.G.J. Brim (Eds.), *Life span development and behavior* (104-135). Academic Press.
[237] Holiday, S.G., & Chandler, M.J. (1986). *Wisdom: Explorations in adult competence: Contributions to human development*, Vol. 17. Basel. Also, Erikson, J.M. (1988). *Wisdom and the senses: The way of creativity*. Norton. Also, Sternberg. Also, Jarvis, P. (1992). *Paradoxes of learning: On becoming an individual in society*. Jossey-Bass. Also, Kramer, D.A., & Bacelar, W.T. (1994). The educated adult in today's world: Wisdom and the mature learner. In J.D. Sinnott (Ed.), *Interdisciplinary handbook of adult lifespan learning*. Greenwood Press. Also, Bennett-Woods, D. (1997). Reflections on wisdom. (Unpublished paper). University of Northern Colorado.
[238] Merriam, S.B., & Caffarella, R.S. (1999). *Learning in adulthood: A comprehensive guide* (2nd ed.). Jossey-Bass, p. 165.
[239] Erikson, J.M. (1988). *Wisdom and the senses: The way of creativity*. Norton, p. 184.
[240] Trumpa, C. (1991). *The heart of the Buddha*. Shambhala.
[241] Woodman, M., & Dickson, E. (1996). *Dancing in the flames: The dark goddess in the transformation of consciousness*. Shambhala.

[242] Macdonald, C. (1996). Toward wisdom: Finding our way to inner peace, love, and happiness. Hampton Roads, p. 1.
[243] Costa, J.D. (1995). *Working wisdom: The ultimate value I the new economy*. Stoddart, p. 3.
[244] Sternberg, p. xviii.
[245] Russell, P. (2007). *The awakening earth: The global brain*. Floris Books.
[246] Lachman, p. 129.
[247] Ibid., p. 130.
[248] Barfield, O. (1988). Saving the appearances. Wesleyan University Press.
[249] *Philosophy, Literature, Mysticism: An Anthology of essays on Swedenborg*. The Swedenborg Society, 2013. as quoted in Lachman, p. 139.
[250] Lachman, p. 133.
[251] Bennet et al., *The profundity and bifurcation of change part III: Learning in the present*.
[252] Silverman, D.P. (Ed.) (1997). Ancient Egypt. Oxford University Press, p. 90.
[253] Blair, H. (2015). Reading on sentence structure from Huge Blair form lectures on rhetoric and Belles letters. http://academic.macewan.ca/einarssonr/files/2009/10/On-Sentence-Structure-by-Blair1.pdf
[254] *Writing: The nature, development and teaching of written communication* (vol. II) (1982). Lawrence Erlbaum Associates.
[255] Excerpts from Cowley, M. (Ed.) (1958). *Writers at work: The Paris review interviews*. The Paris Review.
[256] Lakoff, G., & Nunez, 4. (2000). *Where mathematics comes from*. Basic Books, p. 27.
[257] Maturana, H.R., & Varela, F.J. (1987). *The tree of knowledge: The biological roots of human understanding*. Shambhala.
[258] Edelman, G. (1989). The remembered present: A biological theory of consciousness. Basic Books.
[259] Davis, J. (1997). *Alternate realities: How science shapes our vision of the world*. Plenum Trade.
[260] Carroll, p. 171.
[261] MacFlouer, N. (2004-16). *Why life is ...* Weekly radio shows: BBSRadio.com (#1-#48) and KXAM (#1-#143). (See Chapter X).
[262] Lipton, B. *The biology of belief: Unleashing the power of consciousness*. Hay House.
[263] Roberts, J. (1994). The nature of personal reality. Amber-Allen Publishing.
[264] Lipton, B., & Bhaerman, S. (2009). *Spontaneous evolution: Our positive future (and a way to get there from here)*. Hay House, p. 26.
[265] *Encarta World English Dictionary* (1999). St Martin's Press
[266] Lipton and Bhaerman.
[267] Ikemi, Y., & Nakagawa, S.A. (1962). A psychosomatic study of contagious dermatitis. *Kyoshu Journal of Medical Science, 13*, 335-350.
[268] Edelman, G., & Tononi, G. (2000). *A universe of consciousness: How matter becomes imagination*. Basic Books.
[269] McTaggart, L. (2008). The field: The quest for the secret force of the universe. Harper.
[270] de Chardin, P.T. (1959). The phenomenon of man, p. 63.

[271] Gerber, R. (2000). *Vibrational medicine for the 21st century. The complete guide to energy healing and spiritual transformation*. Eagle Brook, p. 5.
[272] McTaggart, p. 23.
[273] Stonier (1997), p. 14.
[274] Stonier (1990), p. 13.
[275] Boltzmann, L. (1896, 1898). *Lectures on gas theory* (part I and part II) (Trans. S. G. Brush, 1976). University of California Press.
[276] Schrödinger (1944) (Combined reprint, 1967). *What is life?* Cambridge University Press.
[277] Stonier (1997), p. 15.
[278] Ibid, p. 17.
[279] Stonier (1997), p. 70.
[280] MacFlouer, N. (1999). *Life's hidden meaning*. Ageless Wisdom Publishers.
[281] Heisenberg, W. (1949). The physical principles of the quantum theory. Trans. C. Eckart & F.C. Hoyt). Dover Publications, Inc.
[282] Besant, A., & Leadbeater, C.W. (2021). *Thought-forms*. Rolled Scroll Publishing, p. xx.
[283] Bennet, Bennet & Turner, *Expanding the self: The intelligent complex adaptive learning system. A new theory of adult learning*. See also, Bennet, Bennet & Turner, *Unleashing the human mind: A consilience approach to managing self*.
[284] Puthoff, H.E. (1989). Source of vacuum electromagnetic zero-point energy. *Physical Review A*(40), 4857-62. Also, Puthoff, H.,W. (1990). The energetic vacuum: Implications for energy research. *Speculations in Science and Technology, 13*(4), 247.
[285] Stonier (1997).
[286] Laszlo, E. (2004). *Science and the Akashic Field: An integral theory of everything*. Inner Traditions, p. 107.
[287] Ibid., p. 108.
[288] Gell-Mann.
[289] Bennet, A., & Bennet, D. (2004). *Organizational survival in the new world: The intelligent complex adaptive system*. Elsevier.
[290] Cozolino, p. 3.
[291] Bennet, A., Bennet, D., Shelley, A., Bullard, T., & Lewis, J. (2018). *The profundity and bifurcation of change part IV: Co-creating the future*. MQIPress.
[292] Nystrom, H. (1979). *Creativity and innovation*. John Wiley & Sons.
[293] Leonard, D., & Swap, W. (1999). *When sparks fly: Igniting creativity in groups*. Harvard Business School Press, front cover.
[294] Shelley.
[295] Crawford, p. 55.
[296] Bennet, A., & Turner, R. (2023). Relationship network management. In Bennet, A., & Turner, R., *Reblooming the knowledge movement: The democratization of organizations*. MQIPress.
[297] Shelley, A.W. (2021) *Becoming Adaptable*. Intelligent Answers.
[298] Goldberg, E. (2005). *The wisdom paradox: How your mind can grow stronger as your brain grows older*. Gotham Books.
[299] Ross.
[300] *American Heritage Dictionary of the English Language* (4th ed.) (2006). Houghton Mifflin Company.

[301] Csikszentmihalyi, M. (2014). *The systems model of creativity: The collected works of Mihaly Csikszentmihalyi.* Springer, p. 70.
[302] Ibid.
[303] Ibid.
[304] Long, T.A. (1986). Narrative unity and clinical judgment. *Theoretical Medicine 7*, 75-92.
[305] Lewis, J. (2019). *Story thinking: Transforming organizations for the fourth industrial revolution.* Amazon KDP.
[306] Ibid.
[307] Ibid.
[308] Ramon, S. (1997). *Earthly cycles: How past lives and soul patterns shape your life.* Pepperwood Press, p. 48.
[309] Searle, J.R. (1983). *Intentionality: An essay in the philosophy of mind.* Cambridge University Press, p. ix.
[310] Ibid.
[311] Prinz, W. (2005). An ideomotor approach to imitation. In S. Hurley & N. Chater, *Perspectives on imitation: From neuroscience to social science vol. 1: Mechanisms of imitation and imitation in animals* (141-156). MIT Press.
[312] Bennet, Bennet, & Turner, *Expanding the self: The intelligent complex adaptive learning system.*
[313] Amen, D.G. (2005) *Making a good brain great.* Harmony Books, p. 115.
[314] Csikszentmihalyi, *The systems model of creativity: The collected works of Mihaly Csikszentmihalyi.*
[315] Crawford, p. 73.
[316] Lachman, p. 26.
[317] Creswell, J. W. (2014). *Research design: Qualitative, quantitative, & mixed methods approaches.* SAGE.
[318] Bennet, A., & Scott, C.L. (2019). *With passion, we live and love: Research, prose, verse and music.* MQIPress.
[319] Bennett-Goleman, T. (2001). *Emotional alchemy: How the mind can heal the heart. Harmony Books.*
[320] Belitz, C., & Lundstrom, M. (1997). *The power of flow.* Harmony Books.
[321] Melendez, S.E. (1996). An outsider's view of leadership. In F. Hesselbein, M. Goldsmith & R. Beckhard, *The Drucker Foundation: The leader of the future.* Jossey-Bass, pp. 293-302.
[322] Senge.
[323] Cools, J. (2023). Crystallizing the symphony of passions. In Bennet, A., & Baisya, R. (Eds.), *INside INnovation: Looking from the inside out*, pp. 271-298. MQIPress, p. 271.
[324] Belitz & Lundstrom, p. 57.
[325] Ibid.
[326] Cools, p. 280.
[327] Goleman, D. (1995). *Emotional Intelligence.* Bantam Books, p. 228.
[328] The KMTL Study is a 2005 research study that reached out to 34 Knowledge Management Thought Leaders located across four continents. The intent was to explore the aspects of KM that contributed to the passion expressed by these thought leaders.

[329] MacFlouer (2004-16).
[330] *American Heritage Dictionary of the English Language* (4th ed.), p. 919.
[331]Crandall et al.
[332] Klein, G. (2003). *Intuition at work: Why developing your gut instincts will make you better at what you do.* Doubleday, p. 13.
[333] Damasio, A.R. (1994). *Descartes' error: Emotion, reason, and the human brain.* G.P. Putnam's Sons, p. 188.
[334] Cooper, L.R. (2005). *The grand vision: The design and purpose of a human being.* Planetary Heart.
[335] Anderson, J.R. (1983). *The architecture of cognition.* Harvard University Press.
[336] Damasio, p. 139.
[337] Bennet, A., & Bennet, D. (2007). CONTEXT: The shared knowledge enigma. *VINE, 37*(1), pp. 27-40.
[338] Reber, A.S. (1993). *Implicit learning and tacit knowledge: An essay on the cognitive unconscious.* Oxford University Press. Also, Kirsner, K., Speelman, C., Mayberry, M., O'Brien-Malone, A., Anderson, M., & MacLeon, C. (Eds.) (1998). *Implicit and explicit mental processes.* Lawrence Erlbaum Associates, Publishers.
[339] Reber, p. 23.
[340] Matthews, R.C. (1991). The forgetting algorithm: How fragmentary knowledge of exemplars can yield abstract knowledge. *Journal of Experimental Psychology: General, 120*, pp. 117-119.
[341] Polanyi, M. (1967). *The tacit Dimension.* Anchor Books, , p. 108.
[342] Polanyi, M. (1958) *Personal knowledge: Towards a post-critical philosophy.* The University of Chicago.
[343] Merriam, S.B., Caffarella, R.S., & Baumgartner, L.M. (2006). *Learning in adulthood: A comprehensive guide.* John Wiley & Sons.
[344] Damasio, 1994, p. 188.
[345] Bennet, D., & Bennet, A. (2008). Engaging tacit knowledge in support of organizational learning. *VINE, 38*(1), pp. 72-94.
[346] Klein.
[347] Ibid.
[348] Damasio, 1994.
[349] Adolphs, R. (2004). Processing of emotional and social information by the human amygdala. In Gazzaniga, M.S. (Ed.), *The cognitive neurosciences III.* The Bradford Press, p. 1026.
[350] Haberlandt, K. (1998). Human memory: Exploration and application. Allyn & Bacon.
[351] Mulvihill, M.K. (2003). The Catholic church in crisis: Will transformative learning lead to social change through the uncovering of emotion?. In Weissner, C.A., Meyers, S.R., Pfhal, N.L., & Neaman, P.F. (Eds.), *Proceedings of the 5th International Conference on Transformative Learning*, pp. 320-323. Teachers College, Columbia University, p. 322.
[352] For an in-depth treatment of the emotions in terms of emotional intelligence, see Goleman (1995).
[353] Bennet & Bennet, The knowledge and knowing of spiritual learning, pp. 150-168.
[354] Ibid.
[355] Bennet, D. (2006) Expanding the knowledge paradigm. VINE, 36(2), pp. 175-181.

[356] White, R.W. (1959). Motivation reconsidered: The concept of competence. *Psychological Review, 66*, pp. 297-333.
[357] Nouwen, J.J.M. (1975). *Reaching out: The three movements of the spiritual life*. Doubleday.
[358] Sternberg.
[359] Zohar, D., & Marshall, I. (2000). Connecting with our spiritual intelligence. R. R. Donnelley and Sons Company, pp. 2-3.
[360] Csikszentmihalyi, M. (1990). *Flow: The psychology of optimal experience*. Harper & Row.
[361] Merriam et al. (2006), p. 195.
[362] Amann, T. (2003). Creating space for somatic ways of knowing within transformative learning theory. In C.A. Wiessner, S.R. Meyer, N.L. Pthal, & P.G. (Neaman (Eds.), *Proceedings of the Fifth International Conference on Transformative Learning*. Teacher's College, Columbia University, pp. 26-32.
[363] Damasio, 1994.
[364] Eich, E., Kihlstrom, J.F., Bower, G.H., Forgas, J.P., & Niedenthal, P.M. (2000). *Cognition and emotion*. Oxford University Press.
[365] Hodgkin, R. (1991, September 27). Michael Polanyi—Profit of life, the universe, and everything. In Times Higher Educational Supplement, p. 15.
[366] See Bennet, A. & Bennet, D. (2014). Knowledge, theory and practice in Knowledge Management: Between associative patterning and context-rich action. *Journal of Entrepreneurship, Management and Innovation 10*(1), pp. 7-55. www.jemi.edu.pl
[367] Polanyi, 1958
[368] Pinker (2007). Also, Nelson, C.A., deHaan, M., & Thomas, K.M. (2006). *Neuroscience of cognitive development: The role of experience and the developing brain*. John Wiley & Sons. Also, Gazzaniga, M.S. (2008). *Human: The science behind what makes us unique*. HarperCollins.
[369] Ellinor, L., & Gerard, G. (1998). *Dialogue: Rediscover the transforming power of conversation*. John Wiley & Sons, p. 26.
[370] Rock, A. (2004). *The mind at night: The new science of how and why we dream*. Basic Books.
[371] Kounios, J., & Beeman, M. (2014). The cognitive neuroscience of insight. *Annual Review of Psychology 65*(1), pp. 71-93. Also, Gilsinan, K. (2015). The Buddhist and the neuroscientist: What compassion does to the brain. [Blog] *The Atlantic*. theatlantic.com/health/archive/2015/07/dalai-lama-neuroscience-compassion/397706/
[372] Zeidan, F., Johnson, S., Diamond, B., David, Z., & Goolkasian, P. (2010). Mindfulness meditation improves cognition: Evidence of brief mental training. *Consciousness and Cognition 19*(2), pp. 597-605.
[373] Davidson, R. J. (2010). Empirical explorations of mindfulness: conceptual and methodological conundrums. *Emotion*, *10*(1), 8–11. https://doi.org/10.1037/a0018480
[374] Colzato, I., Ozturk, A., & Hommel, B. (2012). Meditate to create: The impact of focused-attention and open-monitoring training on convergent and divergent thinking. *Frontiers in Psychology, 3*.
[375] Kabat-Zinn, J. (1982). An outpatient program in behavioral medicine for chronic pain patients based on the practice of mindfulness meditation: Theoretical considerations and preliminary results. *General Hospital Psychiatry*, *4*(1), 33–47.

[376] Bishop, S. R., Lau, M., Shapiro, S., Carlson, L., Anderson, N. D., Carmody, J., & Devins, G. (2004). Mindfulness: A proposed operational definition. *Clinical Psychology: Science and Practice, 11*(3), 230–241. https://doi.org/br6rx6
[377] Dane, p. 1000.
[378] Brown, K. W., Ryan, R. M., & Creswell, J. D. (2007). Mindfulness: Theoretical Foundations and Evidence for its Salutary Effects. *Psychological Inquiry*, *18*(4), 211–237. https://doi.org/10.1080/10478400701598298
[379] Kelzer, K. (1987). The sun and the shadow: My experiment with lucid dreaming. ARE Press.
[380] Bennet & Bennet, The human knowledge system: Music and brain coherence.
[381] Oster, 94-102.
[382] Ritchey (2003).
[383] Mavromatis (1991); Atwater (2004); Fischer (1971); West (1980); Delmonte (1984); Goleman (1988); Jevning et al. (1992).
[384] Colino, S. (2023, December 12). What is lucid dreaming—and how can you learn it? National Geographic Science, Mind, Body. *National Geographic.*
[385] Csikszentmihalyi, M. (2003). *Good business: Leadership, flow and the making of meaning.* Viking, p. 60.
[386] The Knowledge Management Thought Leader (KMTL) Study conducted in 2004-2005 engaged 34 KM thought leaders spanning four continents. Ten years later a 2014 Sampler Call reengaging nine of those early participants and adding three additional thought leaders reaffirmed the direction Knowledge Management was heading. The results of these studies, sponsored by The Mountain Quest Research Institute, are detailed in Chapter 5 of the 2023 release *Reblooming the Knowledge Movement: The Democratization of Organizations.*
[387] Seligman, M.E.P. (2011). Flourish: A visionary new understanding of happiness and well-being. Free Press, pp. 11-12.
[388] Maslow, A. (1965). Humanistic science and transcendent experience. *Journal of Humanistic Psychology, 5*(2), 219-27. Also, Maslow, A. (1968). *Toward a psychology of being.* Van Nostrand.
[389] Hebb, D.O. (1955, July). Drive and the CNS. *Psychological Review,* 243-52. Also, Hebb, D.O. (1966). *The organization of behavior.* Wiley & Sons. Also, Harlow, H.F. (1953). Mice, monkeys, men, and motives. *Psychological Review 60*, 23-32. Also, Butler, R.H., & Alexander, H.M. (1955). Daily patterns of visual exploratory behavior I the monkey. *Journal of Comparative and Physiological Psychology, 48*, 247-9. Also, White.
[390] deCharms, R., & Muir, M.S. (1978). Motivation: Social approaches. *Annual Review of Psychology, 29*, 91-113.
[391] Deci, E.L. (1971). Effects of externally mediated rewards on intrinsic motivation. *Journal of Personality and Social Psychology, 18*, 105-15. Also, Deci, E.L. (1972). Intrinsic motivation, extrinsic reinforcement, and inequity. *Journal of Personality and Social Psychology, 22*(1), 113-20. Also, Deci, E.L. (1975). *Intrinsic motivation.* Plenum.
[392] Lepper, M.R., Greene, D., & Nisbett, R.E. (1973). Undermining children's intrinsic interest with extrinsic reward: a test of the "over justification" hypothesis. *Journal of Personality and Social Psychology, 28*(1), 129-37
[393] Csikszentmihalyi, *Flow: The psychology of optimal experience*, p. 15.

[394] Ibid., p. 3.
[395] Csikszentmihalyi, M. (2003). *Good business: Leadership, flow and the making of meaning*. Viking, p. 39.
[396] Csikszentmihalyi, M. (1975) *Beyond boredom and anxiety*. Jossey Bass. Also, Csikszentmihalyi, *Creativity: Flow and the psychology of discovery and invention.*
[397] Dietrich, A. (205). *How creativity happens in the brain*. Palgrove Macmillan.
[398] Amabile, T. (2005). Affect and Creativity at Work. Administrative Science Quarterly, 50, pp. 367-403.
[399] Csikszentmihalyi (1990)
[400] Brown, K.W., & Ryan, R.M. (2003). The benefits of being present: Mindfulness and its role in psychological well-being. *Journal of Personality and Social Psychology*, 84(4), 822-848.
[401] Creswell, J.D. (2017). Mindfulness interventions. *Annual Review of Psychology, 68*(1), 491-516, p. 492.
[402] Kabat-Zinn, J. (2003). Mindfulness-based interventions in context: Past, present, and future. *Clinical Psychology: Science and Practice, 10*(2), 144-156.
[403] Hawkins and Blakeslee, p. 137.
[404] Scharmer, C.O. (2009). *Theory U: Leading from the future as it emerges*. Berrett-Koehler.
[405] Senge, P.M., Scharmer, C.O., Jaworski, J., & Flowers, B.S. (2004). *Presence: Exploring profound change in people, organizations and society*. Random House, Inc.
[406] Ibid.
[407] Forwarded in the January 08, 2017, daily quote from Abraham-Hicks Publications.
[408] Csikszentmihalyi, *Flow: The psychology of optimal experience*, p. 41.
[409] Paul Potts was the winner of the Britain's Got Talent competition. See Paul Potts *One Chance* music CD (SYCOmusic, 2007); also see www.youtube.com/watch?v=9hlq_GGiln4 for his incredible performance in the finals.
[410] Dobbs, D. (2007). Turning off depression. In F.E. Bloom (Ed.), *Best of the brain from Scientific American: Mind, matter, and tomorrow's brain*, p. 22.
[411] Immordino-Yang, M.H. (2016). The smoke around mirror neurons: goals as sociocultural and emotional organizers of perception and action in learning. In M.H. Immordino-Yang (Ed.), *Emotions, learning, and the brain: Exploring the educational implications of affective neuroscience.* Norton.
[412] For more information on mirror neurons, see Gazzaniga, M.S. (2004). *The cognitive neurosciences III.* MIT Press.
[413] Ericsson, K.A., Charness, N., Feltovich, P.J., & Hoffman, R.R. (Eds.) (2006). *The Cambridge handbook of expertise and expert performance.* Cambridge University Press.
[414] Ross.
[415] For additional information on the development of expertise see Ericsson et al.
[416] For a good explanation of Emotional Intelligence see Goleman (1995) AND Goleman, D. (1998). *Working with Emotional Intelligence*. Bantam Books.
[417] Rescher, N. (2001). *Paradoxes: their roots, range, and resolution*. Open Court.
[418] Sallinsbury, R.M. (1988). *Paradoxes.* Cambridge University Press.
[419] Van Heijenoort, J. (Ed.) (1967). *From Frege to Gödel: A source book in mathematical logic. 1879-1931*. Harvard University Press.

[420] Two excellent references are *Paradoxes: Their Roots, Range and Resolution* by Nicholas Rescher (which also includes a history of paradox) and *Paradoxes from A to Z* by Michael Clark.
[421] Klein, p. 13.
[422] Tallis, p. 182.
[423] Carter, R. (2002). *Exploring consciousness*. University of California Press.
[424] Bennet & Bennet, The knowledge and knowing of spiritual learning, pp. 150-168.
[425] Ibid.
[426] Pert, C.B. (1997). *Molecules of emotion: A science behind mind-body medicine*. Touchstone.
[427] Kahneman, D. (2013). *Thinking, fast and slow*. Farrar, Straus & Giroux.
[428] Gladwell, M. (2005). *Blink: The power of thinking without thinking*. Little, Brown.
[429] Lachman, p. 171.
[430] Main, R. (1997). *Jung on synchronicity and the paranormal*. Princeton University Press, p. 18.
[431] de Laszlo, V. (Ed.) (1958). *Psyche & symbol: A selection from the writings of C.G. Jung*. Anchor Books, p. 261.
[432] Kammerer, P. (1919). *Das Gestex der Serie*. Deutsche Verlaga-Ansalt. Quoted in Koestler, A. (1972). *The roots of coincidence*. Random House.
[433] Peat, F.D. (1988). *Synchronicity: The bridge between matter and mind*. Bantam Books, p. 16.
[434] Hall, C.S., & Nordby, V.J. (1973). *A primer of Jungian Psychology*. New American Library, p. 39.
[435] Peat, p. 16.
[436] Hume, D. (1978). Selby-Bigge, I.A., & Nidditch, P.H. (Eds.). *Treatise of human nature*. Oxford University Press.
[437] Pert, p. 42.
[438] Alberts, D.S., & Hayes, R.E. (2005). *Power to the edge: Command, control in the information age*. Command & Control Research Program.
[439] Senge et al., p. 160.
[440] Sheldrake.
[441] Cooper.
[442] Iacoboni, M. (2008). *The new science of how we connect with others: Mirroring people*. Farrar, Straus & Giroux.
[443] Rizzolatti, G. (2006, November). Mirrors in the mind. *Scientific American*, p. 60.
[444] Ibid, p. 56.
[445] Ibid, p. 61.
[446] Ibid.
[447] Bennet, Bennet, & Turner, *Expanding the self: The intelligent complex adaptive learning system*.
[448] Damasio, p. 188.
[449] Quoted from Wilson, as cited in Hodges, D. (2000). Implications of music and brain research. *Music Educators Journal, 87*(2), 18.
[450] MacFlouer (2004-16).
[451] Ritsema, R., & Karcher, S. (Trans.) (1995). *I Ching: The classic Chinese oracle of change* (The first complete translation with concordance). Barnes & Noble, p. 11.
[452] Ibid, p. 12.

[453] Legge, J. (Trans). (1996). *I Ching: Book of changes: The ancient Chinese guide to wisdom and fortunetelling.* Random House Value Publishing.
[454] Ritsema and Karcher.
[455] Legge, p. xi.
[456] Ibid, p. ix.
[457] Ritsema and Karcher, p. vii.
[458] Wing, R.L. (Trans.) (1986). *The Tao of power: Lao Tzu's classic guide to leadership, influence, and excellence.* Doubleday.
[459] Ibid., p. 11.
[460] Ibid.
[461] Bennet, A. (2018). *Possibilities that are YOU! Volume 3: Engaging forces.* MQIPress.
[462] Ibid, p. 22.
[463] MacFlouer (2004-2016).
[464] Rizzolatti, p. 61.
[465] Bennet, A., & Turner, R. (2023). *Reblooming the knowledge movement: The democratization of organizations.* MQIPress.
[466] Jones, M. (n.d.). *Rediscovering a mythic worldview.* Management issues at the heart of the changing workplace. httpls://www.management-issues.com/opinion/6983/rediscovering-a-mythic-worldview/
[467] McWhinney, W. (1992). *Paths of change: Strategic choices for organizations and society.* SAGE Publications.
[468] Ibid., p. 43.
[469] Bradley, F.H. (1966/1893). *Appearance and reality.* Oxford University Press, p. 218.
[470] LeShan, L. (1976). *Alternative realities.* Ballantine, p. 90.
[471] Carse, J. P. (1986). *Finite and infinite games.* Ballantine, p. 168.
[472] Ibid.
[473] de Unamuno, M. (1967). *Our Lord Don Quixote* (Anthony Kerrigan, Trans.). Princeton University Press.
[474] Ibid., p. 142.
[475] Michael, D.N. (1977). Planning's challenge to the systems approach. In H.A. Linstone & W.H.C. Simmonds, *Futures research: New directions.* Addison-Wesley Publishing Company, Inc.
[476] McWhinney.
[477] MacFlouer (2004-2016).
[478] *The Urantia Book* (1955). URANTIA Foundation.
[479] Ibid., p. 1295-1296.
[480] Bennet & Turner.
[481] Yang, K., Ribiére, V., & Bennet, A. (2023). Can we really hide knowledge? Unpublished paper. Also, Bogilović, S., Černe, M., & Škerlavaj, M. (2017). Hiding behind a mask? Cultural intelligence, knowledge hiding, and individual and team creativity. European Journal of Work and Organizational Psychology, 26(5), 710-723. Also, Černe, M., Hernaus, T., Dysvik, A., & Škerlavaj, M. (2014). What goes around comes around: Knowledge hiding, perceived motivational climate, and creativity. *Academy of Management Journal, 57*(1), 172-192.
[482] Ibid.

[483] MacFlouer (2004-2016).
[484] Bennet, Bennet, & Turner (2015).
[485] Brown, T. (2009). *Change by design: How design thinking transforms organizations and inspires innovation*. HarperCollins, front flap.
[486] Ibid.
[487] Ibid, p. 4.
[488] McTaggart (2002)
[489] Goswami, A. (2000). *The visionary window: A quantum physicist's guide to enlightenment*. Quest Books, Theosophical Publishing House, p. 30.
[490] Planck, M. (1920, June 2). The genesis and present state of development of the quantum theory. (Nobel Lecture).
[491] Wallas, G. l. (1931/1926). *The art of thought*. Johnathan Cape
[492] Bennet, *Possibilities that are YOU! Volume 3: Engaging forces*.
[493] Houston, J. (2000). *Jump time: Shaping your future in a world of radical change*. Penguin Putnum, Inc.
[494] Fricker, M. (2007). *Epistemic justice: Power and the politics of knowledge*. Oxford University Press.
[495] Ritsema & Karcher, p. 11.
[496] Sternberg.
[497] Ibid.
[498] Galenson, D. (2013). The wisdom and creativity of the elders in art and science. Blog. David Galenson is Professor of Economics at the University of Chicago.
[499] Ibid.
[500] Sternberg.
[501] The definition of intelligent activity forwarded in this text is a state of interaction where intent, purpose, direction, values and expected outcomes are clearly understood and communicated among all parties, reflecting wisdom and achieving a higher truth.
[502] MacFlouer, 2004-16.
[503] Ibid.
[504] Morgan, G. (2006). *Images of Organization*, Sage Publications.
[505] Pert, p. 276.
[506] Hawkins and Blakeslee.
[507] Kuntz, P.G. (1968). *The concept of order*. University of Washington Press, p. 162.
[508] Hawkins and Blakeslee, p. 109.
[509] Ibid.
[510] Bennet, A., & Bennet, D. (2013). *Decision-making in the new reality*. MQIPress.
[511] James.
[512] Published as a chapter in Bennet & Bennet, 2013)
[513] Clavell, J. (Ed.) (1983). *The art of war: Sun Tzu*. Dell Publishing.
[514] Barthes, R. (1985). *In the responsibility of forms*. Hill and Wang.
[515] Wycoff, J. (1991). *Mindmapping: Your personal guide to exploring creativity and problem-solving*. The Berkley Publishing Group.
[516] For details see Kahneman, D., Slovic, P., & Tversky, A. (1982). *Judgment under uncertainty: Heuristics and biases*. Cambridge University Press.
[517] Tiller, W. (2007). *Psychoenergetic science: A second Copernican-scale revolution*. Pavior.

[518] Senge.
[519] Goleman (1995).
[520] Goleman (1995) and Goleman (1998).
[521] Argyris, C. (1990). *Overcoming organizational defenses: Facilitating organizational learning*. Prentice Hall.
[522] Bohm, D. (1992). *Thought as a system*. Routledge.
[523] Nonaka, I., & Takeuchi, H. (1995). *The knowledge-creating company: How Japanese companies create the dynamics of innovation*. Oxford University Press. See also Polanyi, M. (1958). *Personal knowledge: Towards a post-critical philosophy*. The University of Chicago.
[524] Peek, P. M. (Ed.) (1991). *African divination systems: Ways of knowing*. Indiana University Press.
[525] Ibid, p. 37.
[526] Douglas, M. (1984). If the Dogon … *Implicit Meanings: Essays in Anthropology*, 124-141, p. 129.
[527] Lévi-Strauss, C. (1966). *The savage mind*. University of Chicago Press.
[528] Mendonsa, E. L. (1976). Characteristics of Sisala diviners. In A. Bharati (Ed.), *The realm of the extra-human: Agents and audiences*. The Hague, Mouton, 179-95.
[529] Whyte, S. R. (1991). Knowledge and power in Nyole divination. In P. M. Peek (Ed.), *African divination systems: Ways of knowing*. Indiana University Press, 153-172.
[530] Meyer, P. (1991). Divination among the Lobi of Burkina Faso. In P. M. Peek (Ed.), *African divination systems: Ways of knowing*. Indiana University Press, 91-100.
[531] Blier, R. (1991). Diviners as alienists and annunciators among the Batammaliba of Togo. In P. M. Peek (Ed.), *African divination systems: Ways of knowing*. Indiana University Press, 73-90.
[532] Shaw, R. (1991). Splitting truths from darkness: Epistemological aspects of Temne divination. In P. M. Peek (Ed.), *African divination systems: Ways of knowing*. Indiana University Press, 137-152.
[533] Almquist, A. (1991). Divination and the hunt in Pagibeti ideology. In P. M. Peek (Ed.), *African divination systems: Ways of knowing*. Indiana University Press, 101-111.
[534] Parkin, D. (1991). Simultaneity and sequencing in the oracular speech of Kenyan diviners. In P. M. Peek (Ed.), *African divination systems: Ways of knowing*. Indiana University Press, 173-190.
[535] Callaway, H. (1991). The initiation of a Zulu diviner. In P. M. Peek (Ed.), *African divination systems: Ways of knowing*. Indiana University Press, 27-36.
[536] Peek, p. 193.
[537] Devisch, R. (1991). Mediumistic divination among the Northern Yaka of Zaire: Etiology and ways of knowing. In P. M. Peek (Ed.), *African divination systems: Ways of knowing*. Indiana University Press, 112-132.

References

Adolphs, R. (2004). Processing of emotional and social information by the human amygdala. In Gazzaniga, M.S. (Ed.), *The cognitive neurosciences III*. The Bradford Press.

Alberts, D.S., & Hayes, R.E. (2005). *Power to the edge: Command, control in the information age*. Command & Control Research Program.

Almquist, A. (1991). Divination and the hunt in Pagibeti ideology. In P. M. Peek (Ed.), *African divination systems: Ways of knowing*. Indiana University Press, 101-111.

Amabile, T. (2005). Affect and Creativity at Work. *Administrative Science Quarterly, 50*, pp. 367-403.

Amabile, T.M. (1983). *The social psychology of creativity*. Springer.

Amabile, T.M. (1996). *Creativity in context*. Westview.

Amann, T. (2003). Creating space for somatic ways of knowing within transformative learning theory. In C.A. Wiessner, S.R. Meyer, N.L. Pthal, & P.G. (Neaman (Eds.), *Proceedings of the Fifth International Conference on Transformative Learning*. Teacher's College, Columbia University, pp. 26-32.

Amen, D.G. (2005) *Making a good brain great*. Harmony Books.

American Heritage Dictionary of the English Language (4th ed.) (2006). Houghton Mifflin Company.

Anderson, J.R. (1983). *The architecture of cognition*. Harvard University Press.

Andreasen, N. (2005). *The creating brain: The neuroscience of genius*. The Dana Foundation.

Argyris, C. (1990). *Overcoming organizational defenses: Facilitating organizational learning*. Prentice Hall.

Arieti, S. (1976). *Creativity: The magic synthesis by Silvano Arieti*. Goodreads.

Armstrong, D.M. (1989). *Universals: An opinionated introduction*. Westview Press.

Atwater, F.H. (2004). *The Hemi-Sync process*. The Monroe Institute.

Avedisian, J., & Bennet, A. (2010). Values as knowledge: A new frame of reference for a new generation of knowledge workers. *On the Horizon, 18*(3), pp. 255-265.

Baltes, P.B., & Smith, J. (1990). The psychology of wisdom and its ontogenesis. In R.J. Sternbert (Ed.), *Wisdom: Its nature, origins and development*, Cambridge University Press, 87-120.

Barfield, O. (1988). Saving the appearances. Wesleyan University Press.

Barthes, R. (1985). *In the responsibility of forms*. Hill and Wang.

Begley, S. (2007). *Train your mind change your brain: How a new science reveals our extraordinary potential to transform ourselves*. Ballantine Books, p. 69.

Belitz, C., & Lundstrom, M. (1997). *The power of flow*. Harmony Books.

Bennet, A. & Bennet, D. (2014). Knowledge, theory and practice in Knowledge Management: Between associative patterning and context-rich action. *Journal of Entrepreneurship, Management and Innovation 10*(1), pp. 7-55. www.jemi.edu.pl

Bennet, A. (2018). *Possibilities that are YOU! Volume 3: Engaging forces*. MQIPress.

Bennet, A. (2018). *Possibilities that are YOU! Volume 20: The humanness of humility*. MQIPress.
Bennet, A. (2018). *Possibilities that are YOU! Volume 10: Knowing*. MQIPress.
Bennet, A., & Bennet, D. (2004). *Organizational survival in the new world: The intelligent complex adaptive system*. Elsevier.
Bennet, A., & Bennet, D. (2007). CONTEXT: The shared knowledge enigma. *VINE, 37*(1), pp. 27-40.
Bennet, A., & Bennet, D. (2007). The knowledge and knowing of spiritual learning. *VINE, 37*(2), pp. 150-168.
Bennet, A., & Bennet, D. (2008). The human knowledge system: Music and brain coherence. *VINE: The Journal of Information and Knowledge Management Systems, 38*(3), 277-295.
Bennet, A., & Bennet, D. (2013). *Decision-making in the new reality: Complexity, knowledge and knowing*. MQIPress.
Bennet, A., & Scott, C.L. (2019). *With passion, we live and love: Research, prose, verse and music*. MQIPress.
Bennet, A., & Turner, R. (2023). *Reblooming the Knowledge Movement: The Democratization of Organizations*. MQIPress.
Bennet, A., Bennet, D. & Avedisian, J. (2018). *The course of knowledge: A 21st century theory*. MQIPress.
Bennet, A., Bennet, D., Shelley, A., Bullard, T., & Lewis. J. (2020). *The profundity and bifurcation of change part II: Learning from the past*. MQIPress.
Bennet, A., Bennet, D., Shelley, A., Bullard, T., & Lewis, J. (2020). *The profundity and bifurcation of change part III: Learning in the present*. MQIPress.
Bennet, A., Bennet, D., Shelley, A., Bullard, T., & Lewis, J. (2020). *The profundity and bifurcation of change part IV: Co-creating the future*. MQIPress.
Bennet, D. (2006) Expanding the knowledge paradigm. *VINE, 36*(2), pp. 175-181.
Bennet, D. (2023). Systems and complexity thinking. In Bennet, A., & Turner, R., *Reblooming the knowledge movement: The democratization of organizations*, pp. 456-486. MQIPress.
Bennet, D., & Bennet, A. (2008). Engaging tacit knowledge in support of organizational learning. *VINE, 38*(1), pp. 72-94.
Bennet, D., Bennet, A., & Turner (2018). *Expanding the self: The intelligent complex adaptive learning system. A new theory of adult learning*. MQIPress.
Bennet, D., Bennet, A., & Turner, R. (2022). *Unleashing the human mind: A consilience approach to managing self*. MQIPress.
Bennett-Goleman, T. (2001). *Emotional alchemy: How the mind can heal the heart. Harmony Books*.
Bennett-Woods, D. (1997). Reflections on wisdom. (Unpublished paper). University of Northern Colorado.
Berman, S., & Korsten, P. (2010). *Capitalizing on complexity: Insights from the global chief executive officer (CEO) study*. IBM Institute for Business Value.
Besant, A., & Leadbeater, C.W. (2021). *Thought-forms*. Rolled Scroll Publishing.
Bishop, S. R., Lau, M., Shapiro, S., Carlson, L., Anderson, N. D., Carmody, J., & Devins, G. (2004). Mindfulness: A proposed operational definition. *Clinical Psychology: Science and Practice, 11*(3), 230–241. https://doi.org/br6rx6

Blair, H. (2015). Reading on sentence structure from Huge Blair form lectures on rhetoric and Belles letters. http://academic.macewan.ca/einarssonr/files/2009/10/On-Sentence-Structure-by-Blair1.pdf

Blier, R. (1991). Diviners as alienists and annunciators among the Batammaliba of Togo. In P. M. Peek (Ed.), *African divination systems: Ways of knowing*. Indiana University Press, 73-90.

Boden, M. (1991). The creative mind, myths & Mysticism. Basic Books.

Bodhi, B. (1984). *The noble eightfold path: Way to the end of suffering*. Pariyatti.

Bogilović, S., Černe, M., & Škerlavaj, M. (2017). Hiding behind a mask? Cultural intelligence, knowledge hiding, and individual and team creativity. European Journal of Work and Organizational Psychology, 26(5), 710-723. *Academy of Management Journal, 57*(1), 172-192.

Bohm, D. (1980). *Wholeness and the implicate order*. Routledge & Kegal Paul.

Bohm, D. (1992). *Thought as a system*. Routledge.

Boltzmann, L. (1896, 1898). *Lectures on gas theory* (part I and part II) (Trans. S. G. Brush, 1976). University of California Press.

Bradley, F.H. (1966/1893). *Appearance and reality*. Oxford University Press.

Brown, K. W., Ryan, R. M., & Creswell, J. D. (2007). Mindfulness: Theoretical Foundations and Evidence for its Salutary Effects. *Psychological Inquiry*, *18*(4), 211–237. https://doi.org/10.1080/10478400701598298

Brown, K.W., & Ryan, R.M. (2003). The benefits of being present: Mindfulness and its role in psychological well-being. *Journal of Personality and Social Psychology*, 84(4), 822-848.

Brown, T. (2009). *Change by design: How design thinking transforms organizations and inspires innovation*. HarperCollins, front flap.

Bullard, B., & Bennet, A. (2018). *Remembrance: Pathways to expanded learning with music and meta-music®*. MQIPress.

Butler, J. (1906). *The analogy of religion, natural & revealed*. J.M. Dent & Company.

Butler, R.H., & Alexander, H.M. (1955). Daily patterns of visual exploratory behavior in the monkey. *Journal of Comparative and Physiological Psychology, 48*, 247-9.

Byrnes, J.P. (2001). *Minds, brains, and learning: Understanding the psychological and educational relevance of neuroscientific research*. The Guilford Press.

Callaway, H. (1991). The initiation of a Zulu diviner. In P. M. Peek (Ed.), *African divination systems: Ways of knowing*. Indiana University Press, 27-36.

Caine, G., & Caine, R.N. (2006). Meaningful learning and the executive functions of the brain. In S. Johnson & K. Taylor (Eds.), *The neuroscience of adult learning: New directions for adult and continuing education* (pp. 71-86). Jossey-Bass.

Campbell, D.T. (1960). Blind variation and selective retention in creative thought and other knowledge processes. *Psychological Review, 67*, 380-400.

Capurso, V., Fabbro, F., & Crescentini, C. (2014). Mindful creativity: the influence of mindfulness meditation on creative thinking. *Frontiers in Psychology*.

Carroll, G.D. (1986). *Brain hemisphere synchronization and musical learning*, reprint of paper published by University of North Carolina at Greensboro, N.C.

Carroll, S. (2016). *The big picture: On the origins of life, meaning, and the universe itself*. Dutton.

Carse, J. P. (1986). *Finite and infinite games*. Ballantine.
Carter, R. (2002). *Exploring consciousness*. University of California Press.
Černe, M., Hernaus, T., Dysvik, A., & Škerlavaj, M. (2014). What goes around comes around: Knowledge hiding, perceived motivational climate, and creativity. *Academy of Management Journal, 57*(1), 172-192.
Checkland, P. (1999). Systems thinking, systems practice: Include a 30-year retrospective. John Wiley and Sons, Inc.
Christos, G. (2003). *Memory and dreams: The creative human mind*. Rutgers University Press.
Clark, M. (2002). *Paradoxes from A to Z*. Third Ed. Routledge.
Clavell, J. (Ed.) (1983). *The art of war: Sun Tzu*. Dell Publishing.
Clayton, V., & Birren, J.E. (1980). The development of wisdom across the lifespan: A reexamination of an ancient topic. In P.B. Baltes & O.G.J. Brim (Eds.), *Life span development and behavior* (104-135). Academic Press.
Colzato, I., Ozturk, A., & Hommel, B. (2012). Meditate to create: The impact of focused-attention and open-monitoring training on convergent and divergent thinking. *Frontiers in Psychology, 3*.
Cools, J. (2023). Crystallizing the symphony of passions. In Bennet, A., & Baisya, R. (Eds.), *INside INnovation: Looking from the inside out*, pp. 271-298. MQIPress.
Cooper, L.R. (2005). *The grand vision: The design and purpose of a human being*. Planetary Heart.
Cornell, A.W. (1990). *The power of focusing: A practical guide to emotional self-healing*. MJF Books, front cover.
Cornford, F. (1991). *From religion to philosophy*. Princeton University Press.
Costa, J.D. (1995). *Working wisdom: The ultimate value in the new economy*. Stoddart.
Cowley, M. (Ed.) (1958). *Writers at work: The Paris review interviews*. The Paris Review.
Cozolino, L., & Spokay, S. (2006). Neuroscience and adult learning. In S. Johnson & K. Taylor (Eds.), *The neuroscience of adult learning: New directions for adult and continuing education* (pp. 71-86). Jossey-Bass.
Cozolino, L.J. (2006). *The neuroscience of human relationships: Attachment and developing social brain*. W.W. Norton.
Crampton, M. (1975). Answers from the unconscious. *Synthesis 1*(2), 140-141.
Crandall, B., Klein, G., & Hoffman, R.R. (2006). *Working minds: A practitioner's guide to cognitive task analysis*. The MIT Press.
Crawford, R.P. (1954). *The techniques of creative thinking: How to use your ideas to achieve success*. Hawthorn Books, Inc.
Creswell, J. W. (2014). *Research design: Qualitative, quantitative, & mixed methods approaches*. SAGE.
Creswell, J.D. (2017). Mindfulness interventions. *Annual Review of Psychology, 68*(1), 491-516.
Csikszentmihalyi, M. (1975) *Beyond boredom and anxiety*. Jossey Bass.
Csikszentmihalyi, M. (1990). *Flow: The psychology of optimal experience*. Harper & Row.
Csikszentmihalyi, M. (1996). *Creativity: Flow and the psychology of discovery and invention*. HarperCollins Publishers.

Csikszentmihalyi, M. (2003). *Good business: Leadership, flow and the making of meaning*. Viking.

Csikszentmihalyi, M. (2014). *The systems model of creativity: The collected works of Mihaly Csikszentmihalyi.* Springer.

Csikszentmihalyi, M., & Csikszentmihalyi, I.S. (Eds.) (1988). *Optimal experience: Psychological studies of flow in consciousness*. Cambridge University Press.

Damasio, A.R. (1994). *Descartes' error: Emotion, reason and the human brain*. G.P. Putnam's Sons.

Dane, E. (2011). Paying attention to mindfulness and its effects on task performance in the workplace. *Journal of Management, 37*(4), pp. 997-1018.

Davidson, R. J. (2010). Empirical explorations of mindfulness: conceptual and methodological conundrums. *Emotion, 10*(1), 8–11. https://doi.org/10.1037/a0018480

Davis, J. (1997). *Alternate realities: How science shapes our vision of the world.* Plenum Trade.

de Bono, E. (1992). *Serious creativity: Using the power of lateral thinking to create new ideas.* HarperCollins.

de Chardin, P.T. (1959). *The phenomenon of man.*

de Charms, R., & Muir, M.S. (1978). Motivation: Social approaches. *Annual Review of Psychology, 29*, 91-113.

de Laszlo, V. (Ed.) (1958). *Psyche & symbol: A selection from the writings of C.G. Jung.* Anchor Books.

de Unamuno, M. (1967). *Our Lord Don Quixote* (Anthony Kerrigan, Trans.). Princeton University Press.

Deci, E.L. (1971). Effects of externally mediated rewards on intrinsic motivation. *Journal of Personality and Social Psychology, 18*, 105-15.

Deci, E.L. (1972). Intrinsic motivation, extrinsic reinforcement, and inequity. *Journal of Personality and Social Psychology, 22*(1), 113-20.

Deci, E.L. (1975). *Intrinsic motivation*. Plenum.

Delmonte, M.M. (1984). Electrocortical activity and related phenomena associated with meditation practice: A literature review. *International Journal of Neuroscience, 24*, 217-231.

Devisch, R. (1991). Mediumistic divination among the Northern Yaka of Zaire: Etiology and ways of knowing. In P. M. Peek (Ed.), *African divination systems: Ways of knowing*. Indiana University Press, 112-132.

Dietrich, A. (205). *How creativity happens in the brain*. Palgrove Macmillan.

Dittmann-Kohli, F., & Baltes, P.B. (1990). Toward a neofunctionalist concept of adult intellectual development: Wisdom as a prototypical case of intellectual growth. In C. Alexander & E. Langer (Eds.), *Beyond formal operations: Alternative endpoints to human development*. Oxford University Press.

Dobbs, D. (2007). Turning off depression. In F.E. Bloom (Ed.), *Best of the brain from Scientific American: Mind, matter, and tomorrow's brain*.

Douglas, M. (1984). If the Dogon … *Implicit Meanings: Essays in Anthropology*, 124-141, p. 129.Dreher, D. (1995). *The Tao of personal leadership*. HarperBusiness.

Drucker, P. F. (1967). *The effective executive*. Harper & Row.

Edelman, G. (1989). *The remembered present: A biological theory of consciousness*. Basic Books.

Edelman, G.M., & Tononi, G. (2001). *A universe of consciousness: How matter becomes imagination*. Basic Books.

Eich, E., Kihlstrom, J.F., Bower, G.H., Forgas, J.P., & Niedenthal, P.M. (2000). *Cognition and emotion*. Oxford University Press.

Ellinor, L., & Gerard, G. (1998). *Dialogue: Rediscover the transforming power of conversation*. John Wiley & Sons.

Encarta World English Dictionary (1999). St Martin's Press.

Ericsson, K.A., Charness, N., Feltovich, P.J., & Hoffman, R.R. (Eds.) (2006). *The Cambridge handbook of expertise and expert performance.* Cambridge University Press.

Erikson, J.M. (1988). *Wisdom and the senses: The way of creativity*. Norton.

Eysenck, H.J. (1993). Creativity and personality: A theoretical perspective. *Psychological Inquiry, 4*, 147-178.

Feldman, D.H. (1999). The development of creativity. In R. J. Sternberg (Ed.), *Handbook of creativity*, 169-186. Cambridge University Press.

Finke, R.A., Ward, T.B., and Smith, S.M. (1992). *Creative cognition: Theory, research, and applications*. MIT Press.

Fischer, R. l (1971). A cartography of ecstatic and meditative states. *Science, 174*(12), 897-904.

Formica, M. J. (March 6, 2015). *Mindfulness and cultivating creativity*. Find a Therapist.

Freud, S. (1926). *Collected papers*, Vol. 4. Hogarth Press.

Fricker, M. (2007). *Epistemic justice: Power and the politics of knowledge.* Oxford University Press.

Galenson, D. (2013). The wisdom and creativity of the elders in art and science. Blog.

Gardner, H. (1993). *Creating minds: An anatomy of creativity seen through the lives of Freud, Einstein, Picasso, Stravinsky, Eliot, Graham, and Gandhi*. Basic Books.

Gazzaniga, M.S. (2004). *The cognitive neurosciences III.* MIT Press.

Gazzaniga, M.S. (2008). *Human: The science behind what makes us unique*. HarperCollins.

Gell-Mann, M. (1994). *The quark and the jaguar: Adventures in the simple and the complex.* W.H. Freeman and Company.

Gerber, R. (2000). *Vibrational medicine for the 21st century. The complete guide to energy healing and spiritual transformation*. Eagle Brook.

Gilsinan, K. (2015). The Buddhist and the neuroscientist: What compassion does to the brain. [Blog] *The Atlantic*. theatlantic.com/health/archive/2015/07/dalai-lama-neuroscience-compassion/397706/

Gladwell, M. (2005). *Blink: The power of thinking without thinking*. Little, Brown.

Goh, C. (May 16, 2016). How to apply mindfulness to the creative process. *Mindful: healthy mind, healthy life*.

Goldberg, E. (2005). *The wisdom paradox: How your mind can grow stronger as your brain grows older*. Gotham Books.

Goleman, D. (1995). *Emotional Intelligence*. Bantam Books.

Goleman, D. (1998). *Working with Emotional Intelligence*. Bantam Books.

Goleman, G.M. (1988). *Meditative mind: The varieties of meditative experience.* G.P. Putnam.

Goswami, A. (2000). *The visionary window: A quantum physicist's guide to enlightenment.* Quest Books, Theosophical Publishing House.

Goswami, A. (2014). *Quantum creativity: Think quantum, be creative*. Hay House, Inc.

Green, R.D. (2016) Conversation from Huffington Post. http://www.huffingtonpost.com/r-kay-green/giving-back)b)3298691.html

Gruber, H.E. (1989). The evolving systems approach to creative work. In D.B. Wallace, & H.E. Gruber (Eds.), *Creative people at work: Twelve cognitive case studies*. Oxford University Press, 3-24.

Grudin, R. (1984). The ethics of inspiration. In Rizzoli, *The phenomenon of CHANGE*. Cooper-Hewitt Museum, The Smithsonian Institution's National Museum of Design.

Gruzelier, J. (2008). A theory of alpha/theta neurofeedback, creative performance enhancement, long distance functional connectivity and psychological integration. Cognitive Processing *10*(81), pp. 101-109.

Guengerich, G. (2015). *The four stages of desire: From everything to one thing: Why we should stop wanting everything and focus on what matters most*. Blog posting.

Guilford, J.P. (1950). Creativity. *American Psychologist, 5*, 444-454.

Haberlandt, K. (1998). *Human memory: Exploration and application.* Allyn & Bacon.

Hall, C.S., & Nordby, V.J. (1973). *A primer of Jungian Psychology*. New American Library.

Harlow, H.F. (1953). Mice, monkeys, men, and motives. *Psychological Review 60*, 23-32.

Harman, W., & Rheingold, H. (1984). Higher creativity: Liberating the unconscious for breakthrough insights. Jeremy P. Tarcher/Putnam.

Hawkins, D.R. (2002). *Power vs force: The hidden determinants of human behavior*. Hay House.

Hawkins, J. (2021). *A thousand brains: A new theory of intelligence*. Basic Books.

Hawkins, J., & Blakeslee, S. (2004). *On intelligence: How a new understanding of the brain will lead to the creation of truly intelligent machines*. Times Books.

Hebb, D.O. (1955, July). Drive and the CNS. *Psychological Review,* 243-52.

Hebb, D.O. (1966). *The organization of behavior*. Wiley & Sons.

Heijnen, R.D. (2022). Desire—Life as a drama based game or the thermodynamics of everything. In S.B. Schafer & A. Bennet (Eds.), *The handbook of global media's preternatural influence on global technological singularity, culture and government* (pp. 214-242). IGI Global.

Heisenberg, W. (1949). The physical principles of the quantum theory. (Trans. C. Eckart & F.C. Hoyt). Dover Publications, Inc.

Hink, R.F., Kodera, K., Yamada, O., Kaga, K., & Suzuki, J. (1980). Binaural interaction of a beating frequency following response. *Audiology, 19*, 36-43.

Hobson, J.A. (1999). *Consciousness*. Scientific American Library.

Hodges, D. (2000). Implications of music and brain research. *Music Educators Journal, 87*(2), 18.

Hodgkin, R. (1991, September 27). Michael Polanyi—Profit of life, the universe, and everything. In *Times Higher Educational Supplement*.

Holiday, S.G., & Chandler, M.J. (1986). *Wisdom: Explorations in adult competence: Contributions to human development*, Vol. 17. Basel.

Holton, R. (n.d.). Belief/desire psychology, the Human theory of motivation & emotions. *Moral Psychology, 24*(120).

Houston, J. (2000). *Jump time: Shaping your future in a world of radical change*. Penguin Putnum, Inc.

Hume, D. (1978). Selby-Bigge, I.A., & Nidditch, P.H. (Eds.). *Treatise of human nature*. Oxford University Press.

Hutchins, R.M. (1952). *Great Books of the Western World*. William Benton Publisher.

Iacoboni, M. (2008). *The new science of how we connect with others: Mirroring people*. Farrar, Straus & Giroux.

Ikemi, Y., & Nakagawa, S.A. (1962). A psychosomatic study of contagious dermatitis. *Kyoshu Journal of Medical Science, 13*, 335-350.

Immordino-Yang, M.H. (2016). The smoke around mirror neurons: goals as sociocultural and emotional organizers of perception and action in learning. In M.H. Immordino-Yang (Ed.), *Emotions, learning, and the brain: Exploring the educational implications of affective neuroscience*. Norton.

Isakson, S.G., & Parnes, S.J. (1985). Curriculum planning for creative thinking and problem solving. *Journal of Creative Behavior* 19, 1-29.

James, J. (1996). *Thinking in the future tense: A workout for the mind*. Touchstone.

Jarvis, P. (1992). *Paradoxes of learning: On becoming an individual in society*. Jossey-Bass.

Jeffrey, S. (2008). *Creativity revealed: Discovering the source of inspiration*. Creative Crayon Publishers.

Jeving, R., Wallace, R.K., & Beidenbach, M. (1992). The physiology of meditation: A review. *Neuroscience and Behavioral Reviews, 16*, 415-424.

Johnson, S. (2006). The neuroscience of the mentor-learner relationships. In S. Johnson & K. Taylor (Eds.), *The neuroscience of adult learning: New direction for adult and continuing education* (pp. 63-70). Jossey-Bass.

Jones, M. (n.d.). *Rediscovering a mythic worldview*. Management issues at the heart of the changing workplace. https://www.management-issues.com/opinion/6983/rediscovering-a-mythic-worldview/

Kabat-Zinn, J. (1982). An outpatient program in behavioral medicine for chronic pain patients based on the practice of mindfulness meditation: Theoretical considerations and preliminary results. *General Hospital Psychiatry, 4*(1), 33–47.

Kabat-Zinn, J. (2003). Mindfulness-based interventions in context: Past, present, and future. *Clinical Psychology: Science and Practice, 10*(2), 144-156.

Kahneman, D. (2013). *Thinking, fast and slow*. Farrar, Straus & Giroux.

Kahneman, D., Slovic, P., & Tversky, A. (1982). *Judgment under uncertainty: Heuristics and biases*. Cambridge University Press.

Kammerer, P. (1919). *Das Gestex der Serie*. Deutsche Verlaga-Ansalt. Quoted in Koestler, A. (1972). *The roots of coincidence*. Random House.

Kandel, E.R. (2006). *In search of memory: The emergence of a new science of mind.* W.W. Norton & Company.

Kaufman, J., & Sternberg, R. (2011). *The Cambridge handbook of creativity.* Cambridge University Press.

Kelzer, K. (1987). *The sun and the shadow: My experiment with lucid dreaming.* ARE Press.

Kipling, R. (1985). Working-tools. In B. Ghiselin (Ed.), *The creative process: A symposium.* Berkeley, CA, University of California Press, 161-163. (Original article published in 1937).

Kirsner, K., Speelman, C., Mayberry, M., O'Brien-Malone, A., Anderson, M., & MacLeon, C. (Eds.) (1998). *Implicit and explicit mental processes.* Lawrence Erlbaum Associates, Publishers.

Klein, G. (2003). *Intuition at work: Why developing your gut instincts will make you better at what you do.* Doubleday.

Koestler, A. (1975). *The act of creation.* Macmillan.

Kolb, D.A. (1984). *Experiential learning: Experience as the source of learning and development.* Prentice Hall.

Kounios, J., & Beeman, M. (2014). The cognitive neuroscience of insight. *Annual Review of Psychology 65*(1), pp. 71-93.

Kramer, D.A., & Bacelar, W.T. (1994). The educated adult in today's world: Wisdom and the mature learner. In J.D. Sinnott (Ed.), *Interdisciplinary handbook of adult lifespan learning*. Greenwood Press.

Kudesia, R. S. (July 05, 2015). Mindfulness in the workplace. In J. Reb & P. W. B. Atkins (Eds.), *Mindfulness in Organizations: Foundations, Research, and Applications*, pp. 190-212.

Kuntz, P.G. (1968). *The concept of order*. University of Washington Press.

Lachman, G. (2017, 2022). *Lost knowledge of the imagination*. Floris Books.

Lakoff, G., & Nunez, 4. (2000). *Where mathematics comes from*. Basic Books.

Laszlo, E. (2004). *Science and the Akashic Field: An integral theory of everything*. Inner Traditions.

LeDoux, J. (1996). *The emotional brain: The mysterious underpinnings of emotional life.* Touchstone.

Legge, J. (Trans). (1996). *I Ching: Book of changes: The ancient Chinese guide to wisdom and fortunetelling.* Random House Value Publishing.

Leonard, D., & Swap, W. (1999). *When sparks fly: Igniting creativity in groups.* Harvard Business School Press.

Lepper, M.R., Greene, D., & Nisbett, R.E. (1973). Undermining children's intrinsic interest with extrinsic reward: a test of the "over justification" hypothesis. *Journal of Personality and Social Psychology, 28*(1), 129-37

LeShan, L. (1976). *Alternative realities*. Ballantine.

Lévi-Strauss, C. (1966). *The savage mind.* University of Chicago Press.

Lewis, J. (2019). *Story thinking: Transforming organizations for the fourth industrial revolution*. Amazon KDP.

Lipton, B. *The biology of belief: Unleashing the power of consciousness*. Hay House.

Lipton, B., & Bhaerman, S. (2009). *Spontaneous evolution: Our positive future (and a way to get there from here)*. Hay House.

Liu, E., & Noppe-Brandon, S. (2009). *Imagination first: Unlocking the power of possibility*. Jossey-Bass.

Long, T.A. (1986). Narrative unity and clinical judgment. *Theoretical Medicine 7*, 75-92.

Lovejoy, A.O. (1976) *The great chain of being*. Harvard University Press.

Macdonald, C. (1996). *Toward wisdom: Finding our way to inner peace, love, and happiness*. Hampton Roads.

MacFlouer, N. (1999). *Life's hidden meaning*. Ageless Wisdom Publishers.

MacFlouer, N. (2004-16). *Why life is* ... Weekly radio shows: BBSRadio.com (#1-#48) and KXAM (#1-#143).

Machlup, F. (1962). *The production and distribution of knowledge in the United States*. Princeton University Press,.

Main, R. (1997). *Jung on synchronicity and the paranormal*. Princeton University Press.

Marchese, T.JU. (1998). The new conversations about learning: Insights from neuroscience and anthropology, cognitive science and workplace studies. www.newhorizons.org/lifelong/higher)ed/marchese.htm

Martindale, C., & Mines, D. (1975). Creativity and cortical activation during creative, intellectual and EEG feedback tests. *Biological Psychology 3*(2), pp. 91-100.

Marton, F., & Booth, S. (1997). *Learning and awareness*. Lawrence Erlbaum Associates.

Maslow, A. (1965). Humanistic science and transcendent experience. *Journal of Humanistic Psychology, 5*(2), 219-27.

Maslow, A. (1968). *Toward a psychology of being*. Van Nostrand.

Matthews, R.C. (1991). The forgetting algorithm: How fragmentary knowledge of exemplars can yield abstract knowledge. *Journal of Experimental Psychology: General, 120*, 117-119.

Maturana, H.R., & Varela, F.J. (1987). *The tree of knowledge: The biological roots of human understanding*. Shambhala.

Mavromatis, A. (1991). *Hypnagogia*. Routledge.

May, R. (1970). *The courage to create*. Bantam.

McCabe, T. J. (2017). *Expanded consciousness: The many dimensions of our thoughts*. Self-published.

McGilchrist, I. (2009). *The master and his emissary*. Yale University Press.

McHale, J. (1977). Futures problems or problems in futures studies. In H.A. Linstone & W.H.C. Simmonds (Eds.), *Futures research: New directions*. Addison-Wesley Publishing Company, Inc.

McTaggart, L. (2008). *The field: The quest for the secret force of the universe*. Harper.

McWhinney, W. (1992). *Paths of change: Strategic choices for organizations and society*. SAGE Publications.

Melendez, S.E. (1996). An outsider's view of leadership. In F. Hesselbein, M. Goldsmith & R. Beckhard, *The Drucker Foundation: The leader of the future*. Jossey-Bass, pp. 293-302.

Mendonsa, E. L. (1976). Characteristics of Sisala diviners. In A. Bharati (Ed.), *The realm of the extra-human: Agents and audiences*. The Hague, Mouton, 179-95.

Merriam, S.B., & Caffarella, R.S. (1999). *Learning in adulthood: A comprehensive guide* (2nd ed.). Jossey-Bass, p. 165.

Merriam, S.B., Caffarella, R.S., & Baumgartner, L.M. (2006). *Learning in adulthood: A comprehensive guide.* John Wiley & Sons.

Metcalf, B. (2016). Field Effect Audio Technology™ (F.E.A.T.™) FAQ shared with author by Metcalf on 11/05/2016.

Meyer, P. (1991). Divination among the Lobi of Burkina Faso. In P. M. Peek (Ed.), *African divination systems: Ways of knowing*. Indiana University Press, 91-100.

Michael, D.N. (1977). Planning's challenge to the systems approach. In H.A. Linstone & W.H.C. Simmonds, *Futures research: New directions.* Addison-Wesley Publishing Company, Inc.

Minsky, M. (2006). *The emotion machine: Commonsense thinking, artificial intelligence, and the future of the human mind.* Simon and Schuster.

Moon, J.A. (2004). *A handbook of reflective and experiential learning: Theory and practice.* RoutledgeFalmer.

Moore, A., & Malinowski, P. (2009). Meditation, mindfulness and cognitive flexibility. *Consciousness and Cognition, 18*(1), 176-186.

Morgan, G. (2006). *Images of Organization*, Sage Publications.

Mulvihill, M.K. (2003). The Catholic church in crisis: Will transformative learning lead to social change through the uncovering of emotion? In Weissner, C.A., Meyers, S.R., Pfhal, N.L., & Neaman, P.F. (Eds.), *Proceedings of the 5th International Conference on Transformative Learning*, pp. 320-323. Teachers College, Columbia University.

Murphy, M. (1992). The future of the body. Tarcher.

Nelson, C.A., deHaan, M., & Thomas, K.M. (2006). *Neuroscience of cognitive development: The role of experience and the developing brain.* John Wiley & Sons.

Nonaka, I., & Takeuchi, H. (1995). *The knowledge-creating company: How Japanese companies create the dynamics of innovation.* Oxford University Press.

Nouwen, J.J.M. (1975). *Reaching out: The three movements of the spiritual life.* Doubleday.

Nystrom, H. (1979). *Creativity and innovation.* John Wiley & Sons.

Osborn, A.F. (1953). *Your creative power.* Scribner.

Oster, G. (1963). Auditory beats in the brain. *Scientific American, 229*, 94-102.

Parkin, D. (1991). Simultaneity and sequencing in the oracular speech of Kenyan diviners. In P. M. Peek (Ed.), *African divination systems: Ways of knowing.* Indiana University Press, 173-190.

Peat, F.D. (1988). *Synchronicity: The bridge between matter and mind.* Bantam Books.

Peek, P. M. (Ed.) (1991). *African divination systems: Ways of knowing.* Indiana University Press.

Perkins, D.N. (1995). *Outsmarting IQ: The emerging science of learnable intelligence.* Free Press.

Pert, C.B. (1997). *Molecules of emotion: A science behind mind-body medicine.* Touchstone.

Peterson, B. (2022). *Grand Experience Leonardo da Vinci, 500 Years of Genius*, A Legends of Art and Innovations Publication at Biltmore, North Carolina.

Philosophy, Literature, Mysticism: An Anthology of essays on Swedenborg. The Swedenborg Society.

Pinker, S. (2007). *The stuff of thought: Language as window into human nature.* Viking.

Planck, M. (1920, June 2). The genesis and present state of development of the quantum theory. (Nobel Lecture).

Poincaré, H. (2001). *The Value of Science: Essential Writings of Henri Poincaré.* Random House (Modern Library Science).

Polanyi, M. (1958) *Personal knowledge: Towards a post-critical philosophy*. The University of Chicago.

Polanyi, M. (1967). *The tacit dimension*. Anchor Books.

Prinz, W. (2005). An ideomotor approach to imitation. In S. Hurley & N. Chater, *Perspectives on imitation: From neuroscience to social science vol. 1: Mechanisms of imitation and imitation in animals* (141-156). MIT Press.

Puthoff, H.E. (1989). Source of vacuum electromagnetic zero-point energy. *Physical Review A*(40), 4857-62.

Puthoff, H.,W. (1990). The energetic vacuum: Implications for energy research. *Speculations in Science and Technology, 13*(4), 247.

Ramon, S. (1997). *Earthly cycles: How past lives and soul patterns shape your life.* Pepperwood Press.

Reber, A.S. (1993). *Implicit learning and tacit knowledge: An essay on the cognitive unconscious*. Oxford University Press.

Rescher, N. (2001). *Paradoxes: their roots, range, and resolution*. Open Court.

Ritchey, D. (2003). *The H.I.S.S. of the A.S.P.: Understanding the anomalously sensitive person.* Headline Books.

Ritsema, R., & Karcher, S. (Trans.) (1995). *I Ching: The classic Chinese oracle of change* (The first complete translation with concordance). Barnes & Noble.

Ritsema, R., & Karcher, S. (Trans.) (1995). *I ching: The classic Chinese oracle of change* (the first complete translation with concordance). Barnes & Noble, Inc.

Rizzolatti, G. (2006, November). Mirrors in the mind. *Scientific American.*

Roberts, G. (2006). *Free your mind: A scientific approach to unleashing creativity.* [Blog] independent.co.uk

Roberts, J. (1994). *The nature of personal reality*. Amber-Allen Publishing.

Rock, A. (2004). *The mind at night: The new science of how and why we dream*. Basic Books.

Ross, P.E. (2006, August). The expert mind. *Scientific American.*

Rossman, J. (1931). *The psychology of the inventor: A study of the patentee.* Inventors Publishing.

Russell, P. (2007). *The awakening earth: The global brain*. Floris Books.

Ryle, G. (1949). *The concept of mind.*

Salk, J. (1973). *The survival of the wisest.* Harper & Row.

Sainsbury, R.M. (1988). *Paradoxes.* Cambridge University Press.

Scharmer, C.O. (2009). *Theory U: Leading from the future as it emerges*. Berrett-Koehler.

Schrödinger (1944) (Combined reprint, 1967). *What is life?* Cambridge University Press.

Searle, J.R. (1983). *Intentionality: An essay in the philosophy of mind.* Cambridge University Press.

Searle, J.R. (2000). Consciousness, free action, and the brain. *Journal of Consciousness Studies*, 7(10).

Seligman, M.E.P. (2011). *Flourish: A visionary new understanding of happiness and well-being*. Free Press.

Senge, P.M. (1990). *The fifth discipline: The art and practice of the learning organization*. Currency/Doubleday.

Senge, P.M., Scharmer, C.O., Jaworski, J., & Flowers, B.S. (2004). *Presence: Exploring profound change in people, organizations and society*. Random House, Inc.

Shand. A.F. (1920). *The foundation of character* (2nd ed.).

Shaw, B. (1934). *The compete plays of Bernard Shaw*. Odhams Press.

Shaw, R. (1991). Splitting truths from darkness: Epistemological aspects of Temne divination. In P. M. Peek (Ed.), *African divination systems: Ways of knowing*. Indiana University Press, 137-152.

Sheldrake, R. (1989). *The presence of the past: Morphic resonance and the habits of nature*. Vintage Books.

Shelley, A. (2007). *Organizational zoo: A survival guide to work place behavior*. Asian Publishing.

Shelley, A.W. (2021) *Becoming Adaptable.* Intelligent Answers.

Shorter Oxford English Dictionary 5th ed, vol 1.

Silverman, D.P. (Ed.) (1997). *Ancient Egypt.* Oxford University Press.

Simonton, D.K. (1999). Talent and its development: An emergenic and epigenetic mode. *Psychological Review, 106*, 435-457.

Smith, J., Dixon, R.A., & Baltes, P.B. (1987).

Stein, M.I. (1967, 1974). *Stimulating creativity*. Academic Press.

Steiner, G. (1978) *Has truth a future?* BBC Publications, p. 16.

Sternberg, R.J. (2003). *Wisdom, intelligence, and creativity synthesized.* Cambridge University Press.

Sternberg, R.J. (Ed.) (1990). *Wisdom: Its nature, origins and development*. Cambridge University Press.

Stonier, T. (1990). *Information and the internal structure of the universe*. Springer-Verlag.

Stonier, T. (1997). *Information and meaning: An evolutionary perspective*. Springer-Verlag.

Swann, R., Bosanko, S., Cohen, R., Midgley, R., & Seed, K.M. (1982). *The brain—A user's manual*. G.P. Putnam & Sons.

Tallis, F. (2002). *Hidden minds: A history of the unconscious*. Arcade.

Taylor, I.A. (1959). The nature of the creative process. In P. Smith (Ed.), *Creativity*. Hastings House.

Taylor, K. (2006). Brain function and adult learning: Implications for practice. In S. Johnson & K. Taylor (Eds.), *The neuroscience of adult learning: New directions for adult and continuing education* (pp. 71-86). Jossey-Bass.

Tchaikovsky, M. (1906). *The life and letters of Peter Ilich Tchaikovsky*. John Lane Company.

Templeton, Sir John (2002). *Wisdom from world religions: Pathways toward heaven on earth*. Templeton Foundation Press.

The Urantia Book (1955). URANTIA Foundation.

Tiller, W. (2007). *Psychoenergetic science: A second Copernican-scale revolution*. Pavior.

Torrance, E.P. (1974). *Torrance tests of creative thinking*. Personnel Press.

Trumpa, C. (1991). *The heart of the Buddha*. Shambhala.

Van Heijenoort, J. (Ed.) (1967). *From Frege to Gödel: A source book in mathematical logic. 1879-1931*. Harvard University Press.

Vaudeville, C. (2017). *A weaver named Kabir: Selected verses with a detailed biographical and historical introduction*. Motilal Banarsidass Publishers.

Wade, J. (1996) *Changes of mind: A holonomic theory of the evolution of consciousness*. SUNY Press.

Wagner, A. (2023). *Sleeping beauties: the mystery of dormant innovations in nature and culture*. One World.

Wallas, G. l. (1931/1926). *The art of thought*. Johnathan Cape

Warmington and Rouse (1984). *Great dialogues of Plato*.

Weisbert, R.W. (1999). Creativity and knowledge: A challenge to theories. In R.J. Sternberg (Ed.), *Handbook of creativity* (226-250). Cambridge University Press.

West, M.A. (1980). Meditation and the EEG. *Psychological Medicine, 10*, 69-375.

White, R.W. (1959). Motivation reconsidered: The concept of competence. *Psychological Review, 66*, pp. 297-333.

Whyte, S. R. (1991). Knowledge and power in Nyole divination. In P. M. Peek (Ed.), *African divination systems: Ways of knowing*. Indiana University Press, 153-172.

Wilber, K. (2000) Integral psychology: Consciousness, spirit, psychology, therapy. Shambhala Publications.

Wilson, C. (1965). *Beyond the Outsider*. Houghton Mifflin Co.

Wilson, E.O. (1998). *Consilience: The unity of knowledge*. Alfred A. Knopf.

Wing, R.L. (Trans.) (1986). *The Tao of power: Lao Tzu's classic guide to leadership, influence, and excellence*. Doubleday.

Woodman, M., & Dickson, E. (1996). *Dancing in the flames: The dark goddess in the transformation of consciousness*. Shambhala.

Writing: The nature, development and teaching of written communication (vol. II) (1982). Lawrence Erlbaum Associates.

Wycoff, J. (1991). *Mindmapping: Your personal guide to exploring creativity and problem-solving*. The Berkley Publishing Group.

Yang, K., Ribiére, V., & Bennet, A. (2023). Can we really hide knowledge? Unpublished paper.

Zeidan, F., Johnson, S., Diamond, B., David, Z., & Goolkasian, P. (2010). Mindfulness meditation improves cognition: Evidence of brief mental training. *Consciousness and Cognition 19*(2), pp. 597-605.

Zohar, D., & Marshall, I. (2000). *Connecting with our spiritual intelligence*. R. R. Donnelley and Sons Company.

Subject Index

The Ever-new Dawn !

As you discover creative capacities
Enriching vistas come into view.
Your labors deepen and expand,
curiosities blossom,
Fascination yields benefits and breakthroughs,
Relationships deepen,
And life reveals and touches new summits.
-Robert Turner

About the Authors

Dr. Alex Bennet is a Professor with the Innovation and Knowledge Institute Southeast Asia, Bangkok University, and the Director of the Mountain Quest Institute, a research and retreat center located in the Allegheny Mountains of West Virginia. Through three quests – the quest for knowledge, the quest for consciousness, and the quest for meaning – the Institute is dedicated to helping individuals achieve personal and professional growth, and organizations create and sustain high performance in a rapidly changing, uncertain, and increasingly complex world. Alex is the former Chief Knowledge Officer and Deputy CIO for Enterprise Integration of the U.S. Department of the Navy, having previously served as Acquisition Reform Executive and Standards Improvement Executive, and is recipient of the Distinguished Public Service Award, the highest civilian honor from the Secretary of the Navy. She has published hundreds of papers and journal articles, and over 40 books, primarily with her life partner, Dr. David Bennet, a nuclear physicist and neuroscientist. Together, the Drs. Bennet have spoken and taught around the world. Her latest publications are *Reblooming the Knowledge Movement: The Democratization of Organizations* (with Robert Turner), *INside INnovation: Looking from the Inside Out* (edited with Rajat Baisya), *Playing in the Mind Field Volume 1: Life in the Field*, *Unleashing the Human Mind: A Consilience Approach to Managing Self* (with David Bennet and Robert Turner), and an accompanying Field Guide which includes the lovable Organizational Zoo Critters developed by Arthur Shelley. Alex believes in the multidimensionality and interconnectedness of humanity as we move out of infancy into full consciousness. She may be contacted at alex@mountainquestinstitute.com

Dr. Arthur Shelley is a collaborative community builder, multi-awarded learning facilitator and creative education designer with over 30 years of professional experience across the international corporate, government and tertiary education sectors. He is the author of four books, has worked in 12 countries, is a mentor in several international communities, and has supervised PhD candidates in five countries. Arthur is passionate about creativity in learning and innovation to cocreate the flow of new knowledge and value. He has collaborated with organisations as diverse as NASA, Cirque Du Soleil, Local and National Governments, Universities, start-ups, SMEs, and multinational corporations. https://www.linkedin.com/in/arthurshelley/ "Asking which is my favourite OrgZoo critter is like asking a parent who is their favourite child! If only one, I feel that the Owl is who I would identify with the most – knowledge sharing, mentoring and supportive of learning for others, as he displays throughout this text – behaviour I have invested in most in my professional work." He may be contacted at Arthur@IntelligentAnswers.com.au

Charles Dhewa is a proactive Knowledge Management specialist, evaluator and thought leader on African food systems, rural development and indigenous knowledge systems. Working at the intersection of formal and informal agricultural markets across Africa, his organization, Knowledge Transfer Africa also known as eMKambo (www.knowledgetransafrica.com / www.emkambo.co.zw trends around food systems to ensure agricultural value chains are driven by knowledge, technology and innovation. He is always clarifying opportunities and influencing policy through his thought leadership blog https://emkambo.wordpress.com as well as Ted Talks like this one https://www.youtube.com/watch?v=zVMCfCMFJOo. At the international level, Charles is a Core Group member of the Knowledge Management for Development D-Group (www.km4dev.org) as well as a communication and evaluation consultant under the IDRC-supported initiative known as Designing Evaluation & Communication for Impact (DECI) https://evaluationandcommunicationinpractice.net/.

Among other qualifications, Charles holds a Master of Philosophy in Information and Knowledge Management from Stellenbosch University, South Africa). He is currently completing PhD studies at the Knowledge, Technology and Innovation (KTI) department, Wageningen University & Research (WUR) in The Netherlands, as part of a special cohort of PhDs-for-professionals.

Recent Offerings from MQIPress

Reblooming the Knowledge Movement: The Democratization of Organizations (2023)

Alex Bennet and Robert Turner with Foreword by Rory Cross and chapters contributed by Francisco Javier Carrillo, Mark Boyes, Florin Gaiseanu, Chulatep Senivongse, and Milton de Sousa

Reblooming unfolds on millennia of human challenges and advances. Now, at every level and at every reach across organizations, networks, and nations there is a new coalescing of democratization, intelligent learning, and capacity for surmounting complexity. With freedom of thought, freedom of expression, and freedom of association, ideas beget ideas. The emergent result is the rich globalization of knowledge and its close companion, innovation.

INside Innovation: Looking from the Inside Out (2023)

Dr. Alex Bennet and Dr. Rajat Bais (Eds.) with Prologue by Dr. Leif Edvinsson and Foreword by Dr. Massimo Pregnolato

In addition to a collection of insightful innovation case studies, this book offers an unusual look at creativity and innovation from the inside out. Three innovators – a scientist, an organizational guru, and an artist – share the personal passions that have driven their success. "And, then, looking from the inside out, readers are provided the opportunity to evaluate their own organizations against the Most Innovative Knowledge Organization (MIKE) international study program and awards criteria, thus engaging their own innovative juices."

Unleashing the Human Mind: A Consilience Approach to Managing Self (2022)

David Bennet, Alex Bennet, Robert Turner
with Foreword by Florin Gaiseanu

What does it mean to be human? Increasingly, we recognize that we are infinitely complex beings with immense emotional and spiritual, physical and mental capacities. Presiding over these human systems, our brain is a fully integrated, biological, and extraordinary organ that is preeminent in the known Universe. Its time has come. This book is grounded in the Intelligent Complex Adaptive Learning System (ICALS) theory based on over a decade of researching experiential learning through the expanding lens of neuroscience.

Review Bites from Around the World:

Once in a while, I am exposed to a work so profound that it literally causes a massive shift in my own thinking and beliefs ... I found myself riveted to each paragraph as I embarked on a journey that vastly deepened my understanding of the learning process.

-Duane Nickull, Author, Technologist, and Seeker of Higher Truth, Canada

Every now and then a book comes along that compels your spirit. In these times of uncertainty and even great danger for humanity, this book reminds us of what it means to be human, our infinite potential and innate ability to learn and to love.

-Dr. Milton deSousa, Associate Professor, Nova School of Business and Economics, Portugal

Very few people have the gift to integrate such complex ideas, especially those about learning ... this work can be likened to the Webb Telescope, which gives us more clarity into our mysteries.

-Michael Stankosky, DSc, Author, Philosopher, Professor, Editor-Emeritus, Member of the Academy of Scholars, USA

And the ***Unleashing Field Guide: An OrgZoo Quest***

Alex Bennet, Robert Turner, Arthur Shelley, Jane Turner and Mark Boyes (Illustrator) (2022)

Arthur Shelley's beloved OrgZoo critters – the voices in our heads – join us in a learning quest up the mountain to unleash the human mind.

The Mountain Quest Institute located in the Allegheny Mountains of West Virginia is a research, retreat, and learning center dedicated to helping individuals achieve personal and professional growth, and organizations create and sustain high performance in a rapidly changing, uncertain, and increasingly complex world. MQI has three quests: the Quest for Knowledge, the Quest for Consciousness, and the Quest for Meaning. MQI is scientific, humanistic, and spiritual and finds no contradiction in this blend.

Project & Technology Management Foundation (PTMF) is a not-for-profit organization promoted by a group of very senior academicians, researchers, industry leaders and academic administrators in India with an objective to disseminate knowledge and provide training and accreditation in the area of project, program and technology management by organizing conferences, workshops, publications, syndicating research, arranging training and teaching program and courses and collaborating and dynamically networking with other global organizations for knowledge creation. See www.ptmfonline.com

Other titles from MQIPress:

The Profundity and Bifurcation of Change: Parts I – V (2017; 2020)

Possibilities that are YOU! (a 22-volume conscious look book series) (2018)

The QUEST: Where the Mountains Meet the Library (2021)

The Course of Knowledge: A 21st Century Theory (2015)

Decision-Making in The New Reality: Complexity, Knowledge and Knowing (2013)

Expanding the Self: The Intelligent Complex Adaptive Learning System (2015)

Leading with the Future in Mind: Knowledge and Emergent Leadership (2015)

With Passion, We Live and Love: Research, Prose, Verse and Music (2021)

Freeing
Preparing
IC
Accessing
Focusing

Made in the USA
Coppell, TX
29 March 2024

30679624R00184